Negotiating Democracy and Religious Pluralism

MODERN SOUTH ASIA

Ashutosh Varshney, *Series Editor*
Pradeep Chhibber, *Associate Series Editor*

The Other One Percent
Sanjoy Chakravorty, Devesh Kapur, and Nirvikar Singh

Social Justice through Inclusion
Francesca R. Jensenius

Dispossession without Development
Michael Levien

The Man Who Remade India
Vinay Sitapati

Business and Politics in India
Edited by Christophe Jaffrelot, Atul Kohli, and Kanta Murali

Clients and Constituents
Jennifer Bussell

Gambling with Violence
Yelena Biberman

Mobilizing the Marginalized
Amit Ahuja

The Absent Dialogue
Anit Mukherjee

When Nehru Looked East
Francine Frankel

Capable Women, Incapable States
Poulami Roychowdhury

Farewell to Arms
Rumela Sen

Negotiating Democracy and Religious Pluralism

India, Pakistan, and Turkey

Edited by

KAREN BARKEY, SUDIPTA KAVIRAJ, AND
VATSAL NARESH

UNIVERSITY PRESS

OXFORD
UNIVERSITY PRESS

Oxford University Press is a department of the University of Oxford. It furthers
the University's objective of excellence in research, scholarship, and education
by publishing worldwide. Oxford is a registered trade mark of Oxford University
Press in the UK and certain other countries.

Published in the United States of America by Oxford University Press
198 Madison Avenue, New York, NY 10016, United States of America.

Library of Congress Control Number: 2021904812

ISBN 978-0-19-753002-3 (pbk.)
ISBN 978-0-19-753001-6 (hbk.)

DOI: 10.1093/oso/9780197530016.001.0001

1 3 5 7 9 8 6 4 2

Paperback printed by Marquis, Canada
Hardback printed by Bridgeport National Bindery, Inc., United States of America

To the late Alfred C. Stepan, mentor, colleague, friend, and preeminent scholar of democracy, toleration, and authoritarianism. May his ceaseless advocacy for democracy and his infinite wisdom guide our path.

Contents

Acknowledgments

This project began with a generous grant from the Henry Luce Foundation. Alfred C. Stepan inspired and supported it from inception. Toby Volkman watched over this project with attentive care throughout.

Our first meeting was held at Columbia University, under the auspices of the Center for Democracy, Toleration and Religion (CDTR), in 2016. Some of our wonderful collaborators participants there and at our second meeting at Berkeley indelibly shaped this volume for the better, and we gratefully acknowledge their contribution: Asad Q. Ahmed, Manan Ahmed, Yesim Arat, Koray Çaliskan, Thomas Blom Hansen, Mehdi Hasan, Suat Kiniklioglu, Ravish Kumar, Basharat Peer, Raka Ray, Senator Sherry Rehman, Yasmin Saikia, Tolga Tanis, Mark Taylor, and Ozan Varol.

The team at CDTR made the laborious task of conference-organising a genuinely enjoyable exercise. Without Jessica Lilien's ingenuity and meticulous attention to detail, this project would never have taken off. Mariam Elnozahy and Menna El-Sayed's crucial assistance, academic and logistical, brought cheer when it was most needed. We also thank the department of Middle Eastern, South Asian and African Studies at Columbia University for their financial support.

We continued the project under the auspices of Social Science Matrix at University of California-Berkeley. There, Erica Browne and Dasom Nah provided stellar logistical and editorial assistance. The collaboration would not have continued without the financial and intellectual backing of the Haas Institute for a Fair and Inclusive Society (now the Othering and Belonging Institute). We thank John Powell, Taeku Lee, Raka Ray, and Eva Seto.

Bhawna Parmar worked with us patiently to illustrate a thoughtful book cover. Holly Mitchell at OUP was the epitome of forbearance in seeing us through. We thank her and David McBride, as well as the team at Newgen.

Contributors

Nosheen Ali is a sociologist serving as Global Faculty-in-Residence at the Gallatin School, New York University. Ali works on state-making, ecology and Muslim cultural politics with a focus on Pakistan and Kashmir. Her book *Delusional States: Feeling Rule and Development in Pakistan's Northern Frontier* (Cambridge University Press, 2019) examines state power and social struggle in Gilgit-Baltistan, a contested border zone that forms part of disputed Kashmir. Ali is the founder of *Umangpoetry*, a digital humanities endeavor for documenting contemporary poetic knowledges in South Asia, and Karti Dharti, an alternative space for ecological inquiry.

Ateş Altınordu is Assistant Professor of Sociology at Sabancı University, Istanbul. His work focuses on religion and politics, secularization and secularism, and the cultural sociology of contemporary Turkish politics. His articles have been published in the *Annual Review of Sociology, Politics and Society, Kölner Zeitschrift für Soziologie und Sozialpyschologie*, and *Qualitative Sociology*.

Senem Aslan is Associate Professor of Politics at Bates College. She was previously a post-doctoral fellow in the Department of Near Eastern Studies at Princeton University between 2008 and 2010. Dr. Aslan's book *Nation-Building in Turkey and Morocco: Governing Kurdish and Berber Dissent*, was published by Cambridge University Press in 2014. Her other works have been published in the *International Journal of Middle East Studies, Nationalism and Ethnic Politics, Nationalities Papers, Oxford Handbook of Turkish Politics*, and the *European Journal of Turkish Studies*. At Bates, she teaches courses on Middle East politics, state-building, and nationalism. Her recent research focuses on the different governments' politics of symbolism and imagery in Turkey.

Rochana Bajpai is Associate Professor of Politics at SOAS University of London. She is the author of *Debating Difference: Group Rights and Liberal Democracy in India* (Oxford University Press 2011, sixth impression). Dr Bajpai has published widely on the Indian Constituent Assembly debates; conceptions of secularism and minority rights; debates on social justice and affirmative action in India and Malaysia. Her current project focusses on the theory and practice of political representation, with reference to minority representation in Indian Parliament. Dr Bajpai is a founding member of the SOAS Centre for Comparative Political Thought and a co-convenor of the London Comparative Political Thought Group.

Karen Barkey is the Haas Distinguished Chair of Religious Diversity at the Othering & Belonging Institute and Professor of Sociology at the University of California, Berkeley. She is also the Director of the Center for the Study of Democracy, Toleration, and Religion (CDTR). Barkey's books include *Shared Sacred Sites: A Contemporary Pilgrimage* (2018, with Dionigi Albera and Manoël Pénicaud), *Choreographies of Shared Sacred*

Sites: Religion, Politics, and Conflict Resolution (2014, co-edited with Elazar Barkan), *Empire of Diversity* (2008), and *Bandits and Bureaucrats* (1996).

Amrita Basu is Domenic J. Paino 1955 Professor of Political Science, and Sexuality, Women's and Gender Studies at Amherst College. Her scholarship explores women's activism, feminist movements, and religious nationalism in South Asia. Her most recent book, *Violent Conjunctures in Democratic India* (Cambridge University Press, 2015), explores when and why Hindu nationalists engage in violence against religious minorities. She is also the author of *Two Faces of Protest: Contrasting Modes of Women's Activism in India* (1992) and has edited several anthologies which focus on women's activism and movements across the globe.

Fatima Y. Bokhari is a legal practitioner and researcher with over a decade of experience working on criminal justice reform, focusing on gender rights and legal empowerment of marginalized groups. At present, she leads Musawi – an independent research organiza- tion in Pakistan, which works to support government and non-government stakeholders to affect evidence-based legal and policy reforms.

Faisal Devji is a Professor in History and Fellow of St Antony's College at the University of Oxford, where he is also the Director of the Asian Studies Centre. Dr. Devji is the author of four books, *Muslim Zion: Pakistan as a Political Idea* (2013), *The Impossible Indian: Gandhi and the Temptation of Violence* (2012), *The Terrorist in Search of Humanity: Militant Islam and Global Politics* (2009), and *Landscapes of the Jihad: Militancy, Morality, Modernity* (2005).

Humeira Iqtidar is a Reader in Politics at King's College London. She is a co-convenor of the London Comparative Political Theory Workshop and editor of the McGill-Queens Studies in Modern Islamic Thought. She is the author of include *Secularising Islamists? (2011),* and *Tolerance, Secularisation and Democratic Politics in South Asia (2018, co- edited with Tanika Sarkar).* Iqtidar is currently working on two projects. The first focuses on non-liberal conceptions of tolerance through an engagement with 20th century Islamic thought. The second, titled *Justice Beyond Rights,* builds on her research with refugees and migrants from the tribal areas of Pakistan.

Mathew John is Professor and Executive Director at the Centre on Public Law and Jurisprudence at Jindal Global Law School. He has graduate degrees in law from the National Law School, Bangalore and the University of Warwick, and completed his doc- toral work at the London School of Economics on the impact of secularism on Indian con- stitutional practice. He has previously worked at the Alternative Law Forum, Bangalore on social justice lawyering; he was a law and culture fellow at the Centre for the Study of Culture and Society, Bangalore; and has been a visiting fellow at the Centre for the Study of Law and Governance, Jawaharlal Nehru University.

Sudipta Kaviraj is Professor of Indian Politics and Intellectual History at Columbia University in the City of New York. Kaviraj's books include *The Imaginary Institution* *of India* (2010), *Civil Society: History and Possibilities* co-edited with Sunil Khilnani (2001), *Politics in India* (edited, 1999), and *The Unhappy Consciousness: Bankimchandra Chattopadhyay and the Formation of Nationalist Discourse in India* (1995).

Uday S. Mehta is Distinguished Professor of Political Science at the Graduate Center – City University of New York. He is the author of two books, *The Anxiety of Freedom: Imagination and Individuality in the Political Thought of John Locke* (1992) and *Liberalism and Empire: Nineteenth Century British Liberal Thought* (2000), and is currently completing a book on M. K. Gandhi's critique of political rationality.

Vatsal Naresh is a PhD student in Political Science at Yale University. His research focuses on democratic theory, political violence, constitutionalism, and South Asian politics. Naresh co-edited *Constituent Assemblies* (Cambridge University Press 2018, with Jon Elster, Roberto Gargarella, and Bjorn-Erik Rasch).

Matthew J. Nelson is Professor of Politics at SOAS University of London. His first book *In the Shadow of Shari'ah: Islam, Islamic Law, and Democracy in Pakistan* was published in 2011 (Columbia University Press). Dr Nelson is a founding member of the Centre for Comparative Political Thought and the Centre for the International Politics of Conflict, Rights, and Justice at SOAS. His current research focuses on comparative constitutional politics and the politics of sectarian and doctrinal diversity in Islamic law and education.

Christine Philliou is Associate Professor of History at the University of California, Berkeley. She is the author of *Biography of an Empire: Governing Ottomans in an Age of Revolution* (University of California Press, 2011) and *Turkey: A Past Against History* (University of California Press, 2021). Philliou's next book, "The Post-Ottoman World," looks at the death of the Ottoman Empire through the lens of Greek and Turkish nation-state formation in the nineteenth and twentieth centuries.

Sadia Saeed is an Assistant Professor of Sociology at the University of San Francisco. She is the author of *Politics of Desecularization: Law and the Minority Question in Pakistan* (Cambridge, 2017). Saeed is currently working on a book manuscript on the triangular relationship between sovereignty, law and religious difference in pre-modern Muslim societies.

Itineraries of Democracy and Religious Plurality

Karen Barkey, Sudipta Kaviraj, and Vatsal Naresh

I.1 Introduction

This volume focuses on the relation between the functioning of democracy and the prior existence of religious plurality in three societies outside the West: India, Pakistan, and Turkey. The existing literature on "the spread of democracy" relies primarily on the power or the example of the West for democratic government to spread to other societies. The intellectual and sociocultural traditions of specific societies are rarely analyzed in detail. Often discussions of democracy examine how individual religious traditions relate to the demands of democratic politics: is Islam or Hinduism conducive to or compatible with democracy? The central question we seek to address in this volume is different. Democracy is centrally concerned with political pluralism in many ways. Democratic procedures of collective decision-making presuppose a social condition in which different, often conflicting social interests press a plurality of demands on the state. Constitutional features of democracy—like freedom of expression and association—contribute to a situation where the those who exercise power lack the capacity to stamp out different points of view. It is only recently that Western European countries have had to recognize and rethink the role of religious and ethnic pluralism in the unfolding of democratic decision-making. In many non-Western countries, adaptation to democratic politics has meant struggling with the legacy of historical religious pluralism since before modern states were established.

Early scholars of democracy primarily examined divergences of constitutional legal design—presidential or parliamentary forms, or federal or unitary structures—across a range of countries in the modern West that were similar in the sociological composition of their electorates, and had similar historical traditions drawn from the settlement of Westphalia. In sociological terms, these states were relatively homogeneous: some were so as a result of the powerful, coercive, violent processes following the rise of the modern state system. This settlement encouraged the creation of religiously unified polities. In the nineteenth

Karen Barkey, Sudipta Kaviraj, and Vatsal Naresh, *Itineraries of Democracy and Religious Plurality* In: *Negotiating Democracy and Religious Pluralism.* Edited by: Karen Barkey, Sudipta Kaviraj, and Vatsal Naresh, Oxford University Press.
© Oxford University Press 2021. DOI: 10.1093/oso/9780197530016.003.0001

century, these states developed strong nationalist sentiments around a single language, religion, culture, and history—all included in the standard definitions of the nation-state. As modernization theory became dominant after the Second World War, the non-Western world was deemed both more backward and bound to follow in the footsteps of the West through sheer cultural imitation (see, for example, Apter 1965; Geertz 1963; Lerner 1958; Rudolph and Rudolph 1967). As a project, the study of democracy now has to deal with a much wider and consequently more diverse world; the present challenge of democratic government is far more complex. Academic research in the past decades has gradually formed a picture of democratic systems that is more critical and has expanded its study to a larger variety of cases. Consequently, explaining variations in democratic experience requires close attention to the sociological structure of each society in which democratic politics operates, and to the historical traditions of political life. This volume contributes to this new line of enquiry into comparative politics with a deeper critical historical understanding.

In parallel, scholars of religious history and intellectual historians have also questioned the Enlightenment conception of religious traditions as merely superstitious and uniformly exclusivist. The concisely simple philosophy of history that underpinned traditional studies of politics saw the rise of European modernity as the emergence of a uniquely rationalistic civilization that spread intellectual enlightenment and introduced ideas of human dignity against other religious cultures that were discriminatory and intolerant. Comparative historical sociology today is obliged to reopen these assumptions and re-examine questions about the historical trajectories of politics in different parts of the world. As it has embarked on this analysis of varieties of historical trajectories and conceptions of religious history, comparative historical sociology has pioneered a richer and more capacious field of study. This collection of chapter represents the extension of such an expansion of the fields of study linking religious traditions to political outcomes.

In the countries of interest, Turkey, India, and Pakistan, religious pluralism was part of successful accommodation in the past. Under new political arrangements, religious pluralism has come under severe threat. With the rise of majoritarian domination, the future of pluralism, tolerance, and democratic norms is in peril. It is this particular theoretical and comparative concern, from the transition to modern statehood to the present day, that has directed the work of this volume. In this introduction, we begin by discussing critical theoretical and methodological issues that such comparative historical work should address. We then present the historical arcs of Pakistan, India, and Turkey before their transition to modern statehood to serve as a framing tool for the chapters in the volume. Finally, we speak to a series of contemporary questions that present themselves through the analysis of the three cases.

I.2 Concepts

Social science analysis of historical processes like the establishment of democratic government or religious change and secularization—the two processes
this volume is concerned with—must use a preformed language of social science theory. Its central concepts, such as calling economic changes "capitalist
industrialization," or labeling religious transformations "secularization," are predominantly drawn from analytical reflections on nineteenth-century European
history—the only theater of serious social science discussion at that time.
One of the major problems of modern social science is the way such theoretical constructs are used for comparative historical analysis. In the first stage of
the development of social science, historical disciplines engaged in two kinds
of cognitive and epistemic activities: first, empirical descriptions of social processes, followed by the production of theoretical constructs as such empirical
information accumulated and became more elaborate. Theoretical concepts like
secularization, disenchantment, and the rise of capitalism were all products of
this second intellectual practice. In the next century and beyond, social scientific
inquiry expanded exponentially across the globe incorporating historical knowledge about cultures, societies, states, and institutions outside Western Europe.

A central shortcoming of this process of the cognitive expansion of social science was the asymmetry of the two levels. While empirical historical research
became increasingly expansive, the corpus of theoretical concepts remained restricted to the original cluster devised mainly in the classical phase of theoretical
development. Social science thinking developed a strange "triangular" structure.
The theoretical constructs used were invariably drawn from European theoretical models of development of capitalism, the modern state, secularization,
and urbanism. Instead of looking for new constructs of theory, rich empirical
material and historical evidence were sought to be forced into the theoretical
constructs drawn from early modern social theory. This theoretical problem
works sometimes at an even deeper level, as empirical descriptions of social reality cannot use a theory-independent language; and the obligatory use of the
conventional language obstructs a clearer apprehension of reality or obfuscates
understandings of real patterns in historical events. Studies in our collection illustrate the necessity of greater awareness of these questions for social theory. In
this section, we examine the conceptual foundations that initiated the collabo-
rative project: the internal heterogeneity of democracy; pluralism; and identity;
and a particular consequence of their mixture, "majorities" and "minorities."

An interesting feature of scholarly literature on democracy is that democracy
itself is rarely historicized. The standard procedure for the analysis of democracy
and its historical tribulations is to focus on a constitution that is viewed as democratic and to record occasional decline and the rise of authoritarian rule in its

place. However, a closer reading of the internal records of all democratic societies should promote a more intrinsically historical approach to the existence of democracy itself. Society does not become uniformly democratic for all its citizens simply by the adoption of a universal franchise or competitive elections, even on a procedural account. It is a historical fact that legal frames engage citizens in self-rule and protect groups from arbitrary power to quite different degrees. Democracy is an internally uneven system in practically all its real incarnations. Democracy—if it indicates a political experience of procedural equality, the secure enjoyment of rights, and protection from avoidable, arbitrary power—is internally heterogeneous in all instances across various criteria—in terms of class, caste, region, and historical period. Democracy in Britain in the 1950s and 1960s incorporated the government of Northern Ireland, where Catholics suffered forms of legalized exclusion. That Black Americans in the United States were widely disenfranchised, could not enter restaurants, or ride in front seats of buses in the postwar decades did not lead political scientists to declare America a non-democratic polity. Northern Ireland—like Kashmir in South Asia—is an example of regional unevenness in the enjoyment of democratic rights. The treatment of African Americans—like Dalits in India or Ahmadis in Pakistan—is illustrative of the domination of persons along the lines of race, caste, and religion. The case of Dalits in India reveals further that even when there is legal equality, the practical enjoyment of democratic rights can be uneven. Similarly, for Alevis and Kurds in Turkey, democratic rights are unevenly distributed and enjoyed. While some scholars, especially in comparative politics, view the process of democratization to be complete upon the institution of competitive elections, we posit that it continues as a process thereafter as well.

The institutional requirement in a democratic constitution of abstractly equal rights can work against domination. Excluded groups can use the declared principles of democratic constitutions to protest against domination, often allowing them to achieve actual improvement in their political condition. Democracy remains an ideal: a political system can slide toward lesser or greater enjoyment of actual democratic rights by ordinary people across a scale. A realistic picture of democracy can only arise if this internal unevenness and heterogeneity is acknowledged and recorded in our political analyses. This collection tries to understand how the internal heterogeneity of democracy affects the prospects of pluralism and vice versa in Pakistan, India, and Turkey.

Pluralism, the other central concept of this volume, also requires definition. Pluralism does not inevitably follow from plurality. Sudipta Kaviraj (in his chapter) defines religious plurality as "the brute fact of existing differences between religious groups," whereas religious pluralism refers to a "cognitive and ethical attitude . . . allowing all faith-groups to practice their religious life without hindrance from other faiths or from the state." Where diversity and difference are endemic, pluralism, as a politically accommodative recognition of difference, can reduce the possibility of domination.

The term "identity" itself—which plays such an essential role in all our chapters—requires a clearer and more refined definition. In our analysis, the idea of identity always has at least two meanings: the identity of the *individual*, and the identity of the *collectivity*. Under modern conditions, identity becomes vital in both senses, because modernity transforms both types of identity and gives them a new intensity. Modern individuals are incited to choose their identities by the constant interpellation of intellectual forces and modern institutions, acting most powerfully through their peers. Even if individualism is not widely embraced as a moral-philosophical ideal, waves of influence of liberalism, socialism, and other modernist political ideologies usually encourage a strong emphasis on the individual's selection of positions. Yet many of these modern ideologies urge modern assertive individuals to view themselves as members of a large, agentive collective identity—like the nation, or the people, or the religious community, or regional culture. Political modernity might contribute to the intensification of both senses of community—individual and collective. This is particularly true because in many cases, the politically assertive individual chooses a collective identity—like the nation, people, or religious community— to mark herself. Identification with a larger collective identity—which a person considers imperiled, or from which a person draws sustenance—is often folded into the making of individual identity itself.

A persistent difficulty with identity is that self-identification is usually inextricably linked to other-identification as well. The self—especially collective ones—tends to be identified by attributes that are marked off against others. In this sense, identities are relational. Consider the demands to define "Muslim" in a restrictive fashion in Pakistan, which pushed Ahmadis outside its boundaries. The Ahmadis—when they defined themselves—did not see the boundaries falling that way. But modern identities are ordinarily political—in the sense that our identity is constituted by what we think we are, but also by what others think we are. Moreover, since their thinking is reflected in their *acting* toward us in a particular way, it forces us to take that view of ourselves into account, and act back toward it. Conceptions of identities are, in this sense, generally agentive. The complex interactions between different religious communities—through their self-definition and other-definition—chronicled in the studies included in this volume raise the question of reviewing the conceptual grids that social scientists employ.

When situated in the discourse of modern government, the distinction between majorities and minorities emerges as a prism for understanding political conflict. Varying ideas of popular sovereignty and nationalism encourage the belief that the state "belongs" to its people. If the people have internal divisions, there is a drift toward the idea that the "majority" has a prior claim. Remarkably, this is a quintessentially modern claim made on the state; premodern states did not have to contend with an equivalent political-moral notion for two reasons. First, as boundaries of empires tended to fluctuate constantly, it was difficult to set up a relation of this kind between the state and its people, besides the fact of the concentration of sacralized authority in a single person. Second, premodern states often worked based on various levels of allocation of political authority that were subordinate to the higher level, but which also had substantial power— an arrangement of political power quite different from modern notions of sovereignty. Although the terms "sovereign" and "sovereignty" were used widely to refer to the highest imperial authorities and the ultimacy of their power, neither word carried the legal connotation of modern sovereignty.

There are two different uses of the language of majority and minority that need to be differentiated. In the idealized account of democratic theory, legitimate decisions have to be taken by the majority principle. Majorities are abstract collectives created in the moment of a political decision constituted by the aggregation of individual wills. They are episodic and random in the sense that an individual falling into a majority in case of a vote on one issue can be in the minority on another. Being part of a decisional minority does not give rise to resentment against being outside of the decision-making process altogether. This is different from when the language of majority/minority tracks identity divisions, which are stickier. Falling into a minority as an identity category can mean systematic exclusion from citizenship status and from major decisional processes of a society. In such cases, the possibility of being in the decisional majority is significantly lower. However, as we saw earlier, even such designations of majority/ minority status depend crucially on the way a state and its people, or its "nation," are defined. With an internally pluralistic definition of Islam, sects like the Ahmadiyya would be counted as part of the political community. A more restrictive notion would, by contrast, not merely extrude the Ahmadiyya outside the Muslim community, but tend to restrict itself further to exclude groups like the Shia. Comparably, a pluralist notion of the nation in India can view Muslims as equal citizens. In contrast, a restrictive conception of the nation around a Hindu nationalist self-conception would tend to reduce them to a condition of domination before turning on itself and narrowing the definition of Hindus. Once the identitarian language of majority/minority enters the political life of a society, its effects have proved irreversible.

In Pakistan, India, and Turkey, majority and minority communities are constituted by inheritances of imperial pasts that, while subjugating these groups, created some frameworks for the management and regulation of difference. In Turkey, republican leaders sought a rupture from the Ottoman Empire across domains, including an inversion of a spirit of toleration into a secularized state based upon the primacy of ethnically Turkish Sunni Muslims. India's elites committed themselves to institutionalized pluralism in a negotiated settlement that balanced the imperatives of modern, individuated, liberal democracy and long-standing religious traditions and caste inequities. Pakistan's elite settlement was less definitive and more protracted. The result, however, was an explicit endorsement of an Islamic state and the institutionalized domination of Bengalis, and Ahmadis and other minorities. The contemporary trajectories of all three cases highlight deepening domination and perilously poised democratization. In Turkey, "political Islam" under Recep Tayyip Erdoğan has encouraged greater religiosity among Sunni, and thereby, displaced the prevailing republican secularism. While India's constitutionally entrenched principles of equality and secularism always remained somewhat aspirational, the rise of Hindu nationalism threatens even its symbolic dominance. Pakistan's nascent democratization has had little observable effect on minority domination, and the future of democracy and of pluralism there remains uncertain.

I.3 Histories

I.3.1. The Transition in Turkey

Turkey's transition from empire to nation-state marks a transformation from imperial to national rule, with particular implications for religious and other forms of diversity. The Young Turks tried initially to save the empire and, after failing to do so, to build a new entity. The Ottoman Empire was a multireligious and multiethnic imperial society with a long tradition of state-managed diversity. In the transition, non-Muslim communities moved from being autonomous, tolerated, and protected "millets" to equal citizens exposed to the vagaries of transitional violence. From the empire's violent dissolution emerged a Turkey that was somewhat easily demarcated and territorially sound.

Ottoman society might be one of the better cases of imperial accommodation of religion with a state carefully attending to religious differences and defining the role religion played in the imperial polity (Barkey 2008). Starting in the late thirteenth century, the Ottomans conceived a polity that was open to diversity. This accommodation was largely due to the particular regional and demographic conditions of conquest, the Turkic experience in the steppes of Central Asia and in the Seljuk empire that had preceded the Ottomans. Mixing this experience with a particular understanding of Islam that guided Muslim rulers to accept Christians and Jews as People of the Book, they established a tolerant imperial society that refrained from large-scale persecution of diversity. This difference, which Ottomans realized had *to be managed rather than eliminated*, became one of the most important aspects of the relationship between state and religious communities. Mostly, the imperial recognition of the value of diversity trumped the possibility of religious exclusion, especially as the Ottoman state remained vigilant about its control over religious extremes. The tightly supervised supremacy of the state over the predominant religion also helped contain the deleterious effects of Islamic orthodoxy. Despite such imperial jurisdiction, the forces that controlled religion also contributed to its entrenchment. The ulema built tremendous institutional competence and continuity through Ottoman history, most clearly visible at critical moments of the transition from empire to nation-state and thereafter. That is to say, the institutional representatives of an Orthodox version of Islam remained steadfast in their preferences on societal oversight even as the secular state insisted on "laic secularism." Such institutional continuity—and complexity—remains part of the contemporary rise of political Islam.

In the Ottoman Empire, ethnic and religious communities had different structural and cultural profiles. After the conquest of Constantinople in 1453, Mehmed II established particular compacts with each religious community (millets), marking a relationship of governance through dependency and autonomy. The Ottomans adopted the Greek Orthodox system of centralized, hierarchical governance for all Orthodox Christians. The compact with the Jews established a decentralized organizational framework around multiple lay leaders, and an intermediate form governed Armenians. Imperial rulers reconfigured these relations in the era of reforms between 1839 and 1856. From quasi-contracts renewed time and again, millets became formally structured and bounded entities, simultaneously endowed with equality and freedom. The citizenship law of 1869 declared full equality under the law. However, the language of "millet" was still used, and communities continued to think of themselves as millets. The contradictions were vast, signaling equality and yet assuming difference through formal "millet" boundaries; wanting to construct a loyal citizenry with Ottomanism as a central concept, while tampering with the internal autonomy of communities by introducing new structures of millet governance. Affording non-Muslims equality under Western European pressure also angered Muslim populations, who perceived Jews and Christians as having too many privileges. This became especially challenging as Muslim refugees poured into the shrinking empire.

The reform era mobilized religious communities qua communities and accelerated the process of individual identity formation, which culminated in the post-1908 revolutionary celebrations as well as in the elections that followed. After the unraveling of the revolution and the subsequent counterrevolution, these communities' "dreams were shattered" to different degrees, as Bedross der Matossian (2014) demonstrates. Through the European powers' interwar occupation of the Ottoman territories, each of the millets confronted different challenges. The Armenians, who had experienced pogroms following Russian intervention in eastern provinces, lived through the Ottoman massacres of 1895–96, which escalated into the genocide of 1915. Greeks faced various iterations of war and the flight of western Anatolian populations for Greece that culminated in the formal population exchanges of 1923. Jews, among the least politicized by the transformations, suffered the consequences of rising anti-millet sentiment through the wars. As the Balkans fell apart despite the zealous Young Turks' increasingly desperate and violent attempts to save the empire, the millets lost their privileges and autonomy and faced imminent extermination and expulsion. Those who escaped that fate became minorities.

In the denouement of this transition from empire to the nation-state, millets became minorities, a new vocabulary with negative implications for understandings of belonging in the new polity. The Treaty of Lausanne formally inaugurated the shift from millet to minority in 1923. Turkish nationalists came to view the politics of "minority rights" with contempt partly because the discourse emerged while the empire was being dismembered. They saw it as a concession to contemporary Western discourses on religious freedom and minority rights. The appellation of minority was applied to non-Muslim communities and underscored a potential unwillingness to accept them as part of the Turkish nation (Rodrigue 2013). The ethnic and religious groups within Islam, the Kurds and Alevis respectively, were subjected to forcible assimilation. In other words, non-Muslims, precluded from full belonging, became minorities, while the "Turkish" label veiled difference internal to Islam. The Turkish state did not demand loyalty by conversion (especially since the rhetoric of the state was strictly secular). However, the elite institutionalized distinctions between Muslims/Turks and non-Muslims in everyday life. Campaigns such as "Citizens Speak Turkish!" clearly discriminated against minorities who spoke various languages and were uncomfortable with the new Turkish language. In the absence of the millet's institutionalized protections, minorities felt unmoored. Finally, while the millet was perceived positively in imperial idiom, "minority" was and still is a vilified label.

Most scholars of Turkish secularization accept the conventional description of Turkish secularism: the ruling elite prohibited the public display of Muslim religiosity, while controlling religious life through a dedicated bureaucracy. We suggest that secularization proceeded at two levels, one restricting the formal and informal representations of Islam, the other allowing for continuity in clerical institutions under the aegis of the state. First and foremost, secularization modeled on the French experience affected the public display of religion. In the Anatolian countryside, away from the gaze of the state, conservative Islamic practice endured. The policies of the new republican state most adversely impacted

Sufi orders and heterodox groups on the margins of Ottoman religiosity, most of which were eliminated or went underground.

Second, even though the state strictly controlled it, religion continued to have an institutional existence. In the nineteenth and twentieth centuries, the religious bureaucracy had remained integrated into the state of Abdülhamit but also through the centralization policies of the Young Turks, and in the particular secular politics of Kemalist Turkey. Religious mobilization in the name of Islam was instrumental in rallying troops to fight the War of Independence. With the establishment of the Republic, control over Sunni practice remained with the Directorate of Religious Affairs (an organization similar to the Ottoman Seyh-ül-Islam). Even though the directorate's initial mandate was restricted, its role expanded, especially following the 1980 parchment-barrier constitution, whence it became the institution tasked with promoting Sunni Islamic religiosity. Although laicity eliminated public symbols of religion, Sunni Islam was privileged, and the directorate promoted institutionalized religiosity. Turkish secularism was not position-neutral; it favored Sunni Islam, just as Turkishness privileged ethnic Turks over other ethnic and religious groups.

Unlike the Jewish and Orthodox millets, the Kurdish and Alevi populations identify as Muslim. The new state's Turkification program subjected them to forced assimilation. This entailed the abandonment of the Kurdish language and Alevi religious traditions and disavowing all displays of Kurdish and Alevi cultural difference. The Sunni Muslim masses and their ulema were also disappointed, for they saw their sacrifices for nation-building abandoned in favor of a secular ideal. The new modern, westernized Turkey jettisoned pluralism and rendered both minorities and majorities uneasy, albeit asymmetrically. Today, under the leadership of Erdoğan and the Adalet ve Kalkınma Partisi (AKP), nationalism has become entwined with Sunni Islam much more forcefully, with the state backing the rejection of all other forms of Islamic belonging.

In sum, during the transition from empire to national state Turkey refashioned its relations with diversity, turning the three millets into minorities, subduing the Sunni Islamic population's religiosity while defining the nation through their identity, and repressing Muslim others into submission. Even though non-Muslim minorities have been affected by this transformation, their numerical insignificance (Jews, Armenians, and Greeks comprise less than 1 percent of the population) has mitigated their fate. They have remained on the margins of political life. Kurds and Alevis, however, have organized at different historical moments, with varying success. The significant institutional continuity bolstered the ascendancy and dominance of Sunni Muslims that their faith enjoyed, while observers mistakenly fixated on the formal and informal structures of secularism.

I.3.2. Unmaking British India

In the subcontinent, too, the arrival of political modernity spelt a profound transformation of state institutions and the historical transference from an empire-state to something like a nation-state. However, the imagination of the "nation-state" was both complex and fragmented. Unlike Turkey, the territorial space now called India was rarely securely unified under a single political regime, except short periods when a great line of empires—the Mauryas (first century BC), the Guptas (fourth century AD), the Delhi Sultanate (twelfth–sixteenth centuries AD) and the Mughal Empire (sixteenth–eighteenth centuries AD)— touched the highest point of their expansion. Even during these interregnums, the territorial expanse contained a variety of kingdoms and political authorities and different models of rulership. However, social history shows the existence of several large religious communities from ancient times. Political rulers were faced from the time of the Mauryas with a choice between aligning the state exclusively with a single religious group, and subordinating or extruding the others, or following a policy of accommodation toward a diversity of religious communities. At least since the time of Asoka, the general response of imperial rulers to religious diversity or plurality was accommodation in some form rather than exclusion. Mughal rulers followed this pragmatic tradition. Although they were formally adherents of Sunni Islam, they maintained close ties with the neighboring Persian empire and fostered the practice of Shia Islam among their subjects. More significantly, the dominant sections of their subject population consisted of Hindu sects. Despite evidence of sporadic incidents of temple destruction, the Mughals pursued a policy of accommodation toward differing strands of Islamic and Hindu sects. If we use the conceptual distinction between plurality—the brute fact of diversity of faiths—and pluralism—an ethical acknowledgment of the value of differing religious paths, and in some cases, even a celebration of the ethical, philosophical, cultural multiplicity this produced—the Mughal state was certainly animated by a *pluralist* political and cultural principle. Besides this political doctrine, religious life in everyday practice was dominated on the Islamic side by Sufi doctrines, on the Hindu side by followers of bhakti saints—like Vaishnavas, and by nascent syncretic traditions like those of the Sikhs. These sects followed a principle of mutual everyday toleration, giving rise to syncretic devotion at the popular level, and in some cases to innovative forms that combined and transcended the two primary faiths.

The initial stages of British expansion in India were accompanied by the arrival of Protestant missionaries who saw an immense opportunity for proselytization assisted by a Christian colonial power. However, pragmatic considerations of colonization and imperial expansion soon dispelled such trends. The colonial administration mostly refused the missionary temptation of expanding a spiritual empire of Christianity and discouraged the use of official patronage for Christians. The British colonial state, especially after the rebellion of 1857–58, positioned itself as a neutral arbiter between contending religious communities and their occasionally conflicting demands. Colonial scholarship, policy, and overt propaganda increasingly represented the historical relationship between Hindus and Muslims as one of eternal conflict. After James Mill's highly influential work on the history of the empire, the colonial knowledge complex portrayed Muslim rule as an earlier form of colonization. The specter of conflict between communities, primarily Hindus and Muslims, became a perpetual anxiety through the late nineteenth and early twentieth centuries. Simultaneously, technologies of rule, like the census, allowed states to acquire information, and thereby to manage communities. The census became a project of enumeration that produced these communities—Hindu, Muslim, scheduled castes, and so on—across the territorial expanse of British India. Late colonial policies like the introduction of separate electorates in limited representative institutions fixed and facilitated aggregated religious-political communities. Nevertheless, there was a long historical lineage behind the idea that the state should not become affiliated with a single religious community, and the British frequently appealed to their distance from both communities to legitimate their arbitration.

In British India too, not surprisingly, something akin to the contrast between millets and minorities was played out in political discourse. As the idea of the modern state with representative institutions became familiar in Indian political discourses, some Muslim thinkers, often based in Muslim-minority provinces, expressed anxiety about the future status of Muslims if the British Empire ended. The prospect of turning from an aristocratic minority into a minority under representative institutions was viewed with grave misgiving by a long line of Muslim leaders. Political debates before Indian independence consequently turned on the crucial question of representation of majorities and minorities in a modern "nation-state." Muslim political thought gradually divided into two traditions.

Leaders in the Muslim League eventually accepted the "two-nation theory," which claimed that the two religious communities were so fundamentally different that they could not coexist in a common "nation-state." But another section of the Muslim leadership agreed with leaders of the Indian National Congress in conceiving of its nation pluralistically, according minorities special protection in the constitution. The irreconcilable divergence between these two conceptions of the state led to the partition of British India and the death and displacement of millions. The state that the Indian constitution designed, and called by the name "nation-state," was a substantially different imaginative construct from the standard version of the European nation-state. The Congress elites sought to avoid forming a "nation" around a single group of people that would reduce others to unequal partners in the political community with long-standing relations of antagonism and domination. After independence, in India, this non-homogeneous, pluralist conception of the people and its state remained the dominant political discourse. It seemed that the ideal of a religious-pluralist "secular" political order had triumphed; providing a secular basis to India's democracy—although its image of secularity was vastly different from the French ideal of laïcité.

The events leading to the partition of British India, however, revealed that the existence of a plurality of religious groups as brute fact did not necessarily lead to the growth of pluralist philosophical or political traditions. Precisely this common past was read in radically opposed ways between two influential sets of political elites. India and Pakistan had a shared history—but this was interpreted by their politically dominant elites in entirely opposite ways. If the Nehruvian leadership in the Congress sought to build its constitutional design on the pluralist interpretation of the historical past, Pakistan under Jinnah was predicated on an opposite reading of this identical history. The independence of India was, from this angle, a profoundly ambiguous event: the creation of two states legitimizing two different readings of a shared past. India's political trajectory after independence showed internal complexities. Even though Nehru came to office, many in his party retained proclivities for domination over minorities. Hindu nationalist political parties suffered a temporary defeat, but remained a strident presence in political life. On a subtler level, Hindu nationalism as a political sentiment persisted in varying degrees among members of quite different political groups. For instance, segments of the Congress, and even some sections of the socialist political groups, expressed milder and fragmentary forms of Hindu nationalist sentiment. Yet there is a significant paradox in Indian democratic politics that demands some explanation. An array of factors, including the enumerative logic of democratic competition, led to a re-emergence of Hindu nationalist politics from the 1980s. After a period in which successive Hindu nationalist and pluralist coalition governments ruled at the center, in the 2014 general elections, Hindu nationalists came to office with a simple majority. Thereafter, democracy has been beset by majoritarian domination rather than straightforward authoritarianism or populism.

The Muslim League, led by Jinnah, was successful in establishing a separate state for Muslims in the subcontinent. Pakistan's founding, unlike India and Turkey, was not marked by a definitive elite settlement. We cannot say with certainty whether the legacy of Pakistan's founding moment was Jinnah's oft-quoted vision of religious freedom for minorities within a state created for South Asian Muslims or an Islamic republic ruled according to Maududi's ordering of divine and democratic sovereignty. By 1970, few dominant voices remained to defend the more "secular" conception of the state. The constitutional process of negotiating between these visions, staged in Pakistan's first Constituent Assembly, failed in 1954, and Pakistan's establishment as an Islamic state in 1956 was soon followed by military rule. The creation of Bangladesh in 1971 shattered the rhetoric of a nation for all South Asian Muslims. In its aftermath, through periods of democratic rule and military government, systemic violence and exclusion against religious minorities have intensified. The legacy of General Zia ul-Haque's derided "Islamization" has scarcely eroded. Elected governments following Zia's demise have actively sought to restore civilian power. However, civilian Prime Ministers, and Musharraf's military regime alike have not reversed state-sponsored Sunni domination.

Imran Khan's Pakistani Tehreek-i-Insaf Party's victory in 2018 heralds an unpredictable future for Pakistan's democratic future. It is also unclear whether democracy in Pakistan will mean religious domination, especially when violence and exclusion elicit wide popular support. One disheartening feature of the functioning of democratic institutions is the stark demonstration of the helplessness of democracy against itself. There are few barriers in the path of politicians who enjoy the support of a majority and seek to undermine democratic institutions.

I.4 Historical Perspectives

In this section, we compare aspects of the Ottoman and British Empires, and the modern states that emerged as their successors. Sadia Saeed's chapter foregrounds this comparative disposition. Saeed presents an intertemporal comparison of Safavid Iran and Mughal India, and contemporary Iran and Pakistan. Discussions on the relation between religion and sociological plurality are sometimes conducted in a rather one-sided manner: the central question is whether religious doctrines acknowledge the socially existing diversity, and make an effort to treat adherents of other religious faiths with dignity. This is a question about the doctrines internal to religious thought. But for premodern societies, which are often deeply religious, an argument about toleration and accommodation of religious diversity might come from an entirely different source— the *political* logic of imperial state formations. Imperial states have fluctuating boundaries, and when states expand very rapidly across territory, they acquire political control over increasingly diverse populations. An argument for toleration or accommodation arises at times from a purely political requirement of imperial states. Since converting these new subjects, or removing them through expulsion or extermination, is not a practically feasible option, imperial ruling elites sometimes craft political arguments for toleration. This can happen despite the existence of anti-pluralist ideas in religious doctrines.

Saeed challenges the notion that Islamic regimes' uniformly violate "minority rights" and that they have done so by following sharia. She argues that civilizational accounts of Islam's management of heterodoxy select particular features amenable to comparison with Western modernity and sometimes reductively posit sharia as the central principle of premodern Islamic societies. Whereas the Safavid rulers under Shah Abbas and thereafter persecuted and expelled the Nuqtavis, the Mughals, especially under Akbar, consciously promoted accommodation and toleration. Saeed shows that sharia, as a vocabulary of law and legitimacy, was not the primary motivation in either regime's disposition toward minorities. Contemporary Iran and Pakistan are more similar than their imperial precursors—both regimes persecute religious heterodoxies like the Baha'i and the Ahmadis. However, Saeed suggests that sharia could also legitimate opposition to Ahmadi exclusion, thereby demonstrating the versatility of Islamic religious vocabularies and emphasizing that political decisions do not follow inevitably from religious texts.

Both the Ottoman and the Mughal Empires acknowledged the presence of diversity, even though sociologically, the two empires were very different. In Turkey, other religious communities—the Christians and the Jews—were smaller groups living under the rule of a state that presided over a predominantly Muslim population. In India, this relation was reversed: even at its apogee, the Mughal Empire's subjects were mostly Hindus. However, Hindus rarely identified themselves as a single faith until the nineteenth century, in contrast to Jews and Christians. Unlike in Turkey, the presence of Islam in South Asia was socially dispersed, similar to the social organization of the Hindus, not organized by a state-recognized religious bureaucracy.

Over centuries, the bare political compulsion of tolerance became an institutionalized ethic of toleration and political pluralism. The Ottomans allocated specific privileges to the non-Muslims in the primarily Muslim center of the empire. In its external dominions, the empire had to administer areas that were primarily inhabited by non-Muslim subjects. The empire-state under the Mughals had to follow policies that reckoned with the established condition that Hindus vastly outnumbered their Muslim subjects. In the world outside the modern West, such practices of religious pluralism were intellectually established and turned into state policies much earlier than the rise of modern political toleration in Western political theory. However, both the fundamental principles of such accommodative politics and its institutional form were quite different, understandably, from Western secularism. When democratic forms of government were established in these societies, they had a long historical lineage of indigenous political theory and practice upon which they could draw.[1]

---

[1] It is not our suggestion that these legacies were symmetric. Both empires had significant fluctuations in imperial policy over time, and the Mughal Empire's effective sovereignty over large parts of India had begun to collapse as early as 1712. British rule interrupted this legacy and radically

The various inherited "usable pasts" were treated differently by the political elites in India, Pakistan, and Turkey. Our contributors examine the array of intellectual currents that circulated for approval in the twilight of empire. Two dissimilarities between the three cases are strikingly evident. First, as the Ottoman Empire shrank disastrously after the First World War, Turkey became more religiously and ethnically homogeneous. Turkish elites opted to obstruct the public display of Muslim religiosity while regulating religious life, notably through its ecclesiastical bureaucracy. Simultaneously, they endorsed symbolic primacy for ethnically Turk and religiously Sunni Muslim identity. In modern Turkey, continuity with the older forms of pluralism nearly disappeared, while the legacy of state-controlled Islam continued. Christine Philliou's chapter chronicles the decline of a counterfactual possibility. She demonstrates how the liberal, pluralist elite who had backed the Tanzimat reforms were steadily sidelined from politics as the Young Turk faction gained prominence and established a nationalist, authoritarian agenda to salvage the empire. The reformist liberal elites saw the future of the empire as a renewed imperial formation shaped by the confessional and ethnic pluralism that had been the backbone of imperial strength. Even though they represented another path to modernity and nationhood, they lacked ties to the crucial institutions and were overcome by nationalist forces. Their defeat led to the discursive superimposition of treason and liberalism. Liberal reformists were persecuted, and with their defeat, the Young Turks tied liberalism and toleration to treachery and betrayal of the nation. Their defeat narrowed the trajectory of the transition, and notwithstanding ebbs and flows in the practice of democracy, liberalism has not resurfaced in Turkey's political mainstream.

Meanwhile, the last decades of British rule in undivided India saw fervent intellectual activity undergirding movements for independence, religious reform, and the overthrow of the caste system. Faisal Devji's chapter recounts influential theorists' attempts to subvert colonial assumptions about the banality of religious conflict and the bankruptcy of South Asian political thought. The figures Devji discusses, exemplars of Hindu, Muslim, and Dalit politics, engage in a project that clarifies the problem of *rational* interest in colonial religious and caste politics. They reject the colonial framing of impassioned, irrational natives destined for perpetual bloodshed and consider anew the causes of and motivations for communal conflict, and what to do about it. For B. R. Ambedkar, contestation over rational interests was impeded by collective mobilization at the expense of individual rationality among Hindus and Muslims, and, more significantly, by the perversity of caste, which misrepresented the interests of upper castes

altered language and idiom in public life. It is an open question whether political elites were inspired by more than a distant historical memory of negotiated toleration.

as those of all Hindus. Reformulating religious mobilization was a priority for Muslim separatists and Hindu nationalists alike. M. A. Jinnah and V. D. Savarkar understood extant religious conflict as born from the history of intimate relations, and both sought to *rationalize* the basis of their community's engagement with the other and within itself. Whereas Jinnah sought to create a mutual interest in harmony, Savarkar sought to produce for the Hindu community a more instrumentally rational political lexicon. M. K. Gandhi stood apart in rejecting rationality, and interest, especially of property, as the basis of harmonious cooperation. Mohammad Iqbal was also suspicious of the notion that a society based on interest was desirable. But he prescribed a spiritual solution steeped in the unique intellectual traditions of South Asian Islam, quite distinct from Gandhi's emphasis on everyday sacrifice and self-abnegation.

Uday Mehta's chapter presents an examination of Gandhi's critique of the dominant approaches to religious diversity, including that of postcolonial India's constitution. Mehta suggests that Gandhi rejected fundamental assumptions about religious conflict, such as its inevitable escalation, and instead saw it as self-regulating and contained. Gandhi opposed understanding and articulating religious diversity and conflict in modern political terms because these traditions had unexceptional, long-standing histories in South Asia. In contrast with a securitized vision in which the state resolved such conflicts, Gandhi ardently opposed the idea of an intermediary authority. Secularism, on this account, was a form of mediation between abstract claims and values, not a practical enterprise grounded in everyday life. Moreover, Mehta suggests, it was part and parcel of a project of radical social transformation that Gandhi had little interest in pursuing. Gandhi's solution lay instead in an invocation of religion, which alone could inspire *patience* and thus, coexistence. Mehta's chapter is both a critique of the project of negotiation between state and religion and an invitation to consider religion anew, devoid of the pernicious logics produced within it by statist discourses.

Humeira Iqtidar's chapter examines the thought of Vinayak Damodar Savarkar and Abul A'la Maududi, whose followers claim them as the originators of Hindu nationalism and Islamism, respectively. Unlike Gandhi, Savarkar and Maududi articulated a "modernist conception of religiosity," thereby contributing to a "secularization" of multifarious practice-oriented faiths. Savarkar's *The Essentials of Hindutva* is steeped in a nationalist vocabulary drawn from his interpretation of European nationalism. Savarkar's priority was the construction of an inclusive, territorially linked nation with hierarchical claims based on greater attachment—that of coinciding ancestral and religious allegiance to India, which would never be available to Muslims and Christians. Maududi, on the other hand, critiqued the uncritical imitation of European nationalism, which was incompatible with Islam and contained the possibility of unbridled racial domination. Maududi suggested that the extent of religious plurality in British India necessitated political nationality—a framework for the negotiation of political differences—rather than cultural nationalism, based on the homogeneity of social conditions. However, both assumed and accepted what they took to be democracy's central imperative: constituting and sustaining a "majority." For Savarkar, this majority was a Hindu majority, defined by the coincidence of holy and ancestral territory. For Maududi, the majority included the Muslims of the world, motivated to support democracy for the furtherance of ethical principles compatible with Allah's sovereign will. Democracy itself would not have a settled relationship with pluralism, and the projects that claim inspiration from Savarkar and Maududi would benefit from a reliance upon majority will in democratic and military rule alike.

Pakistan's 1956 constitution declared it an Islamic state and equipped it with an institutional apparatus to ensure adherence to certain religious precepts. The Pakistani elite permitted only the public religiosity of Sunni Islam even as the persecution of Ahmadis began before the constitution's enactment and intensified in the following decades. Even as the Indian and Pakistani trajectories differed, alternative "usable pasts" remain alive within their traditions as, for instance, Savarkar's imaginary of a Hindu nationalist India finds resurgence under the Bharatiya Janata Party (BJP).

In political life, all moments or all periods are not equal. There can be two different spans of equal time—let us say a decade—that are of quite unequal historical importance. Founding moments might determine the future course of history, precisely because these are moments in which framing institutions are often shaped: a constitution formed, or state boundaries established. These events are themselves products of contingent moments, but they serve to constrain the range of options available to later generations of political actors. In this respect, the founding moments in India, Pakistan, and Turkey are interesting to compare, especially because unprecedented mass violence accompanied each transition.

For Turkey, the postwar years saw the vast Ottoman Empire shrink into a state that was territorially much smaller. Because a large inward migration of populations accompanied the collapse of the empire, the residual state was more homogeneous in terms of religion and ethnicity. The Armenian genocide and forced exchanges were absorbed as necessities and their genocidal impact denied in official histories. Independence for India was a profoundly ambiguous event: the celebration of freedom was inextricable from the political failure to prevent a territorial partition of British India into two separate, eventually hostile states, and more significantly, from the massacre of millions of people caught in the transfer of populations. The Indian political elite sought to fashion a constitution that could render such events less probable in future.

Through a negotiated process, they established universal franchise democracy and enshrined minority protections in the constitution. Although the actual enjoyment of minority rights was sometimes constrained in political life, these were protected in cultural and educational life. The same event—partition—was a moment of triumph in Pakistan, the culmination of a successful movement for a state for South Asian Muslims. In this sense, it acted not to constrain elites, but to empower claims for a state that gave symbolic primacy to Islam. Partition's material effects—relatively disadvantageous for Pakistan in economic and military resources—only exacerbated the challenges to democratic compromise.

The second axis of comparison concerns the career of democracy in each society. Turkey's modern transformation has often been overtly authoritarian, with long spells of military government and formal one-party rule. Republican elites, parties, and the military, as the guardians of secularism and claimants to Ataturk's legacy, colluded to keep power in their hands to the detriment of the Anatolian hinterland. This latter group, more conservative and overtly religious, over time became increasingly dissatisfied with the ruling parties. The dissatisfaction of religious Muslims mapped onto an anti-authoritarian impulse—from which the AKP benefited in the initial stages of its ascendance. In Pakistan too, democratic competition was frequently interrupted by long spells of military rule. Among the four coup spells, Zia ul-Haq's regime from 1977 through 1988 has perhaps had the most significant impact upon politics thereafter. Religious domination—through coerced public religiosity of the majority and violence against the minorities—intensified, and political competition became subservient to military-determined national security concerns. India's competitive democratic system was formally interrupted only briefly, by the Congress, in the "Emergency" from 1975 to 1977. Most of the constitutional changes initiated during the Emergency were reversed upon the resumption of democratic rule, but the first non-Congress government retained the commitment to a "secular" republic. In the following decade, political parties across the spectrum began making majoritarian appeals and promoting violence—especially against Sikhs and Muslims—rendering the "secular" label aspirational rather than achieved.

Our historical comparison alludes to different explanatory challenges in each case, based upon our shared anxiety about the relationship between democracy and religious pluralism since the modern foundation of these polities.

I.5 Genealogies of State and Religion

Many of our chapters deal with the founding moments of these polities—Turkey's foundation through the Kemalist constitution, India's Constituent Assembly and interim government, and Pakistan's more indecisive and protracted process of settling down into an institutional system determined by its constitution. In these cases, and elsewhere in the non-European world, this constituted a period of transition in a peculiar sense. Most non-European states were some form of empire-states or their successors, which may not have inherited their vast territorial extent but continued with the features of their political institutions. For instance, the empire-states did not demand too close a connection between the rulers and their subjects, notions of popular sovereignty, or European-style "nationalism." Thus, what the process of transition was from was quite clear: it was a breakdown of imperial systems and replacement of empire-states by states of some different form. What would emerge from the transition was much less clear for two reasons. First, the conversion into another form of state took decades, even centuries, and was not evident, in the sense of being unconcluded for some time; and second, the transition was not to a single form of the state. Indeed, what the form was to be was both contested and multiple.

We need to observe an interesting feature of these foundations: these are all equally foundational moments in the life of their states, but they are not foundations of the same thing. If we set aside the misleading idea from international law that "all states are nation-states" or that "we live in a time of nation-states," we shall realize an important truth about the international state order—that the nation is not primarily a legal category: it is a sociological category to which the international order gives a uniform, legal recognition a posteriori. The nation-state, to be meaningful, must be a kind of state. Historically, the term emerged as a new kind of state emerged in Europe out of the slow decline and fragmentation of imperial states—the destruction of the Holy Roman Empire, the Spanish and Portuguese empires, and the imperial structures of the French state. Imperial states had constantly fluctuating boundaries, and therefore the relation between their structures and their populations were not stable. As a further consequence, these states were far more accustomed to dealing with and acknowledging diversity among their subjects. The states that emerged after the disruption of the imperial orders were far more homogeneous, with fixed boundaries and fixed populations, which were systematically homogenized by orderly ethnic cleansing now described as the Westphalian process. This form came to be defined as the nation-state.

The states that emerged from the foundational moments of the non-Western world were quite heterogeneous. In our three cases, the state outcomes were quite divergent. Turkey decided in favor of the typical European state, specifically a French model—secular, ethnically homogeneous (or pretending to be), and based on a uniform national citizenry. Pakistan, at least formally, also adopted the European model of a sociologically singular nation of citizens—stressing their identity of the Muslim religion, and ignoring other, especially linguistic, forms of diversity. India, by contrast, adopted through its constitution a

model of a state based explicitly on a diverse group of peoples—separated by religion, caste, language, regional culture, and so forth—an internally plural political community. Yet these were all called by the international community equally
"nation-states"; and more confusingly, they themselves applied that descriptive
term to themselves. Pakistan and Turkey conceived themselves as nation-states,
as did India—though far more implausibly. In our historical analysis, therefore,
we have to be skeptical about this false and entirely misleading homogenization
and pursue the logic of very different kinds of state-making in each case.

In her contribution to this volume, Rochana Bajpai examines how the Indian
state has negotiated between the claims of different religious groups and the
effects of state policies on societal pluralism. A state's approach to religious plurality is itself plural at any given time and over time. Bajpai's typology of political
pluralism unsettles the narrative of the state as an unchanging agent of homogenization over time. Precolonial regimes adopted "hierarchical pluralism," where
the dominance of one religion was recognized, while others were tolerated
within an asymmetric hierarchy produced by caste. Thereafter, following British
rule, the Indian constitution heralded four forms of negotiation: weak multicultural, integrationist exclusionary, integrationist inclusionary, and strong multicultural. Weak multiculturalism describes limited self-regulation for minorities,
with the acknowledgment that the state's prerogatives are prior, as in the case
of the constitution's recognition of group rights and autonomy for minorities in
the practice and propagation of religion and in cultural and educational affairs.
Strong multiculturalism refers to internal regulation valued for itself, as in the
Congress's problematic support for the Muslim orthodoxy in the Shah Bano case.
Integrationist exclusionary measures included the disestablishment of separate
electorates and the refusal to reserve constituencies for religious minorities in
their stead. Scheduled castes and tribes were treated somewhat more inclusively,
with reserved constituencies defended as serving integrative as well as social
justice goals simultaneously. Bajpai argues that majoritarian assimilationism,
with similarities to Sri Lanka and Pakistan, has supplanted these approaches to
diversity under Hindu nationalist rule in India. Unlike integrationism, assimilationism denies the legitimacy of pluralism and seeks to impose majority
practices, symbols, and control on minorities.

Ateş Altınordu introduces a different logic of state-religion engagement in
his examination of the prospects of postsecularism in contemporary Turkey.
Postsecularism, in Jürgen Habermas's formulation, describes a new phase in the
relationship between state and religion, wherein secular and religious actors develop the capacity for mutual respect and complementary learning. Altınordu's
empirical analysis focuses on compulsory religious instruction in primary and
secondary schools, the status of public atheism, and complementary learning
processes between religious and secular citizens during the Gezi protests of 2013.

He shows that far from being able to develop complementary learning processes that lead to mutual respect, neither religious nor secular actors have been able to become respectful of the other, partly due to political polarization. Altınordu concludes by suggesting that Habermas was insufficiently attentive to the state's power over discourse, and the possibility that this power might be actively exercised to prevent the advent of postsecularism.

Matthew Nelson highlights the plurality of approaches to pluralism by examining the puzzle of the Constituent Assembly of Pakistan's adoption, retention, and reinterpretation of religious rights articles from Irish and Indian antecedents to explain how a constitutional clause can have varied effects in different contexts. The importation of constitutional text becomes a lens through which Nelson explains changing motivations, and as a result, consequences for religious pluralism. He argues that borrowed constitutional provisions are merely "empty signifiers" that acquire new meanings when read in conjunction with contextual legal and political changes. Religious freedom rights that protected minorities in India and Ireland later specified and legitimated Ahmadi persecution as a non-Muslim minority in Pakistan. Nelson's chapter shows how locating Zia ul-Haq's dictatorship as the beginning of Ahmadi discrimination effectively conceals the complicity of secular parties and politics in creating and sustaining the constitutional architecture that undermined pluralism before and after the lengthy military interlude.

In suggesting that democracy and religious pluralism must be negotiated, we must disambiguate the actors *negotiating* that relationship. Mathew John's chapter traces the Indian Constituent Assembly and, subsequently, the Supreme Court of India's interventions in regulating state interference in religion. John argues that the Supreme Court's use of "essential practices" doctrine has served to constrain the exercise of religious liberty and diminish the extent of religious pluralism. Under this doctrine, the Supreme Court has adjudicated which practices are essential to religious worship and which are not, leaving the latter within the domain of legitimate state intervention. Over time, the court has protected a shrinking set of core practices from state intervention. Further, despite its recognition of the plurality of traditions and practices of Hindu religiosity, the Supreme Court has synthesized a doctrinal account of Hindu religion. John argues that an alternative interpretive framework would better protect religious pluralism and empower state intervention in discriminatory practices.

Sudipta Kaviraj's chapter demonstrates the decline of state pluralism, the logic of aggregative identities in political mobilization in independent India, and, in closing, the moral psychology and institutional structure of democratic violence. Kaviraj argues that caste's hierarchical and segmenting features produced a logic of mobilization that, over time, accorded legitimacy to identitarian aggregation of all shades—not just those identified by the constitution-makers as deserving of recognition on the grounds of social justice. When Dalits, other backward classes (OBCs), and Adivasis created political parties and built extensive social networks, the logic of collective mobilization became a tool for their relative empowerment. However, when these parties struck bargains to acquire political power, they evoked disillusionment among supporters and the ire of upper-caste groups who saw the redistribution of wealth and power as illegitimate. The Congress justified its varied social coalitions with Nehruvian pluralism. Over time, both the party and its purported pluralism were discredited, most successfully and definitively by the BJP in 2014 and 2019. As Savarkar suggested, the composition of Hindus as a political community entailed the thinning of the ethical and practical core of religious practice to erase differences across regions, traditions, and castes. Simultaneously, the definition of Hinduness acquired meaning through differences with Muslims and Christians. Electorally, this identity took shape only over the past three decades, and the BJP's electoral rise and sustenance have come alongside a rise in "everyday violence." Kaviraj explores the conditions of possibility for such violence—the complexity of agential structures in the modern Indian state; the nature of mob violence; and mismatch between a social organization's incentives and a political party's compulsions. The forms and characteristics of violence bring us to the volume's final section.

I.6 Violence and Domination

Conventional accounts of democracy treat the absence of political violence as a necessary condition for democracy to exist. Further, political theorists often imply that democracy prevents political violence between groups competing for power. Following Schumpeter, Western observers of democracy have examined democracy primarily as a *steady-state* framework for political life, rather than a historically unfolding process. In doing so, these thinkers have winnowed numerous forms of political violence to that between elite factions competing for state power. Western theorists presume that political violence, narrowly construed, is kept in abeyance by democracies as found in Western nation-states. Persistent violence against minorities—as in the case of Black Americans—does not affect the prospects of democracy, because it is deemed social and not political. Such a position forecloses careful analyses of the causes and consequences of violence on the institutions of democratic rule. Our contributors thus confront a twofold problem. First, as in the West, the problem of violence has not been settled before the modern state's founding. Second, persistent collective violence against groups has significant consequences for democratic institutions and political activity. The chapters in this volume demonstrate how democratic logics of mobilization and contestation can cause varied forms of social and political violence imbricating religious communities, practices, and symbols. Reflexively, contributors also describe how acts of violence shape democracy and religious life.

Fatima Bokhari's chapter discusses the transformation of Pakistan's blasphemy laws from legal pluralism provisions that protected group rights into an instrument of domination for the majority community against perceived slights by minorities. She argues that under Zia ul-Haq's rule, the regime amended colonial-era laws regulating speech and offense, formalizing a pattern of discrimination already prevalent in the mobilization against Ahmadis, as discussed in Nelson's chapter. These changes formally restricted the application of blasphemy laws to the protection of Islamic sentiment, as opposed to the sentiment of Pakistan's numerous religious minorities. Bokhari shows how those accused under these laws, their lawyers, prosecutors, judges, and state officials are routinely threatened and have been murdered by those seeking pronouncements of guilt, whether as a judicial verdict or social condemnation. The judicial system in Pakistan does not resolve blasphemy cases; it has instead become a site for the broader political domination of Ahmadis and other minorities.

In India, accusations of cow slaughter, or "love jihad," have acquired a similar status as blasphemy in the popular fury they elicit and the violence that ensues. There is a striking resemblance in the form of violence directed against alleged blasphemers and supposed cow slaughterers. In some cases, groups of men assault and murder victims, often on camera, with the confidence that it was the actions of their peers that resulted in murder. In other cases, they celebrate the victim's death, and proudly proclaim their deed. Social and political organizations provide legitimacy to these actions by commemorating them or even offering them nominations to seek political office. The state and its law enforcement apparatus remain inert, or offer tacit material and symbolic support, signaling that such acts of violence are permissible and possibly desirable.

Amrita Basu chronicles these and other instances of violence in contemporary India. She argues that unlike the BJP-led government of 1998–2004, the second and third BJP-led national governments' tethering of religious nationalism to right-wing populism has led to greater violence against minorities. Selective violence against minorities proliferates below a threshold of casualties that the state has conventionally recorded as mass violence, thereby furthering political polarization without incurring the substantial political costs of a "riot." After 2002, when Narendra Modi's government in Gujarat presided over deadly riots, an earlier model of mobilization by polarization became ineffectual. Pogroms on a large scale seemed to cause unassailable political costs imposed by news media as public opinion, and by associations of industry. Basu extensively chronicles lists "small scale" violence and "hate crimes" against religious, caste, and gender minorities carried out with the complicity—a priori or belated—and support of the state. These incidents serve both to secure electoral victories and to redescribe the founding narrative of the Indian state.

The fate of ethnic and religious minorities in Turkey has ebbed and flowed through the republican period, with periods of intense violence against Kurdish populations of eastern Turkey, especially under one-party and military rule, and since 2013. The Kurds have been involved in a consistently violent confrontation, fighting against state repression and autonomy. The Alevis have historically been more widely dispersed, and have faced discrimination that bears similarity to the Ahmadiyya in Pakistan. The Diyanet, especially under the AKP regime, classifies the Alevis as Sunni, influenced by Sufism, instead of recognizing their claim to being a non-Sunni Muslim community. The result is that they cannot claim state support for their religious institutions and practices. Unlike recognized minorities, the Alevis are also subjected to compulsory Sunni religious instruction in schools. Jews and Greek Orthodox Christians, insignificant in demographic terms, have a long history of incorporation through indirect rule under the millet system under Ottoman rule, and continue to articulate group claims through community leaders. Violence against minorities in Turkey has taken varied forms, including targeted atrocities, such as the 5–6 September 1955 or the 2 July 1993 attacks against Alevis and a protracted civil war against the Kurdish population. As Turkey attempted to join the European community in the late 1990s, it accepted judicial stipulations from the European Court of Human Rights that portended the possibility of more robust minority protections.

Senem Aslan examines the consequences of this legal shift for state-minority relations in Turkey. She argues that Turkey's courts have developed a statist jurisprudence that continually undermines minority interests and, further, that the judiciary has failed to ensure executive compliance with ECtHR judgments and even Turkish precedents. Aslan illustrates the failure of Alevi judicial activism by considering compulsory religious instruction in schools, religious identification on identity cards, and the construction of cem houses. In each instance, ECtHR jurisprudence was unequivocal in its direction to Turkish authorities, but executive authorities at local and national levels cited domestic law and national courts to disregard, sabotage, or delay implementation. Kurdish legal activism, Aslan suggests, has been comparatively more successful because it was accompanied by widespread social and political mobilization and emerged against the backdrop of a devastating civil war. Activism around the use of Kurdish names and the Kurdish language ultimately achieved its ends through political action that modified Turkish law through legislation. Aslan shows that discrimination may be better observed in the state's use of administrative tools than in legal pronouncements alone. After the attempted coup in 2016, the Turkish state has vigorously attacked minority rights, highlighting Aslan's central claim: political and social mobilizations are essential to securing pluralism in modern Turkey. As of this writing, the prospects for pluralism are bleak.

Nosheen Ali's chapter observes an interesting feature of identity politics that is often left unremarked in the literature. Even before the creation of Pakistan, some major Islamic writers, including Iqbal, demanded a consensus around the idea that Ahmadis are not Muslims. This immediately suggests that the creation of a state for *all* Muslims was less simple than it initially appeared because there could be indeterminacy in the definition of who was a Muslim, and therefore identification of *all* the Muslims of South Asia. Ali's chapter examines a subsequent stage of the search for progressively purer versions of Muslimness, and a redefinition of a Muslim around an exclusivist and purist Sunni identity that goes on to find Shias of uncertain or questionable status. This is reflected in the widespread violence against Shias in a state that was meant to provide security to all Indian Muslims against the persecution of Hindus. A definition around a religious identity can turn into a problem precisely because it can be defined more and more tightly around narrower definitions of that identity. The force of Ali's argument comes from the theoretical insight: identities can be defined in terms of purity or in terms of grades of intensity. When the latter process unfolds, a dominant subgroup can turn against and persecute groups hitherto considered within the fold with the enormous force of the state. To describe such a scenario, it is important for scholarly vocabulary to be cognizant of the power that permeates difference. Ali therefore encourages the replacement of "sectarianism," a power-neutral concept, with "sectism," which more effectively communicates the normative stakes of the Shia-Sunni relationship in contemporary Pakistan.

The volume closes with Karen Barkey and Vatsal Naresh's comparative analysis of majoritarian domination in Turkey and India. Barkey and Naresh identify majoritarian domination as the transposition of a sociological, enumerated majority upon the idea of majority rule, resulting in the avoidable and arbitrary interference in the basic interests of minorities. They suggest that although India's and Turkey's respective founding moments bequeathed different legacies for the negotiation between democracy and religious pluralism, the two polities have since converged. The fate of religious minorities—and of democracy— hangs perilously in both societies, as well as in Pakistan. This volume offers no predictions or prescriptions. We hope to provide instead a set of historically grounded chapters that help explain the past and present.

References

Apter, David E. 1965. *The Politics of Modernization*. Chicago: University of Chicago Press.
Barkey, Karen. 2008. *Empire of Difference: The Ottomans in Comparative Perspective*. Cambridge; New York: Cambridge University Press.

Matossian, Bedross. 2014. *Shattered Dreams of Revolution: From Liberty to Violence in the Late Ottoman Empire*. Stanford: Stanford University Press.

Geertz, Clifford. 1963. *Old Societies and New States: The Quest for Modernity in Asia and Africa*. London: The Free Press.

Gerschenkron, Alexander. 1962. *Economic Backwardness in Historical Perspective*. New York: F. Praeger. http://catalog.hathitrust.org/api/volumes/oclc/7391717.html.

Lerner, Daniel. 1968. *The Passing of Traditional Society: Modernizing the Middle East*. New York: Free Press.

Rudolph, Lloyd I. and Susanne Hoeber Rudolph. 1967. *The Modernity of Tradition: Political Development in India*. Chicago: University Of Chicago Press.

Rodrigue, Aron. 2013. "Reflections on Millets and Minorities: Ottoman Legacies." In *Turkey between Nationalism and Globalization*, edited by Riva Kastoryano. New York: Routledge.

SECTION I
HISTORICAL PERSPECTIVES

1

Islam, Modernity, and the Question of Religious Heterodoxy

From Early Modern Empires to Modern Nation-States

Sadia Saeed

Questions centered on apostasy, heresy, and blasphemy are critical public issues in contemporary Muslim societies. A plethora of prominent examples can be readily identified, ranging from globally contentious incidents (e.g., the fatwa issued by Iran's Ayatollah Khomeini against Salman Rushdie for writing *The Satanic Verses* in 1989; global outcry in the wake of printing of satirical cartoons depicting Prophet Muhammad in Danish and French publications) to nationally contentious issues (e.g., the controversies surrounding the religious status of the Ahmadiyya communities in a host of Muslim countries; the supposed apostasy of Nasr Abu Zayd in Egypt). In response, Muslim political authorities have often enacted laws that criminalize blasphemy, heresy, and/ or apostasy. In other words, states in Muslim majority societies have been actively engaged in defining what can be broadly termed religious heterodoxy. Consequently, elaborate official, legal, and public narratives have emerged that aim to specify what constitutes blasphemy, who is a heretic, and the constitutional limits of religious freedoms. At stake in these narratives are quintessentially modern issues pertaining to secularism, nationalism, state formation, and liberal constitutional rights (e.g., Ahmed 2009; Hirschkind 1995; Saeed 2017).

While these core issues are distinctly modern, "tradition" critically informs these contemporary debates. In the imagination of Muslims, typically Islamists and ulema, who are engaged in establishing the public import of punitive positive laws criminalizing what they perceive as religious heterodoxy, maintaining coherent and readily intelligible distinctions between religious orthodoxy/ orthopraxy and heterodoxy/heteropraxy is important because of requirements of sharia (e.g., Maududi 1977). Often, this maintenance is also perceived as being integral to defining the boundaries of the Muslim umma so that the latter may effectively manage threats against itself not only from non-Muslims but also

Sadia Saeed, *Islam, Modernity, and the Question of Religious Heterodoxy* In: *Negotiating Democracy and Religious Pluralism*. Edited by: Karen Barkey, Sudipta Kaviraj, and Vatsal Naresh, Oxford University Press. © Oxford University Press 2021. DOI: 10.1093/oso/9780197530016.003.0002

from the transgressors, impostors, and deviants within.[1] In response, critics and opponents of these positions have posited alternative understandings of the ethos of sharia, pointing to tolerance and freedom of religious beliefs as fundamental Islamic imperatives for crafting modern Muslim polities (An'Naim 2008; Afsaruddin 2008). Analytically, then, contemporary preoccupations with Islamic heterodoxy unfold on contested discursive terrains in which various interlocutors attempt to address and negotiate the relationship between tradition and modernity, (positive) law and ethics, Muslim nationhood and state formation, and the boundaries between public morals and private beliefs.

In fact, the issue of curbing (or tolerating) religiously heterodox aspirations, commitments, and worldviews has been a perennial feature of Islamic history. It preoccupied the first caliph, Abu Bakr, who orchestrated the Wars of Apostasy to discipline, among others, those Muslims who stopped paying taxes to the state, thereby becoming lax in fulfilling their Islamic obligations, after Prophet Muhammad's death in AD 632 (Donner 1981: 85–86). It occupied the Abbasid rulers as they dealt with the detested *zandaqa* and their "heresies" through an active policy of persecution.[2] We can witness similar anxieties about heretical *madhhabs* (Islamic schools of law), Sufi orders, and "troublesome" individuals under subsequent Islamic political regimes, extending all the way into the early modern period and subsequently entering the modern period.

Even a cursory glance at this history shows that the very complexion of "apostates" and "heretics" has varied dramatically across Islamic history, ranging from amorphous grouping such as *zandaqa*; now-extinct *madhhabs* such as the Karramiyya (Malamud 1994); prominent individuals such as Mansur al-Hallaj (848–922); bygone Sufi orders such as the Nuqtavis (Babayan 2002); and contemporary revivalist movements such as the Baha'is and the Ahmadiyya (Cole 1998; Friedmann 1989). Scholarship on these have emphasized factors such as the quest for political legitimacy, popular sentiments, considerations of law and order, and sharia injunctions about unbelief (*kufr*), apostasy (*ridda*), and heresy (*ilhad*) to properly contextualize these various instances.

Taking the previously mentioned contested discursive terrains as its point of departure, this chapter posits the following questions: how have distinct understandings about sharia—its broader aims, spirit, and ethos, as well as its positive injunctions—shaped concrete state responses toward managing "heterodox" religious communities across time and space? I address this question

---

[1] This was the South Asian Muslim poet Muhammad Iqbal's justification in 1935 for demanding that British colonial authorities in India cease to include the "heretical" Ahmadiyya community in the Indian Muslim category. See Iqbal (1976).

[2] The *zandaqa* connote a loose grouping of individuals who were persecuted in the early Abbasid Empire for their heresies, in particular for secretly harboring dualist Manichaean beliefs. See Ibrahim (1994).

through a comparative and historical approach. First, I analyze how rulers in two early modern Muslim empires, Safavid Iran and Mughal India, dealt with the same heterodox group, the Nuqtavi Sufi order. Next, I focus on how two contemporary Muslim-majority states that emerged from these empires, Iran and Pakistan, have sought to regulate and discipline "heretical" groups in their midst—Baha'is in Iran and the Ahmadiyya in Pakistan.

My aim in posing the question (and method of inquiry) thus is twofold. First, I seek to interrogate how the management of religious heterodoxy has evolved in the shift from early modern Muslim empires to modern nation-states. I ask: is the temporal break between early modern/premodern empires and modern states— a break that is fundamentally inscribed within our accounts of modernity—able to account for actually existing historical differences? How exactly are early modern empires different from modern Muslim states in managing religious heterodoxy? Can we identify patterns that crosscut these political forms? This line of inquiry, I argue, is critical for moving away from civilizational accounts that seek to capture supposedly essential features of Muslim societies, and for moving toward comparative and historical studies that are able to identify analytically sound connections and comparisons among and beyond Muslim societies. This, in turn, is critical for formulating accounts of transitions to modernity that are not beholden to teleological Eurocentric notions that emphasize and normalize notions of unredeemable and non-usable pasts and always-already open and progressive futures.

Second, this chapter seeks to throw light on how sharia, both as a religious symbol and as a repository of concrete and practice-oriented injunctions, has functioned historically in state management of religious heterodoxy. It is now commonplace to assert, following Talal Asad's classic statement on the subject, that Islam as an object of study is best approached as a discursive tradition, that is, as a historically contingent and evolving set of discourses that inform the practices and institutions of Muslims (Asad 1986). However, it also remains the case that this discursive tradition is often at play only selectively, if at all, and is invoked and drawn upon in variable ways in different historical contexts. An inquiry into these variations clears important analytical space for contextualizing and historicizing both positive injunctions and more general and diffuse understandings of sharia.

Based on these two entwined lines of inquiry, this chapter demonstrates that there were significant historical variations between early modern Muslim empires with respect to religious policy toward heterodox groups. While Safavid Iran provides a striking example of religious persecution of "dissenting" religious orders, the case of the Mughal Empire depicts an active political commitment toward providing a safe haven and a welcoming abode for persecuted groups. In contrast to these *multiple pasts*, contemporary Muslim-majority states exhibit considerable similarities vis-à-vis state policies toward heterodox groups. Iran and Pakistan continue to criminalize Baha'is and the Ahmadiyya respectively as a matter of considered state policies that have been legitimized through quintessentially modern, constitutional, and nationalist means. Iran and Pakistan thus enjoy a shared present that needs to be accounted for. Furthermore, in none of the four cases was the response of any polity structured by positive sharia injunctions. Instead, distinct politico-cultural imaginaries about governing religious differences have shaped different state responses. These imaginaries, I argue, are an outcome of concrete geopolitical, demographic, and ideological milieus and not derivatives of Islamic juristic laws (i.e., *fiqh*). On the whole, by comparing the variable state responses and social meanings of sharia within and across these different political forms, this chapter makes a case for incorporating notions of multiple Muslim pasts and an increasingly convergent and shared Muslim modernity within our accounts of transitions to modernity.

In what follows, I begin with a critical discussion of civilizational analyses in the study of Muslim societies. Next, deploying the question of religious pluralism and heterodoxy, I proceed to make a case for a historical and comparative sociology of Muslim societies that is foregrounded in the multiple pasts of Muslim societies. I follow this discussion with a historical analysis of the previously mentioned cases—the Nuqtavi order in Safavid Iran and Mughal India, the Ahmadiyya movement in Pakistan, and the Baha'is in Iran.

1.1. Islam and Civilizational Analyses

The question of how to define Islam as an object of study has been central to scholarship on Islam. A significant trend in this scholarship is the quest to identify the essential characteristics of Islamic tradition and how these impact Muslim societies across space and time. I characterize this scholarship as driven by civilizational analyses, and argue that it occludes systematic inquiry into how Muslim societies have historically resembled or differed from each other with respect to core and recurrent political, religious, and social issues. One result of this is the analytical marginalization of the differential ways in which the Islamic tradition, typically coded as "sharia law," has been concretely deployed across time and space.

The most sustained theoretical treatment of the subject of civilizational analyses has been developed by S. N. Eisenstadt through the framework of multiple modernities. The term was explicitly aimed at a critique of modernization theories that proceed from classical sociological works of Marx, Weber, and Durkheim. There were two broad critiques leveled at the latter's teleological rendering of modern social change as a transition from backward, archaic, and antiquated "tradition" to rational, scientific, and essentially Western "modernity." First, Eisenstadt critiqued the assumptions that there *ought* or even *could* be a single endpoint (so to speak) of modernity. Not only do different people hold "very different views on what makes societies modern," they also operate as active agents to reconstitute societies in order to realize their preferred cultural visions and programs (Eisenstadt 2000: 2). Second, Eisenstadt (and collaborators) sought to temper the homogenization of "tradition" implicit in teleological accounts of modernity, instead drawing attention to the diversity of premodern "civilizations" that ultimately contributed to "multiple modernities." This latter line of inquiry proceeded from Eisenstadt's related interest in the multiple axial age civilizations (Eisenstadt 1986).

Many scholars working on non-Western societies have enthusiastically embraced the notion of multiple modernities, taking it as a point of departure for developing related notions of "Islamic modernities," "Chinese modernity," "European modernity," and so on. However, some postcolonial scholars have critiqued the notion of multiple modernities on the grounds that it is essentially Eurocentric since it locates the origins of modernity in developments deemed endogenous to the West. Instead, the notion of "connected histories" is proposed to draw attention to shared and connected pasts that enabled a global and collective, albeit diverse, entry into modernity (e.g., Bhambra 2010). From this perspective, the products of modernity, such as human rights and industrialization, are collective achievements and not European creations that subsequently diffused to the rest of the world. This line of critique is focused on global connections that have been constitutive of modernity and is hesitant to stray into the premodern period.

The question of religious rights, however, poses a number of unique issues. Although capitalism, industrialization, and liberalism are modern phenomena that can be more or less precisely timed and situated in concrete spatial and connected contexts, the question of religious rights has been a vital political, intellectual, and theological question across many premodern societies. Within the hegemonic Eurocentric discourse of modernity, however, religious rights and freedoms are situated as a uniquely modern (and by extension Western) achievement. On the one hand, this assertion does do justice to a European history that was punctuated by wars of religion, persecutions, expulsions, and inquisitions. From the French Revolution to the colonization of North America, which allowed respite to nonconformist sects, modern Western history attests to the distance that has been covered vis-à-vis its earlier wars of religion punctuated by religious intolerance and persecutions. On the other hand, the hegemonic presence of this discourse implicitly suggests, first, that non-Western societies were similarly characterized by religious intolerance and, second, that liberal rights can readily provide solutions for religious conflicts and discriminations in

Muslim societies. In other words, the multiple and historically distinct trajectories of religious freedom that, as I show later, have been a part of Muslim histories get subsumed into an overarching Eurocentric narrative that posits a passage from persecutory traditional societies to free and progressive modern societies.

Civilizational analyses also tend to flatten premodern Islamic histories in other ways, most notably by inflating the role of sharia (or some other historical feature of Muslim societies) in shaping Muslim societies. Marshall G. S. Hodgson's magisterial *The Venture of Islam* exemplifies the best of this scholarly tradition of inquiry. Covering the entire history of Islam all the way up to the "Great Western Transmutation" (Hodgson 1974b: 176–79) that led the world into modernity, the *Venture* is a self-conscious celebration of the Islamic "citied and lettered life" (Hodgson 1974a: 91) both in its "Islamic" (understood as properly religious, sharia based) and nonreligious but culturally shared (literary culture, philosophy, poetry, etc.) dimensions (Hodgson 1974a: 59, 75). Together, these features constitute the "Islamicate" civilization. Talal Asad's focus on Islam as a "discursive tradition," while opening up considerable space for examining how Muslims reason through historically constituted and shifting discourses grounded in "the founding texts of the Qur'an and the Hadith," is focused on examining how authoritative "orthodoxies" are formed and how they shape practices (Asad 1986: 14). Ultimately, both these interventions place undue focus on textual traditions as primary determinants of how Muslims think and do things.

The Islamic legal scholar Wael Hallaq has recently taken up the issue of the fate of sharia, the premier text-based tradition in Islam, in the transition from premodern Islamic governance to modern states. Hallaq vigorously argues that Islam is inherently incompatible with modern political institutions, in particular the modern state (Hallaq 2013). The reason is that the modern state stands in a sharp and unbridgeable contrast with institutions of premodern Islamic governance because the two are paradigmatically, that is, in essence, different. The "central domain," or the pivot around which all else in society rotates, of the paradigmatic Islamic governance was sharia, the "moral law" of God. Sharia represented an "overarching moral apparatus" that was an end in itself and to which techniques of law (in the modern sense) were made subservient. This sharia developed through the participation of the Muslim community by organically producing its own experts who were not subservient to the will of the ruler. Instead, it was the ruler's law that was subservient to sharia. Jurists and legists held on steadfastly to their judicial independence so as to ensure justice, the moral accountability of rulers, and ethical considerations in society. The modern state, on the other hand, rests on notions of state (and not God's) sovereignty. It places distinctly modern obligations on citizens on the basis of its own morality grounded in the law/violence nexus, rational bureaucracy, and cultural hegemony. Ultimately, Hallaq argues, the idea of an Islamic state is self-contradictory because sharia cannot accommodate the institutions of the modern state while retaining its essence.

Hallaq is clear in suggesting that his elaboration of these paradigmatic features, which rests on a philosophical and not a historicist mode of inquiry, can help us grasp the fundamental contrast between premodern and modern Muslim societies. Yet the question remains whether Hallaq's thesis is sustainable when scrutinized from a historical sociological lens. Note that Hallaq's paradigmatic features do not function like Weberian ideal types that are heuristic devices used by the researcher to aid historical inquiry. Instead, Hallaq's paradigmatic features, particularly the primacy of sharia, self-consciously function to present an ahistorical claim about a singular essence of lived experiences in Muslim societies. However, any claim that rests on the ubiquity of sharia in large swaths of premodern Muslim societies across centuries must be made amenable to historical and comparative inquiry.

Hallaq's emphasis on sharia as the central organizing principle of premodern Muslim societies essentially makes a civilizational claim. I raise his work here also from a methodological standpoint since the tendency to generalize about the features of a singular "civilization" is endemic to civilizational analyses (Arjomand 2011: 322). In this sense, Hallaq's work closely aligns with the project of comparative (axial) religious civilizations that seeks to explain the enduring features and dynamics within any given civilization. However, there is also a critical difference in that generalizations within the "comparative civilizations" framework in principle proceed from historical inquiries. For example, Said Amir Arjomand draws on Eisenstadt to demonstrate the importance of considering not only the endemic tensions among patrimonial Muslim rulers and intolerant "fundamentalist" movements across Islamic civilization but also the critical role played by various heterodox movements in tipping the balance (2011: 329). This clears important conceptual ground for incorporating the potentially constitutive role of contentious dynamics that may differ from place to place. It is important to note, however, that Arjomand maintains an overarching commitment to a civilizational analysis even though a specific place (Iran/Persia), and not the totality of Islamic civilization, is the primary focus of inquiry.

On the whole, civilizational analyses of Muslim societies analytically privilege particular features or dynamics in Muslim societies, even when it is routinely conceded that these features are historically contingent, part of a larger "living tradition," and not immune from change. However, this privileging, as I demonstrate subsequently, is analytically and empirically untenable. I thus propose a tempering of civilizational analyses through a comparative and historical approach that is explicitly aimed at considering how local and shared problems that arise across so-called civilizational landscapes produce highly distinct practical solutions. In the present context, such an approach allows an identification of what I term the multiple pasts of religious heterodoxy in Muslim societies.

1.2. Historicity, Religious Heterodoxy, and the Transition to Modernity

Why is it important to identify these multiple pasts with respect to the question of religious heterodoxy? Let's turn back to the framework of multiple modernities. One of the key interventions of the framework is its insistence that there have historically existed a diversity of cultures and a plurality of civilizations. These cultures and civilizations have subsequently interacted with Western modernity differently, producing their own syntheses and forging their unique ways of responding to a basically Western modernity. Along this vein, it can be argued that decentering a single civilizational unit illuminates yet more diversity—of culture, political forms, and intellectual traditions. In the sphere of Muslim histories, it allows an explicit recognition and problematization of distinct modalities of addressing shared social, political, and religious concerns (in the present case, governing religious differences) within seemingly homogenous cultural milieus.

First, consider the case of three early modern Muslim empires—Ottoman, Mughal, and Safavid. Marshall Hodgson (1974b) famously termed these the "gunpowder empires," and numerous scholars have subsequently found these empires to be comparable units of analysis (e.g., Dale 2010; Streusand 2010). Despite the historical affinities between these three empires, scholars have also noted important points of difference that occlude civilizational analyses. For example, Rudi Matthee (2009) engages the question whether Safavid Iran was an empire given its various eccentricities. For example, the Safavid polity had a distinct ideological orientation due to its extreme commitment to Twelver Shiism, which was declared the official religion of the realm under the first Safavid ruler, Shah Ismail I (r. 1501–34). On the question of accommodation of religious difference, Sanjay Subrahmanyam notes the similarity between Safavid Iran, Tokugawa Japan, and the Habsburg Empire on the grounds that all demonstrated a sort of religious intolerance that was absent in other contemporary empires (Subrahmanyam 2006: 78). Abbas Amanat equates the Safavid Empire with the "persecuting societies" of medieval Europe, noting the former's dissimilarities with its neighboring Muslim empires (Amanat 2014: 369). In other words, when the primary focus of scholars is on how, where, and with outcomes Muslims *do* things, they find that Muslim societies often had more in common with non-Muslim societies than with each other. Although a banal observation from the historian's perspective, the question remains how these historical differences and similarities can be analytically deployed to generate non-Eurocentric accounts of Muslim transitions to modernity.

Second, there is the question of what sociologists term "path dependency" (Mahoney 2000). Do these multiple pasts of Islamic history continue to exert effects today? If yes, how? Also, how have encounters with European colonial powers interrupted the significance of these pasts? As ample scholarship has noted, one of the effects of the colonial encounter in India—and indeed Islam more broadly—was the production and dissemination of a view of Islam as intolerant and the West as a liberal civilizing force that would bring equality to previously discriminated-against religious communities. The project of crafting postcolonial modernities in Muslim societies has entailed an engagement with these colonialist assumptions, and through them, with Islamic pasts, real or imagined. For the project of a historical sociology of religious pluralism in Muslim societies, it is imperative to understand the ongoing effects of these pasts on current practices.

Third, and with reference to the specific issue at hand, it is notable that the question of religious heterodoxy continues to be a vexing and unsettled issue across a range of Muslim majority societies. The Ahmadiyya communities in Indonesia and Pakistan, Baha'is in Egypt and Turkey, and Alevis in Turkey represent some of the more prominent modern "cases" of religious heterodoxy. Are contemporary political engagements with the supposed heterodoxies of these groups a relic of an Islamic past? Or are these current debates a site of reform and renewal of Islam, as is claimed by many an Islamist? Or does this engagement point to the will and power of modern secular states to control all spheres of life, including and specifically religion, itself a modern category of organizing experiences and ordering the social world (Asad 2003)?

Following Sudipta Kaviraj, I contend that the question of religious heterodoxy in contemporary Muslim societies ought to be approached simultaneously as a "traditional" and a "modern" issue. As Kaviraj aptly notes, "modernized" practices often "carry on many residues of older habitual conduct, and the meanings and habits of older processes affect and modify modern forms" (2005: 518). Hence, these practices "cannot be reduced to either purely Western or traditional forms" (519). From this perspective, the persistence of the question of religious heterodoxy in countries such as Iran and Pakistan cannot be fully explained without paying heed to the concern of many vocal Muslims that sharia enjoins that heterodoxy cannot be tolerated in Muslim lands. Consequently, we may speak of a shared Muslim imperative of determining and responding to heterodoxy across time and space.

However, there are critical structural differences between premodern and modern societies. First, and most obviously, premodern patrimonial-bureaucratic empires have been replaced by modern states. Muslim rulers such as the Mughal emperor Akbar (1542–1605) and the Safavid emperor Shah Abbas I (1571–1629) were led by ideological orientations that evolved and took shape in concrete political contexts defined by imperial imperatives of managing diverse peoples across wide swaths of territory. Today, the personalities and inclinations of rulers have become significantly less important as étatist reason (governmentality, monopolization of use of violence within a clearly demarcated territory, enumeration of populations, management of hierarchies among them, etc.) aided by unprecedented powers of state penetration into society have become the norm.

Another critical difference is the impulse toward homogenization that characterizes modern states. In contrast to premodern empires, modern Muslim states are geographically smaller, more homogenous, and embedded in an international system structured by the ideology of nationalism. The modern state seeks to efface difference within its territorial boundaries, either through proposing civic criteria of belonging, in which case differences get subsumed under abstract criteria of citizenship, or through proposing, as the Muslim nation-state does, religious boundaries whereby non-Muslims start receding from national life. This tendency is reflective of a *shared modernity* across modern states that crystallizes in instances such as ethnic conflicts, marginalization of racialized minorities, xenophobia, and, of course, religious violence across societies and traditions (Balibar 204; Mann 2005; Omi and Winant 2014; van der Veer 1994). All of these cases point to the tendency toward majoritarianism that is built into the very logic of modern politics through the exclusionary logics of modern nation-building processes and mass democratic politics. In modern Muslim states, it manifests itself through the formulation of official nationalist ideologies that seek to define, adjudicate, and ultimately legitimize the aspirations of their majority Muslim subjects qua Muslims.

The politics of heterodoxy in modern Muslim states is shaped by this dynamic of majoritarianism, which finds sustenance through institutions and practices of mass politics. When mass politics is linked with religion without proper institutional safeguards for tempering majoritarianism, the likely outcome is that religious differences are hierarchized through religious nationalist discourses that are often legitimized by the authority of the state. The agency of social actors, typically ulema and Islamists, is a key factor here since these groups have been at the helm of demands that the state deploy top-down positive law to punish heterodoxy. In the final analysis, Hallaq is indeed correct in arguing that the classical institutions surrounding sharia, notably the jurists' monopolization of determination of sharia-based responses to pressing ethical and moral questions, are incompatible with modern political institutions. However, contra Hallaq, these were also in tension with the exercise of sovereignty by early modern kings ruling over sprawling empires.

1.3. The Multiple Pasts of Religious Heterodoxy

On Thursday, 5 August 1593, the fifth Safavid shah (monarch) of Persia, Shah Abbas I (r. 1587–1629), abdicated his throne for a period of three days. In his place, Ustad Yusuf Tarkishduz, a member of the esoteric Nuqtavi order, was made king. People from near and far, including Shah Abbas I himself, bowed before the new king and followed the full range of accouterments accompanying the throne. Three days later, on 8 August 1593, Ustad Yusuf was shot and killed by a firing squad and his body hung for public view. Following this, Shah Abbas I reclaimed his throne.

This strange episode in Safavid history anchors Kathryn Babayan's gripping account of shifting landscapes of religion and politics, history and memory, and conversion and translation in Safavid Iran (Babayan 2002). The Nuqtavis, who have assumed a striking significance in scholarship on the early modern Indo-Persianate world, were a religious group that emphasized belief in cyclical renewal beyond Islam, apocalypticism, messianic ideas, continuous prophecies, and Gnosticism.[3] Situated in a critical period of "heterodox" resurgence in the Indo-Persianate world, the Nuqtavis drew from ancient Greco-Persian beliefs, predecessors like Nizari Isma'ilis and the Hurufi movement, and Sufi pantheistic traditions within Islam itself.

The early Safavid mystics and their supporters, the Qizilbash (Red Heads), had closely identified with the spiritual landscape of Mazdean groups such as the Nuqtavis that were deeply immersed in pre-Islamic Persian idioms of *ghuluww* (exaggeration) (Babayan 2002: 33). As their temporal authority gained ground, Safavid shahs began to distance themselves from their earlier syncretism and define a new Shia orthodoxy. This process was accelerated by a geopolitical context defined by enmity with the neighboring Sunni Ottoman Empire. Safavid shahs not only adopted an official creed, Twelver Shiism, but also undertook measures to marginalize heterodox groups like the Nuqtavis, who appear to have enjoyed some popularity among the people, including the Qizilbash.

In this context and under Shah Abbas I, Nuqtavi predictions about the end of the Arab "cycle" (read Islam) and the transition to a post-Islamic Persian period (*daur-e-Ajam*) that would supposedly take place at the cusp of the approaching and widely anticipated Islamic millennium began to seem more and more sinister. The bizarre throning of the Nuqtavi Ustad Yusuf was a response to a specific Nuqtavi prophecy that predicted that a bad omen would befall the Persian shah during an approaching conjunction of Saturn and Jupiter at the turn of the millennium. In order to ward off this celestial catastrophe, Shah Abbas

---

[3] See Amanat (2009: 73–89) for a historical account of the origins and development of the Nuqtavi movement.

I abdicated his throne so that the bad omen might fall on the unlucky Nuqtavi king. Following this event, Nuqtavis were systematically persecuted, leading to many of them taking refuge in the neighboring Mughal Empire. Eventually, Nuqtavis vanished from the Iranian cultural milieu. Overall, in Babayan's work, Nuqtavis serve as a reminder of a forgotten Islamic past in which different cultural and spiritual idioms—*guwluww*, Alid loyalty, and Sufism—mingled, mutually shaped and reshaped each other, increased or decreased in importance, and eventually disentangled to give way to a new mainstream orthodoxy.

There is another way that the heterodoxy of Nuqtavis has been invoked in scholarship on Indo-Persianate world. Sanjay Subrahmanyam (1997) deploys Nuqtavis in the course of making a case for "connected histories" over "comparative histories." Subrahmanyam argues for the importance of drawing out connections among different geographical entities that are today deemed to be holistic containers of neatly trimmed histories by virtue of forming modern nation-states. Connected histories allow entry into distinct geographical milieus characterized by profound ideational and symbolic exchanges as well as shared political and cultural idioms. In this vein, Subrahmanyam draws attention to the profound influence of millenarian ideas around 1000 A.H. (1591–92) in Ottoman, Mughal, Safavid, and even Southeast Asian lands. He draws on the episode related by Babayan to argue that millenarianism was able to serve as a resource for the centralizing monarch Shah Abbas I to rein in opposition and attempt to establish cultural uniformity across his empire.

The theme of a shared Indo-Persian cultural and political landscape has been recently further elaborated by the historian A. Azfar Moin, who depicts the centrality of millenarian expectations and kingly "sainthood" for articulations of political sovereignty in the Mughal Empire through its encounters with Safavid Iran (Moin 2012). Not surprisingly, Nuqtavis appear in Moin's work as a bridge between the Safavid and Mughal Empires, at one time forming the basis for the Mughal emperor Akbar writing to Shah Abbas I and asking him to show tolerance toward those of different faiths (Moin 2012: 165).

The focus on shared and connected milieu of the Indo-Persian world of Mughals and Safavids, with the Ottomans lurking in the shadows, serves as a powerful caution to denaturalize the boundaries of contemporary nation-states in order to delve into worlds bygone that were profoundly characterized by a distinct and shared ethos of time, place, movement, and circulation. At the same time, from the perspective of comparative and historical sociology, a striking aspect of Nuqtavis is the ways in which they were persecuted in Safavid Iran and accommodated in Mughal India. In Persia, there were at least two major rounds of persecution of Nuqtavis that were known as "heretic killing" (*mulhid-kushi*). The first transpired circa 1575–76 under the reign of Shah Tahmasp (r. 1524–76) and the second under Shah Abbas I circa 1590–91, around the turn of the Islamic millennium (Amanat 2014: 369). Consequently, a number of Nuqtavis left for Mughal India, where they were well received in Akbar's court until they organically vanished from India's religio-intellectual landscape sometime around the turn of the eighteenth century.

The difference between Safavid Iran and Akbar's Mughal India is not surprising and has been extensively commented upon, as for example, in most of the works referenced in this section. The most critical factor, no doubt, is the different demographic landscape of the two empires. While Safavid Iran was markedly homogenous in religious terms, at least in comparison with the neighboring Mughal and Ottoman Empires, Muslim rulers in India had always had to contend with a highly diverse religious landscape. In fact, Muslims formed a numerical minority in India. Consequently, Muslim rulers as far back as the Delhi Sultanate (1206–1526) had sought to induct at least a few Hindu officers into high positions (Khan 2016: 2). It was this policy that was adopted and expanded, first under the Afghan Surs and later under the Mughal emperors Babur, Humayun, and, of course, Akbar.

Furthermore, Akbar, as is well known, was quite heterodox himself, as attested by his explicit adoption of the doctrine of *sulh-i-kull* (Universal Reconciliation) in 1581. This concept, formulated either by him or for him by his minister Abul Fazl, denoted "a principle capable of promoting amity among divergent groups on a culturally plural situation" (Khan 2016: 163; Kinra 2013). It signified a critique of exclusivist religion, that is, the identification of the state with any one religion. It drew on theories of just rule that enjoin the ruler to extend his benevolence and protection to all his subjects, irrespective of race and religion (Khan 2001: 31). Even earlier in his rule, Akbar abolished the pilgrimage tax in 1562 and the *jizya* in 1564.[4] At that time, however, Akbar was driven more by exigencies of ruling over a religiously diverse empire than by considerations of religious tolerance or intellectual influences. Thus, Akbar accompanied these policies with efforts that were explicitly aimed at "placating orthodox Muslim sentiments" (Khan 2016: 123–24).

It was slowly and over time that Akbar shed what appear to have been his genuinely held prejudices against Hindus, Shias, and heterodox orders such as Mahadavis earlier in his rule (Khan 2016: 156). This slow change has been attributed to a number of factors such as his practice of taking Rajput (Hindu) wives and engaging in worship with them, and a growing interest in philosophy that ultimately led to the creation of his *ibadat-khana* (literally, house of worship) (Khan 2016: 159–60). Here, religious and philosophical debates were routinely staged among adherents of various religions, atheists, agnostics, and

---

[4] The *jizya* was subsequently reimposed in 1575 and abolished for a second time in 1580. It remained abolished until 1679, when it was reimposed by Aurangzeb's rule (1658–1707).

antinomians beginning from 1575. It was in this cultural milieu that prominent Nuqtavis escaping Safavid Iran ultimately found themselves (Amanat 2014).

Safavid monarchs, on the other hand, were keen to distance themselves from their earlier associations with pre-Islamic spiritual and philosophical idioms. This entailed eradication of not only extremist millenarian movements like Nuqtavis but also persecution of popular Sufism, suppression of Sunnism, and the active propagation of Twelver Shiism (Arjomand 1981: 3). Under Shah Tahmasp's rule, for example, art forms such as poetry and music that are traditionally frowned upon by sharia were prohibited *but only when* they did not in some way praise the Twelve Imams (Johnson 1994: 126). A number of royal policies were put into place to pressure the population into accepting Twelver Shiism. They included reducing taxes in districts that could prove that the populations therein had been committed to Ali or Twelver Shiism prior to Safavid rule, and replacement of Friday prayers that Sunni hold integral to Islamic worship with ritual cursing of the first three caliphs (Abu Bakr, Omar, and Uthman) (Johnson 1994: 128–29). Sunni routinely underwent extortion, intimidation, and harassment, and consequently, the practice of giving a "protection fee" by a Sunni in exchange for buying testimony to his Shiism by a Shia emerged (Johnson 1994: 131). The history of the Safavid Empire is also ripe with instances of forced conversions of non-Muslims, an issue to which I will return.

A comparison of the treatment of the same entity, the Nuqtavis, across two different but contemporaneous premodern contexts allows us to appreciate the highly variable responses to the question of heterodoxy. Certainly these variations can readily be explained by a number of contingent and interacting factors such as structures and forms of imperial networks, personalities and dispositions of rulers, ethnic and religious makeup of imperial societies, and political, intellectual, and symbolic traditions around sovereignty, justice, and kingship, to name a few. Yet, as argued earlier, these differences are routinely overlooked in *analytical* discussions about Muslim societies, with the result that the diversity of Muslim pasts is flattened by their insertion into civilizational analyses.

In fact, a striking aspect of both the Mughal and Safavid response is that neither is anchored in considerations of sharia. Consider, first, the Mughal case. If Akbar tolerated heresies of Nuqtavis in his famous *ibadat-khana*, it was certainly not grounded in the Quranic injunction that there is no compulsion in religion. Although an engagement with this ethical spirit of Quran was certainly present within the Mughal intellectual milieu through *akhlaq* texts (Alam 2004), Akbar's religious policies were also motivated by pragmatic considerations of ruling over and accommodating a majority Hindu society with a powerfully entrenched indigenous hierarchy. These factors must have mingled with his personal proclivities, intellectual quests, and interests in comparative religion. Equally significantly, Akbar was deeply steeped in the millenarian mood of his times, and the Nuqtavi claim that Akbar was the next millennial prophet-bearer must have endeared them to him even more. Finally, as Azfar Moin's (2012) work has demonstrated, premodern kings of the era, including Akbar, positioned themselves as sacred *millenarian* sovereigns who, by this virtue, stood above the law. Consequently, a number of Nuqtavis thrived in Akbar's court, where they found a hospitable environment to share and disseminate their views, and perhaps influence Akbar's own developing views on *sulh-i-kull* and his emerging personal sect of *din-i-ilahi* (Amanat 2016: 374–76).

Now consider the Safavid case. Although different Islamic law schools (madhhabs) have different positions on apostasy, atheism, and heterodoxy, all agree that the determination on these issues is to be made by jurists. This is because classically, Islamic law is the jurist's, and not the state's, law (Hallaq 2013). Furthermore, the Shafi'i school, which was practiced in Iran before the Ja'afri school took over in the late Safavid and early post-Safavid period, holds, following the Shafi'ite al-Ghazali, that ordinary people gone astray ought to be given the chance to repent and re-enter the fold of Islam before the imposition of capital punishment (*istiaba*). The right to repent may, however, be taken away from leaders of heretical movements at the discretion of the jurist *if* heresies are being spread for worldly possessions or political power or to cause political rebellion (Griffel 2001: 353; Johansen 2003: 687–88).

In persecuting Nuqtavis, however, Safavid shahs were not following established and authoritative sharia injunctions. As Abbas Amanat (2014: 370–71) reveals about seventeen known Nuqtavis who died during the Safavid persecution of the late sixteenth century:

> Twelve were perished; either executed as *mulhids* [atheists] by government agents (some personally in the hands of 'Abbas I) and others killed by the mob. Of the remaining three, one was blinded and only two were saved after they repented. In a few cases, executions were endorsed by jurists but in other cases the killings were apparently the outcome of the Shah 'Abbas's own initiative and as a reaction to fear of a Nuqtawi-provoked uprising at the turn of the Islamic millennium (1591–92).

Not surprisingly, Safavid rulers levied charges of political rebellion in order to crack down on Nuqtavis. Political rebellion, as noted earlier, is a legitimate reason in sharia to punish heresy. The Nuqtavi Darvish Khusraw underwent an inquisition led by ulema on charges of heresy and was subsequently put to death (Arjomand 1981: 9). At the same time, other modes of persecution such as mob killings, executions undertaken by the shah himself without the mediation of jurists, and cruel punishments such as blinding that are not authorized in sharia were also deployed.

Indeed, the Safavid Empire for much of its history appears to have been primarily driven by "realpolitik and/or expediency" and "reasons of state," which necessitated eradication of volatile millenarian expectations (Gregorian 1974: 655; Arjomand 1981: 34). This can be seen by periodic episodes of forcible conversion of non-Muslims, including Jews and Christians, groups that are accorded the status of protected People of the Book, or *dhimmis*, in sharia. While Armenians and Georgians on the whole enjoyed greater accommodation within the empire, in the face of political expediency, this accommodation was readily abandoned. For example, Shah Abbas adopted a "scorched earth" policy in 1604 to thwart Ottoman advances that ultimately led to forced conversion of around twenty thousand Armenians who were forced to migrate elsewhere in the empire (Abisaab 2004: 62). Notably, forced conversions had routinely been repudiated by prominent Shia ulema since the beginning of Safavid rule. Instead, these ulema preferred to take the orthodox theological position that individuals ought to be encouraged and persuaded to accept Shiism (Abisaab 2004: 13, 35). Clearly, these sharia injunctions were conveniently and routinely ignored. When possible, recourse was made to sharia to justify forced conversions, as for example when, Jews, Christians, and Georgians were taken as captives in the course of war with the Ottomans in 1605, and charged with fighting Muslim forces (Abisaab 2004: 62, 63). However, as Rula Jurdi Abisaab concludes, "Far from being a fixed policy toward non-Muslims of the empire, the Shah [Abbas I] took diverse approaches toward them depending on historical circumstances and political expediency" (2004: 63).

In the final analysis, neither Mughal accommodation nor Safavid persecutions can be laid at the door of the jurist-centered sharia. The Nuqtavi example clearly indicates that, historically, Muslim societies do not have an inherent or predetermined relationship even with thorny heterodox groups. In the case of non-Muslims, the question of religious difference has always been crucially entangled *both* with considerations of political power and imperial forms and governance (Barkey 2008; Burbank and Cooper 2010), political theologies (Moin 2012) *and* with ethical and intellectual traditions that often transcend what Marshall Hodgson termed "Shariah-mindedness" and what Hallaq terms paradigmatic sharia (Alam 2004; Kinra 2013).

But the case of heterodox groups such as Nuqtavis is conceptually different since they tend to be smaller, more diffuse, and already suspect in the eyes of vanguards of religious orthodoxy. It may be that persecuting such groups is more politically expedient for the ruler than accommodating them. Although sharia injunctions do not allow persecution of groups, ulema across Islamic history have certainly endorsed inquisitions and persecutions of individuals belonging to such groups. Consequently, it is particularly striking not only that the question of religious heterodoxy in early modern Muslim empires not produce a "typical" response but also that the responses were oftentimes not guided by sharia injunctions. Neither the fact of a common political form (premodern empire) nor that of a shared cultural and religious landscape (Indo-Persianate Islam) led to similar policies toward the same religious group, the Nuqtavis. The Mughal emperor Akbar chose to accommodate Nuqtavis, while the Safavid shahs opted for persecution in a bid to arrive at doctrinal uniformity in their realms. Both responses emerged from dynamics specific to the two empires. However, these *multiple pasts* of religious heterodoxy in premodern Muslim societies, I argue in what follows, continue to seep into the present times.

1.4. Politics of Heterodoxy in Pakistan

Let us fast-forward to the twentieth century. The day in question is 5 August 1974, and the site is Pakistan's National Assembly, incidentally the first formed democratically through general elections. On this day, the Assembly met as a "Special Committee" wherein all members of the National Assembly (MNAs) would deliberate, on camera, the religious status of the Ahmadiyya movement. Leaders of the Ahmadiyya movement were invited to present their views and to answer questions posed by MNAs. In the words that abound in the proceedings themselves, Ahmadiyya leadership was "cross-examined" by Pakistan's attorney general, Yahya Bakhtiar, who assumed a position akin to a "lawyer" (National Assembly of Pakistan 1974: 60). Speaker of the National Assembly Sahabazada Farooq Ali chaired the proceedings. Any MNA who wished to pose a question to the Ahmadi representatives had to hand it in written form to the attorney general, who would then proceed with the questioning. The Ahmadi representatives were to be "witnesses" and the MNAs "judges." The proceedings thus assumed the air of a formal courtroom. Subsequently, on 7 September 1974, Ahmadis were unanimously voted a non-Muslim minority. A constitutional amendment was made whereby Pakistan's constitution now formally defines a non-Muslim:

> A person who does not believe in the absolute and unqualified finality of The Prophethood of Muhammad (Peace be upon him), the last of the Prophets or claims to be a Prophet, in any sense of the word or of any description whatsoever, after Muhammad (Peace be upon him), or recognizes such a claimant as a Prophet or religious reformer, is not a Muslim for the purposes of the Constitution or law.[5]

---

[5] Constitution (Second Amendment) Act of 1974, Constitution of Islamic Republic of Pakistan.

The Ahmadiyya movement originated in colonial India under the leadership of Mirza Ghulam Mohammad (1835–1908), who made a series of claims, spread out over time and expounded in writings, about being a Muslim reformer, the Mahdi, Messiah, and finally, a prophet who was in communication with God (Friedmann 1989). As we know, such post-prophetic groups constitute a significant tradition in Islamic history of which the Nuqtavis are but one small part. Although they were categorized as a "sect" of Islam by the British colonial state in India, Indian Muslim ulema increasingly came to hold Mirza Ghulam Ahmad, subsequent leaders of the movement, and its followers as deviants, apostates, and/or heretics. The Ahmadiyya community on its part not only resisted these characterizations but also claimed to adhere to the most authentic and correct Islam.

There is nothing inherently novel about either Mirza Ghulam Ahmad's so-called heresies or the vociferous disputes that immediately began to proliferate around them under colonial rule. Assessments of religious claims, pronouncements of heresy, and popular prejudices against deviant groups can be seen in diverse historical contexts across Islamic history. What is different, however, is that these conversations were being held in a milieu in which Europeans and not Muslims held political power. The British colonial state was principally opposed to entertaining questions of apostasy and heresy within colonial law unless they related to the now delimited and carefully circumscribed area of family law that was governed by sharia (Saeed 2016).

An element of novelty, of something historically unprecedented, however, is visible when we move to postcolonial Pakistan and witness sustained social movements by right-wing religious groups demanding that the Pakistani state officially declare Ahmadis a non-Muslim minority in the interest of the Muslim nation-state (Saeed 2012). These movements, which became particularly intense in 1947, 1952–53, and then 1974, firmly belong in modernity since their legitimacy is underpinned by political and not religious reasons. Most notably, they are anchored in a social space that is structured by democratic politics, wherein the interests of the national collectivity are articulated toward the end of being recognized by and realized in the state.[6]

Strikingly, the justifications given for declaring Ahmadis non-Muslim during the course of the Special Committee's proceedings were not grounded in traditional sharia rulings but in wholly modern claims about the imperatives of democratization in a Muslim nation-state. However, the issue was brought to the National Assembly on largely Islamic grounds. The twenty-two MNAs belonging to opposition parties (mostly Islamist) who were at the forefront of the campaign

[6] See Hirschkind (1997) for a good conceptual discussion of how Islamist movements are underpinned by the reason of the modern state.

to get the state to declare all followers of Mirza Ghulam Ahmad "not Muslims" justified their demands on the following grounds: Mirza Ghulam Ahmad's "false declaration to be a prophet, his attempts to falsify numerous Quranic texts and to abolish Jihad were treacherous to the main issues of Islam"; Mirza Ghulam Ahmad "was a creation of imperialism for the sole purpose of destroying Muslim solidarity and falsifying Islam"; the entire Muslim umma considers Ahmadis "outside the pale of Islam"; and Ahmadis are "indulging in subversive activities internally and externally by mixing with Muslims and pretending to be a sect of Islam" (National Assembly of Pakistan Debates 1974: 1306). The issues at hand, therefore, were derived from Islamic imperatives, some of which have roots in sharia injunctions (e.g., curbing heresy) and others that are clearly beyond the pale of sharia (forcible declaration of persons who claim to be Muslim as non-Muslim). Nonreligious considerations were also raised, for example, that the Ahmadiyya movement was a political creation of the British rule and was deployed by the latter to disrupt the unity of Indian Muslims. During the course of the inquiry, all of these issues were repeatedly raised by the ulema MNAs.

This discourse notwithstanding, the attorney general provided the primary justifications for the inquiry, in his capacity as the representative of the state, on strictly secular and constitutional grounds.[7] A brief discussion on the first day of the proceedings explicitly dealt with the issue of the authority of the Pakistani state to determine the religious status of Ahmadis. Although Ahmadiyya community representatives consented to appearing before the National Assembly, their spiritual head, Mirza Nasir, intimated that religion was a matter of "heart and conscience" and that the very fact of the proceedings interfered with the constitutional right, enshrined in Article 20 of the Pakistani constitution, to freedom of religious expression. It thus became incumbent on the state to present statist reasons and justifications for the proceedings.

Some of these justifications included, first, the "hurt sentiments" of Pakistani Muslims, which is a modern nationalist argument. Second, it was noted that limits to freedom of religious belief and expression were practiced even by liberal secular states, as seen, for example, by abolition of Hindu practice of sati (widow burning) in British India. In this instance, justifications for setting limits to religious freedoms, which is undertaken (at least in theory) by liberal states to curb illiberal religious practices, were invoked by an illiberal but democratic state to curb a constitutionally guaranteed right. Third, reference was also made to the preamble to Pakistan's constitution as well as specific constitutional clauses. These included Article 20 (mentioned already) that makes religious freedoms "subject to law, public order and morality"; the clause in the preamble

---

[7] This discussion is adopted from Saeed (2017: 128–33), but see also National Assembly of Pakistan (1974).

that enjoins the Pakistani state to take steps that enable Muslims to live their individual and collective lives in accordance with the teachings and principles of Islam; and Article 2 of the Pakistani constitution, which declares Islam the state religion of Pakistan.

As noted earlier, sharia-based rulings on heresy were practically absent as justifications for the inquiry and its eventual outcome. Also absent was the issue of how Islamic legal norms address the issue of the forcible expulsion from Islam of those individuals and communities who claim to be Muslim. Mirza Nasir Ahmad had explicitly claimed that Islam provides no justification for such legislative action. One MNA belonging to an Islamist party attempted to address this issue by arguing that the forcible declaration of Ahmadis as non-Muslim was justifiable from within the Islamic legal tradition. However, Chairman Farooq Ali declared that these arguments pertained to mere "intricacies" that were better left for mosques and not the National Assembly. Another MNA argued that Ahmadis were apostates and hence could be legitimately murdered or expelled from Pakistan. Unsurprisingly, this line of inquiry too was discouraged by Farooq Ali. Another MNA argued that he was incompetent to engage with the issue of the religious status of Ahmadis because "he was not an expert on Islam, studied Islamiat [Islamic studies], or was a professor of Islamiat." He maintained that as a "lay-man" on these matters, it was not only difficult for him to serve as a judge but that it was also "unfair" for him to be expected to do so. However, the cross-examination proceeded with the understanding that ulema MNAs would provide the necessary Islamic knowledge when needed.

A number of reasons can be mentioned to explain this occlusion of Islamic legal norms. For one, it is not immediately obvious how charges of apostasy can be pinned on Ahmadis in a context in which they openly pronounce *shahada* (Islamic declaration of faith), revere the Quran and Prophet Muhammad, and follow shared injunctions of Islam regarding prayers, fasting, and so on (Burhani 2014: 296).[8] Similarly, it is not readily obvious how Ahmadis can be declared apostates since apostasy is a status that has historically been attributed to individuals and not whole groups. Furthermore, apostasy applies in cases where the individual in question visibly converts away from Islam and not cases like most of the Ahmadis, who are born into the faith. Third, a significant tradition in Islamic law allows apostates to repent and thereby return to the fold of Islam (*istiaba*). Assuming that the charges of apostasy could be legitimately levied against an Ahmadi, from a technical-sharia point of view, she or he would have to be given the option of repenting. In instances where repentance is not forthcoming, the jurist would then authorize the state to administer Islamic punishment.

---

[8] Jihad, however, is a highly contentious issue since Mirza Ghulam Ahmad explicitly reinterpreted jihad as referring to nonaggressive tactics such as proselytization and persuasion.

Ultimately, what crystallizes in the debates is that the Pakistani state sought to establish the heretical nature of Ahmadis for the purposes of crafting gradations of citizenship, as opposed to responding to Islamic imperatives about curbing heresy that would entail giving juristic authority to ulema. Modern states can more readily respond to claims about boundaries of citizenship inclusion and exclusion that are rendered in nationalist terms. Modern democratic politics is centered on precisely such contentious claims that are couched in a language of distribution of social, cultural, and political rights across different social groups. For these reasons, ultimately a Muslim nationalist discourse was combined with religiously derived charges of heresy to justify the symbolic exclusion of Ahmadis.[9]

The Islamic historical consciousness at play in the inquiry is clearly more reminiscent of Safavid Iran than Mughal India. In Muslim-majority countries such as Pakistan that constitutionally privilege a religiously based national identity over liberal rights, it is almost a bygone conclusion that religiously orthodox social elements such as ulema and Islamists will find fertile ground to push for exclusion and criminalization of groups and individuals that they deem religiously heterodox. After all, this is a prominent historical dimension of Islamic history that is justifiable from within sharia but within clearly defined constraints and limits. Since these latter are structurally undermined by modern institutions of governance, recourse is taken to modern secular and nationalist arguments such as "hurt religious sentiments" to enact and justify exclusions.

However, it would be a mistake to think that arguments for accommodation and tolerance of religious differences on Islamic grounds have no place to thrive within modern states systems. In Pakistan, for example, the argument that the ethos of accommodation of religious difference is an Islamic imperative has been made in the most unlikely of sites, the superior courts, by secularly trained judges. In a number of important legal cases surrounding the issue of religious rights of the Ahmadiyya community, both before and after 1974, judges routinely supplemented their legal argumentations by drawing on Quranic injunctions about religious freedoms as well as on distinct readings of the Muslim past emphasizing toleration on part of Muslim rulers (Saeed 2017: ch. 5).

For example, in a case dealing with rights of a journal editor to publish polemics against Ahmadiyya movement, the judge drew on a number of Quranic verses to argue that discrimination against Ahmadis was "opposed to the true Islamic precepts and injunctions."[10] He invoked verse 256 of chapter 2 of the Quran, "which guarantees freedom of conscience in clear mandatory terms," and

[9] Eventually, in 1984, punitive measures against Ahmadis were enacted in Pakistan's criminal code. The state also instituted Pakistan's controversial blasphemy laws as well as a number of Hudood ordinances that introduced Islamic punishments.

[10] *Abdul Karim Shorish Kashmiri v. The State of West Pakistan* PLD 1969 Lahore 289.

another verse that states: "Let there be no compulsion in Religion." Another verse (3:79) was drawn on in which "there is also a positive injunction . . . prohibiting man—even though a prophet—from imposing his will upon others." It was concluded, "Freedom of thought and conscience could not have been guaranteed in clearer terms [in the Quran]."

In this case, which was concluded in 1969, the spirit of sharia that was invoked is reminiscent of the best of the Mughal tradition that had been encapsulated in *akhlaq* literature. The invocation of an egalitarian sharia remained a feature of jurisprudence on religious rights of Ahmadis until the 1980s, when there was a turn toward defining and including punitive Islamic punishments within criminal law.

1.5. Politics of Heterodoxy in Iran

Before turning to some concluding points, I will very briefly consider the case of modern post-revolutionary Iran, which presents a much greater continuity with its Safavid past than Pakistan does with its Mughal past. As mentioned earlier, the Safavid Empire undertook extensive measures to ensure religious conformity among the populace, a policy that entailed persecutions, forced conversions, and institutionalized marginalization of groups that did not belong to the empire's official religion of Twelver Shia Islam. Strikingly, despite the history of acute persecutions, post-Islamic movements continued to arise in the region, notably the Baha'i movement. The Baha'is are an outgrowth of another "heterodox" group, the nineteenth-century Babi movement that originated in Persia under the leadership of the Iranian prophet Sayyid 'Ali Muhammad Shirazi (1819–1850), called the Bab. The only significant millenarian movement in Shia Islam during the nineteenth century, it was brutally crushed due to its complete break with Islamic orthodoxy and its attempt to forge a new spiritual and religious code. Its message, nonetheless, continues in the Baha'i faith, which began as a Babi sect under the spiritual leadership of Mirza Husayn Ali Baha'u'llah (1817–92). It went on to gain considerable success inside Iran, where it constitutes a large religious minority, as well as elsewhere in the Middle East, in Asia, and in Europe.[11] Baha'is are widely perceived as a heretical sect that emerged from within the Islamic tradition, although Baha'is subsequently repudiated the claim that they are a sect of Islam and now claim independence from Islam.[12]

---

[11] See Cole (1998) for a history of the Baha'i movement.

[12] Baha'is reject the finality of Muhammad's prophecy while accepting that Muhammad was a sacred prophet. Bahaullah declared himself to be a prophet and set down principles of Baha'i faith in the *Holy Book* (*Kitab al-Aqdas*).

Although there are a large number of Baha'is in Iran, the official state policy of various Iranian ruling regimes has been one of legal nonrecognition. Thus, Baha'is were not a recognized religious minority in either the Pahlavi dynasty (1925–79) or the Islamic republican state (1979–present). It is this nonrecognition that is of conceptual interest. Even under secularizing regime of Pahlavi shahs, while Zoroastrians, Jews, Armenians, and Assyrians were recognized as minorities and entitled to a degree of autonomy in personal status and family laws, non-Shia Muslims and Baha'is were not recognized. Clearly, this policy of nonrecognition allowed the regime to avoid legislating on Baha'is. Since Baha'is are widely considered heretical and true "infidels," a policy of nonrecognition emerged as a viable response given the currents of that time. On their part, Baha'is were able to rise to positions that were prohibited to other recognized minorities and for which only Muslims were eligible. Baha'is thus actively supported the Pahlavis, even though the regime tended to side with anti-Baha'i groups in instances of religious conflicts, such as the 1955 anti-Baha'i riots. Furthermore, "Nonrecognition did make it difficult for Baha'is to register marriages and births, publish religious literature, or run their own schools, and they were subject to discrimination on an individual basis" (Higgins 1984: 53).

After the 1979 revolution, Baha'is continued to be unrecognized in the constitution. It is significant that the fact of recognition allowed other religious groups in Iran to participate in post-revolutionary constitutional debates and voice their specific fears and aspirations in a public forum (Sanasarian 2000: ch. 2). The theological nature of subsequent state structure has certainly ensured the maintenance of hierarchical distinctions between Muslims and non-Muslims. However, legal recognition has allowed for at least a social space from which to make claims. For Baha'is, on the other hand, legal nonrecognition now meant that they were subjected to more intense measures at being silenced and persecuted. Their persecution has been well documented and has entailed individual attacks that the government does not punish, execution of a number of Baha'i leaders on grounds of spying, and denying national identity cards to Baha'is on grounds that they are not a recognized religion. These practices are generally met with silence in Iranian society because, among other things, there is a deep-seated perception among Iranians that Baha'is disproportionately benefited from Pahlavi patronage, engage in anti-state conspiracies, and hold cosmopolitan and "western" ideas (Chehabi 2008). Overall, nonrecognition has allowed different Iranian regimes to manage the Baha'i question differently across time.

On the whole, the legal nonrecognition of Baha'is can be interpreted as a deliberate strategy adopted by the Iranian state to avoid making official pronouncements on the heterodoxy of Baha'is while keeping the space open for measures that may, at least theoretically, be either more persecutory or more accommodative than endorsed by Islamic legal rulings grounded in sharia. However, given the intense nature of anti-Baha'i polemics in Iran, championed most often by religious clerics through recourse to sharia injunctions about heresy and apostasy (Sanasarian 2000: 24–30), it seems unlikely that accommodation of Baha'is will be undertaken by the state anytime soon. Despite the popularity of this narrative, it is notable that the Baha'i question is ultimately managed primarily through political fiat and not through application of sharia. In this, Iran is comparable to Pakistan, since it is ultimately the modern imperatives of defining national identity in exclusionary terms and responding to popular religious sentiments that form the basis for discriminating against Baha'is.

1.6. Conclusion

This chapter has examined the changing configurations between Islam and religious heterodoxy in the shift from premodern Muslim empires to modern nation-states. Specifically, it has addressed how a number of premodern and modern Muslim political entities have dealt with religious groups deemed heterodox. Although the Quran does not provide prescriptions for dealing with religious heterodoxy, it immediately emerged as a critical issue in sharia, with different madhhabs adopting distinct positions. It continues to be a socially resonant issue in contemporary Muslim societies, as can be seen by the considerable body of modern state laws, regulations, and jurisprudence that deals with issues of blasphemy, apostasy, and heresy across Muslim countries. Through a critical engagement with how various Muslim political entities have dealt with groups deemed religiously heterodox, this chapter has drawn attention to the *multiple pasts* and a *converging present* of Muslim societies.

A comparative and historical approach to the question of heterodoxy in Muslim societies leads away both from the Enlightenment conceit that respect for rights, entitlements, and dignity due to others who are different is a modern (read Western) phenomenon *and* from equally ahistorical blanket arguments of the order "Islam allows/disallows religious freedom." Deploying the example of Nuqtavis in the early modern Muslim empire, I have made a case for considering the multiple pasts of religious heterodoxy in Muslim history. This analysis also reveals the highly contingent nature of sharia in the practical management of heterodoxy. This line of inquiry explicitly questions civilizational analyses of Islamic history that privilege similarities at the cost of systematic inquiries into differences, contrasts, and variations among various premodern Muslim polities. This, I have argued, is critical for formulating properly historicist accounts of Muslim pasts and moving toward new non-Eurocentric and non-teleological accounts of transitions to modernity.

Second, this chapter has sought to showcase the continued importance of a historical consciousness about sharia and memories of the Islamic past in contemporary debates about religious heterodoxy. This consciousness, however, is sustained in a political milieu in which nationalism exerts hegemonic force. Given the increasing salience of religious nationalism across Muslim societies, critical resources present in the Islamic past for accommodation of religious differences have become less accessible within modern state institutions. Majoritarianism and the homogenizing tendencies of modern nation-state formation have introduced novel problems and disabilities for minority religious groups. Ultimately, the continuing significance of the question of religious heterodoxy in contemporary Muslim countries is reflective of both traditional and modern imperatives. A further comparative engagement with how the Islamic tradition and modern imperatives intermingle in different places can further enhance our understandings about the multiple modernities that characterize the world today.

Acknowledgments

In addition to the editors of this volume, I would like to thank Azfar A. Moin and Thomas Blom Hansen for their incisive comments. I also benefited greatly from presenting this essay at the conference "Muslim Thought and Practice in South Asia: New Practices and Directions" at Boston University (27 October 2016).

References

Abisaab, Rula Jurdi. 2004. *Converting Persia: Religion and Power in the Safavid Empire.* London: I.B. Tauris.

Afsaruddin, Asma. 2008. "Making the Case for Religious Freedom within the Islamic Tradition." *Review of Faith & International Affairs* 6(2): 57–60.

Ahmed, Asad A. 2009. "Spectres of Blasphemy: Macaulay, the Indian Penal Code and Pakistan's Postcolonial Predicament." In Raminder Kaur and William Mazarella, eds., *Censorship in South Asia: Cultural Regulation from Sedition to Seduction*, 172–205. Bloomington: Indiana University Press.

Alam, Muzaffar. 2004. *The Languages of Political Islam: India, 1200–1800.* Chicago: University of Chicago Press.

Amanat, Abbas. 2009. *Apocalyptic Islam and Iranian Shi'ism.* London: I.B. Tauris.

Amanat, Abbas. 2014. "Persian Nuqtawīs and the Shaping of the Doctrine of 'Universal Conciliation' (*ṣulḥ-i kull*) in Mughal India." In Orkhan Mir-Kasimov, ed., *Unity in*

Diversity: Mysticism, Messianism and the Construction of Religious Authority in Islam, 367–92. Leiden: Brill.

An-Na'im, Abdullahi. 2008. *Islam and the Secular State: Negotiating the Future of Shari'a*. Cambridge, MA: Harvard University Press.

Arjomand, Saïd Amir. 1981. "Religious Extremism (Ghuluww), Ṣūfism and Sunnism in Safavid Iran: 1501–1722." *Journal of Asian History* 15(1): 1–35.

Arjomand, Saïd Amir. 2011. "Axial Civilizations, Multiple Modernities, and Islam." *Journal of Classical Sociology* 11(3): 327–35.

Asad, Talal. 1986. "The Idea of an Anthropology of Islam." Occasional Paper Series, Washington, DC: Georgetown University Center for Contemporary Arab Studies.

Asad, Talal. 2003. *Formations of the Secular: Christianity, Islam, Modernity*. Stanford, CA: Stanford University Press.

Babayan, Kathryn. 2002. *Mystics, Monarchs, and Messiahs: Cultural Landscapes of Early Modern Iran*. Cambridge, MA: Harvard University Press.

Balibar, Etienne. 2004. *We, the People of Europe? Reflections on Transnational Citizenship*. Princeton, NJ: Princeton University Press.

Barkey, Karen. 2008. *Empire of Difference: The Ottomans in Comparative Perspective*. New York: Cambridge University Press.

Bhambra, Gurminder K. 2010. "Historical Sociology, International Relations and Connected Histories." *Cambridge Review of International Affairs* 23(1): 127–43.

Burbank, Jane, and Frederick Cooper. 2010. *Empires in World History: Power and the Politics of Difference*. Princeton, NJ: Princeton University Press.

Burhani, Ahmad Najib. 2014. "Treating Minorities with Fatwas: A Study of the Ahmadiyya Community in Indonesia." *Contemporary Islam* 8(3): 285–301.

Chehabi, Houchang E. 2008. "Anatomy of Prejudice: Reflections on Secular Anti-Baha'ism in Iran." In Dominic Parviz Brookshaw and Seena B. Fazel, eds., *The Baha'is of Iran: Socio-Historical Studies*, 184–99. London: Routledge.

Cole, Juan R. I. 1998. *Modernity and the Millennium: The Genesis of the Baha'i Faith in the Nineteenth-Century Middle East*. New York: Columbia University Press.

Dale, Stephen F. 2010. *The Muslim Empires of the Ottomans, Safavids, and Mughals*. Cambridge: Cambridge University Press.

Donner, Fred McGraw. 1981. *The Early Islamic Conquests*. Princeton, NJ: Princeton University Press.

Eisenstadt, S. N., ed. 1986. *The Origins and Diversity of Axial Age Civilizations*. SUNY Press.

Eisenstadt, S. N. 2000. "Multiple Modernities." *Daedalus* 129(1): 1–29.

Friedmann, Yohanan. 1989. *Prophecy Continuous: Aspects of Ahmadi Religious Thought and Its Medieval Background*. Berkeley: University of California Press.

Gregorian, Vartan. 1974. "Minorities of Isfahan: The Armenian Community of Isfahan 1587–1722." *Iranian Studies* 7(3–4): 652–80.

Griffel, Frank. 2001. "Toleration and Exclusion: Al-Shāfi'ī and al-Ghazālī on the Treatment of Apostates." *Bulletin of the School of Oriental and African Studies* 64(3): 339–54.

Hallaq, Wael B. 2013. *The Impossible State: Islam, Politics, and Modernity's Moral Predicament*. New York: Columbia University Press.

Higgins, Patricia J. 1984. "Minority-State Relations in Contemporary Iran." *Iranian Studies* 17(1): 37–71.

Hirschkind, Charles. 1995. "Heresy or Hermeneutics: The Case of Nasr Ḥamid Abu Zayd." *American Journal of Islamic Social Sciences* 12(4): 463–77.

Hirschkind, Charles. 1997. "What Is Political Islam?" *Middle East Report* 27: 12–14.

Hodgson, Marshall G. S. 1974a. *The Venture of Islam: Conscience and History in a World Civilization*. Vol. 1: *The Classical Age of Islam*. Chicago: University of Chicago Press.

Hodgson, Marshall G. S. 1974b. *The Venture of Islam: Conscience and History in a World Civilization*. Vol. 3: *The Gunpowder Empires and Modern Times*. Chicago: University of Chicago Press.

Ibrahim, Mahmood. 1994. "Religious Inquisition as Social Policy: The Persecution of the Zanadiqa in the Early Abbasid Caliphate." *Arab Studies Quarterly* 16(2): 53–72.

Iqbal, Muhammad. 1976. *Islam and Ahmadism*. Lahore: Muhammad Ashraf, Kashmiri Bazar.

Johansen, Baber. 2003. "Apostasy as Objective and Depersonalized Fact: Two Recent Egyptian Court Judgments." *Social Research* 70(3): 687–710.

Johnson, Rosemary Stanfield. 1994. "Sunni Survival in Safavid Iran: Anti-Sunni Activities during the Reign of Tahmasp I." *Iranian Studies* 27(1–4): 123–33.

Kaviraj, Sudipta. 2005. "An Outline of a Revisionist Theory of Modernity." *European Journal of Sociology* 46(3): 497–526.

Khan, Iqtidar Alam. 2001. "State in the Mughal India: Re-Examining the Myths of a Counter-Vision." *Social Scientist* 29(1): 16–45.

Khan, Iqtidar Alam. 2016. *India's Polity in the Age of Akbar*. New Delhi: Permanent Black.

Kinra, Rajeev. 2013. "Handling Diversity with Absolute Civility: The Global Historical Legacy of Mughal Ṣulḥ-i Kull." *Medieval History Journal* 16(2): 251–95.

Mahoney, James. 2000. "Path Dependence in Historical Sociology." *Theory and Society* 29(4): 507–48.

Malamud, Margaret. 1994. "The Politics of Heresy in Medieval Khurasan: The Karramiyya in Nishapur." *Iranian Studies* 27(1–4): 37–51.

Mann, Michael. 2005. *The Dark Side of Democracy: Explaining Ethnic Cleansing*. New York: Cambridge University Press.

Matthee, Rudi. 2009. "Was Safavid Iran an Empire?" *Journal of the Economic and Social History of the Orient* 53(1): 233–65.

Maududi, Abul A'la. 1977. *Human Rights in Islam*. Lahore: Islamic Publications.

Moin, A. Azfar. 2012. *The Millennial Sovereign: Sacred Kingship and Sainthood in Islam*. New York: Columbia University Press.

National Assembly of Pakistan. 1974. *Proceedings of the Special Committee of the Whole House Held in Camera to Consider the Qadiani Issue, August 5, 1974–September 7, 1974*. Islamabad: Government of Pakistan Press.

National Assembly of Pakistan Debates. June 30, 1974. Islamabad: Government of Pakistan Press.

Omi, Michael, and Howard Winant. 2014. *Racial Formation in the United States*. 3rd ed. London: Routledge.

Saeed, Sadia. 2012. "Political Fields and Religious Movements: The Exclusion of the Ahmadiyya Community in Pakistan." *Political Power and Social Theory* 23: 189–223.

Saeed, Sadia. 2016. "Imperial Ideologies, Transnational Activism: Questioning the Place of Religious Freedom from British India." *Comparative Studies of South Asia, Africa and the Middle East* 36(2): 229–45.

Saeed, Sadia. 2017. *Politics of Desecularization: Law and the Minority Question in Pakistan*. New York: Cambridge University Press.

Sanasarian, Eliz. 2000. *Religious Minorities in Iran*. New York: Cambridge University Press.

Streusand, Douglas E. 2010. *Islamic Gunpowder Empires: Ottomans, Safavids, and Mughals*. Boulder, CO: Westview Press.

Subrahmanyam, Sanjay. 1997. "Connected Histories: Notes towards a Reconfiguration of Early Modern Eurasia." *Modern Asian Studies* 31(3): 735–62.

Subrahmanyam, Sanjay. 2006. "A Tale of Three Empires: Mughals, Ottomans, and Habsburgs in a Comparative Context." *Common Knowledge* 12(1): 66–92.

van der Veer, Peter. 1994. *Religious Nationalism: Hindus and Muslims in India*. Berkeley: University of California Press.

2

Liberalism and the Path to Treason in the Ottoman Empire, 1908–1923

Christine Philliou

The question of pluralism in the Ottoman Empire has long occupied historians and social scientists alike.[1] Was the multiplicity of confessional, ethnic, and linguistic communities in the empire's domains a cause for its longevity? And was the pluralism the Ottomans inherited in their lands a precipitant of the empire's own devolution in the nineteenth and early twentieth centuries? Most would answer yes to both questions at this point, blaming exclusivist ideologies of nationalism and their European colonial purveyors for destroying an early modern plural(ist) imperial formation. If we take a closer look at the period of final devolution of the empire, between the Constitutional Revolution of July 1908 and the dissolution of the sultanate and establishment of the Turkish Republic in 1922–23, however, we can see that there were other dynamics at play as well, and that the transition from a diverse empire to a homogeneous nation-state was hardly predetermined or clean. As early modern pluralism met its existential enemy, modern exclusivist nationalism, there was a group—liberals—who seemed to be trying to forge a different path. Such a path would have, perhaps, maintained a kind of pluralism by reconstituting the basis for politics and sovereignty, allowing for the participation of and dialogue between multiple political parties as well as social, ethnic, and confessional groups. In what follows I trace the path of liberalism in the late Ottoman Empire, down to its tragic end in the birth of the Turkish republic, and argue that the fate of liberalism was intextricalby bound up with a particular understanding of and space for pluralism. I argue furthermore that this process was articulated with a vocabulary of patriotism, when seen from the inside.

Liberalism in an Ottoman idiom grew out of a language of patriotism, and for that reason it is necessary to consider the meanings of that term as a precursor

---

[1] A version of this chapter, "Liberalism as Treason in the Ottoman Empire," was presented in St. Petersburg in June 2015 at a conference, "Cultures of Patriotism in World War One," organized by Laura Engelstein and Boris Kolonitskii and held at the American University in St. Petersburg. I draw from some of the same material that forms the basis of *Turkey: A past against History* (Berkeley, CA: University of California Press, 2021).

Christine Philliou, *Liberalism and the Path to Treason in the Ottoman Empire, 1908–1923* In: *Negotiating Democracy and Religious Pluralism*. Edited by: Karen Barkey, Sudipta Kaviraj, and Vatsal Naresh, Oxford University Press. © Oxford University Press 2021. DOI: 10.1093/oso/9780197530016.003.0003

to the story of liberalism. The term "patriotism" would have been—and was—translated into an Ottoman milieu in at least three variants, reflecting the tripartite nature of the Ottoman language itself: the Persian/Turkish *vatanperestlik*, the Arabic *hubb al-vatan*, and sometimes the Turkish *vatan sevdası/sever*, all meaning literally "love of country/homeland." As in English, all three terms for patriotism appear to transcend the political. Also as in English, the concept turned out to be deeply political, and inextricable from the troubling nineteenth- and twentieth-century questions surrounding the bases for sovereignty and affiliation across the territories and groups that constituted the Ottoman Empire. Likewise, the term *vatan*, or "country/homeland," used in all three variants of Ottoman terms for "patriotism," is seemingly generic (country, homeland) but in actuality is used to mean an Ottoman (turned-Turkish) political/cultural and linguistic space (alt. *anavatan*, motherland).

Patriotism (love of the *vatan*), and the perceived and real lack thereof, was, of course, a fundamental factor in the devolution of the Ottoman Empire in the course of the nineteenth century, beginning with the Greek War of Independence in the 1820s. Could and would non-Muslims be patriotic as they became eligible for belonging in alternative countries/motherlands? Could they, and did they really want to, love the Ottoman motherland? And this only prompted a further cascade of questions for Ottoman elites about what the Ottoman motherland was and could be, for Muslims as well as non-Muslims. As the principle of nationalism evolved to vie with imperial loyalties, Greeks, Serbs, and ultimately Bulgarians and Romanians developed a love for "their" countries, carved out of Ottoman territories, while Christians (and, in smaller numbers, Jews) remaining in the Ottoman Empire struggled to articulate a basis for loyalty and patriotism.

This discursive basis for non-Muslim loyalty to the Ottoman sultanate (or sultan? or government? or homeland?) was made possible by the Tanzimat reforms of the mid-nineteenth century (1839–76), wherein a language of equality and we might say secularism (even if routed through, and ultimately reinforcing, the boundaries of confessional communities) accompanied by de jure equality and citizenship (by 1856) was born. In the conventional narrative of the Ottoman nineteenth century, the pendulum of reforms continued to swing in the direction of liberal parliamentary constitutionalism *alla franga* until the establishment of an actual parliament and promulgation of an actual constitution (Kanun-i Esasi) in 1876–77.[2] A few months after the accession of Sultan Abdülhamit II to the throne, and with the resumption of Ottoman-Russian military conflict in the Balkans and eastern Anatolia (in regional rehearsal for the Great War to come), the constitution was suspended and a period

---

[2] See the classic Roderic Davison, *Reform in the Ottoman Empire, 1856–1876* (Princeton, NJ: Princeton University Press, 1963).

of neo-absolutist despotism (*istibdad*) began, replete with unabashed censorship and surveillance, thanks to a burgeoning proto-modern security apparatus. Thereafter, liberalism, constitutionalism, and by extension notions of patriotism directed at any entity beyond the person of the sultan became suspect, whether for Muslims or for non-Muslims.

It was in the underground and émigré spaces of the Hamidian period (1876–1908/9) that new iterations of patriotism and sovereignty developed, which included constitutionalism, or at least the reflex-like desire for the restoration of the 1876–77 constitution as a solution to the impasse of governance. Ironically, a major such "underground" space was within the Ottoman military itself post-1878. These Young Turk officers saw themselves as acting out of true (and from our perspective extreme) patriotism, after having watched helplessly as the Balkans, where many of them were born and raised, were wrenched from Ottoman control by European imperial(ist) powers in conjunction with non-Muslim nationalists/patriots/brigands. They saw the cultured Tanzimat statesmen of the previous generation, for all of their ecumenical "Ottomanism," as painfully ineffective at governing and promoting the interests of the central state. Furthermore, they saw the "neo-absolutist" sultan Abdülhamit, for all of his strongarm tactics and paranoia, as equally ineffective at accomplishing what really counted: defending the empire and its territorial integrity, let alone defending their own manhood as the empire's military forces at the Balkan front lines.

When the Young Turks finally succeeded in having the constitution restored in July 1908, these new iterations of patriotism, and new combinations of constitutionalism and authoritarianism, gradually came to the fore. One of many factors that makes the period between 1908 and 1923, when the empire was finally dissolved, difficult to appreciate is the fact that there was no unitary, explicit, fully elaborated ideology of the Committee of Union and Progress (CUP) , the organization that took control of the Ottoman government and state.[3] But liberalism and pluralism—as in political pluralism in the form of a system with multiple parties, or confessional/ethnic pluralism, as in a federalist vision for imperial governance—was at the heart of the conflict that motivated the CUP. The "triumvirate" of Talaat, Cemal, and Enver Pasha, who effectively ran the party and the empire from at least 1913 until their flight in the wake of the Ottoman defeat in October–November 1918, never announced their program, and in fact often deliberately shrouded their intentions and policies in secrecy.[4] For this

[3] This is made quite clear in M. Şükrü Hanioğlu's recent *Atatürk: An Intellectual Biography* (Princeton, NJ: Princeton University Press, 2011); he even goes so far as to say that pragmatism was the ideology of Mustafa Kemal Atatürk, and therefore of his antecedents, the Young Turks / CUP.

[4] There are, of course, texts that were published in this time that are credited with having had great influence over various tendencies of the Young Turk movement and the CUP in particular, such as *Üç Tarz-ı Siyaset* (Three Styles of Politics) by Yusuf Akçura, and the writings of Ahmet Ağaoğlu/Agaev

reason we often must deduce what it was they were fighting for, beyond the mere territorial integrity of the empire. They of course considered themselves patriots, whose goal was to "save the empire," but what precisely that entailed was not always clear.

The meanings of Ottoman patriotism in the course and aftermath of World War I, then, cannot be understood without a preliminary analysis of what patriotism was coming to mean in the prewar years of the Second Constitutional (July 1908 to the autumn of 1914). To grasp what patriotism could mean in those years, in turn, necessitates an appreciation of the enemies against which the Young Turks–turned-CUP defined themselves and took shape as a movement: enemies that included the European great powers, non-Muslim Ottoman subject populations, forces of Muslim religious "reaction" (*irtica*), and no less important, but much less appreciated in scholarship, the focus of this chapter: the liberals among their own fellow Turks and Muslims.

Leaders of the CUP would never have admitted openly that they were enemies of liberals or liberalism, in part because, as will be pointed out repeatedly in what follows, their very raison d'être and basis for popular support was the restoration of the liberal constitution. And yet for contingent as well as structural reasons they consistently worked to marginalize individual liberal intellectuals and politicians, labeling them not as liberals but as reactionaries (*mürteci*), and therefore anti-constitutionalists who supported a return to *istibdad* (absolutism), a discursive move that is likely familiar to students of Russian/Soviet history.

I maintain here that liberalism and the liberal iteration of patriotism—which was little more than a holdover of the Ottoman Tanzimat mentality—came to acquire the status of treason in the short period between the Constitutional Revolution of July 1908 (the goal of which was to restore the (liberal) constitution that had been suspended in 1876–77) and the outbreak of World War I. This fact has been thoroughly obscured by the dominant narrative at the time and since, until only a few decades ago, in Turkey and among many scholars of Ottoman/Turkish history abroad; a narrative constructed and propagated by CUP partisans that appropriated the state apparatus and the very concept of patriotism in the Ottoman, and then Turkish, national milieu.

But the evidence is clear, especially when we look to the Armistice period (1918–23), when elements of the CUP regrouped in Anatolia and launched the Turkish national movement, eventually succeeding in nullifying the 1920 Treaty

and Ismail Gasprinski, Ziya Gökalp, and Munis Tekinalp (Moiz Kohen). But my point here is that there was no ideological consensus regarding the meaning of "Turk" or "Ottoman," or the preference of pan-Turkism as opposed to pan-Islamism or pan-Turanianism, and therefore about the basis for sovereignty (and patriotism) in the Second Constitutional period. It is also interesting to note that of the major ideologues and theorists noted previously, three were Russian Muslim/Turkish émigrés, one was a Jew from Salonika, and one was of Kurdish descent from Diyarbakir.

of Sèvres and achieving independent Turkish statehood with the 1923 Treaty of Lausanne. During this period, all of the top liberals (Ali Kemal, Rıza Tevfik, Damat Ferit Pasha, etc.) were labeled not merely reactionaries, but traitors to the nation (*vatan haini*), and therefore the antithesis of patriots. The fact that they were indeed working in cooperation with British occupation authorities, and the national movement was launched to end that occupation, heaped more meaning on these charges. Indeed, this only reveals that there are many steps and contingencies between the outbreak of World War I and the final victory of the Turkish nationalists under Mustafa Kemal in late 1922, but liberalism had already started on the path to treason before the Great War broke out. Thus, to follow the development of liberalism and its opposite just before World War I in light of what would transpire at the war's end affords us not just an ear onto voices previously left unheard, but a deeper understanding of the Great War as a historical and political process in both the final devolution of the empire and the shaping of the modern nation-state of Turkey.

2.1. Ottoman Liberals: Journalism and Treason

While the wing of the Young Turk coalition that evolved into the Committee of Union and Progress (which itself was transformed from a secret society to an organization, and finally a political party) was predominantly of military background, the wing that became the Liberal Party (in a series of incarnations Ahrar Fırkası, Hürriyet ve İtilaf Fırkası, etc.) was more diverse. The Liberal wing was in general composed of mid- and high-level civil servants and "aristocrats," intellectuals, and writers/journalists, as well as some military men who left the CUP at various points. Modern-day historian Feroz Ahmad characterized them as "well-educated, westernised, cosmopolitan, and comfortable with a foreign language or culture, usually French."[5] Their general political orientation tended to be Anglophile, and their liberalism, like the British variant, combined a deeply entrenched elitism (and concomitant association with empire and its hierarchy) with a dedication to liberal/individual freedoms and parliamentary rule.

The right to press freedom was one of the central freedoms that brought the Young Turk coalition together to demand the restoration of the constitution (Kanun-i Esasi) in 1908. Among the ideological differences between the two wings was that the CUP was expressly opposed to "autocracy," which it saw as the rule of the Palace and the Porte (grand vizier), and yet in favor of centralization on the matter of non-Muslim communities (leading to a policy of forced Turkification). The Liberals, in contrast, and led by figures such as Prince

[5] Feroz Ahmad, *The Making of Modern Turkey* (Routledge: New York, 1993), 34.

Sabahettin, a member of the Ottoman royal house, and Damat Ferit Pasha, an aristocrat who had married into the ruling dynasty, were partial to the rule of high bureaucrats, and in favor of decentralization and federalism as a way of managing confessional and ethnic diversity in the lands that remained part of the empire by this point.[6]

When the coalition of these groups, known loosely as the Young Turks, came together in July 1908 and effected the restoration of the 1876 Kanun-i Esasi, it was, in their minds, to rescue the failing empire and salvage remaining imperial territories by establishing a rule of law and a more efficient administration. It was also to alleviate the severe restrictions on press freedoms that had been in effect under Sultan Abdülhamit. Both factions of Young Turks during the reign of Abdülhamit had resorted to publishing their newspapers beyond the reach of Ottoman censors, whether in British/autonomous Egypt, Paris, or Switzerland, and had in general gone to great lengths to circumvent the restrictions on the press within the empire.[7]

Freedom of the press, then, was one of the banner issues of the Young Turk coalition from its inception—both its nationalist, centralist wing (led by Ahmet Rıza, editor of the CUP-in-exile gazette *Meşveret* before 1908) and its liberal, decentralist one (led by Prince Sabahettin). And for this reason, the number of newspapers published in the empire, mainly in Istanbul, proliferated within hours of the constitution being restored in July 1908. Palmira Brummett, historian of the revolutionary press, quotes the 1908 yearbook (*salname*) as having listed 97 publishers, and compares the 103 Turkish-language newspapers that appeared between 1879 and 1907 with the 240 that were published within the first year after the constitutional revolution.[8]

This explosion in press activities in 1908 went hand in hand with the larger euphoria for "freedoms" (*hürriyetler*) that the constitution was assumed to have brought, and part of the climate of a "broad spirit of conciliation."[9] The first newspapers of the constitutional era were, according to one contemporary

---

[6] While one might see decentralization, and possibly regional or communal autonomy, as its extension, as a forward-thinking, if romantic strategy to manage diversity, the Liberals were often protrayed by the CUP adherents as backward reactionaries (*mürteci*) lumped together with opposition among the ulema, and at the very least as elitists who were out of touch with political realities. Among the most prominent Liberals was Prince Sabahettin, a member of the Ottoman dynasty who had spent many years in Paris agitating for change, and who, upon his return in September 1908, helped found the Liberal Union (Ahrar Fırkası).

[7] According to Erol Baykal, "The Ottoman Press: 1908–1923," (PhD dissertation in progress), 1, Abdülhamit had suspended the rather liberal press law that had been enacted under Abdülaziz in 1864. When the suspension was lifted along with the suspension of the constitution in July 1908, there was a great deal of confusion on the part of government functionaries as to what the policy would be toward the private press.

[8] Palmira Brummett, *Image and Imperialism in the Ottoman Revolutionary Press, 1908–1911* (Albany: State University of New York Press, 2000), 3–4.

[9] Michelle Campos, in her *Ottoman Brothers: Muslims, Christians, and Jews in Early Twentieth-Century Palestine* (Stanford, CA: Stanford University Press, 2011), makes central use of newspapers in Jerusalem during this honeymoon phase of the Second Constitutional period (July 1908–April

observer, "nothing but a fervent outcry of joy."[10] In the words of another, "The streets, where people did not usually feel free even to walk fast, lest they attract the attention of spies, were filled with noisy crowds listening joyfully to revolutionary speeches, or making demonstrations before public buildings, newspaper offices, or foreign embassies."[11]

Brummett comments on the role of the press in politics and society after 1908, writing, "The press then addressed both the anxieties created by the disestablishment of the old regime and the underlying forces and conditions that had produced the revolution in the first place: the lack of political and social freedom, the debilitated economy, the obsolete military, the perceived corruption of officials at all levels of the government, the dearth of opportunity for a new class of Western-educated bureaucrats, the prostitution of the Ottoman economy to European economic interests, and the cultural schizophrenia created by Ottoman reform programs and by European dominance."[12] The role of the press in a nominally constitutional, parliamentary regime presented a major contradiction for the Unionists, or the Committee of Union and Progress, as they sought to expand their control over more and more branches of the government and areas of society.

For, while the Young Turks had been in opposition—to Abdülhamit, his bureaucracy, and his security apparatus—it was still unproblematic to stand for freedom of the press. Once the constitution had been restored, allowing de jure freedom of the press was necessary to maintaining any legitimacy, but to allow a de facto freedom was in effect to invite a measure of chaos, and, from the Unionists' perspective at least, to undermine their bid for power. For this reason, post-1908, and especially after the "March 31 Events" of 1909, as we will see later, the mere attempt to develop and sustain an independent press was a catch-22 for both the journalists and those in power: for the journalists, exercising their freedom to criticize the government was on the one hand their raison d'être, and on the other to risk penalty and even prison, and in a few cases, death. As for the Unionists, throughout this period they were, by their own account, fighting to maintain constitutional, parliamentary rule, a key feature of which, they were well aware, was a free press; and yet, because their power was far from unchallenged, many of the organization's leaders felt extremely threatened by the critical articles being published about them and their methods.[13] Journalists, writers,

---

1909), highlighting, often uncritically, the optimistic discourse of freedom and brotherhood among Ottoman citizens of all confessional affiliations.

[10] Ahmet Emin Yalman, "The Development of Turkey as Measured by Its Press," PhD dissertation, Columbia University, 1914, 87.

[11] Yalman, "Development of Turkey," 87.

[12] Brummett, *Image and Imperialism*, 5.

[13] Despite the "complete Unionist victory" in the parliamentary elections of autumn 1908 (Erik Jan Zurcher, "The Ides of April," in *The Young Turk Legacy and Nation-Building: From the Ottoman*

and editors became, quite literally, the crucibles of the Second Constitutional period.

A new and quite liberal press law was enacted in July 1909 and stayed in effect until March 1913, shortly after the CUP had taken total control of the government in the *Babıali* coup d'état in January of that year. So the climate between 1909 and 1913 was one of an ostensibly liberal legal milieu, but with martial law and de facto suppression and intimidation tactics the order of the day. Opposition writers and journalists, then, by merely practicing their profession and trying to foster a debate about freedom and politics in the uncharted waters of a constitutional, parliamentary Ottoman Empire, were often seen as dangerous, and ultimately as seditious—something that was not supposed to be in the new world of freedoms and constitutionalism.[14] The fact that they were increasingly coming to express their criticism through humor in 1910–11—cartoons, satire, and parody—made the situation even more fraught, as criticism quickly blurred into mocking, and attacks, like politics in general, became highly personalized. At stake was the very meaning of a press in Ottoman/constitutional society. The press represented something very different for the Liberals than it did for the CUP/Unionists; while a *free* press was crucial to the vision of politics (and patriotism) held by liberals in the Ottoman Empire, and particularly Istanbul, the press was a crucial tool and vehicle for propaganda in the "top-down" structure and vision of the CUP leadership. In the press we can thus find some of the deepest contradictions and fault lines of the Young Turk project as it devolved into distinct and opposing factions.

Three prominent opposition journalists were even gunned down in Istanbul, exposing the less-than-liberal reality behind the facade of press freedom between 1909 and 1913. All of them, as one of their associates would point out repeatedly, were also killed in close proximity to *karakol*, or police stations in the capital, implying that there was government (Unionist-CUP) involvement in the killings. The first, Hasan Fehmi, a writer for *Serbesti* (Freedom) (liberal Mevlanzade Rıfat's newspaper), was killed in March 1909. The second, Ahmet Samim, who wrote for *Seda-yı Milli* (National Voice), was killed on the Galata Bridge in July 1910. And the third, Zeki Bey, a writer for *İştirak* (Comrade) (İştirakçı/Socialist Hilmi's newspaper), was killed in the seaside village of Bakırköy outside of Istanbul in July 1911. The following section will put these events in the more specific context of politics in Istanbul between 1908 and 1913,

Empire to Ataturk's Turkey [I.B. Tauris: London, 2010], 75), CUP/Unionist fear of opposition only increased.

[14] Refik Halid (Karay) (1888–1965) is a major protagonist in the larger project of which this chapter is a part. See Christine M. Philliou, *Turkey: A past against History* (2021) for an exploration of these issues through his life and work.

leading up to the deportation and internal exile of hundreds of liberal opposition intellectuals and writers in June 1913.

The first major watershed after the constitutional revolution, 1909's "March 31 Events," as they are known (March 31 by the Rumi calendar, April 12–13 by the new calendar), were themselves bound up closely with press-related goings-on, and constituted the breaking point for the two wings—liberal (federalist) and illiberal (unionist)—of the Young Turk coalition. These events served as an end of political innocence for masses and elites alike, and especially for journalistic and literary circles. They also heralded the start of a tense conflict between the ostensible ends of politics—freedom and liberal democracy—and the means— a naked struggle for power between the Unionists, on the one hand, and the Ottoman governing apparatus and individual liberals and "reactionary" or anti-constitutionalist opponents, who allied in different combinations and parties throughout these four years, on the other.

Starting in February 1909, when the CUP effected a vote in parliament to re-place the liberal-minded grand vizier Kıbrıslı Kiamil Pasha with the more closely CUP-affiliated Hüseyin Hilmi Pasha, an all-out war between liberal opposition newspapers (such as İkdam) and CUP organs (such as Tanin) ensued. The con-flict reached a crescendo in early April when a fedai (volunteer/paramilitary) gunned down the opposition journalist Hasan Fehmi, editor of the opposition newspaper Serbesti. His funeral turned into a mass opposition rally the following day, escalating tensions that were already high.[15] A draft law intended to restrict demonstration had been put to the assembly, but was delayed until the 25 of that month due to opposition within the assembly.[16] Grand Vizier Hüseyin Hilmi Pasha had also requested a law curbing press freedoms at this moment. In this political climate an uprising occurred the nature of which is still fiercely debated in Turkey today; it was a self-proclaimed "sharia-ist" (şeriatçı) movement to re-verse the constitutional revolution, which some argue was set up by the CUP to provoke a coup d'état and justify further repression. These events ended the honeymoon period of the Second Constitutional period, and remain among the most controversial events of the twentieth century in Turkey today.[17]

Whatever the root cause of the March 31 Events, the 10 days of revolt and upheaval against the CUP and/or the constitutional regime prompted an un-precedented crackdown, starting with the arrival of the Action Army (Hareket Ordusu) marching into Istanbul from the Balkans, the establishment of

[15] See Zurcher, "The Ides of April," 76 and passim.

[16] Feroz Ahmad, Ittihat Terakki (Istanbul: Kaynak Yayinlari, 1999), 60.

[17] The recent Gezi Park events in Istanbul took place around the site of the barracks where the March 31 Events occurred; Prime Minister Erdoğan made no secret of the fact that he saw himself as fighting the CUP and avenging the injustices they perpetrated on the (Islamist) opposition starting from these events.

martial law, and the removal of Abdülhamit II from the throne (to house arrest in Salonika, the headquarters of the CUP). In a different light, these events have also very much lived on in the imagination of CUP adherents and among secularist/Kemalists in the Turkish republic even to the present day, a reminder of the fact that the government could be lost in an instant to religious reactionaries, rather than (for liberals at the time) as a moment when freedom was violated.

According to Ahmet Emin (Yalman), a prominent intellectual at the time, who switched camps from the liberal to, ultimately, the Turkish nationalists, had this to say already in 1914: "The new era marked the beginning of the end of the Young Turkish idealism. Instead of sticking to the letter of paper laws and the ideas of 'liberty, equality, and fraternity,' constitutional rights were suspended under extraordinary measures, a state of siege was proclaimed, and control by direct force, instead of by impression and prestige, was sought."[18]

The liberal opposition had been rendered dormant in the wake of the March 31 Events and continuing martial law, but began to come back out into the open, as the power of the CUP began to wane only two years later. In the absence of foreign invasion in 1910 and much of 1911, the government, and within it the CUP, was consumed with the dilemmas of actually governing the remaining territories of the empire, and in working out the logistical and procedural realities of a constitutional, parliamentary government (we should keep in mind that the First Consitutional period was less than a year long, hardly allowing the time to work out these issues). The day-to-day tasks of governing in peacetime almost did the organization in, as it struggled to deal with internal conflicts between the military (War Ministry) and the CUP; conflict over troubled financial reform surrounding the Ottoman loan of 1910; and the persistence of martial law since mid-1909.[19] It was only wars with foreign enemies that gave the CUP renewed strength.

The press, now a force to be reckoned with since the proliferation of so many gazettes in 1908–9, was connected to these fissures and conflicts on a number of levels. In the press were debates (or at least positions expounded upon in Unionist or Liberal papers) about the more straightforward issues of non-Muslim belonging and regional government (centralization/decentralization) and fiscal policy. But the press was also an important locus for testing the democratic process itself. Government treatment of the press was, therefore, a litmus test of the freedoms that were claimed when the constitution was restored. By extension, criticism of the government and/or the CUP in the press was seen as a right to be exercised by informed citizens, at least in the view of liberals. To

[18] Yalman, "Development of Turkey," 98–99.
[19] This is all solidly argued throughout Feroz Ahmad's classic, *The Young Turks: The Committee of Union and Progress in Turkish Politics, 1908–1914* (New York: Columbia University Press, 1969; 2010), 67.

be a *muhalif*, or opponent, in this period, then, was a deliberate (often liberal) stance meant at once to test the mettle and real intentions of the CUP in its bid for power, and to act as a check on specific policies and legislation they tried to enact.

By October 1912, a new period of domestic polarization and hot wars with foreign powers had begun. The Liberal opposition to the CUP was now in power, having been freely elected in 1911, and the Ottoman-Italian War was underway (until September 1912, when the Ottomans sued for peace due to the Balkan ultimatum)—this led directly to the (first) Balkan War (October 1912–May 1913), an unmitigated disaster for the Ottomans and for Muslim populations of the Balkans. This defeat, and the loss of territories and uprooting of Muslims communities throughout the Balkans, became a major catalyst for the next round of violence against Ottoman Armenians and other Christians in Anatolia in the course of World War I.[20] Because the Liberals were in power, they were of course deemed responsible for the defeat; it therefore constituted the most powerful springboard for the CUP to regain control of the government, and ultimately the state.

2.2. June 1913: Liberalism Displaced

In January 1913 the CUP, in response to the defeat in the (first) Balkan War, initiated a coup, storming the Sublime Porte (*Babıali*), the seat of government, determined to gain total control this time around.[21] A few months later, in June of that year, elder statesman and grand vizier / *sadrazam* Mahmut Şevket Pasha was assassinated, prompting nothing short of panic among CUP leaders. Cemal Pasha, a member of the so-called triumvirate of the CUP, according to his own memoirs, had already started preparing a list of people to arrest in this dangerous (to him) climate.[22] In June 1913, within days after the assassination, over 800 "opponents," many of them liberal writers, publishers, and journalists, were arrested and put on the ship *Bahri Cedit* ("New Sea") to the eastern Black Sea coastal town of Sinop.[23] In Cemal Pasha's view, he had compiled the list of

[20] Several recent works elaborate on this, including Ryan Gingeras, *Sorrowful Shores: Violence, Ethnicity, and the End of the Ottoman Empire, 1912–1923* (Oxford: Oxford University Press, 2009).

[21] I refer to the "CUP" as one body as shorthand. Scholars are well aware there were different figures and factions even within the CUP, and that because of the secrecy of the organization-turned-party it is often impossible to know who initiated which decisions and why, and whether anyone from within opposed such decisions.

[22] See Djemal Pasha, *Memoirs of a Turkish Statesman, 1913–1919* (New York: George H. Doran, 1922), chap. 1.

[23] There is relatively little information about these events, the particular people who were exiled, and their experience in exile, in the major historical/scholarly works of this period. On the one hand, this is surprising, given that the group amounted to more or less the entire intelligentsia of the capital, and by extension the empire. On the other hand, it makes a great deal of sense, given that CUP

intellectuals to be removed from the capital so as to keep them safe. It seems clear from the goings-on in the years leading up to 1913 that intellectuals were deemed a threat to a regime that was already insecure and under siege from several directions.[24]

It is interesting, however, that these intellectuals, not yet openly labeled traitors but removed ostensibly for their own safety, were anything but ill-treated in their internal exile. It was meant to be a comfortable exile indeed. Some who had been working as civil servants before the deportation continued to receive their salaries or pensions; some were sent an allowance by their families in Istanbul. And the town of Sinop was not the worst locale for exile: a beautiful and quaint coastal town on the Black Sea, lying on an isthmus with a medieval castle-turned-prison, and a sizable Greek community to supply plenty of raki and tavernas for the Istanbul natives, as we know from some of the literary work that these exiles produced about their experience.[25]

What does this mean, that intellectuals had to be removed from the capital, and yet treated with kid gloves? For one thing, we can see that in this period, before the outbreak of World War I, some in the CUP leadership were far from resolved that liberalism was tantamount to treason. Some in the CUP seemed to see a place for liberals and intellectuals, if nothing else than because they were often from prominent families associated with the bureaucracy and the ruling dynasty, and therefore could not be treated as expendable, but were at the same time deeply uncomfortable with the question of how they fit together with the CUP leaders' own aspirations for total control of the state. This would stand in contrast to the situation after the war's end, when the nationalist movement took shape in Anatolia. In 1913 liberals were threatening, dangerous, and endangered even, but perhaps not yet treasonous. Many of the 800 exiles were allowed back to Istanbul or other nearby sites of exile already the following year. Others remained stranded in Anatolia for most of the duration of the war, labeled as "not trustworthy" in Ottoman documents.

partisans, later to become Turkish nationalists, generated the dominant narrative of history until very recently. Even Feroz Ahmad, whose analysis of the period, *Young Turks*, has yet to be superseded, tells the story from the perspective of the CUP, and accordingly offers only a passing mention of this event.

[24] A wonderfully vivid description of what it felt like to be engaged in politics and the press at this time can be found in Refik Halid (Karay)'s "Bu da bir keyiftir" (This, too, is a kind of pleasure). He described the adrenaline rush of feeling that one could be seized by police at any moment, whether out in public or in one's own home. In a sense, Cemal was correct to take this measure of deporting these intellectuals to keep them safe, since clearly they were not safe (from Cemal's own police force) in the capital.

[25] See, for instance, Refik Halid (Kaaray)'s "Şaka" (The Joke), a short story evocative of de Maupassant, about three (exiled) men in Sinop who fall into a tragic adventure after a night of drinking at a Greek tavern in the town.

2.3. Epilogue/Postscript: 1914–1923

By 1914 we can already start to see a fusing together of party (CUP), government, state, and homeland (*vatan*). Among the results of this process was that the CUP had appropriated and, as we will see subsequently, obstructed nearly the entirety of the discursive space of constitutionalism, nation, and homeland. Thus "patriotism" was becoming inextricable from (CUP) partisanship. Supporting the homeland in the war effort meant consent to the CUP and its policies, without an elaborate justification of why such an effort was worthwhile for the good of any—Ottoman or Turkish—nation.[26]

Erol Köroğlu demonstrates the results when partisanship was turned into patriotism in his *Ottoman Propaganda and Turkish Identity: Literature in Turkey during World War I*. Thanks to severe censorship and a virtual press blackout for much of the duration of the war—by 1918 there were only 14 newspapers being published in Istanbul—and no supply of paper that would make possible even illegal publications, any opposition, liberal or otherwise, was out of the question.[27] Several prominent liberals remained in exile within the empire or abroad, some as late as January 1918, making them powerless bystanders to the repression (hangings of the many deserters from the Ottoman army in Anatolia, as in the Arab provinces) and genocide going on around them. Intellectuals who did participate in the war effort were those closely aligned with the CUP. Those with looser connections or outright hostile relations to the party chose to oppose CUP policies by remaining silent, not by publishing their dissenting opinions, making it hard to pinpoint precisely how and when they differed from the party/patriotic line.[28]

The project to forge a homogeneous national culture also resumed as the world war drew to a close, when sociologist, writer, and ideologue of Turkish Ziya Gökalp re-established *Yeni Mecmua* (New Magazine) from before the war and tried to enlist a few writers of the opposition in addition to the standard CUP adherents.[29] But in the interim, unresolved splits within the elite made it impossible to consolidate an ideological basis for Ottoman, or Turkish, nationalism, which would have been a prerequisite for patriotism. By mid-1914 there was

---

[26] New critical scholarship of this period and such issues has proliferated in the past 5–10 years, exemplified by the work of Uğur Ümit Üngör, Fuat Dündar, Michael Reynolds, Mehmet Beşikçi, and Ryan Gingeras, not to mention Taner Akçam, Michael Mann, and Erol Köroğlu.

[27] In August 1914 a temporary press law was introduced that forbid the founding of any new papers or press agencies, banned newspapers from publishing any extra editions, and mandated that all newspapers would only be distributed after having been brought to the censorship room at the Istanbul Post Office. In addition, no telegrams were to be sent in any language other than Turkish, Arabic, or French. See Erol Köroğlu, *Ottoman Propaganda and Turkish Identity: Literature in Turkey during World War One* (London: I.B. Tauris, 2007), 13 n. 28.

[28] Köroğlu, *Ottoman Propaganda*, 78.

[29] Köroğlu, *Ottoman Propaganda*, xxiii.

little consensus even within the government about the patriotic justification for getting involved in what had been an intra-European war. The inference made at the time and since is that Ottoman/CUP involvement in the war on the side of Germany was nothing more than a last-ditch attempt to salvage the empire. Accordingly, it was difficult to create a discursive edifice for patriotism, let alone pluralism, or a cultural/historical justification for the many sacrifices imposed on Ottoman subjects in the course of the war.

Lacking, then, was a framework in which to produce patriotic propaganda, and more broadly a culture of nationalism with any room or justification for pluralism. Thus, it is not surprising to see a contemporary and intellectual like Ahmet Emin (Yalman), connected in varying degrees to the CUP, writing, "Educational war propaganda was extraordinarily neglected in Turkey. The main activity in this regard was negative. Everything was done to hinder the spreading of truth. The positive work coexisted [*sic*, consisted] in publishing the illustrated and popular *Harp Mecmuası* [War Review] and a series of books."[30]

By the final year of the war, censorship eased significantly, but liberal writers who were coming back out into the open were still cautious with their words. Topics that were deemed safe to discuss in print during the war often revolved around the morality of activities such as war profiteering and the phenomenon of the *harp zengini*, or "war rich" (black marketeers) in a time of severe scarcity and rationing; not, of course, the broader questions about the decision to enter the war or the policy decisions about how to conduct it.[31]

While such an intolerant climate for opposition may have been the norm for countries at war (then, as now), it is important to keep in mind in part because it determined much about the dynamic of politics as the empire emerged, devastated, from the war in late 1918. When the empire conceded total defeat in late 1918, it was also, by all accounts, the end of the CUP as a party and a movement. Liberals came back in full force—as full as was possible after the utter devastation and profound existential crisis that the war experience had brought about. As the Ottoman capital was occupied by the British, French, and American victors and the institutions of the sultanate and caliphate were effectively under British control, the meaning of Ottoman or Turkish nationalism was not immediately clear in anyone's mind. The idea of pluralism therein was embroiled in the state violence perpetrated against Armenian and other non-Muslim civilian populations in the course of the way, and in the question of culpability and reckoning.

Liberals, who as a whole had maintained a more conciliatory stance toward non-Muslims and therefore toward pluralism, were allowed back in the open as the remnants of the CUP retreated into the background—and into Anatolia to

---

[30] Köroğlu, *Ottoman Propaganda*, 5.
[31] Köroğlu, *Ottoman Propaganda*.

gather arms for the next round of armed conflict. The press again proliferated, as it had in July 1908, and open discussions of culpability and accountability for war crimes, which included massacres of Armenian civilian populations (the word "genocide" had not yet been coined), were featured in Ottoman as well as minority Armenian newspapers.[32] Military tribunals were convened at the behest of the British to bring CUP perpetrators of war crimes to justice, and the last Ottoman parliament, which met in late 1918, openly discussed measures to hold accountable the individuals and organizations that were deemed responsible for this violence.[33]

Liberals found themselves again in positions of power in the Ottoman government, often working closely with British military and occupation authorities. Some liberals even welcomed British, and more so American, involvement, expressing an interest in tutelage and/or an actual mandate administration to remake the Ottoman government into a parliamentary system that would retain the institution of the sultanate (akin to Britain's monarchy, one may presume). They, too, saw themselves as patriots, working to restore an Ottoman sultanate badly damaged by the illiberal CUP, which had unnecessarily thrown the empire headlong into a self-destructive war. And they saw the terms of defeat as necessary to accept, along with the responsibility for a war they themselves did not choose.

This—acceptance of the terms of defeat and the ensuing Treaty of Sèvres negotiated by prominent Ottoman liberals such as Riza Tevfik—would be among the many accusations against them in the case for treason. Leaders of the reconstituted CUP, now the Turkish national movement, had developed a different and conflicting notion of patriotism wherein the institution of the sultanate was considered compromised, and the Turkish "nation" had to be defended against annihilation. At the time the nationalists came to Istanbul and declared final victory over British, French, and Greek occupation forces in the autumn of 1922, the first and major liberal casualty would be Ali Kemal, a dyed-in-the-wool liberal and Anglophile who had worked with British occupation forces and openly against Mustafa Kemal's national movement, and had supported the terms of Sèvres. Ali Kemal was lynched after being seized from his home in Istanbul and while en route to be tried by nationalists (and former CUP members) in Ankara, the new national capital, in late 1922.

[32] I have not yet checked the Greek-language newspapers but would imagine there are similar discussions going on there. For the Armenian case, see Lerna Ekmekcioglu, "Improvising Turkishness: Being Armenian in Post-Ottoman Istanbul, 1918–1933," PhD dissertation, New York University, 2010.
[33] See Ayhan Aktar, "Debating Armenian Massacres in the Last Ottoman Parliament, November–December 1918," *History Workshop Journal* 64 (2007): 240–270.

By the time the Turkish nation-state was safely established, liberalism could be openly equated with treason, capping off a long story that had begun in 1908. The circle of liberal intellectuals that had long opposed CUP tactics and policies, and in the wake of the Ottoman defeat in World War I had formed the "Friends of England Society" in early 1919 (Ali Kemal, Halide Edip, Sait Molla, and Refik Halid, among them), in fact turned out to be *the* number one enemy of Mustafa Kemal after he had consolidated his power and finally offered an official history of the national movement in his 1927 speech, *Nutuk* (The Speech). The opening pages of the 700-plus-page speech focus entirely on the (liberal) Friends of England Society and their traitorous collaboration with the British, which compromised the nation and the sultanate, making necessary his own national movement. Liberals, and liberalism as a political tradition and a set of sensibilities, then, had gone from being a crucial constituent element in the Young Turk rise to power in 1908, to being synonymous with treason to the nation, and therefore fundamentally at odds with "patriotism"—they were literally labeled *vatan haini* (traitors to the nation) rather than its opposite, *vatanperest/vatansever* (patriots) by the time the Turkish republic was established in 1923. As for the liberals: those who did not recant and join forces with the nationalists ended up on the "List of 150 Undesirables," stripped of citizenship in the new Turkish nation-state and exiled beyond its borders until 1938, just before Atatürk's death.

Nationalism, then, in the last Ottoman decade, turned out to be synonymous with CUP-turned-Kemalist partisanship, a fact that had tremendous ramifications not just in how the crimes of World War I would be remembered and suppressed, but for the structures of power in the new Turkish republic. If liberals could not be Turkish nationalists, what could it mean for the horizons of possibility in republican Turkey when it came to questions of pluralism?

Acknowledgements

A version of this chapter, "Liberalism as Treason in the Ottoman Empire," was presented in St. Petersburg in June 2015 at a conference, "Cultures of Patriotism in World War One," organized by Laura Engelstein and Boris Kolonitskii and held at the American University in St. Petersburg. An earlier version of this paper has been published in Russian in Kristin Filliu. 2020. Liberalizm kak put' k gosudarstvennoi izmene v Osmanskoi imperii, 1908–1923 gg. in Kul'tury patriotizma v gody Pervoi mirovoi voiny: sbornik statei. Edited by Konstantin A. Tarasov, compiled and with a foreword by Boris I. Kolonitskii. 'Epokha voin i revoliutsii' series, vol. 13. St Petersburg: Izdatel'stvo Evropeiskogo universiteta v Sankt-Peterburge, 299–315. I draw from some of the same material that forms the basis of *Turkey: A past against History* (Berkeley, CA: University of California Press, 2021).

3

Fatal Love

Intimacy and Interest in Indian Political Thought

Faisal Devji

The history of religious but also economic and political differences between Hindus and Muslims in India is a lengthy one. Indeed, among scholars it has come to constitute one of the world's most important examples of communal conflict in modern times. Resulting as it apparently did in the violent partition of British India and the creation of Pakistan, the repercussions of this conflict continue to define the relations of Hindus and Muslims within and between these countries. Whether or not this history is seen as being either particularly religious or inevitably primordial, and however novel or contingent many of its instances might be, most accounts of Hindu-Muslim conflict tend to emphasize the growing distance between these admittedly shifting and changing communities. But my argument in this chapter shall do exactly the opposite, showing that this relationship was in fact marked by great intimacy, which made for the possibility both of harmony and violence.

To be more precise, I will describe how Indian politicians, in the period leading up to their country's independence and partition in 1947, were able to engage in a debate about the problem that intimacy and even love rather than distance posed for Hindu-Muslim relations. In doing so they managed to exit the colonial problematic of managing communal difference that, we shall see, defined, and continues to define, the political as much as scholarly accounts of religious conflict in India. Unlike these accounts, the new language was not purely instrumental or administrative in character, but dealt with the problem of disagreement and violence in normative terms as part of what we might call modern Indian political thought. While this novel language continues to exist in popular culture, however, it seems to have largely disappeared from political thought in the period after independence, with the old vocabulary of the colonial state reinstated in the analysis of religious conflict in all the successor states of the Raj.

Whether by scholars, journalists, politicians, or indeed participants in some riot, religious conflict in India tends to be seen in very similar ways. However simple or complex the explanation proffered, such conflict is understood as being made up of inherited prejudices and repackaged sentiments, both embedded

Faisal Devji, *Fatal Love* In: *Negotiating Democracy and Religious Pluralism.* Edited by: Karen Barkey, Sudipta Kaviraj, and Vatsal Naresh, Oxford University Press. © Oxford University Press 2021. DOI: 10.1093/oso/9780197530016.003.0004

within a changing structure of social or economic relations. True or false as these analyses may be, interesting is their ubiquitous character as a kind of common sense. This suggests that they are themselves stereotyped products of a given order. Whatever their differences, after all, these accounts rarely integrate religious conflict into any conceptual framework. At most it is attributed to everyday political instrumentality, with otherwise latent religious views being exploited for electoral or commercial purposes by unscrupulous officials, hand in hand with criminals and local youth organizations.[1]

Emerging in colonial times, such explanations are linked to what Bernard S. Cohn called an imperial sociology of knowledge, in which the social sciences as they came to be known were deployed to make sense of conflict, if only with a view to control it.[2] As actual or would-be instruments of the British and later Indian governments, these accounts were never meant to address religious conflict as anything other than a problem, and certainly not by considering it in conceptual or normative terms as part of a political order. Ironically, it was the older language of orientalist scholarship in the eighteenth and early nineteenth centuries, as well as that of religious debate and missionary activity during this period, that stood alone in taking these enmities seriously, rather than seeing them merely as examples of social dysfunction or the epiphenomena of economic struggles, to say nothing about the ambitions of strongmen.

While there have been a few excellent studies, mostly anthropological, that exit a colonial sociology of knowledge in exploring the local languages and internal logics of religious conflict in India,[3] what I am interested in is the making of a new political vocabulary to understand it. In particular, I shall be occupied with the way in which leading politicians from the Indian National Congress, the All-India Muslim League, the Hindu Mahasabha, and the Scheduled Castes Federation sought to remake the political language of their country. They did so by radicalizing a classically imperialist argument, that India was marked by its lack not of wealth or power so much as of ideas and principles, and it was this situation that made British rule possible as well as necessary. So the apparently ceaseless and inevitable animosity between Hindus and Muslims was said to require the presence of a foreign power to keep the peace between them.

Although there were many ideas and principles that Indians supposedly lacked, among them individualism or the ability to separate political from religious life, it is the alleged absence of interest as a political category (but strangely

---

[1] Of the many authors writing in this vein, Paul Brass (2003) is perhaps the most influential one today.

[2] See, for example, Cohn 1996.

[3] See, for instance, the work of Arjun Appadurai, such as *Fear of Small Numbers: An Essay on the Geography of Anger* (2006) and Veena Das, *Life and Words: Violence and the Descent into the Ordinary* (2006).

not an economic one) that I am concerned with. On the one hand Indians were taken to be so consumed by a generally pecuniary form of self-interest that they were willing to stoop to the most brutal violence in order to achieve it, even if this meant putting the greater good of the country and so their own future at risk. This narrative still characterizes much of the social science analysis of religious and other forms of conflict in India. But on the other hand Indians seemed willing to sacrifice their interests and even lives in superstitious or fanatical actions that were as much religious as political. And if some of these actions could be attributed to ignorance and poverty, the participation in them of prosperous and educated Indians always rendered such distinctions ambiguous, a puzzlement that characterizes Indian journalism then as now.

Naturally interests come in different sizes and shapes, including various gradations of individual and collective identity, each of which may contradict any of the others. So the problem supposedly posed by India's simultaneously excessive and recessive interests had to do not with their plurality so much as with their irrationality, which is to say their counterproductive character. Given their great internal differences, for example, how might Hindus and Muslims constitute political interests, unless it was negatively or due to mutual and hereditary antipathies? Why were economic, regional, or indeed truly national forms of collective life unable to compete with caste or religious ones? The answers to these and other similar questions also involved pointing to some absence, whether of education, administration, or independence, and thus doing little more than doubling the colonial narrative of lack as a category constitutive of India's political life.

Now the colonial state was not the only agency that promoted the idea that India's politics was constituted by absence. Indians themselves did the same, trying to address this lack either by seeking to fill it with more "rational" class or national interests, or by claiming that such an absence was a positive one and marked India's peculiar genius as opposed to that of Europe. Both of these approaches, of course, were apologetic ones, but they were also, as I have suggested, radicalized into a new kind of argument as part of a conversation between Indian politicians from different parties. We shall see that this conversation brought together as well as divided such figures quite differently from the way in which they are otherwise related in history. And if it turned an old imperial argument into a new Indian one, this was not least because the colonial state was no longer part of this conversation.

While the English word "interest" was used by all of the figures I deal with in this chapter, it is also important to note that the term has no exact equivalent in Indian languages. So the idea of self-interest, for instance, may be conveyed by the term *swarth*, more commonly selfishness, while that of advantage more generally might be called *fayda*, or benefit. It is then the English original that allows one to make sense of such redefined Indian terms, whose multiplicity indicates another kind of absence or inability, perhaps even the refusal to constitute a complete or one-to-one translation of interest in its theoretical and political sense into Indian vernaculars. That this is not due to ignorance of such an original is clear enough, and thus calls for an explanation of the difference in linguistic usage. Provisionally it might be possible to suggest that this difference indicates the ambiguity with which the word was and continues to be invested.

3.1. Making Interests out of Religion

Bhimrao Ramji Ambedkar, India's foremost Dalit, or "Untouchable," leader, was interested in conflict between Hindus and Muslims for at least two reasons. One had to do with the fact that he was a severe critic of Hinduism and sought to draw his people out of its embrace, eventually converting to Buddhism for this purpose. But Ambedkar was also resentful that Muslims, or rather the Muslim League, had practically colonized all forms of opposition to both Hinduism and the Congress, leaving him to follow its much more powerful lead as an occasional and subordinate ally of the party. He tried positioning himself between the Congress and League, or the Hindus and Muslims, as a third party much as the British did, so as to render a supposedly neutral judgment on their quarrel in good liberal as much as colonial terms. One example of this is a passage from Ambedkar's letter on 14 May 1946 to A. V. Alexander, one of the members of the cabinet mission that had arrived from England to consult Indian leaders on the constitutional future of their country:

> To my mind, it is only right to say that the Hindus and the Muslims are today mentally incompetent to decide upon the destiny of this country. Both Hindus and Muslims are just crowds. It must be within your experience that a crowd is less moved by material profit than by a passion collectively shared. It is easier to persuade a mass of men to sacrifice itself collectively than to act upon a cool assessment of advantages. A crowd easily loses all sense of profit and loss. It is moved by motives which may be high or low, genial or barbarous, compassionate or cruel, but is always above or below reason. The common sense of each is lost in the emotion of all. It is easier to persuade a crowd to commit suicide than to accept a legacy. (Ambedkar 1991: 492–3)

Even a cursory look at Ambedkar's letter should make it clear that he quickly turned a colonial position and terminology to quite different purposes. To begin with, he followed good liberal precedent in attributing interests to property or at least a sense of ownership, even if only of oneself, as John Locke might have said. The problem with Hindus and Muslims, in other words, was not that they were religions, as opposed to, say, classes, but that these communities were not defined by property and ownership, and so could not deal with each other contractually. While the rival claims of the Congress, League, and Mahasabha seemed to bely his argument, since their leaders made claims to very specific rights and powers, whether territorial, electoral, or administrative, Ambedkar had another point to make. This had to do with what he saw as the highly risky brinksmanship of religious conflict in India, as well as its sacrificial character, particularly evident in Gandhi's political opinions as much as practices.

Ambedkar thought it was the caste system, more than religious conflict, that made interests impossible in India. For by refusing to allow Dalits to own property, bear arms, or be educated, high-caste Hindus also disallowed the generalization of ownership and so interest as a social category. Property couldn't therefore constitute the basis of Indian politics. And what this resulted in was interest as a particular rather than universal form, which meant that instead of rationalizing Indian society and so sustaining it, interest as a purely upper-caste category ended up destroying it. So in his 1945 book, *What Congress and Gandhi Have Done to the Untouchables*, Ambedkar describes the "anti-social" character of high-caste Hindus in the following way:

> The isolation and exclusiveness following upon the class structure creates in the privileged classes the anti-social spirit of a gang. It feels it has interests "of its own" which it makes its prevailing purpose to protect against everybody even against the interests of the State. (Ambedkar 1991: 285)

Just as caste Hindus comprised a "gang," then, for Ambedkar Hindus and Muslims were "crowds" rather than interests. This was because whatever the claims their leaders made, they were not defined by property and ownership, described as "material profit" and a "legacy," that of a single country bequeathed by the British, which would have forced them to deal with each other by a "cool assessment of advantages." Instead they were willing to destroy the country itself as well as large numbers of their own community in collective acts of "sacrifice" and "passion" that were only made possible because they were not tied to the conservative, or perhaps more appropriately, conservationist, logic of property and ownership. Indeed, Ambedkar was acute enough to note that such a sacrificial politics, by which he no doubt meant Gandhi's nonviolent mobilizations, could result in "compassionate" as much as "cruel" actions, since both nonviolence "above reason" and violence "below reason" were products of the same unanchored passions, which not coincidentally also characterized the Mahatma's followers.

In making this argument, Ambedkar was not only putting himself in the traditionally British position of a third party, adjudicating between the rival claims of Hindus and Muslims, he was also making a claim of his own. For in the revised edition of his book on Pakistan, published in 1946, Ambedkar recommended the partition of India, if only to make Hindus and Muslims into interests by attaching these communities each to its own national state. We shall see that Muhammad Ali Jinnah, the Muslim League's president, held much the same view. But Ambedkar also sought to place his own Dalits in the position vacated by the Muslims, as India's leading minority with its own rights and politics. And if he was temporarily forced to take on the role of the colonial state or the Muslim League, it was because the Dalits, too, were not constituted as an interest but, far more than Muslims, who at least possessed regional majorities, were scattered across the country and divided by language, ethnicity, class, and sect. And unlike Muslims, they had no elite defined by land, capital, or education.

After independence, then, Ambedkar in his new position as leader of India's Constituent Assembly as well as law minister, worked hard to make Dalits into a political interest by replacing the old system of separate electorates and reserved places in the civil and other services that had been put into place primarily for Muslims, with caste-based reservations instead. Though he had wanted separate electorates as well, these Ambedkar did not succeed in achieving, but instead created a kind of property for Dalits by constitutional fiat. Not satisfied with this purely legal and administrative act, however, Ambedkar also sought to endow Dalits with a sense of self-ownership by having them abandon Hinduism, describing their conversion in terms of obtaining property. In fact, his settling on Buddhism as the religion of choice was due not simply to its historical enmity with Hinduism, for example on the matter of caste, but perhaps also because as a practically dead faith in much of the country, it could be fully owned by Dalit converts who would only have become clients of the more numerous Christians and Muslims.

If I have described Ambedkar's views on religious conflict in India, it is not because they were particularly original. Indeed, he used the same terms and conceptions as other Indian politicians, which was what made a conversation between them possible. What his ideas demonstrate, rather, is how generalized this argument was, moving well beyond the ethnographic or historical particularity of Hindu-Muslim relations, to pose interest as a problem at the conceptual level. For Ambedkar refused to see it as natural or given in any sense, and, as we have seen, sought to create interests where they didn't exist. Moreover, his argument was self-illustrative, insofar as Ambedkar was himself forced to occupy the roles of others, as long as he could not represent Dalits as an interest. For without interests, and the contractual agreements that were meant to characterize their relations, conflict not only remained unregulated, but came to be defined by an intimate logic of mutual substitution.

The intimacy between religious rivals, then, seemed to result from their inability to constitute interests. Quite apart from attempts to imitate or take each other's place, this intimacy was brought to light in an explicitly erotic way by the Hindu nationalist leader Vinayak Damodar Savarkar. In his 1923 tract *Essentials of Hindutva*, Savarkar was chiefly concerned with defining Hindus as a political rather than religious community. While he valued the religious beliefs and observances of Hindus as constituting their historical and existential sense of nationality, Savarkar also saw them as being so diverse and fragmented as to render their political unity impossible. So he began the text with a disquisition on the name "Hindu," which in the view of historians was an insulting one given by the Persians to Indians, who had no collective designation for themselves:

> We hope that the fair Maid of Verona who made the impassioned appeal to her lover to change a name that was "nor hand, nor foot, nor arm, nor face, nor any other part belonging to a man" would forgive us for this our idolatrous attachment to it when we make bold to assert that "Hindus we are and love to remain so!" (Savarkar 1969: 1)

Savarkar's reference, of course, was to Shakespeare's *Romeo and Juliet*, a play about two lovers doomed because of their feuding families. In particular, he compared the apparently foreign name "Hindu" with that of Romeo, which Juliet wished so fervently was one that belonged to another. Not only did their Muslim enemies in some sense give Hindus their identity in this historical narrative, but Savarkar also appeared to compare the two communities to Shakespeare's lovers. Indeed, he went on to expand upon the comparison:

> Would the fair Apostle of the creed that so movingly questioned "What's in a name?" have liked it herself to nickname the God of her idolatry as "Paris" instead of "Romeo"? Or would *he* have been ready to swear by the moon that "tipped with silver all the fruit tree-tops," that it would serve as sweet and musical to his heart to call his "Juliet" by "any other name" such as for example— "Rosalind"? (Savarkar 1969: 2)

The problem with religious conflict in India, therefore, was not that the two communities were strangers to one another, but instead that they were so intimate as to be described as lovers doomed by an inherited enmity. So by the middle of his text, Savarkar switched from *Romeo and Juliet* to another one of Shakespeare's plays, *Coriolanus*, the tale of a Roman general who, when dishonored by the Senate, turned for assistance in betraying it to his old enemy Aufidius. The

following passage, for example, on how Muslim terms and practices had infiltrated Hindu devotions so deeply as to have become part of their identity, seems to be a reference to that part of the play where Aufidius recognizes his great enemy Coriolanus by the scars he has inflicted upon the latter:

> The words darbar, Diwan-Bahadur, have crept like thieves to the very heart of our Harimandirs. They are the scars of our old wounds. The wounds are healed but the scars persist and seem to be incorporated with our form. As long as any attempts to scratch them out threaten to harm us more than profit, all that we can do is to tolerate them; for after all they are the scars of the wounds received in a conflict that we have won in a gory field in which we remained as the victors of the day. (Savarkar 1969: 78)

While Savarkar didn't elaborate on the idea of interest in the way that Ambedkar and some of the other figures we shall be looking at did, he was the only one to invoke an almost erotic intimacy between Hindus and Muslims, derived, we might argue, from their inability to constitute separate and independent interests. An instance of this in Savarkar's text comes when he describes the numerically insignificant but economically important Gujarati Muslim trading castes of the Khojas, Bohras, and Memons. Favorably noting their "pure Hindu blood" and retention of many Hindu customs and beliefs, Savarkar is nevertheless distressed by this very intimacy. For if such communities were to be acknowledged as Hindus, then the category possessed neither integrity nor politics. Yet any stringent definition risked excluding the very groups that Savarkar did want to include as Hindu, given their great and even contradictory diversity:

> He is, so far as the three essentials of nation (Rashtra), race (Jati) and civilization (Sanskriti) are concerned, a Hindu. He may differ as regards a few festivals or may add a few more heroes to the pantheon of his supermen or demigods. But we have repeatedly said that difference in details here or emphasis there, does not throw us outside the pale of Hindu Sanskriti. The sub-communities amongst the Hindus observe many a custom, not only contradictory but even conflicting with the customs of other Hindu communities. Yet both of them are Hindus. So also in the above cases of patriotic Bohra or Christian or Khoja, who could satisfy the required qualifications of Hindutva to such a degree as that, why should he not be recognized as a Hindu? (Savarkar 1969: 101–2)

While hoping for the reconversion of the Memons, Khojas, and Bohras, then, Savarkar regretfully excludes them from *Hindutva*, or Hindu-ness, by reluctantly turning to religious forms of identification—of the kind he had initially wanted to exclude, because of their sheer diversity—from his strongly territorial, genealogical, and cultural definition of Indian nationality. Only those communities could therefore be described as Hindu that took India both as their fatherland and holy land, which in Savarkar's opinion automatically excluded even the most sympathetic Christians and Muslims. The shift of his argument, in which a couple of minor Muslim heresies compel Savarkar to reclaim the Hindu religion, is clearly a theatrical one, demonstrating the difficulty of demarcating clear interests in India's religious geography, and emphasizing yet again the enormous problem that closeness rather than distance played in the simultaneously intimate and inimical relations between Hindus and Muslims.

The problem posed by the Khojas, Bohras, and Memons on a small scale, and in the present, was for Savarkar mirrored in the past on an incomparably larger canvas by Buddhism. For here, too, was an instance of a phenomenon, purely Indian in origin, that by universalizing itself adopted other homelands. Quite apart from the historical struggle between Buddhism and Hinduism, then, which concerned Savarkar very little, the problem posed by the former had to do with its advocacy of nonviolence on the one hand, which he thought had rendered India effeminate, and its opening to the outside world on the other. After all, it was through Buddhist Central Asia that Muslim invaders came to turn the tide of India's spiritual expansion backward and conquer her in the process.

But given the fact that ancient India's greatest empires had been Buddhist rather than Hindu ones, Savarkar couldn't entirely dismiss it as being either a foreign religion or one fit only for weaklings. He thus had to use curious turns of phrase, stating, "We feel it incumbent to render an apology to ourselves. We have while writing this section wounded our own feelings" (Savarkar 1969: 35). Surely this splitting of the Hindu self, and the hurtful criticism of one of its parts, for which apology must then be made, offers another example of the fundamentally theoretical rather than merely anti-Muslim or Christian problem that intimacy played in Savarkar's thought. But perhaps his most intimate enemy was the most important Hindu figure of his day, Gandhi, who was also associated with the doctrine of nonviolence. Savarkar never mentioned the Mahatma in *Hindutva*, though his criticism of nonviolence in the name of a Buddhism that was practically dead in India, may be seen as a veiled reference to Gandhi's vast mobilizations of Hindus and Hinduism, which cut too close to the bone of Savarkar's enterprise.

It is no small irony that Muhammad Ali Jinnah, the man who became India's most important Muslim leader, was not only himself a Khoja and as irreligious a man as Savarkar could have wished for, but had also once entertained the ambition of becoming a Shakespearian actor and playing the role of Romeo. Indeed, there were occasions when both men, along with Ambedkar, stood together as allies against their mutual enemy Gandhi. Given his family background as well as his early political life in Congress, Jinnah could hardly be said to possess any

inherited prejudices or indeed emotional sensibility as a Muslim, and so like
Ambedkar if not Savarkar, his dealings with religion were highly rationalized
and took the explicit form of political principles.

Having apparently despaired of setting apart India's religious prejudices
from the work of politics, for which he blamed Gandhi's encouragement of religious and especially Islamic pieties in public life, Jinnah decided to turn these
sentiments into interests. So in his presidential address to the Lahore session of
the All-India Muslim League in 1940, Jinnah offered a portrait of Hindu-Muslim
relations that Savarkar might have found agreeable:

> The Hindus and Muslims belong to two different religious philosophies, so-
> cial customs, literatures. They neither intermarry nor interdine together and,
> indeed, they belong to two different civilizations which are based mainly on
> conflicting ideas and conceptions. Their aspects on life and of life are different.
> It is quite clear that Hindus and Musalmans derive their inspiration from dif-
> ferent sources of history. They have different epics, different heroes, and dif-
> ferent episodes. Very often the hero of one is a foe of the other and, likewise,
> their victories and defeats overlap. (Ahmad 1942: 15)

But like Savarkar's narrative of Hindu-Muslim opposition, Jinnah's, too, was
marked by the anxiety of intimacy. For he suggested that their mutual violence
was due to the intertwined character of these communities, whose heroes and
villains as much as defeats and victories tended to "overlap." What was required,
then, was a kind of separation or divorce, one that Jinnah sometimes compared
to the work he did as a lawyer, in reconciling two brothers quarrelling over a pa-
ternal inheritance by partitioning it between them. This would make brothers
into friends, substituting the irrational intimacies of a hereditary bond with
the reasonable instrumentality of a friendship freely chosen. And to transform
brothers into friends meant forsaking passion and prejudice to create what
Jinnah repeatedly called a social contract between Hindus and Muslims.

The problem, in his view, was that Congress and its upper-caste Hindu leadership didn't want a social contract. Like Ambedkar, Jinnah thought this refusal
had to do with the hierarchies of the caste system, which thus had to be broken
not by persuasion but by power. Taking advantage of the limited if gradually
increasing electoral opportunities that the colonial state was making available
to Indians, Jinnah sought to achieve this power by way of popular mobilization, and he did so primarily to insist upon the fact that Hindus, with their caste
divisions, were not a majority, and Muslims, with their large numbers and regional concentrations, were not a minority, as Congress leaders insisted on assuming. Asking them to give up such European delusions and recognize India's
distinctive reality, Jinnah argued that no nation existed in the country.

Now Muslim politicians had long sought to cut down Hindu numbers, and claims to constitute a democratic majority in India, primarily by campaigning to exclude lower castes from them. In doing so they rejected the category of the minority as well, and tried to imagine a pluralistic polity antagonistic to the very idea of a nation-state. What Jinnah did was to reclaim the nation from these generally imperial or internationalist visions of India's future, by making the case that Hindus and Muslims represented two nationalities, rather than a majority and a minority respectively, and thus had to be treated as equals. Yet pressing for "parity" did not necessarily mean conceiving of the nation in conventional terms as any kind of fulsome identity, since for Jinnah Muslim nationhood in particular seems to have been rather empty, more a legal, contractual category than an ontologically weighty one.

In addition to dispensing with the unequal categories of majority and minority, identifying as a nation was simply one way to achieve parity in negotiation and form a social contract with Hindus. And the purpose of this was to make brothers into friends and so religious communities into political interests. But even these remained negative and legalistic ones, for Jinnah thought that in a democracy real interests could never be permanent or communal ones, but had to be open and changeable so that in elections a minority always had the opportunity of becoming a majority and vice versa. This notion was nothing but good liberal orthodoxy, which Jinnah managed to imagine anew. The problem with India, then, was that as long as there existed an apparently permanent communal majority and minority in the country, no democracy was possible but only the brute domination of one over the other.

Eventually Jinnah came to think that only India's partition could destroy these false or religious majorities and minorities, if only by constituting Hindus and Muslims as, respectively, a demographic majority and minority in India, with their status in Pakistan being of course reversed. This would then allow religious identity to become part of private life and sink into the background, so that true interests might emerge to form variable and clearly political majorities and minorities in both countries. This is why Jinnah found it so easy to describe the Muslims who remained in India as a "sub-national minority" after its partition, because Pakistan had overnight deprived them of their empty or negative character as a nation and finally made them into a minority. And so his celebrated address to Pakistan's Constituent Assembly in Karachi on 11 August 1947 was not paradoxical at all, as some historians have held, but entirely in keeping with Jinnah's views:

Today, you might say with justice that Roman Catholics and Protestants do not exist; what exists now is that every man is a citizen, and equal citizen of Great Britain and they are all members of the Nation. Now, I think we should keep that in front of us as our ideal and you will find that in course of time Hindus would cease to be Hindus and Muslims would cease to be Muslims, not in the religious sense because that is the personal faith of each individual, but in the political sense as citizens of the State. (Burke 2000: 28–9)

Taking liberal and democratic theory to their political limits, Jinnah's apparent and self-proclaimed realism can also be seen, as Gandhi did, to be the most ideal-istic form that politics took in India. For even more ambitiously than Ambedkar or Savarkar, Jinnah sought to retrieve interests from religion, or to create them where they didn't seem to exist.

3.2. A Disinterested Politics

While Gandhi started with the same premise as the Indian politicians we have looked at so far, all of whom thought that interests didn't exist in India, or at least didn't define social relations there, he typically reversed its polit-ical meaning. For instead of attributing India's colonization to such a lack of national or even religious interest, the Mahatma argued that it was Indian self-interest that had in fact enabled British rule. So in a chapter of his 1909 tract *Hind Swaraj*, or *Indian Home Rule*, called "Why Was India Lost?," Gandhi blamed colonialism not on the force of arms but rather the mutual interests of British and Indian in commerce:

> Some Englishmen state that they took, and they hold, India by the sword. Both these statements are wrong. The sword is entirely useless for holding India. . . . Then it follows that we keep the English in India for our base self-interest. We like their commerce, they please us by their subtle methods, and get what they want from us. (Gandhi 2003: 41)

For Gandhi, then, interest was primarily an economic rather than political cate-gory, and it therefore resulted in not resistance so much as an all-too-easy acqui-escence to the lure of wealth and comfort. And this meant that if colonialism was to be defeated, interest had to be rejected for sacrifice and duty as their own re-ward. This was one aspect of his famous doctrine, taken from the Bhagavadgita, of desire-less action or forsaking ends for means. In any case Gandhi imagined that since property was not the basis of Indian society, it was neither possible nor desirable to found Indian social relations on interest, and in fact argued that it was only the establishment of the colonial state as a neutral or third party be-tween Indians that made some kind of interest possible, though in a very lim-ited sense.

In other words, Indians were compelled to adopt the character of interest groups whenever they dealt with the colonial state, which, by constituting itself as a mediator between parties, sought to engineer and guarantee contractual relations among them. When speaking about the relations of Hindus and Muslims in particular, Gandhi often described this form of mediation, and its creation of contractual relations through the sole agency of the state, as a system of "divide and rule." By this he didn't necessarily mean that the British were deliberately fooling their naive Indian subjects into quarreling with one another, but rather that the very structure of interest and contract was divisive by definition, because it set the state up as mediator and guarantor for interests that were not at all natural but decided by its workings.

In *Hind Swaraj* it was doctors and lawyers who exemplified the workings of the colonial state, and not only because their authority was accredited by this state. Doctors mediated between the patient and his own body, robbing him of any control over it by sedulously inducing a dependence on medication instead. In this way the *swaraj*, or self-rule, of the individual was destroyed even at the most intimate, corporeal level, and he became a mere cog in the system of imperialism, with its medical and pharmaceutical establishment itself supported by British capital and the greed for profits. As for lawyers, they separated both individuals and groups from each other by interposing the law as a mediator between Indians in such a way as to deprive them of any direct dealings with one another that might result in a friendly or at least mutually agreeable resolution of their disagreement. By delivering justice as a third party, the law instead made amicable resolution impossible, and indeed relied upon forced settlements that could only prolong and embitter the rivalry between individuals as much as communities.

Had the state managed to universalize interest and make of it the basis of all social relations, however, it might have served to pacify India if only in a thoroughly unjust and exploitative way. But the problem was that interest did not define most of the ways in which Indians dealt with each other, for the colonial state's reach was not total and it could therefore only make interests of those who came before its institutions, the courts of law in particular. It was therefore the contradiction between the interests of colonial society on the one hand, and the religious and other ways in which Indians dealt with each other on the other, that made for conflict and violence. And if the reach of the state was limited, it was because interest and contract were ideas that required private property to constitute the basis of society, for it was this over which individuals and groups fought to define themselves as interests.

Like Ambedkar in some way, Gandhi thought that property could not constitute the basis of Indian society, and that interests could not therefore define its manifold relations. This was because most Indians had no property of any kind, something the Mahatma saw as both a curse and a blessing in disguise. After all the fact that property and so interests could not dominate Indian social relations meant that these latter, however oppressive they might otherwise be, could serve eventually to roll back and displace any political or economic order founded on property and its necessary inequalities. As was his wont, the Mahatma made the weakest and most vulnerable sections of Indian society into the vanguard of this nonviolent revolution, a problematic instance of which can be seen in his correspondence with a female disciple, Raihana Tyabji, who had written him about the importance of securing women equal rights of inheritance:

> Why should women have either to beg or to fight in order to win back their birthright? It is strange—and also tragically comic—to hear man born of woman talk loftily of "the weaker sex" and nobly promising "to give" us our due! What is this nonsense about "giving"? Where is the "nobility" and "chivalry" in restoring to people that which has been unlawfully wrested from them by those having brute power in their hands? (As cited in Gandhi 1929: 4)

Publishing her letter in the journal *Young India* on 17 October 1929, Gandhi responded to it by arguing that while he would never countenance unequal treatment of men and women under the law, Tyabji's desire was nevertheless one that sought to expand the role of property in defining Indian social relations. Given the country's poverty, however, the inclusion of women among property-owners could only be accomplished by further entrenching class differences in India:

> But I am uncompromising in the matter of woman's rights. In my opinion she should labour under no legal disability not suffered by man. . . . But to remove legal inequalities will be a mere palliative. The root of the evil lies much deeper than most people realize. . . . Man has always desired power. Ownership of property gives this power. Man hankers also after posthumous fame based on power. This cannot be had, if property is progressively cut up in pieces as it must be if all the posterity become equal co-sharers. Hence the descent of property for the most part on the eldest male issue. Most women are married. And they are co-sharers, in spite of the law being against them, in their husbands' power and privileges. . . . Whilst therefore I would always advocate the repeal of all legal disqualifications, I should have the enlightened women of India to deal with the root cause. Woman is the embodiment of sacrifice and suffering, and her advent to public life should therefore result in purifying it, in restraining unbridled ambition and accumulation of property. Let them know that millions of men have no property to transmit to posterity. Let us learn from them that it is better for the few to have no ancestral property at all. (Gandhi 1929: 4)

Gandhi's recommendation, that women emphasize their received and undoubtedly patriarchal role as embodiments of sacrifice to undo the dominance of property in social relations, was perhaps rather impractical, though of the same
nature as the communist vision of the proletariat or the half-developed colonial
world as, respectively, the vanguard and weakest link in the chain of capitalism.
He gave the same advice to Dalits as well, as recounted angrily by Ambedkar
(1990: 291). If all this tells us anything, it is that the Mahatma's criticism of interest and its basis in property was a properly theoretical one, and not just
directed at women or Dalits for entirely prejudicial reasons. So when he came
to speak about religious conflict, Gandhi could draw upon a general theory in
normative political terms. His ambition was to draw out and develop the disinterest or idealism embedded even in the most hierarchical and oppressive social
relations to refashion them in a radical if not revolutionary direction. His great
experiment to do so was made during the Khilafat Movement in the immediate
aftermath of the First World War, when Indian Muslims began to protest British
and French moves to dismember the defeated Ottoman Empire.

Having contributed the bulk of India's troops to the war, especially in the
Middle East, and having been promised by the British prime minister that
Muslim shrines and sanctities would not be interfered with, many Indian
Muslims sought to have their sentiments respected as loyal subjects of the
Empire. And it was to Gandhi that they turned for leadership in a movement
that went on to become the first mass mobilization in Indian history. Apart from
seeing the justice of their claims and counseling a nonviolent approach to the
colonial state, the Mahatma was fascinated by the Khilafat Movement precisely
because it was so difficult to construe it as an interest of any kind. Dedicated to
the preservation of a foreign power, in whose support India's Muslims expended
great efforts and sent large amounts of money, the movement seemed to be a
truly religious and therefore idealistic or disinterested one.

Because it was idealistic, or even fanatical and irrational, and not launched
for an ulterior and therefore interested motive, as the British but also Hindu
nationalists imagined, Gandhi thought Khilafat could transform Indian politics
more generally. Now there were many Hindus and Muslims, too, who sought to
found the movement on a contract and so interest, whereby the former's support would be predicated upon the latter's abandonment of cow-slaughter. But
Gandhi steadfastly rejected such calls, and wanted to base Hindu-Muslim unity
upon the relations of love and sacrifice that he thought marked friendship or
brotherhood as potentially if not always actually disinterested relations. This,
rather than interest and contract, would secure India's unity and freedom:

> The test of friendship is assistance in adversity, and that too, unconditional as-
> sistance. Co-operation that needs consideration is a commercial contract and

not friendship. Conditional co-operation is like adulterated cement which does not bind. It is the duty of the Hindus, if they see the justice of the Mahomedan cause, to render co-operation. If the Mahomedans feel themselves bound in honour to spare the Hindus' feelings and to stop cow-killing, they may do so, no matter whether the Hindus co-operate with them or no. Though, therefore, I yield to no Hindu in my worship of the cow, I do not want to make the stopping of cow-killing a condition precedent to co-operation. Unconditional co-operation means the protection of the cow. (Gandhi 1919: 4)

Like Gandhi, Muhammad Iqbal, the preeminent Muslim poet and thinker of the twentieth century, didn't think a society based on interest was either possible or desirable in India. Thus in his presidential address of 1932 to the All-India Muslim Conference, Iqbal argued that the kind of democracy promoted by Indian nationalists was premised upon what he called the "money-economy of modern democracy." Such a democratic order, in other words, rested upon the assumption that citizens were constituted of individual and self-owning voters for whom interests, too, were understood as properties to be defended. But this form of polity, Iqbal thought, was absolutely foreign to India's peasant majority:

The present struggle in India is sometimes described as India's revolt against the West. I do not think it is a revolt against the West; for the people of India are demanding the very institutions which the West stands for. Whether the gamble of elections, retinues of party leaders and hollow pageants of parliaments will suit a country of peasants for whom the money-economy of modern democracy is absolutely incomprehensible, is a different question altogether. Educated urban India demands democracy. The minorities, feeling themselves as distinct cultural units and fearing that their very existence is at stake, demand safeguards, which the majority community, for obvious reasons, refuses to concede. The majority community pretends to believe in a nationalism theoretically correct, if we start from Western premises, belied by facts, if we look to India. Thus the real parties to the present struggle in India are not England and India, but the majority community and the minorities of India which can ill-afford to accept the principle of Western democracy until it is properly modified to suit the actual conditions of life in India. (As cited in Vahid 1992: 211)

As with Ambedkar and Jinnah, then, Iqbal thought that Congress nationalism, with its focus on electorally defined interests, had either naively or deliberately misread the nature of Indian society by describing it in supposedly universal but in fact specifically European terms. And the repercussions of this misunderstanding, he imagined, were likely to be disastrous. But Iqbal parted ways with this company to join Gandhi in advocating not the creation of interests where they didn't exist, but instead limiting them. For he thought that India's various groups and communities were defined not by property so much as ideals or principles, upon which structures of power, too, were built. However violent such ideals might occasionally be, Iqbal recognized them as extraordinary in their potential to make history out of spirit and principle, which is to say by the transcendental however defined.

While he thought that property had not yet come to define Indian social relations, then, Iqbal saw in nationalism private property writ large as communal ownership, and understood the nation-state as constituting its epitome as much as guarantor. By excluding the transcendent or ideal element of India's existing social relations, and confining them in good liberal fashion to private life, the form of citizenship characteristic of nationalism ended up making public life entirely materialistic and violent in its instrumentality. The nation-state, in other words, professed to include and tolerate religious and other communities based on ideals, but in fact served to destroy or at least hollow them out. And communism, which Iqbal saw as Islam's only rival as a global alternative to the existential violence of capitalism, he thought simply magnified the role of property in public life by giving it into the possession of the state. In a Marxist state, then, citizens were even more enslaved to property than in a capitalist one.

Iqbal's task, then, was to retrieve the ideal or spiritual element in India's social relations. But instead of doing so in Gandhi's way, by magnifying everyday forms of disinterest or sacrifice into world-historical events, Iqbal remained true to his profession as a poet and philosopher by choosing a more intellectual path. In addition to protecting the apparently irrational aspects of inherited religious practice so as to forestall the domination of property and interest, as we have seen the Mahatma did by his encouragement of caste and gender-defined propertylessness, Iqbal strove to elaborate poetically upon the unpropertied social relations that he thought defined India. These he described as representing "invisible points of contact" between Hindus and Muslims in particular. Such relations were invisible not simply because they were increasingly hidden in the shadow of interests, but also due to the fact that visibility immediately rendered these communities into forms of ownership in which Muslims had to protect mosques from Hindu music while the latter protected cows from Muslim slaughter:

> In view of the visible and invisible points of contact between the various communities of India I do believe in the possibility of constructing a harmonious whole whose unity cannot be disturbed by the rich diversity which it must carry within its bosom. The problem of ancient Indian thought was how the one became many without sacrificing its oneness. To-day this problem has come down from its ethical heights to the grosser plane of our political life,

and we have to solve it in its reversed form, i.e., how the many can become one without sacrificing its plural character. (As cited in Vahid 1992: 197)

Plurality was important for Iqbal not simply because he was concerned with the fate of minorities in India, but because ideals were necessarily and substantively different. In other words this was quite unlike a world defined by property, ownership, and interest, which reduced multiplicity to a merely symbolic status in which, from the point of view of the nation-state as a third party, each difference had the same weight as and was substitutable with another. It was only by seeing Hindus and Muslims, or upper and lower castes, as mutually substitutable pairs, after all, however distinctive and unequal they might otherwise be, that they could become competitors as interest groups. Every piece of property, too, however distinctive, was comparable and so substitutable with any other, for they were equalized by being valued in monetary terms through contracts guaranteed by the state as itself a reified form of property. And it was this false intimacy of competition and substitution that Iqbal rejected by focusing on the real and unconvertible differences of all that was ideal, spiritual, or principled.

Precisely because Muslims in India were a diverse and scattered minority, thought Iqbal, they were defined by ideals more than their coreligionists anywhere else in the world. As he put it in an address to the Muslim League in 1930:

It cannot be denied that Islam, regarded as an ethical ideal plus a certain kind of polity—by which expression I mean a social structure regulated by a legal system and animated by a specific ethical ideal—has been the chief formative factor in the life history of the Muslims of India. It has furnished those basic emotions and loyalties which gradually unify scattered individuals and groups and finally transform them into a well-defined people. Indeed it is no exaggeration to say that India is perhaps the only country in the world where Islam as a society is almost entirely due to the working of Islam as a culture inspired by a specific ethical ideal. (As cited in Vahid 1992: 162)

And it was this spiritual sense of community that made Islam so vulnerable to nationalism as much as what he called religious adventurism in a 1934 article on the Ahmadi sect:

Islam repudiates the race idea altogether and founds itself on the religious idea alone. Since Islam bases itself on the religious idea alone, a basis which is wholly spiritual and consequently far more ethereal than blood relationship, Muslim society is naturally much more sensitive to forces which it considers harmful to its integrity. (As cited in Vahid 1992: 248–9)

By deferring and delaying the advent of the nation-state, in recommending, for instance, India's internal redistribution into Hindu- and Muslim-dominated provinces, Iqbal tried to preserve not just the ideal foundation of Islam, but also the invisible points of contact that made up Indian social relations as a whole. And while his political solutions were of a rather negative kind, Iqbal also rehearsed these invisible relations in his poetry and philosophy, where Hindus and Muslims came to stand for metaphysical rather than sociological categories, being removed from the instrumentality of politics and so rendered unfit to become equivalents of one another.

3.3. Conclusion

I have tried to show in this chapter that a new political language or way of thinking emerged during the two or three decades leading up to India's independence in 1947. While it started out by making use of colonial themes and categories, this form of thought quickly radicalized them into something quite novel. So the received notion that Indian society was constituted by a series of lacks or absences, for example, and therefore subject to colonization, was taken up if only to be turned into an idea beyond European recognition. Thus the interests that Indians were supposed to possess either in excess or insufficiently came to provide political thinkers there with ways of reimagining their country. On the one hand figures like Ambedkar, Savarkar, and Jinnah sought to create interests where there were none; and on the other Gandhi and Iqbal tried to further limit if not roll them back, attributing India's religious and caste conflict precisely to the increasing dominance of property and so interests in public life.

Important about this debate was the fact that it managed to exit the largely instrumental and administrative categories of a colonial sociology of knowledge, locating as it did religious relations within the normative arena of what I am calling political thought. And by taking leave of a narrative in which such relations could only figure as problems to be resolved, this conversation between Indian political leaders was able to identify proximity rather than distance, love of some kind rather than hatred, as the sources for religious amity as well as enmity among Hindus and Muslims. The fundamental ambiguity implied by this idea made it impossible to adopt a wholly instrumental explanation of social relations in India. It is almost as if these men had all realized in one way or another that the sense of betrayal informing so much of the language of violence between Hindus and Muslims had its origins in their intimacy. For a stranger, to say nothing of an enemy, could never betray one, something only a friend or, even better, a brother was capable of doing.

If Hindus and Muslims, then, had to be considered intimates of some sort, and their relations therefore marked by ambiguity, they were nevertheless unable to form a couple—except in the minds of those who paradoxically strove to tear them apart. Most strongly evident in the work of Savarkar, this erotic challenge depended, for him as for the others, upon the effort to firmly separate caste from community. Only by excluding caste, whose relations could never be described in the agonistic and fundamentally egalitarian terms of religious love, might community become a site of intimacy. And yet while caste might be hidden, it could not be excised from the narrative of Hindu-Muslim relations, whose violent potential was in fact linked to fears about each one co-opting low castes against the other. And this triangulation of the relationship robbed religious conflict of any integrity. But while many of these themes continue to be visible in contemporary debates about religious conflict in India, the kind of political thought that once defined them has practically vanished from the scene, and all we are left with is the old colonial sociology of knowledge and its narrative of administration.

References

Ahmad, J. (1942). *Some Recent Speeches and Writings of Mr. Jinnah*. Lahore: Sh. Muhammad Ashraf.

Ambedkar, B. R. (1990). *What Congress and Gandhi Have Done to the Untouchables*. Vol. 9 of *Dr. Babasaheb Ambedkar Writings and Speeches*. Pune, India: Education Department, Government of Maharashtra.

Ambedkar, B. R. (1991). Vol. 10 of *Dr. Babasaheb Ambedkar Writings and Speeches*. Pune, India: Education Department, Government of Maharashtra.

Appadurai, A. (2006). *Fear of Small Numbers: An Essay on the Geography of Anger*. Durham, NC: Duke University Press.

Brass, P. (2003). *The Production of Hindu-Muslim Violence in Contemporary India*. Seattle: University of Washington Press.

Burke, S. M. (2000). *Jinnah: Speeches and Statements, 1947–1948*, Karachi: Oxford University Press.

Cohn, B. S. (1996). *Colonialism and Its Forms of Knowledge: The British in India*. Princeton, NJ: Princeton University Press.

Das, V. (2006). *Life and Words: Violence and the Descent into the Ordinary*. Berkeley: University of California Press.

Gandhi, M. K. (1919). Mr. Gandhi's letter. *Young India*, 1 (54), 4.

Gandhi, M. K. (1929). Position of women. *Young India*, 11 (42), 4.

Gandhi, M. K. (2003). *Hind Swaraj and Other Writings*. Cambridge: Cambridge University Press.

Savarkar, V. D. (1969). *Hindutva: Who Is a Hindu?* Bombay: Veer Savarkar Prakashan.

Vahid, S. A. (1992). *Thoughts and Reflections of Iqbal*. Lahore: Sh. Muhammad Ashraf.

4

Conflict, Secularism, and Toleration

Uday S. Mehta

We live in a world in which conflict often occurs along religious lines, and toleration and secularism are understood as essential to mitigating and managing such
conflict. Moreover, because we think of such conflict as being in its very nature
escalatory, as having no internal limit to it, and hence, as something that tends
toward death, disorder, and destruction, toleration and secularism are thought
of as essentially linked with securing the ideal of the peaceful coexistence of diverse groups of people with differing credal convictions, practices, and identities.
Toleration and secularism are thus deemed to be crucial tools for responding to a
world in which peace and order are broadly accepted as foundational ideals, both
in themselves and, additionally, because they support other normative goals, of
which the presence of a diversity religious groups living together is an undeniable fact.

This assumption regarding diversity as a familiar ground of conflict and
the importance of toleration and secularism in mitigating it is not wrong, and
the ideal it aspires to clearly salutary. But its contemporary ubiquity can have
the effect of obscuring other responses to the fact and experience of religious
diversity and to other ideals or modes of living. One need not, after all, assess
the presence of diverse religious groups and practices merely or even primarily
in terms of their potential to induce conflict or disorder; moreover, one might
place an altogether different normative value on conflict, death, and disorder
than the cascading and dire implications with which modern regimes and
modes of thinking typically view such eventualities. A form of religiosity that
is not dependent on an abstract commitment to toleration and secularism may
be a high value in itself, and the conflict and disorder that could stem from the
presence of diverse of religious groups be thought of as a small price to pay for
the flourishing of religious ways of life. Similarly, one might think of religious
conflict as not being in its nature escalatory, and hence not in need of mediation, and instead as something that has its own retardant, which as it were keeps
the conflict within a narrow ambit—without letting it escalate into social and
political mayhem. Such alternate understandings and ideals are typically associated with different values and institutional arrangements and with different
historical moments.

Uday S. Mehta, *Conflict, Secularism, and Toleration* In: *Negotiating Democracy and Religious Pluralism*. Edited
by: Karen Barkey, Sudipta Kaviraj, and Vatsal Naresh, Oxford University Press. © Oxford University Press 2021.
DOI: 10.1093/oso/9780197530016.003.0005

There are plainly various ways of conceiving of religious diversity and the conflict associated with it, along with their relationship to toleration and secularism, and they stem from different normative positions, histories, and experiences and vouch for different modes of existence. This point has been richly elaborated in recent writings, which point to the ways in which toleration and secularism are historically conditioned, and which further suggest that claims to their presumed universality are too easily overdrawn and perhaps limited by their own provincialism.[1]

The main purpose of this chapter is different from the historicist point made previously. I focus on certain ideas and experiences that acknowledged the fact of religious and cultural diversity, but which did not conceive of that fact as requiring a commitment to the abstract value of toleration and the political response associated with the term "secularism." In the Indian context of the twentieth century such ideas were most forcefully elaborated by M. K. Gandhi. Gandhi took religious diversity to be an established and long-standing feature of the civilizational experience of India. But the implications that he thought to be implicit in this, and the responses that they required, were very different from those in the predominant tradition of modern European and nationalist thinking. The categories in which Gandhi thinks often have an archaic quality, but they merit reconsideration at a time when the familiar terms in which the challenge of religious diversity and toleration is discussed feel fatigued.

4.1. The Historical Context and its Implications

The English Civil War in the seventeenth century had religious conflict among sectarian Christian groups as one of its most decisive aspects. Thomas Hobbes articulated its importance with a clarity that explains—even in traditions that modified his absolutist conclusions. For Hobbes, there were four crucial features relating to religious diversity. First, because religion involved matters of

---

[1] Much of the recent writing on secularism and toleration is anchored in an appreciation and critique of Charles Taylor's magisterial work *A Secular Age* (Cambridge, MA: Belknap Press of Harvard University Press, 2007), which details the path of Latin Christianity. Also see *Varieties of Secularism*, ed. Michael Warner, Jonathan Vanantwerpen, and Craig Calhoun (Cambridge, MA: Harvard University Press, 2010); *Beyond the Secular West*, ed. Akeel Bilgrami (New York: Columbia University Press, 2016); Akeel Bilgrami, *Secularism, Identity and Enchantment* (Cambridge, MA; Harvard University Press, 2014), chaps. 1 and 2. Also see the Immanent Frame, 2007: www.ssrc.org/blogs/immanent_frame/2007/. There is of course an older literature on secularism that is also attentive to its historical particularity. Talal Asad in his classic book *Formations of the Secular: Christianity, Islam and Modernity* (Stanford, CA: Stanford University Press, 2003) articulates an important position that questions the presumed universality of secularism. Michael Walzer's *On Toleration* (New Haven: Yale University Press, 1997) is also deeply attentive to the different regimes and norms of toleration. Also see Rajeev Bhargava's edited volume *Secularism and Its Critics* (New Delhi: Oxford University Press, 1998).

individual faith and salvific concerns—that is, the "inner realm"—it sanctioned private judgments. These included ideas about ways of living and valuations regarding what made it meaningful. This implicated religions, even when they professed to be doing the opposite, with the troubling potential of encouraging radical forms of individuality and alternative conceptions of social and political order.[2] Second, sectarian distinctions within Christianity had become the basis of hardened group identities, which were operating in a space where the distinctions between the various groups, most of which were Christian, were fluid and unclear. Third, these various sectarian groupings, by professing an expansive claim to power and authority, vitiated the possibility of establishing, what for Hobbes was the only credible form of political authority, which had to be unified, singular, and, in the main, secular. This had to be a new form of power, namely political power. Finally, the conflict produced on account of diverse religious sects was not amenable to compromise and hence produced, and had the permanent potential to produce, a form of conflict that was endless and devastating to all forms of social order and, at the limit, to life itself. It was this predicament that led Hobbes to conclude that neither individual volition nor the traditional authority of religious groups could produce the order requisite for any form of social enterprise; in fact it was unable ultimately to protect and sustain that which was of primary importance, namely, human life itself. Hobbes's famous solution to this dire prospect was to argue for a state that was absolute in its power and unified in its parts, and which, only because it was absolute and unified, could mediate and settle the contesting claims of various religious groups, or for that matter any other disputes. For Hobbes, the Civil War had made brutally manifest the anarchical implications that were implicit in any form of social diversity that was undergirded by claims of identity and the potential extravagance of private credal convictions. Hobbes was indifferent to the content of religious beliefs because, despite their content, they all contributed to these implications.

Two things are crucial in Hobbes's account: the first is his conception of conflict, and second his understanding of the state as the singular condition for protecting and securing life. For Hobbes, religious conflict was in its very nature escalatory, because it was backed by inner convictions and hardened and plural claims about identity in a context where the distinct claims and boundaries of religious authority between various groups could not be maintained. Religious groups could not secure their distinct claims to authority in part because they were operating within a broadly shared eschatology and set of credal convictions. The combination of such shared convictions and distinct and contesting claims

[2] See Christopher Hill, *The Century of Revolutions* (Edinburgh: Thomas Nelson & Sons, 1961) and *The World Turned Upside Down* (New York: Penguin, 1972).

of authority produced, in effect, a deficit of power, while internally motivating a constant conflict over it. This is what underlies Hobbes's ardent defense of the secular power of the state, and where the experience of the Civil War was decisive. According to the logic that Hobbes takes to be determinative, no alternative to it is stable, in the sense of being able to contain the conflict that follows from rival claimants. Neither intermediary institutions, nor individual self-restraint, nor normative division of power in the manner proposed by Locke and Madison could limit the potential conflict. Anarchy and death are the only default alternatives to a powerful state. A version of this very narrative becomes central to the constitutional founding of the modern Indian state, which lays out the broad mandate of secularism and its view of toleration in India.

The experiences through which Gandhi thinks of the past and the present are the effects of modern civilization, which have to do with the revaluation of the conditions for self-knowledge, security, technology, patience, and courage. Perhaps surprisingly, given Gandhi's views on nonviolence, he does not, at least not as a primary consideration, associate the deleterious and deforming effects of modern civilization with war, massive devastation, or anarchy. Gandhi does not similarly think of security and the preservation of life as foundational ideals, either for individuals or for communities, and hence he does not give them the sort of primacy that Hobbes does. He does not think of order in terms of something that requires the state, which can secure it by having the capacity to intervene in every eruption of conflict and disorder. The sort of order that matters to him is written into the weave of society and extant social norms, at least before they were ravaged by the effects of modern civilization. He thinks of conflict, including religious conflict, as amenable to persuasion and compromise, in the way that interests are thought to be, and when such persuasion and compromise fail, he imagines the ensuing conflict as something that tends in any case to limit itself. It is not of necessity escalatory. For Gandhi, religious diversity is simply a fact, in the Indian case a long-standing and largely untroubling fact. It is a fact about the distinct religious languages and visions through which people imagine theirs lives and what makes them meaningful. It is not, in the main, a fact about the contesting claims regarding authority and power of different religious groups. The threat that the diversity of religions poses—and he does not think of it as a permanent or underlying threat—is of occasional disorder, but never of social devastation. Unlike the tradition of thinking from Hobbes to Weber that has taken anarchy to be the necessary and immediate counterpoint to the absence of political order, Gandhi does not think in terms of such Manichaean contrasts because, as I have said, he finds the extant basis of order in the diffused patterns and minutia of social practices. Late in his life Gandhi, in the context of pending partition, was even prepared explicitly to countenance the possibility of anarchy in

India, which, despite that prospect, did not warrant imperial intervention.[3] And finally, for Gandhi religion in its many forms is above all the language through which individual self-understanding and self-transformation are made possible. It represented those deep inner convictions and that faith through which individuals explored their own selfhood. And crucially it is this feature that gave to religion the potential to facilitate the mutual understanding among different groups, without requiring a commitment to the abstract value of toleration or the backstop of a unified and powerful state.

4.2. Gandhi's Pluralism

To get a sense of Gandhi's views on religious plurality and conflict one needs to consider passages in *Hind Swaraj* where the issue is explicitly considered. Gandhi's interlocutor (in *Hind Swaraj*) raises the matter of the deep enmity between Muslims and Hindus, and how this "fact" undermined the potential unity of the nation and threatened its aspirations to independence from imperial rule. Gandhi disputes both the alleged nature and depth of the enmity and the specific sort of unity that self-rule required. India, for Gandhi, had a unity that predates the arrival of the British. It is a unity that included various religions and a long history of assimilation, "If the Hindus believe that India should be peopled only by Hindus, they are living a dreamland. The Hindus, the Mahomedans, the Parsees and the Christians who have made India their country are fellow countrymen, and they will have to live in unity if only for their own interest. In no part of the world are one nationality and one religion synonymous terms: nor has it ever been so in India."[4] For Gandhi religious diversity and a basic unity, underwritten by civilization's rhythms and not unitary power, are simply facts. They are part of the warp and weft of an ancient land, and for him they provoke none of the anxiety that they do in his nationalist interlocutor. Neither religious diversity nor the sort of unity Gandhi has in mind is freighted by troubling implications; nor, for that matter, is he buoyed by a high idealism that the presence of religious diversity may point to. Again, they are merely facts, banal and scattered in their obvious familiarity. Hindus and Muslims, Gandhi points out, have survived and prospered under rulers of each faith. They are part of a syncretistic way of life that has points of mutual contact and divergence. What matters is simply that "those who are conscious of the spirit of nationality do not interfere with one another's

---

[3] Faisal Devji gives an extremely interesting account of the British imperial thinking on the prospect of anarchy in the early 1940s and Gandhi's heretical embrace of that prospect. See Faisal Devji, *The Impossible India* (London: Hurst, 2012), chap. 6, "Leaving India to Anarchy."

[4] M. K. Gandhi, *Hind Swaraj*, ed. Antony Parel (New York: Cambridge University Press), 52–53.

religion."[5] The crucial feature of the unity Gandhi vouches for is a shared "mode of life" and not a shared and superintending form of political governance.[6] It is a unity tethered to civilizational routines of common and conflicting interests and social norms. It does not have and does not need, in the manner of a typical nationalist and imperialist, clearly defined political boundaries or a clear font of power and obligation.

On the matter of the alleged deep enmity between Hindus and Muslims, Gandhi is again almost cavalier in his denial of such an enmity. Instead he thinks of the enmity (and the conviviality) as occasioned by contingent circumstances that almost always admit of negotiation and persuasion. Even on the freighted matter of the killing of cows by Muslims he says he would "only plead" with Muslims to refrain from such acts, notwithstanding the reverence he, as a Hindu, feels toward cows. "If he [the Muslim] would not listen to me, I should let the cow go for the simple reason that the matter is beyond my ability."[7] Gandhi's apparent pragmatism in this sentence does not call into question his own religiosity. In some other context, one can well imagine him being willing to die for his religious convictions. But his point here is that he does not take the difference between the Muslim attitude toward the cow from his own Hindu reverence for it as sanctioning an escalation of that difference. Gandhi knows and accepts the fact of the occasional conflict between Hindus and Muslims. But what is striking is the degree to which he views such conflict in a lower key that has no necessary escalatory potential. Consider the following passage, also from *Hind Swaraj*.

I do not suggest that the Hindu and the Mahomedans will never fight. Two brothers living together often do so. We shall sometimes have our heads broken. Such things ought not to be necessary, but all men are not equi-minded. When people are in a rage, they do many foolish things. These we have to put with. But, when we do quarrel, we certainly do not want to engage counsel and to resort to English or any law courts. *Two men fight; both have their heads broken, or one only. How shall a third party distribute justice amongst them? Those who fight may expect to be injured.*[8]

What is starkly clear is Gandhi's casual equanimity about the conflict between Hindus and Muslims. There is no suggestion that it stems from a deep friend/enemy animus in which the very distinction can be, or should be, the foundational ground of a political construct that makes possible and urgent a unity forged around that construct. Gandhi never gives an account of such conflict

---

[5] Gandhi, *Hind Swaraj*, 52–53.
[6] Gandhi, *Hind Swaraj*, 48.
[7] Gandhi, *Hind Swaraj*, 54.
[8] Gandhi, *Hind Swaraj*, 57 (emphasis added).

in which it arises from the essential nature of the two religions, or indeed from anything that has a deeper motivational basis. His thought is strikingly free of such underlying mandates, just as it is free of the mandates of political economy or those of class conflict. Instead, in the examples he gives the conflict is almost always occasioned by, and limited by, a narrow set of contextual considerations. In Gandhi's rendering the conflict is merely a foolish act motivated by prosaic anger, a kind of schoolyard brawl that will run its course, without any implied or necessary escalation. Even the possibility of heads being broken, and hence the presence of violence, does not occasion any special concern. Neither does the possibility that perhaps only one party's head gets broken, and hence that the initial conflict may have been between unequally matched opponents. In Gandhi's view such things sometimes just happen. They are acts of almost childlike folly with no grave religious or historical logic underlying them. They are not part of a cascading momentum that embodies as its immanent consequences dire implications about the war of all against all or social devastation. Gandhi never imagines such a pandemic eventuality in the Indian context.

But what did deeply trouble Gandhi, and what at numerous times in *Hind Swaraj* and elsewhere he returns to, is the idea that such conflict required the mediation of "a third party." Gandhi is absolutely insistent in his refusal to countenance such mediation by any third party, be it the law with its warrant of justice, or the imperial state as the guarantor of peace, order, and a progressive historical alignment, or the national state as it vouches for equality and a representational, sanctioned form of acting on behalf of the public interest. Elsewhere in the same chapter of *Hind Swaraj* Gandhi writes, "We [Hindus and Muslims] should be ashamed to take our quarrels to the English," making it clear that for him the issue of seeking mediation was fraught with both psychological and ethical considerations.[9] At its root for Gandhi all such forms of mediation eviscerate the natural and potential integrity of the self by holding out the lure of abstracted forms of substitution, which only third parties could supply and which make their mediation essential. Even Gandhi's extended diatribes in *Hind Swaraj* against lawyers, doctors, and modern forms of travel are part of the same worry regarding mediation and the effects it has on the self. They interject a dependence, which Gandhi thinks is the hidden essence of modern civilization, in which the security and deepest values of the self become reliant on abstracted projections of power.

Secularism for Gandhi was one such form of mediation, which required conceiving of toleration as an abstract value alongside other similarly conceived values. Because of the escalatory implication of conflict in the modern mode of political thinking and the implied threat to all forms social order and life, secularism and toleration present themselves as intervening in thwarting these

[9] Gandhi, *Hind Swaraj*, 57.

consequences from becoming actual. But for Gandhi toleration in many ways was not a normative value; at least not in the sense that it becomes a standard by which the state mediates between it and other values or deploys it to mediate between the practices and believes of various religions. Instead it is simply a description of the fact of religious diversity as Gandhi saw it exemplified in the cursus of Indian civilization. It did not require conceptualizing toleration as a value, understood as a normative ideal that had to be supported by the state (the third party), because the fact that it referred to was itself not burdened by the harrowing implications that secularism as an instrument of the state, and toleration as a value, were meant to manage.

4.3. Secularism and Religious Toleration

The main point that I have been urging can be summarized as follows. Secularism and the linked idea of religious toleration are a response to a conception of conflict, which was in the English case represented by the crisis of the Civil War, in which conflict is thought to be escalatory and devastating of social order and security. For that reason, its effects can only be moderated or managed through the mediation of the state and the power at its disposal. One characteristic feature of such management is the state's commitment to religious toleration. Given this widely held view of religious conflict, secularism becomes all but mandatory, as does the need for a unified state. Religious toleration, as a normative and political ideal that undergirds the fundamental idea of a secular state that mediates between the values and practices of various religions, is reliant on a particular conception of religious conflict and a closely linked conception of the special priority of security as an individual and collective value.

But if, in the manner of Gandhi, one did not subscribe to this understanding of conflict and to the special priority of security, a range of options open up that do not turn on a political settlement or on the power and unity of the state. On this view, religious toleration, understood as a value, and secularism as an orientation of the state, cease to be mandatory, because they refer to a different history and a different grammar of thinking.[10] For Gandhi these options included forms of social organization that were scattered and decentralized; where conflict was quotidian (and not motivated by something essential) and was thus, in principle, contained and available to persuasion; where security of individuals and the collectivity was valued, but did not have a trumping primacy; and where toleration

---

[10] Akeel Bilgrami, while also referring to Gandhi, makes the same claim, though he does not emphasize, as I do, the specific significance of the role of how conflict is conceptualized. See *Secularism, Identity and Enchantment*, 3–57.

was not an abstract value, but referred simply to the long-standing experience of practice and living with religious diversity, and where what was normatively crucial was the preservation of such forms of living together. Gandhi vouched for these alternatives even after it was clear that the end of imperial rule in India would culminate in the birth of two nations whose mode of managing religious diversity was going to be starkly at odds with his own understanding. Indeed, for Gandhi it was precisely the resort to the idea of civil war, the unending basis of the conflict between Hindus and Muslims, and more broadly, the unavoidable proximity of crisis and hence the imperative need for a unified state, that narrowed the options to the point that only partition could be thought of as creating the conditions in which the state, or rather two states, could perform the appropriate form of mediation. This was the foundational and driving premise of M. A. Jinnah's thought.

In the context of the late 1940s in India, when independence was acknowledged to be fated and when the constitutional form of the future state was being considered by the Constituent Assembly (CA, 1946–49) it was precisely the language of crisis, disunity and religious strife that came to haunt the deliberations of the assembly. It was from these deliberations that the idea of religious toleration and secularism came to taken as mandatory. The invocation of crisis, strife, impending disunity, sectarian divisions and the prospect of mayhem are ubiquitous in the reflections of Indian Constituent Assembly Debates that precede the constitution. The British imperial authorities had themselves for long grounded the legitimacy of their rule as the sole basis for avoiding chaos and mitigating the sectarian crisis, which would result from their departure.[11]

The background to many of these apprehensions about civil war and anarchy is a concern with the Muslim question, issues of caste and pervasive inequality and destitution—hence broadly the social question. Following independence and especially following the outbreak of hostilities in 1948 there was the additional and recurrent, and as it turned out the semi-permanent, invocation of the threat of war with Pakistan. It was a picture of a society fraught with the danger of subjective enthusiasms, religious difference and social and economic divisions. The collective image it produces is of a society in which unity had to be crafted through a new settlement. It is of course undeniable that the entire period of the CA, and the early years of the republic, were shadowed by real crises especially after the failure of the cabinet mission, the outrageous expediency of Mountbatten's plans for the transfer of power, the refusal of Muslim Leagues' representatives to join the deliberations, the horror of partition and the assassination of Gandhi. The concern with war, the prospect of disunity, the anguishing worries about social and other forms of destitution typically mark the birth of

---

[11] See Devji, *The Impossible India*, chap. 6, "Leaving India to Anarchy."

nations and so it not surprising that they should be forcefully expressed. Still it is not these facts alone that adequately capture the importance of this recurrent trope in the Constituent Assembly Debates and elsewhere. The facts, while true, are, after all, selective.[12]

How is one to make sense of such insistently grave perorations? Why does the nation, as it comes to self-consciousness, not just in India but elsewhere too, swaddle itself in such mournful garb and dire apprehensions of strife and conflict? More is stake and this and an abstract perspective tells us something beyond what can be gleamed from the historical and contextual orientation.

As an existential contention the narrative of anarchy, civil war is closely linked with the need for unity with an unequivocal center of sovereign power. Again, in the modern era nobody articulated the rippling stakes of this more forcefully than Hobbes. The ultimate purpose of the social contract for Hobbes was to articulate the multitude into a singular entity—"This done, the multitude so united in *one person* is called a *Commonwealth.*"[13] Such unity had to be buttressed by narrative of anarchy and crisis as its counterpoint, it had to make violent death very proximate. The narrative in effect served to delegitimize all alternative claims to authority as satisfying the first virtue of a political order, namely peace and security; and equally, it made that narrative a permanent feature of the political order's continued legitimacy. The very idea of sovereignty as the source of the political identity had to be undergirded by a constant reminder of their intimacy and proximity to their antithesis, namely anarchy, chaos and violent death. The significance of this postulate, and its status as a quasi-metaphysical imperative, can be seen in the fact that no set of historical or extant conditions exempts a society from the implications of its implicit threat. Peace and security required the mediation of the state. They could not be left to the contingent resolutions offered by other social options. As the post 9/11 world has made vivid, the concern with security operates as a kind of permanent backdrop for every future eventuality, neutralizing culture, society or ethics from having an alternative claim to their redress. (I.e., however, minuscule the probability of an explosive device being hidden in ones shoes or other garments, the risk cannot be taken by the "responsible" authorities, who, after all, are functionaries of the state.)

Whatever the social, ethnic, cultural, geographical or other forms of diversity and unity that might characterize a collection of individuals, they must in addition, be forged into "a people" with a distinctive political self-conception or collective identity. A central feature of that political identity—even if it involves a shared and founding allegiance to certain "inalienable rights" and abstract

---

[12] Devji, *The Impossible India*, 153, quotes a letter by Lord Linlithgow to Lord Wavell with the following sentence: "We could not for the peace of the world allow chaos in India."
[13] Hobbes, *Leviathan*, 109. Partial emphasis added (first emphasis added).

normative principles as the American act of "separation" did,—is an aware-ness, that they constitute "one body" with a shared vulnerability. The forging of a distinct political identity, even in a text such as the American *Declaration of Independence* in which the appeal to normative principles was so conspicuous, explicitly stipulated the need "to provide new guards for their future security" and to "have full power to levy war, conclude peace, contract alliances, estab-lish commerce, and to do all other acts and things which independent states may of right do."[14] The *Declaration* did not just indicate a desire to defect from George III's empire; it was a document that professed the formation of some-thing separate, singular and unified—bound together in part by a shared insecu-rity along with the means to contend with that predicament. Hobbes signals the significance of this metamorphosis of individuals into "one body" by invoking the gravity of the Biblical term Covenant, thereby associating the formation of the Commonwealth with a new communion and a radically transformed onto-logical condition. Locke, though his language was less dramatic, was equally ex-plicit, "it is easy to discern, who are, and who are not, in political society together. Those who are united into one body, and have a common established law and judicature to appeal to . . . ."[15] In brief the unity and the diversity of the social, be it the bonds of family, religious orders, professional guilds, territorial and func-tional forms of association such as towns and villages, none of these can serve as a substitute for the unity of the political.

One might say in this tradition security, self-preservation and political unity are literally obsessions, in that no amount of attending to them fully assuages the anxiety they represent. Even with thinkers like Rousseau and Kant who endorsed a federative ideal there was no relaxing on the importance of patri-otism, notwithstanding the civic accent they placed on it. Related to this idea was the emphasis which political societies placed on territorial and other kinds of boundaries, which were to be rigid and not porous. Hegel was summa-rizing the broad orientation of modern political thought and practice when he wrote: "Individuality is awareness of one's existence as a unit in sharp distinction from others. It manifests itself here in the state as a relation to other states, each of which is autonomous *vis- a- vis* the others."[16] And finally the idea points to the thought that in political society there must be central source of power, even if that power is limited or checked by contesting divisions and established norms for the transfer of power.

[14] See text of the Declaration of Independence. http://www.earlyamerica.com/earlyamerica/freedom/doi/text.html.

[15] John Locke, *Two Treatises of Government*, ed. Peter Laslett, 2nd ed. (London: Cambridge University Press, 1967), 367.

[16] Georg Wilhelm Friedrich Hegel, *Hegel's Philosophy of Right*, trans. T. M. Knox (Oxford: Clarendon Press, 1945), 208.

Nations have to articulate themselves as singular political entities. It points to the crucial significance of the singular collective pronoun, "We, the people," as authorizing the constitutional project. In terms of constitutional salience unity is understood not as a social or civilizational category, but rather as something that refers to a political form. In many ways, the generative crucible of modern constitutions and modern politics turns on the metaphor and the idea of destruction and creation. As a coupling it is the font of that particular disposition by which power, in particular political power, becomes, or at least projects itself as, the singular and redemptive energy of a society. This is especially conspicuous in the case of foundational moments, but also, is so often evident in more routinized politics—which, increasingly, invokes the dramaturgy of a revolutionary pretext. Many of the major themes of modern politics: the concern with power, the unity of the state and the nation, social justice and national recognition rely on contrasts of which destruction and creation are the starkest expression.

The idea that political power emerges from the site of destruction or that it should need such an image for its self-generation is revealing of the nature political power itself. At a broad level it points to the fact that power has a strained if not antithetical relationship to the past. In constituting itself through an act of clearing it is markedly different from social authority, which as Weber emphasized, typically relied on continuity as its mode of self-authorization and legitimacy.[17] This is a theme that informs the Indian Constituent Assembly, though often with ironic touches. The Assembly, as is well known, was full speeches and references to India's glorious and multifarious pasts. One can recall Nehru's many invocations of India's 5000-years of history and traditions (which revealing he often characterizes through the metaphor of weight, thereby also suggesting burden), or Dr. Radhakrishnan's frequent references to India's ancient republican traditions or the countless other occasions in the Assembly when the civilizational luster of India was mentioned, usually with triumphal pride. And yet, and this is the irony, the dominant temper of mind in the Assembly was revolutionary, in which the challenge was to build a new society on the ruins of the old. It was that thought that guided the Assembly from its start to its conclusion, and for which the state and political power was deemed to be the necessary instrument. The metaphor of building, of creating something new runs through the CA's deliberations. It is striking that even some of the native princes, who had much to lose from the emerging constitutional depensation, concurred with this sentiment. For example, Nehru in the resolution regarding "Aims and Objects" invokes, with commendation, the American, French, and Russian revolutions it

---

[17] Max Weber, "Legitimation That Stems from Traditional Forms of Authority." *Essays in Sociology* (Routledge, UK, 2009), 207–14.

is because, as he says, they "gave rise a new type of State."[18] For that new state to have the stature and power requisite for the crafting of a new society, the past had to, quite literally, be past. It could survive only as something on which the state can do its work, as though it were an inherited one-dimensional coda, but not as a living force that infused the present. This is how Nehru, for example, typically conceptualizes the relationship of the past and the state. In *Discovery of India* at one point Nehru paints two images of India; in the first it is dotted with innumerable villages, towns, and cities teaming with the masses. The second image is of the snowcapped Himalayas and the valleys in Kashmir "covered," as he says, "with new flowers and a brook bubbling and gurgling through it." And then, in a remarkably self-conscious admission of the romantic's and revolutionary's preference for blank slates and unpopulated places, for geography over history, he says, "We make and preserve the pictures of our choice, and so I have chosen this mountain background rather than the more normal picture of a hot subtropical country."[19] One way of conceptualizing the enduring challenge of the Indian state is to say that it has always attempted to stop the past from tearing the soul of the nation apart, with power as its principal instrument in this therapeutic endeavor.

4.4.

Gandhi, as I have indicated, expressed a view dissenting from this entire grammar of thinking. It was of a piece with his reluctant support of constitutionalism and the need for unity expressed around the mediating power of the state and the narratives of crisis that underwrote it. But there was also another aspect of these narratives whose focus was the social. There is a family of familiar accounts, often linked with the magisterial work of Norbert Elias on the civilizing process, in which civility referred to the slow accretion of new domestic and public practices, which produced what came to known as a civilized society.[20] The broad impetus for this was the intermingling of new groups of peoples who had to accommodate each other's differences. Over time this process produced a society that displaced the older language of etiquette and manners along with feudal and aristocratic norms, and thus paved the way for an ascending liberal and commercial world.

Gandhi abstained from not only the articulation of grand political project, but also these broad narratives of society and social development. He was indifferent

[18] *Constituent Assembly Debates*, Hereafter CAD (New Delhi, Government of India Publications, 1972) Four Volumes, Volume 1, 61.
[19] Nehru, *Discovery of India*, 62–63.
[20] Norbert Elias, *The Civilizing Process*, trans. Edmund Jephcott, 2 vols. (New York: Pantheon, 1982).

to the historicism that is essential to these narratives, because nothing of any importance in Gandhi turns on the logic of historical development. He viewed satyagraha as tangential to the political and social processes with which history was typically concerned—"satyagraha, being natural, is not noted in history."[21] This did not mean that he thought of human beings as living in some timeless zone of immobility, only that he did not accept the typical social and political narratives that history offered up as the bases of individual and collective self-fashioning. He did not, for example, think that Indian civilization had to, or should, conceive of itself as bound to a teleology whose inevitable outcome was the nation-state or a condition of economic modernity. He also abstained from endorsing the driving frictions that are internal to these historical narratives, accounts such as class struggle, the increase of the productive forces, the logic of capitalist development and imperialist expansion, or the impulse to enlarge the domains of social and political freedom through constitutional commitments. Such abstention did not make him indifferent to social and economic woes such as deprivation, gross inequality, exploitation, or the abuse and abridgement of rights. It was just that his views on these matters did not share the urgency and the causal logic that typically organizes such narratives.

He abstains from these accounts for a very simple reason. Gandhi was never drawn to the idea of society as a project in need of wholesale refashioning. His thought is not spurred by the Manichaean contrast that underlies and guides the vision of so much of modern political and social thought, where the only alternative to political order is the asocial and diabolical ravages of anarchy.[22] It is not that Gandhi accepts every extant aspect of society. He clearly did not, as is obvious from his work on the problem of untouchability in the Hindu caste framework and on many other social woes. But even on these matters his emphasis is not on social development or producing a new kind of society marked by a radical rearrangement of social relations or ruptures in the existing patterns of life. He took society, like religion, to be a given, a fact that, despite its vexations and tribulations, had the tensile capacity to produce an order from within which there was the possibility of self-transformation. His ultimate concern was with conditions that made or obscured the possibility of individual self—knowledge. Gandhi was never taken with the dream of a new kind of society or of a new kind of man. His vision comes from a palette that draws from the materials of ordinary life. He could and did imagine a society with different hues and shapes, without, nevertheless, replacing the palette itself. And he did not, like Nehru

---

[21] Gandhi, *Hind Swaraj*, 90.

[22] In the Indian context, the sharpest contrast was with Ambedkar, who in his exchange with Gandhi on the matter of the caste system, famously claimed, "The foremost thing that must be recognized is that Hindu society is a myth.... Hindu society as such does not exist. It is only a collection of castes." B. R. Ambedkar, *Annihilation of Caste* (New York: Verso, 2014), 241–242.

and most nationalists, believe that India had to be inserted into the prevailing rhythms of universal history, or that it had to have a preference for the bucolic valleys of Kashmir.

4.5.

By way of conclusion I want to return to how Gandhi understands religious toleration and the context in which it operates and what he deems necessary to its flourishing. In the final chapter of *Hind Swaraj* Gandhi makes the following observations and claims:

> You English who have come to India are not a good specimen of the English nation, nor can we, almost half-Anglicized Indians, be considered a good specimen of the real Indian nation. If the English nation were to know all you have done, it would oppose many of your actions. The mass of the Indians have had few dealings with you. If you will abandon your so-called civilization, and search into your own scriptures, you will find that our demands are just. Only on condition of our demands being fully satisfied may you remain in India, and if you remain under those conditions, we shall learn several things from you, and you will learn many things from us. So doing, we shall benefit from each other and the world. But that will happen only when the root of our relationship is sunk in a religious soil.[23]

Gandhi is concerned with three issues in this passage. The first is with the fact that the English in India and the half-Anglicized Indians betray their real and best national traditions and inheritances. They are quite literally poor moral specimens of the genus of which, in the present, they are taken to be representatives. Regarding the former group Gandhi elaborates that their actions would be disapproved of by the English nation were it to become fully aware of them. English in India operate in a moral penumbra and perpetrate a kind of moral subterfuge against the English people. It is a subterfuge that is not fully evident to Indians because few of them have any dealings with the English. The theme is one of self-betrayal and moral occlusion, by both the English and the Indians.

The second issue relates to the conditions that distort mutual understanding between the two groups. The reason for this distortion is the imperial context; but Gandhi does not name it as such, with its conspicuous association with a regime of unequal power and racialized differentiation. Gandhi's purposes exceed the political relationship by pointing to something deeper that underlies

---

[23] Gandhi, *Hind Swaraj*, 115.

and disfigures it. Instead he identifies the context through a broader reference, that is, to "your so-called civilization." It is modern civilization that confines the relations between the English and the Indians on a plane that vitiates their ability to learn from each other. The reference to mutual learning or understanding, almost by its banality, is telling, because it suggests that something as elemental as mutual and genuine learning among different groups is made impossible by the mediation of modern civilization with its uniform metrics and material emphasis. What Gandhi has in mind here are the grand historical narratives that are wedded to a conception of progress and a corresponding belief in differential civilizational elevations. Gandhi is contending that such narratives make mutual learning impossible, because they are premised on the immaturity of one group and the temporal assurance of a particular outcome, that is, even if a conversation between the English and the Indians were to occur. It is also what makes it difficult for the English to appreciate the justice of the demands being made by the Indians, because a particular conception of justice has already been written into those historical narratives. Instead Gandhi suggests that mutual learning and the claims of justice would only become clear if the English sought guidance in their "own scriptures" rather than in the warrant of history.

And third, in a more prescriptive voice, Gandhi writes of the conditions that could rectify both the hindrances in the way of mutual understanding and the self-betrayal within each group. Regarding these conditions Gandhi speaks of the essential need to return to scriptures and of rooting the relationship between the English and the Indians "in a religious soil." Gandhi's primary concern is with the need for a self-searching that is internal to each group. On Gandhi's view a return to scripture is essential to this self-searching. But he is insistent that only a relationship anchored in a religious seedbed holds the potential of both groups overcoming their respective self-betrayal and of learning from each other. Moreover, in this repositioned relationship, between the English and the Indians, he says the broader world would learn from their interaction, and suggestively, there would also be the possibility, to which in this passage, as elsewhere, Gandhi makes explicit reference, that there might be no reason for the English to decamp from India.

The themes of self-betrayal, the distortion brought about by modern civilization, and the need to anchor mutual relations in the language of scripture and religiosity are a digest of the broader issues that matter deeply to Gandhi. They suggest both a positive purpose and a refusal to think in familiar terms. Gandhi is refusing the categories that by the early twentieth century and with redoubled zeal in the decades that followed had come to suffuse the discourse of imperial relations from both sides. He does not, for example, speak of exploitation, inequality, racism, differentials of power, absence of political representation, economic immiseration, quotidian forms of violence, or the warrant and urgency of national independence—even though, in different degrees, all these mattered to him. Similarly, from a positive perspective, he does not engage with the idea of progress, the integration of India and the world, a modernity that moved India away from feudal and obscurantist norms and which carried the imprimatur of science, the prospect of democratic self-governance, or other mandates of a progressive future. As he concludes his discourse on home and self-rule, all these categories seem at best secondary to Gandhi's ultimate purposes. Instead his summation, both critically and positively, points to the importance of scriptures and the language of religion. It is the muffling and displacement of this language that obscures what for Gandhi is the most basic and essential fact of the empire and of modern civilization, namely, that it imperils the moral hygiene of both the English and the Indians.

There is something puzzling about this invocation of religion and the thought that it alone could redeem the appropriate link between the English and the Indians. Why is Gandhi so insistent that a relationship fraught with so many obvious political, economic, moral, and cultural vexations should not, as the typical nationalists insisted, be conceptualized in those familiar terms, but instead, through the language of scripture and religion?

Gandhi's views on religion and his own religiosity are highly complex. This is not the context to propose even a cursory summary of their complexity.[24] What is relevant is that he thinks of religion in its diverse forms as something given, into which one is, as it were, arbitrarily cast. Gandhi's main preoccupation is with infusing the mundane aspects of life with meaning and moral depth, which for him turn ultimately on religious considerations that have to do with submission, where submission itself is not understood in terms of a willed act or a choice, but rather as something that "seizes" the person, and which therefore suggests a form of surrender.[25] This is a thought familiar to many religious traditions, regarding how faith is understood. Faith is not chosen but is constitutive of believers. They give themselves up to it. To paraphrase Wittgenstein, we take hold of a picture (or a narrative) of which faith is a part, and hence we become believers. Faith does not frame the picture or hold the narrative together as something prevenient to it. It is simply one part of it.[26] In this sense it is closely linked with Gandhi's understanding of the social as a prevenient mesh of interconnections. This is what allows Gandhi to affirm different religions as being of equal sanctity, while always claiming to be a devout Hindu himself, and it also explained his opposition

<hr/>

[24] For a thoughtful account of Gandhi's religiosity see Akeel Bilgrami's "Gandhi's Religion and Its Relation to His Politics," in *The Cambridge Companion to Gandhi*, ed. Judith M. Brown and Anthony Parel (Cambridge: Cambridge University Press, 2011), 93–116.

[25] See Ajay Skaria, *Unconditional Equality* (Minneapolis: University of Minnesota Press, 1916), who has a nuanced discussion of seizure and Gandhi views on religion.

[26] Ludwig Wittgenstein, *Philosophical Investigations* (1953). New York: Macmillan.

to missionary attempts to change people's religion. Such conversions always required "uprooting" the believer from his or her inheritance, and thus conversions typically relied on some abstraction and mediation—that is some other dramatic narrative. This itself turned on the believer living vicariously, as though she or he living someone else's life. This was the appeal of modern civilization—a mode of existence and identity in which they were fluid constructions.

Gandhi, like Burke, was wary of anything that conceived of the given in reified and cavalier terms and which viewed its evacuation as merely a matter of altered doctrine or political ideology. For Gandhi religion is similar to one's family, one's social location, and even to one's caste. They make up the habitus that marks out the patterns of individual and social embodiment. Religion, with a special poignancy, constitutes the language through which a bounded horizon is navigated and made meaningful to individuals and communities. It limits choice, but also deepens its potential meaningfulness and application. Gandhi never identifies religion as the basis for forging a homogenous unity that could serve as a buttress to the nation or to any broad collective identity. He thinks of religion in terms of faith, which makes possible coexistence, without having to lean on shared identities that must almost of necessity be secured and invigilated by a third party. It is instead a diverse inheritance, the grammar and the minutia through which the pursuit of self-knowledge is carried out in the practice of everyday life. That practice, because it involves a deep and constant attunement to the question of who I am, places a high premium on patience. Its sternest vigilance is directed at everyday activities such as diet, sexual desires, material strivings, and abstracted forms of political expedience, where the underlying passions are likely to distract attention from the self, and where, moreover, there is a heightened possibility of a vicarious lure. As Gandhi says of the author of the Gita, "He has shown that religion must rule our worldly pursuits. I have felt that the Gita teaches us that what cannot be followed out in day-to-day practice cannot be called religious."[27]

Religion does not sanction the logic of history or of politics because they are typically inattentive to a deep and unhurried moral and psychological vigilance. The patience Gandhi urges insists on that vigilance even in the face of manifest moral violations and injustices that were common in the empire, but equally conspicuous to institutions such as the Hindu caste system. It mitigates the potential feelings of resentment, anger, humiliation—in a word, of alienation—that stem from having our hopes thwarted in the present. It restrains the urgency that underlies most forms of violence. It renders fluid the categorical nature and the structures that rely on distinctions such as friend and enemy, insider and outsider, and other compacted identities such as class, caste, race, or ethnicity, all of which ultimately require the mediating intervention of the state. It does not, as an immediate and insistent goal, pursue expressions of unity that typically orient so much political and collective action.

The concentration it does demand is always on the present and on the self, both of individuals and of collectivities. It operates in a register that is not drawn to the grandiosity of changing the world; or rather, it imagines such change as occurring from actions that are attuned to the question, "What am I doing to myself?" Indeed, Gandhi is perhaps singular, both as a leader and as a thinker, in the degree to which he is utterly indifferent to anything that even hints at grandiosity. Nothing that he ever advocated or lent his prestige to could be thought of in the nineteenth- and twentieth-century sense of the term "project," that is, the projection of a grand plan. In many ways his celebration of the village, as the preferred nexus of social and political life, was meant to thwart grand imperial and national projects.

In many ways Gandhi was drawn to mystical and transcendent yearnings. In his autobiography, as elsewhere, he offers a clear sense of them, and that too in terms that make it clear that all his public and political acts were of subsidiary value. He says, "What I want to achieve,—what I have been striving and pinning for these thirty years,—is self-realization, to see God face to face, to attain *Moksha*. I live and move and have my being in pursuit of this goal. All that I do by way of speaking and writing, and all my ventures in the political field, are directed at this same end."[28] But the appeal of transcendence for Gandhi was always tied to a quotidian rigor, to the insistent attention on the routines and minutiae of everyday life. His religiosity, whatever its ultimate purposes, was tied to a worldly engagement. It was this sort of engagement by his compatriots and by the English that he believed could radically recast the imperial connection.

[28] M. K. Gandhi, *Autobiography: The Story of My Experiments with Truth* (New York: Dover, 1983), viii.

5

Representative Democracy and Religious Thought in South Asia

Abul A'la Maududi and Vinayak Damodar Savarkar

Humeira Iqtidar

5.1. Introduction

The late nineteenth and early twentieth centuries saw increasing enthusiasm about mass democratic participation around the world. Two South Asian thinkers, both religious revivalists, articulated influential visions of what democracy would mean to political and social life in the region. Their followers imagine them as offering diametrically opposed aspirations to each other. Their critics see them to be purveying the same wares packaged in different colors: green for the Muslims, and saffron for the Hindus. However, a more detailed look at the political thought of Abul A'la Maududi (1903–1979) and Vinayak Damodar Savarkar (1883–1966) is immensely instructive in highlighting the differences in their engagement with the idea of the nation and representative democracy. I argue here that both participated in the widening enthusiasm for democratic representation. However, both of them were deeply concerned about the content and role of the demos. Savarkar's thought, I argue, shows a deeper imprint of European ideas of nationalism for popular representation. Maududi, on the other hand, articulated a trenchant critique of nationalism but shied away from engaging with the sociological reality of Muslims of India.

I want to start, however, by noting the strange partition that seems to have extended itself to scholarship on Hindu and Muslim revivalist thought. Scholars who work on one strand do not work on the other.[1] This chapter is an initial and preliminary step in addressing that divide. I focus here on a key work by each author: *Nationalism and India* by Maududi and *The Essentials of Hindutva* by Savarkar. Both were prolific writers, although of very different kinds of material. Savarkar's wrote political/historical texts as well as novels in Marathi that

---

[1] A notable exception is Devji, this volume. Of course, many have commented in general terms on both movements, or on the implications of religious revivalism generally.

Humeira Iqtidar, *Representative Democracy and Religious Thought in South Asia* In: *Negotiating Democracy and Religious Pluralism*. Edited by: Karen Barkey, Sudipta Kaviraj, and Vatsal Naresh, Oxford University Press. © Oxford University Press 2021. DOI: 10.1093/oso/9780197530016.003.0006

afforded his ideas extensive circulation, while Maududi too wrote for a wide audience but for a reading public looking for structured analyses in accessible Urdu.[2] My decision to focus on a key text each is in part driven by the value of presenting the arguments, logic, and flow of each text in some detail. I will, however, bring in insights from their wider corpus to build the argument. Grappling with parallel problems regarding the relationship between nation, representative democracy, and a territorial state, the two thinkers built different visions of that mythical entity "the people" to articulate their divergent visions for India. The wider religious tradition that each was working within also afforded them different conceptual opportunities and constraints.

Maududi and Savarkar are both seen as thinkers and activists who are responsible for pernicious versions of religious nationalism. Their ideas are associated with the persecution of religious minorities in India and Pakistan respectively. Neither of them anticipated the dramatic transformations that transpired in the decades following the writing of the texts discussed in this chapter. I point this out not to provide an apologia[3] but to take seriously the question of circulation of ideas and texts beyond the control and intention of authors. Both were writing from what they saw as embattled positions and against dominant discourses. Neither was part of the political or social elite, although they could lay claim to religiously significant lineage. And critically, both received condemnation and criticism from the majority of the religious scholars in their traditions because they articulated a modernist vision of religiosity as ideally homogenized, internally coherent, and rationalized, in terms of being both explained through logical connections and streamlined to conform to an "essence."[4] And to that extent one can argue that both contributed to a qualitative shift in mass political imagination that might be called a secularization in terms of redefining religion as a coherent, internally consistent entity rather than a way of life rife with contradictions. But more fundamentally for our purposes here, it is sobering to note their enthusiasm for democratic procedures. I start below with an outline of their life and ideas particularly pertaining to nationalism, followed by a preliminary comparison of their approaches.

[2] Savarkar had, in fact, written a more scholarly text on the 1857 rebellion a decade before he wrote *Essentials of Hindutva,* and so the comparison between the two texts selected here may not give a full sense of his oeuvre. For his 1857 volume, he worked in the British Library in London to produce a 500-page manuscript that wove together British sources with Marathi folklore and oral history (Bakhle, 2010a: 158, 169–172).

[3] In the context of Hindu nationalist texts Gyanendra Pandey (1998) has rightly argued that we need to pay attention to reasons other than logical coherence and empirical validity to understand their popular circulation.

[4] For readings of Maududi's thought in this manner see Adams 1966; Iqtidar 2011; for Savarkar see Raghuramaraju 2007.

5.2. Vinayak Damodar Savarkar

Vinayak Damodar Savarkar was born into an upper-caste, but by no means rich, Brahmin Marathi family in 1883. His older brother Ganesh, known also as Babarao, was an important influence and was entrenched in anti-colonial politics at the local level when Savarkar came of age. Following in his brother's footsteps, Savarkar organized a revolutionary group with his friends and called it Rashtrabhakta Samuha (roughly Society of Patriots). This later became Mitra Mela (Society of Friends). When he attended college, Savarkar continued his political activities and remained engaged when, in 1906, he went to London to study law. Here he became a member of the India House, a community of anti-colonial nationalist students in London. During these years he was rumored to have received arms training from Russian revolutionaries. He also published a tract titled *History of the War of Independence* that was banned by the British authorities. This book painted a positive picture of Hindu-Muslim unity during that war (Bakhle 2010a: 153, 169–171; Misra 1999: 176–177). In 1909, one of his associates assassinated Lord Curzon Wyllie in London. In addition, Savarkar was implicated in organizing protests against the Minto-Morley reforms of 1909. Arrested in 1910 and sentenced to the Andaman Islands,[5] which served as a penal colony for the British, Savarkar spent 10 years there before being allowed back to India.

Savarkar started his famous book, *Essentials of Hindutva,* in prison in 1921 and published it in 1923. This book forms an important pillar of Hindu nationalist thinking and has had a decisive impact on the course of Indian political history. From the mid-1930s, when Savarkar became politically active again, he often opposed both Gandhi, the leader of the nationalist Congress Party, and Mohammed Ali Jinnah, the leader of the Muslim separatist Muslim League. Moving to Delhi, Savarkar became increasingly active in Hindu cultural and political organizations. He was vehemently opposed to the partition of India and contested Muslim League's plans for greater role for Muslims in a federated India. Arguing that being a minority did not automatically endow special rights, Savarkar opposed any concessions at the political level. In 1948, after the assassination of Gandhi, Savarkar was arrested because Nathu Ram Godse, Gandhi's assassin, was a member of the Hindu Mahasabha, a group Savarkar had led. Savarkar was ultimately released after a trial. However, from then until his death in 1966, he remained a marginal figure in mainstream Indian politics. Nevertheless, this quiet period was a time of consolidation of cadres and development of networks at a local level in Bombay, where he lived, and in surrounding

---

[5] Savarkar's attempted escape from British authorities in Marseilles, reported in *The Times* (London), contributed to his legendary status for many. See Bakhle 2010b for details.

areas. The influence of his book is in part a result of the long-term, below-the-radar mobilization that he and other members of the Mahasabha continued for decades. However, that alone is not the reason for its longevity and influence. We have to also recognize its resonance in the nation-making project that was undertaken by Indian governments of different stripes.

Savarkar's *Hindutva* is an unusual text in many ways. Written in English—whereas up to then he had written primarily in Marathi (the author in the first printing of *Hindutva* is named as just "a Maratha")—the book covers several centuries while retaining a sharp focus on the question of who can be called a Hindu. Bakhle (2010a) has rightly called for a closer look at the structure, rhetoric, and poetics of the book to move beyond the politics of denunciation and apologia. Savarkar starts by asking the rhetorical question: what is in a name? Referring to Shakespeare's play *Romeo and Juliet*, he starts by contrasting his approach to a name—Hindu—with that of the "fair maid of Verona" (2). To him names represent "the soul of a man," as well as "an idea that may live for centuries" (2). Hindutva "is not a word but a history" that transcends the idea of an individual Hindu (3). Hinduism, he says, is just "a derivative, a part, a fraction of Hindutva" (3). It is on elaborating how we can understand Hindutva that Savarkar focuses the whole book.

In the following chapters he starts from the earliest signs of civilization in the region to claim that it was in association with the river Sindh (Indus) that the term "Sindhu," and later "Hindu," arose. The prominence of Buddhism in the region in the following centuries presents a problem to him because Savarkar veers between wanting to claim Buddhism as a variant of Hinduism and wanting to disassociate his vision of Hindutva from the other countries in Southeast Asia that Buddhism traveled to.[6] Hindutva, to him, is very much tied to Indian territory, and Savarkar builds a detailed vision of war and "manly" violence that distances Hindus from Buddhists. This was a deeply political move, as Savarkar was concerned to negate the valorization of nonviolence that Gandhi's movement had built by the 1920s. He disagreed deeply with Gandhi's use of nonviolence and saw himself as providing an alternative to the vision of the effeminate, nonviolent Hindu that the British had built up and that Gandhi was, Savarkar thought, perhaps naively, validating (Chaturvedi 2010; Bakhle 2010a).

This vision of a military and masculine Hindu was also vital for Savarkar because of his reading of the Muslim presence in India. For him, it was with the

---

[6] It is perhaps because of this ambivalence that he argues that the Indians hear of the Buddhist Mauryan dynasty's greatness only because European orientalists have found records of that dynasty. There were, he says, other greater kings and polities (18–19) that have not received as much attention. Thus, "We do not think that the political virility and manly nobility of our race began and ended with the Mauryas alone or with their embrace of Buddhism" (19).

Arab invasion that India had to contend, not just with the Arabs but with all of Asia (38). He claimed:

> The Arabs had entered Sindh but singlehandedly they could do little else. They soon failed to defend their own independence in their own homeland and as a people we hear nothing further about them. But here India alone had to face Arabs, Persians, Pathans, Baluchis, Tartars, Turks, Moguls—a veritable human Sahara whirling and columns coming up bodily in a furious world storm. (38)

The ferocious and rapacious nature of this invasion, he argues, created the first sense of a separate identity of the Hindu people. Skipping ahead a few centuries, he argues that it was in the war against the Mughal emperor Aurangzeb that "the Hindus lost the battle but won the war. Never again would an Afghan dare to penetrate Delhi" (39). He does not clarify what that war might be, but implicitly he suggests that Hindus were successful in developing a profound identity as a group in fighting against Aurangzeb.[7] Subsuming Sikhs into the fold of Hinduism, he proclaims that "our Sikh brothers" carried the battle across the Indus all the way to Kabul. Quoting from a range of sources, from folk songs to Bajirao's (eighteenth-century Maratha general) and Nana Saheb's (nineteenth-century Maratha leader of 1857 rebellion in Kanpur) letters, Savarkar then builds a detailed picture of the composite group Moghul/Muslim and its oppression that was valiantly fought by Hindus of various ethnic groups.

This, however, leads him to reflect on the debate around him at the time about the term "Hindu." He claims that while the term may not have been mentioned in the Vedas, as many had pointed out, it is an apt name for a citizen of India. Who might that citizen be? He argues that an American can very well become a Hindu if, along with the country, he has adopted "our culture and our history, inherited our blood, and has come to look upon our land not only as the land of his love, but even of his worship" (73). It is in this, declaring India the "land of his worship," that the barb against Muslims, Christians, and Jews is hidden. They who might have holy lands elsewhere cannot lay full claim to being Hindu and hence to being Indian. Having started from a relatively capacious vision of the Hindu as one who lives in the land of the Sindh, Savarkar moved to progressively narrower conceptions in later chapters. He argues in Chapter 5 that no people can claim to

---

[7] This might have particular resonance for the regions where Savarkar's family came from, as Marathas had been particularly active against the Mughal Empire during Aurangzeb's rule (Misra 1999: 145–146). Nandy (2014: 96) suggests that Savarkar's family belonged to a caste that was "one of the Brahmin communities to have tasted real political power in the declining years of the Mughal empire," and points out that "Chitpavans were [also] highly successful in the professions under the Raj but seemed to resent their loss of power."

be recognized as a racial unit as much as the Hindus and "perhaps the Jews" (79). A Hindu marrying outside his caste may lose his caste but not his "Hinduness."

This, however, to Savarkar, is not an outright rejection of Indian Muslims. If they are able to switch their allegiance from other holy lands to India, it is clear that they already have Hindu blood in their veins. As Devji (this volume) has noted, there is an intimate connection between Hindu and Muslim in Savarkar's thought. When Savarkar wants to define Hindus as a race, he comes up against the reality of Muslim converts.[8] In the end, it seems a Mohammedan or a Christian Indian contains all the essentials of Hindutva but one. The definitive element they lack is the recognition that "they do not look upon India their as their Holy land" (101). But quickly he distances himself from presenting this only as religious dogma. Savarkar, not a particularly practicing and believing Hindu, insists instead,

> We honestly believe that the Hindu thought—we are not talking of any religion that is dogma—has exhausted the possibilities of human speculation as to the nature of the divine. . . . Are you a monist? a monotheist—a pantheist—an atheist—an agnostic? Here is ample room oh soul! (101)

This expansive move, in fact, places a particular version of Hinduism at the apex of all religious creeds, since all can be subsumed within it.[9]

But why the insistence on the religious and national homeland being the same? Perhaps his insistence on the one difference Muslims could not surmount, not just theologically but also in terms of their history and imagination, is a perverse compliment. Savarkar thought Hindus should be like his reified notion of Muslims: unafraid to wield the sword to spread their ideas (Sharma 2003: 158–159). But to mobilize Hindus to be like Muslims, Muslims had to be both the model and the enemy. By laying out all the qualities that Muslims putatively had and that Hindus should emulate—violent masculinity, virility, cohesion—Savarkar strove to define clearly an attribute Muslims could never acquire in their claim to India.

More importantly, however, Savarkar was parsing out the exact contours of the nation, territory, and self-rule, having imbibed ideas about the spiritual affinity with one's homeland from Giuseppe Mazzini work. Savarkar was deeply influenced by the ideas of Mazzini,[10] and referred to him often as a great

---

[8] The "millions" who were forcibly converted by Muslim rulers remain Hindu, he says (79). Many among them, he points out, have retained many of the same customs, including caste divisions (80), and recent converts like Bohras and Khojas continue to submit to Hindu laws (89).

[9] On the lack of tolerance built into this seemingly tolerant conception of Hinduism and Ambedkara's critique of it, see Kumar 2018.

[10] On the influence of Mazzini on democratic nationalist thought around the world see Bayly and Biagini 2008. See Bayly 2012 for his influence in India.

philosopher. In 1906 he compiled a 300-page collection of Mazzini's writings translated into Marathi and titled *Mazzini Charitra*. In addition to his experience of living in England, where he came across debates about Irish nationalism, Savarkar claimed that in prison he read in detail the works of Herbert Spencer, Johann Kaspar Bluntschli, and Giuseppe Mazzini to learn about the nature of the state and society (Chaturvedi 2010: 422). It is interesting to note that this is where he also studied religious texts in some detail. The religious texts that he read during this period include the Upanishads, the Rig Veda, Ramayana, Mahabharata, Brahma Sutras, Sankhya texts, Yoga Vashishta, and *Imitation of Christ*. What seems to have been particularly compelling for Savarkar is the almost mystical and spiritual relationship with the country that Mazzini advocated. This spiritual, ancestral, and increasingly religious connection between the nation and the territory is a theme that Savarkar developed in *Hindutva* but also in many other writings (Sharma 2003: 181–184).

This is where the mark of European thought is particularly pronounced in Savarkar's ideas. While Mazzini's democratic nationalism was indeed more complex than Savarkar's reading of it, it is important to recognize the deep imbrication of the ideas of homogenization and the nation with representative democracy in European thought. The origins of nationalism in Europe, seen in colonial times as a mark of European advancement and civilization, can, once we take away the colonial hubris attached to being "first" in this regard, be interrogated more critically. In recent decades political theorists have started paying more attention to the various ways in which homogenization has played an important role in European political thought (Tully 1995). Certainly, there was little acknowledgment of or concern with racially diverse positions and visions (Mills 2008; Buck-Morss 2000). The very invisibility of race in European political theory despite its continued importance in political and social life speaks of its naturalization. Similarly, religious difference was for several centuries a problem to be solved, or at best tolerated, rather than celebrated, leading to specific ways in it could be accommodated within a liberal polity. Lockean toleration assumed homogeneity to be the ideal, from which limited and minor forms of deviance could be allowed (Waldron 1998). Indeed, so specific are the forms of accommodation that, once we move beyond the European Protestant vision of religion, liberal values of equality and freedom of conscience often end up in a contradictory relationship with each other rather than a complimentary one (Spinner-Halev 2005).

Nationalist thought in Europe, particularly in the nineteenth century, relied on, and further deepened, an appreciation of cultural and "spiritual" homogeneity to underpin popular sovereignty and democratic rule. As many have noted, liberalism and nationalism developed together, and the relationship between the two was strengthened during the nineteenth century as "romantic ideas of national identity and solidarity [combined with] liberal ideas of political liberty, individual freedom and constitutional government" (Kelly 2015: 338). John Stuart Mill, the influential nineteenth-century British liberal thinker who serves as an inspiration for many contemporary liberal nationalist theorists, saw national belonging as an essential ingredient of representative government, famously arguing that members of a nationality are likely to be "united among themselves by common sympathies which . . . make them co-operate with each other more willingly than with other people, desire to be under the same government, and desire it should be government by themselves or a portion of themselves exclusively" (Mill 1861: 181).

Mill (1861: 182) also endorsed the notion of a hierarchy of nations when he suggested that "inferior and backward" nations such as the Basques in France, and the Welsh in Britain, would benefit from being assimilated into the nation of more "civilized and highly cultured people." In a nuanced analysis Varouxakis (2002: 23–37, 17–21, 39–50, 60–67) has pointed out that Mill's ideas were more complex than portrayed by some critics, and that while Mill shared ideas about difference, and hierarchy, of nations with some contemporaries, he also differed with them over linking biological determinism or race with the nation. Mill was in a sense going against the mainstream. This qualification highlights the complexity of Mill's ideas, but also paradoxically, the dominance of racial nationalism, in both political practice and thinking during Mill's time. Indeed, before, during, and after Mill's time, his native Britain's national belonging was defined very much by its racial, religious, and cultural others (Colley 1992; van der Veer 2001).

The conceptual dominance of nationality for democratic representation compelled many colonized people to make their claims for equality and liberty with the same vocabulary. Mill's ideas about nationality and representative government influenced the Italian nationalist leader Giuseppe Mazzini, who was instrumental in popularizing "democratic nationalism" in the colonized Global South (Bayly and Biagini 2008). Most late nineteenth- and early twentieth-century anti-colonial movements responded to this conflation of nation with democratic self-representation by claiming to be nations that preceded colonial and imperial domination. It was as pre-existing nations or peoples that they demanded independence, equality, and freedom. Similarly, oppressed racial minorities within liberal democracies thought that if they could establish their claims as a nation, they could proclaim greater self-determination. For instance, African American nationalists of the early twentieth century argued there was little reasonable hope of equality under the existing institutional arrangements and demanded secession as "an oppressed nation" (Valls 2010: 469–470). By the twentieth century the idea of a nation conflated with sovereign people, and a state, was such that the nation-state had been naturalized in mainstream liberal thought. Savarkar seems to have internalized the idea that some people will have greater claim to representation within a territory because of their deeper attachment to it.

5.3. Abul A'la Maududi

Abul A'la Maududi is one of the most influential Islamic and Islamist thinkers of the twentieth century, as well as one of the most systematic South Asian thinkers of the century.[11] Maududi became politically engaged when he was in his late teens early in the 1920s. Born in 1903, he was a scion of a family of scholars and intellectuals who had been associated with the Mughal and other princely courts and had fallen to hard times under British rule. Some of his forefathers also held positions of leadership in Sufi networks. By his own accounts, which are somewhat lacking in modesty, he was a gifted and enthusiastic student, and was partly educated at home (Maududi 1971). He also studied with a few well-known ulema. However, the early death of his father interrupted his pursuit of formal education, and at the age of 17 Maududi started working as an editor of an Urdu journal, *Taj*. He continued to educate himself in the languages of the urban, middle- and upper-middle-class, North Indian Muslim of the period: Persian, Arabic, and Urdu. He also learned some English and, in addition to the works of several English historians and philosophers, also read translations of French and German philosophical works. In 1921 he moved to Delhi to become the editor of another newspaper, *Muslim*, and in 1925 he moved to *Al-Jami'yaat*, both affiliated with the Jami'yat Ulema-i-Hind (JUH).

Having initially identified as an Indian nationalist, Maududi began to see the anti-colonial struggle as distinct from nationalism by the late 1920s. He articulated a deep criticism of nationalism, perhaps initially inspired by his own position as a minority, and later strengthened through his critical engagement with the philosophical underpinnings of European nationalism. His concern about Muslims becoming a permanent minority in democratic India was linked very closely to the larger structural changes that had been put into place by the colonial state and that facilitated increasing political and social association with one or the other religious identity (Jalal 1985; Iqtidar 2011: 40–50; Mufti 1995; Gilmartin 1991, 1998). In 1941 Maududi set up the Jama'at-e-Islami with a group of Islamic scholars and activists. The vast majority of these founding members were journalists, school and college teachers, and middle-ranking civil servants. Maududi had opposed the creation of Pakistan precisely because of his opposition to nationalism, but after partition moved there, banking on greater likelihood of success in setting up an Islamic state in a Muslim-majority state. Until

---

[11] For introductions to Maududi's life and work, see Nasr 1996 and Hartung 2013.

his death in 1979, Maududi faced an uphill battle convincing the electorate that he and his party could provide the leadership the country needed. However, soon after his death his party was catapulted to a position of power by the US-supported military dictator General Zia ul-Haque, who relied on Islamization to provide legitimacy to his rule.

In *Nationalism and India*, containing essays written through the late 1930s and published in 1941, Maududi starts by stating his claim in unambiguous terms: "The most important philosophy of life that is today governing not only India, but the entire world is the philosophy of nationalism. The unfortunate passion of nations has made the life of man miserable on this planet" (5). He is most concerned with Muslims who find this to be a persuasive philosophy, and outlines the three arguments that are most commonly made by those supporting nationalism:

1. This is the philosophy of the conquerors of the time, the Europeans, and thus "we must submit to it" (5).
2. In the past "our country" enjoyed an enviable reputation, and we have had a glorious past, but can only recover past glories through copying what Europe has done today (5).
3. In the past, Muslims and Hindus were separate civilizations based on different religions, but today another civilization has imposed itself on them, and this civilization is "divorced from religion." Its foundations rest on "pure science and empirical philosophy"; unless we conform to this new way of thinking, we cannot survive (6).

Maududi goes on to dismiss these arguments as being based on pragmatism and opportunism rather than fundamental principles or moral grounds, suggesting that followers of nationalism are picking up an idea that may have a market at the moment, but which is not based on "scientific analysis and . . . moral judgement" (6).[12] He exhorts Muslims to display at least as much steadfastness as the anti-nationalist Marxists during World War I, when many of them refused to side with their national governments (7–8). Moreover, he claims, many Muslims don't even recognize the reasons and implications of their support for nationalism, "Because to shift ones [sic] position for nothing is sheer weakness, but having shifted to think that one still occupies one's old position carries with it both weakness and stupidity" (8). If one is a Muslim, then everything has to be viewed from the perspective of Islam.

[12] For Maududi the question of moral judgment is central. In a different text Maududi (1938: 28) argued that to oppose the British just because they came from a foreign land does not make sense. Opposition to the British, he argued, had to be based on principle, either of equality or justice, not on nationalism.

Islam and nationalism are, to Maududi, entirely contradictory. "Islam," he says, "deals with man as man" (10). All of humanity is invited to join Islam on the basis of justice and equality, and there can be no distinction on the basis of race or nation. Nationalism, on the other hand, he claims, tends toward imperialism because all those who are not members of the nation in a state cannot be considered equals (10–11). Expanding upon what he calls the "European" conception of nationalism, Maududi starts by stating that Aristotle endorsed slavery for barbarians and declared all non-Greeks to be barbarians. This form of othering, Maududi claims, forms the "germinal constitution" of nationalism in Europe (12). This renunciation of Aristotle is an unusual move given the deep engagement with Aristotle within Islamic thought. Maududi is back on more solid ground within the wider Islamic tradition of recognizing previous Abrahamic faiths as iterations of the same truth, when Maududi argues that the teachings of Christ acted as a bulwark against the steady development of this nationalism in Europe for many centuries, but when the tyrannies of the pope and state as well as their mutual rivalries expanded, the religious and political transformation of the Reformation took place. Noting with approval the turn toward equality that the Reformation promised, Maududi laments that unfortunately this promise was unrealized. Ancient prejudices were buttressed by economic and political interests defined in national terms, and the languages and literatures of people were harnessed to form these groupings (13–14). Referring to European and American research,[13] Maududi asserts that European nationalism developed in essentially competitive terms, pitting nations against each other.

Claiming that the sharia, that is, the principles to guide an Islamic life, is in direct contradiction with nationalism, Maududi argues that while the sharia is oriented toward openness toward all, nationalism promotes a closed mind that does not allow a nationalist to appreciate anything of value in others. The most dramatic example of this is, he claims, the National Socialist movement of Germany. To demonstrate the dangers of nationalism, Maududi argues that Hitler's theory of world domination is based on his vision of the Aryan nation's inherent superiority (24), but versions of this view are easily found in democratic America with regard to "the negro" and every nation of Europe, be it France, Britain, or Holland (24). Such competitiveness anchored only in the idea of a community with some humans, he argued, makes man unprincipled. The key example of such behavior is Mussolini, Maududi suggests, as somebody who made opportunistic moves across the ideological spectrum and explained it in nationalist terms: "In 1919 he

---

[13] For instance, the text refers to Francis W. Corker's notion of imperial nationalism (16–17), to Ernest Haeckel as proposing a kind of racial cannibalism (18), and Karl Pearson's vision of human history as essentially a contest not just between individuals but also between races (18). For the discussion on pages 18–24 Maududi seems to have relied heavily on the book *Social Philosophies in Conflict*, by the American sociologist Joseph Leighton, published in New York in 1937.

was a liberal socialist, in 1920 he became an anarchist, and in 1921 he opposed both socialists and democrats" (25).

For Maududi, this is the most fundamental incompatibility between nationalism and sharia: there is no overarching morality that can contain national competitiveness. Allah's prophets may have been sent in particular times to specific peoples, but, Maududi contends, their message has always been for all of humanity. Nationalists are unable to recognize that. Their distaste for what did not originate in their own nation makes them disregard the universality of those messages (25–30). An example of the absurdity of this position, for Maududi, is the division among the German National Socialists on the question of the origins of Jesus. Some claim that if Jesus was a Jew, then the Aryan people cannot support the moral and political values he promoted, while others claim that Jesus was not a Semite, ignoring historical reality. Ultimately, then, Maududi worries, nationalism becomes a religion, as in the case of the Nazis: "God is the name of that force and life which has incarnated itself into the German nation, and the German nation is the earthly incarnation of this God. Hitler is the prophet and 'national goals' are the religion brought by this prophet" (29).

Given these fundamental problems with nationalism, Maududi asks, why is it that human beings worldwide seem enthralled by this new religion? His answer is that they do not know any other comprehensive moral and political framework of teachings that "may regulate individual and social wants, keep within legal limits desires and ambitions, give right direction to the powers of action" (34). This is where, in his view, Islam and Muslims can play a pivotal role in providing a critical analysis and, an alternative to the world. That many Muslims themselves are falling prey to nationalism is the most grievous tragedy. Here he distinguishes between two types of nationalities. The first is what he calls "political nationality," under which different nations live within a political entity, participate in it, and continue their differences, debates, and contestations with each other (36). The other is "cultural nationality," where homogeneity of religious identity, thought, and sentiments; kinship and marriage relations; and habits and practices are found. This is the type that nationalism has its roots in and develops a kind of " 'national self,' where the self is soon lost" (37–38). The situation in India is definitely not right for cultural nationality, although political nationality, he thinks, might work in India. He argues that, given the distinctions between Muslims and Hindus in India, it would be perverse to imagine a cultural nationality taking root there any time soon, especially when one considers that it took centuries to bring together the Normans, Saxons, and Britons in England to make a nation (43). In conclusion, he advises well-wishers of India to support a federated system post-independence from the British, rather than a nation-state, for the following reasons (46–47):

1. It would be a long and cumbersome journey to freedom if the development of nationalist sentiment and support is seen as a prerequisite for independence, particularly since it would involve subduing different nations within India to form an Indian nation.
2. Even if Indian independence is gained in this way, it would lead to moral degeneration.
3. The internal contention this attempt at creating an Indian nation would give rise to is bound to delay the formation of a united front against the British. This may even lead to the dream of independence never being realized.

In the federated entity he imagined,

> The permanent status and individuality of every nation would be recognised, every one of them would be allowed autonomous and sovereign control over its "subjects," and the different nations should agree upon a joint action in so far as the common interests of the country are concerned. (48)

This vision of a plural state is close to the Ottoman millet system that he had elsewhere argued was a good way of organizing plural societies.[14] Maududi's critique of nationalism was written as a sequel to a series of articles, which he claimed he had written to warn the Muslims of India about the hazards of the situation they faced. He thought that Muslims were sleepwalking into a situation where they would get rid of British colonialism only to fall under the yoke of Hindu majoritarianism, and that would mean the end of a distinctive Islamic way of life. Thus, he argued at the end of that series (1999 [1938]: 78) that for some, freedom as an Indian was most important, but for him it was unthinkable that a "true" Muslim would willingly participate in such a campaign.

For Maududi, then, the problems with nationalism are linked closely to his concerns about the lack of an ethical framework grounding popular sovereignty. Bringing together democratic theory with Islamic thought, Maududi argued for democratic representation, but against popular sovereignty. He distinguished between democratic procedures allowing efficient expression of human rational faculties for making decisions about governance, and popular sovereignty as an idea that legitimated all laws made through democratic

---

[14] The Ottoman Empire, like other empires, provided a more capacious engagement with diversity than the nation-state. Barkey (2010: 92) argues that "the Ottoman solution to the challenges of religious heterogeneity in an overwhelmingly Muslim society was both an early domination of religion by the state, and a capacious administration of diversity that broadly relied on an understanding of difference without the compulsion to transform difference into sameness." However, this was a system that was not based on the idea of equal citizenship.

procedures. The underlying philosophical thrust of popular sovereignty, he worried, untethered human choices from a moral framework. He argued that once humans assume they can make all laws, even if only in a collective capacity, it becomes hard to limit the oppression that humans can inflict on others. He argued that due to epistemological and cognitive limits, human law-making is always deficient. But more critically, it is easy to become unmoored from ethical considerations when humans believe that they alone have the capacity to make all laws. The coming together of nationalism with popular sovereignty was particularly dangerous. He argued that it is important to ac-knowledge a clear, overarching moral framework that will place some limits on human will and thus oppression (Iqtidar 2020).

The framework will, as sharia has been historically, be open to interpreta-tion, but some broad limits will become hard to transgress. Maududi reworked long-held ideas within Islamic thought about Allah as the owner and lawgiver for the universe to make an argument for Allah's *political* sovereignty (Zaman 2015). This was a novel interpretation of Allah's authority as law giver. Framing it in this way, he thought, would force certain limits on the oppression that humans have inflicted on others. This reworking was not easy; it required Maududi to radically reconceptualize sharia as state laws, when historically sharia had been primarily self-imposed, and *din* as religion, a homogenized, streamlined, and logical set of rules that could be used to guide decision-making in a modern state (Iqtidar 2020). This innovation created a set of new problems for Maududi, particularly regarding the sociological reality of Muslim life. Clearly, the vast majority of Muslims and states led by Muslims were not Islamic by Maududi's definition.

Maududi's critique extended to a questioning of the idea of fundamental rights that were not grounded in lived ethical tradition. He thought that ulti-mately liberal rights made the minority entirely dependent upon the goodwill of the majority. These are important concerns that have resurfaced in recent years in different parts of the world, from the United States to India. Maududi's concerns raise questions that remain inadequately addressed by contemporary liberal nationalist theories. Contemporary liberal nationalist theorists such as David Miller (1995, 2000) and Yael Tamir (1993) support nationality as a mechanism for deepening liberal democracy. The emphasize a vision of na-tionality structured around political values such as equality, something akin to Maududi's conception of political nationality, but do not engage with the reality of existing nationalisms in the contexts they write about. In making this claim they assume that matters of inequality and oppression within the nation are addressed if nationality is constructed through public debate along liberal principles (Miller 1995: 120–135, 181–190). Such a vision glosses over the historical reality that appreciation of diversity and greater political role for minorities is a contingent, recent, and fragile development within Euro-American liberal democracies.

Religious, ethnic, and cultural homogeneity formed the norm in these states through much of the twentieth century. Minority rights were being advocated in colonized states at the same time but primarily as a means of entrenching colonial rule (Mahmood 2012). At best only 60 years separate us from lynching of African Americans, even fewer from British race riots and deep, everyday exclusion (Gilroy 1987). Racialized visions of the nation baked into the United Nations charter (Mazower 2009) and imperialism institutionalized in the Security Council remain challenges to be surmounted. Racist nationalism continues to inform Euro-American politics today. At the level of both ideas and political practice, the inclusion of racial and religious others within European nation-states requires a fundamental reimaging of their very origins (Asad 2002), and that has not even started in earnest yet. Post-racial states in Europe require difficult political and conceptual work before one can assume that liberal nationalism will not end up deepening racism. Liberal nationalist theorists have not yet undertaken that reimagining or conceptual labor.

African American rights movements, anti-colonial mobilizations in the Third World, and minority rights activists found a more favorable political climate during the Cold War than at any time before, as the two superpowers competed to prove their credentials as empires of liberation. Whatever successes these movements accrued cannot be attributed in any straightforward manner to a teleological playing out of liberal ideas. As David Scott (2003: 109) has reminded us, the battle of ideas against communist Soviet Union provided the context in which cultural diversity emerged as a central differentiating value for liberal democracies. The claims regarding diversity that these polities could make prior to World War II were decidedly fragile. The ideological and political pressures of this competition allowed greater space for some consideration of the claims of Jewish, Indigenous, and later Muslim citizens, as well as immigrants from other parts of the world. This brought a particular crisis to twentieth-century liberalism that theories of multiculturalism have sought to address.

5.4. Religious Revivalism and Representative Democracy

As is immediately apparent, Maududi and Savarkar are making very different kinds of arguments in relation to nationalism even though both also took positions against British rule. Savarkar is enthusiastic about the idea of defining a national identity for India, and using its Vedic resources to provide the source material for defining that nation and the demos. Maududi on the other hand is deeply antagonistic toward such a nationalist project, yet unwilling to evaluate the exclusivity of his anxieties about Muslims alone. His concerns about nationalism include a critique of the thrust toward homogenization and internal imperialism. Writing early in 1940, Maududi had more opportunity to witness the pressures placed by demands of nationalism not just in India but also in Europe. However, he had been developing a critique of nationalism since the early 1920s in various other writings.[15] Despite these differences, both Savarkar and Maududi are responding to, and taking for granted, a structural imperative within democratic politics: the importance of constituting a majority.

The early and middle twentieth century was a period of rapid contagion of the idea of democratic politics to populations hitherto left out of democratic participation: women in the UK, indigenous peoples and African Americans in the United States, peasants in India, and laborers in Russia. In India debates during the period skated between the concepts of democratic participation, nation, and state. For many Indians nationhood was one of the preconditions to democratic representation. For others democratic entitlement was separate from their claim to nationhood. There can be little doubt, though, that the enthusiasm for the nation was closely bound up with dreams of independence. The possibilities opened up by considering various permutations of emphases between democracy, nation, and state—democratic and independent nation-state, nation but within a federation, democratic state but within the framework of the empire,[16] and so on—caught the imagination of different activists and thinkers across Asia and Africa, and Indian political thinkers too were part of this cosmopolitan conversation.

This was, of course, a particular type of cosmopolitanism: one that was partly structured and sustained by imperial connections (Bose and Manjapra 2010) and aided significantly by the very indeterminacy of the future. Both Savarkar and Maududi had a range of intellectual and political resources available to them. Savarkar had engaged with Russian and French radicals, and imprisonment brought him in contact with a range of Indians. Through his wide reading and involvement with the nationalist JUH, Maududi had access to a deep repertoire of Islamic philosophy and history. He also engaged with nationalist as well as communist activists and developed a clear appreciation for the Leninist party model (Iqtidar 2011: 66).

The global enthusiasm for democratic representation—with or without a nation-state, within or outside of the empire—opened up new ways of

---

[15] He had started associating nationalism with imperialism, and a way of artificially dividing humans, quite early. See, for instance, Maududi 2007 [1930]: 127–129.

[16] Jalal (1985) makes the argument that Mohammed Ali Jinnah, the leader of the Muslim League, which led the demand for Pakistan, was essentially bargaining for a constitutional role for Muslims within a federal Indian state. See also Cooper and Burbank (2010: 7, 369–374) on twentieth-century demands for equal citizenship within empires more generally.

imaging and defining "the people." Some new distinctions had to be made. How, for instance, to distinguish "the people," those worthy of democratic rights, from "the masses," who tended to be irrational and emotional?[17] This question was linked to older concerns about the quality of "the people." In British liberal thought this question took the form of trying to calibrate when an electorate was ready to take on the responsibility of democracy (Mehta 1999). Literacy, gender, race, and cultural norms all played a role in attaining the status of the mythical "people" who were the objects and agents of democracy. In modern Islamic thought these questions became linked with the debate about rule by good men versus rule by laws (Iqtidar 2017: 801–802). In liberal Indian thought of the time, there was a strong tendency toward the privileging of elite tutelage to harness the power of the people—trust in the people came very hesitantly toward the 1930s and remained open to question even after the granting of universal franchise in 1948 (Bayly 2012: 308–309).[18]

One element of this distrust was clearly a concern about letting illiterate, ill-informed masses make poor judgments and electoral choices. A related element of concern was about the utilitarian and quantitative terms in which democracy was imagined. This concern about the democratic impulse toward quantification was expressed by Iqbal, the poet-philosopher, when he wrote in a much-quoted couplet:

> *Iss raz ko ik mard-e farangi nay kiya fāsh*
> *harchand ki dānā issay khola nahin kartay*
> *jamhūriyat ik tarz e hakumat hai kay jiss main*
> *bandon ko ginā kartay hain tolā nāhīn kartay.*
> This secret was revealed by an Englishman
> although the wise know not to reveal it
> Democracy is a form of government in which
> people are counted, not weighed for their quality.

---

[17] For an overview of some of these debates in European social and political theory see Bellamy 2003. He has made a persuasive argument for paying attention to the place of "masses" in theorizing about democracy in early to mid-twentieth-century Europe, and points toward a subtle but important transformation: "The rethinking of democracy that culminated in Weber essentially reversed the priorities of classical democratic theory, turning the democratic process from a means whereby the ruled controlled their rulers into a mechanism for legitimating and improving the quality of control exercised by rulers over the ruled" (100).

[18] Some have argued that perhaps the very malleability of an illiterate and caste-bound people was seen by the politicians of the late 1940s as ideal for perpetuating Congress rule in India and hence became the reason why they advocated universal franchise as soon as India became independent (Jafferelot, *La democratie en Inde: Religion, caste, et politique* [Paris, 1998] as referred to in Bayly 2012: 308).

While democracy, its value and contours, could be interpreted and practiced in a wide range of ways, the expanded reach of the modern state was forcefully experienced by Indians from the late nineteenth and early twentieth centuries (Kaviraj 2005). Who will control the state was part of the problem democracy was meant to solve. It is evident from Savarkar's text that he recognizes that he is calling into being a people who do not yet recognize themselves as a people. Savarkar thought that a democratic majority beyond the amorphous category "the Indian people" needed to be defined. Of course, many leading political figures of the time were committed to sustaining the idea of the Indian people as *the* majority they spoke for, and in whose name they articulated a nationalist vision. Savarkar's desire to create a nation united in religion came up against the sociological reality of diversity of belief and practice within India. He resolved that problem by demanding an indigenization of holy lands from Muslims, Christians, and Jews. With this move, Savarkar betrayed his reliance on a particular reading of the English experience where a foreign religion (Catholicism) was indigenized to produce a local version (the Anglican Church), but more critically the influence of European romantic nationalism more generally.

Savarkar pointed out that though many Japanese and Chinese practiced a religion that had originated in India (Buddhism), they could not be considered Hindu because they did not live in India. For Savarkar, then, the nation was tied inextricably to territory, and those who had first claim were those for whom this was their holy land. One might ask, first claim for what? Here Savarkar doesn't provide any clear answers. One important implication, suggested but not spelled out by him, is those who could make laws had to be those who took the territory to be their holy land as well. Universal suffrage or mass electoral democracy was not an immediate possibility in India at the time, but it was an important element of the future being imagined by all political parties. Savarkar had seen during his stay in England, through the debates on Irish home rule, the importance of preparing majority opinion. The *Essentials of Hindutva* can be seen to lay out the initial requirements for who will form a majority in democratic India. Certainly for Savarkar the importance of differentiating between Hindus and Muslims did not have religious and spiritual benefits. As Nandy (2014: 103) points out, "Savarkar's hatred for Muslims came not from ideas of ritual purity and impurity or caste hierarchy but from his prognosis of communities that could or could not be integrated—assimilated or dissolved—within the framework of a modern Indian state."

Without referring to Savarkar, and using instead the example of the German National Socialists' debate about the origin of Jesus, Maududi argued against the requirements for cultural/religious nationalism on the grounds of its futility as well as its danger in promoting homogenization. Yet Maududi too wants to call a people into being: the diverse, internally divided Muslims of India who did not recognize what they would lose through their enthusiasm for Indian nationalism. For Maududi, moreover, by the 1940s the implications of being what was being called a permanent minority within a democratic India were becoming dramatic.[19] The indeterminacy of the 1920s, when Savarkar wrote *Essentials of Hindutva*, had given way to a clearer recognition that the initial critical dividing line within independent India's democratic politics was to be across Hindu/ Muslim lines, rather than class or caste. Adcock (2014) and Tejani (2008) have both discussed the implications of the Congress Party's version of secular nationalism in India, which required untouchables to be Hindu, and Muslims, thus, to be a minority. Without including Dalits in the category Hindu, the Hindu majority could not be brought into existence. While caste Hindus had long treated Dalits as outside the religious order, modern electoral compulsions, coupled with new imaginaries of quantifiable communities,[20] led to a push to count them as Hindu rather than as a different religious grouping altogether. In this the Congress had moved closer to the views of groups like Arya Samaj and individuals like Savarkar than it cared to acknowledge.

Critically, both thinkers were not arguing against democratic politics if by that we mean electoral politics. Savarkar's attempt at creating a unified nation of Hindus makes sense only if we recognize that he relied upon electoral politics to deliver his vision of Hindus ruling Hind. In contrast, Gandhi, whom Savarkar was accused of conspiring to kill and whom Savarkar saw as his main political competitor, kept moving out of the logic of democratic politics. Gandhi also did not apportion the same rights to the state in the management of minority relations that democrats were likely to, as Mehta (this volume) has suggested.

Maududi too had a political competitor he thought was leading Muslims astray: Mohammed Ali Jinnah. Muslim nationalism founding a secular Muslim state, the aim of Jinnah's party, was anathema to Maududi. It divided the Muslims of India on the basis of a fallacious notion that control of territory and religious identity went together. To Maududi the project of making a nation-state also distracted Muslims from their main task, that of promoting an Islamic vision of justice. Critically, if Muslims were not creating Pakistan to set up an Islamic state—one where Allah's sovereignty over lawmaking would be recognized explicitly and no laws would be made in contravention to the framework of Islamic justice—then what was the point of making a separate state? Maududi carved out a difficult space between nationalist Muslims (who supported Congress as Indian nationalists) and Muslim nationalists (who supported the Muslim League

[19] Devji (2013: 73–88) provides a good insight into the momentum such fears built up in the 1930s and 1940s.
[20] See Kaviraj 2010 for a nuanced account of how electoral quantification impacted conceptualization of the community in the Indian context. He argues that a "thick," socially embedded notion of what formed a community was replaced by a "thin," abstracted one.

not for principled reasons but just because they happened to be born Muslim) to argue for democratic politics to further ethical development rather than as an end in itself.

Savarkar's *Essentials of Hindutva* is emotive, poetic, and suggestive. Maududi's text is drier; he was a much more systematic thinker than Savarkar in terms of analyzing the philosophical foundations and political implications of nationalism, which he saw as a European idea. Both were political actors who continued to expand upon and elaborate their ideas beyond their texts. The exigencies of the Cold War; the dynamics of two different states, India and Pakistan; rapid decolonization around the world; the rise of Chinese socialism; sociological changes in terms of literacy and social mobility—all these transformations lent cadence, variation, and resonance to their ideas over the decades. What united them was an enthusiasm for democratic politics that relied heavily on an invigorated people to realize the full potential of the electoral mechanism. Their visions of democracy were not the same, nor do they conform easily to other visions of democracy that rest on egalitarianism.[21] Yet it is important for critics to recognize that a call for democratic politics by itself may not provide enough political and ideational resources to combat the politics deriving inspiration from these religious revivalists. This call is already built into the claims that Savarkar and Maududi are making; the dominance of Hindutva in India through electoral politics is reminder enough of that. A sharper, clearer articulation of what exactly alternative visions of democracy will provide, and to whom, is needed now.

Acknowledgments

Jyotirmaya Sharma very helpfully shared material and ideas for this chapter. I am very grateful to him. I would also like to thank Karen Barkey, Sudipta Kaviraj, and in particular, Vatsal Naresh.

References

Adams, Charles. 1966. "The Ideology of Mawlana Mawdudi." In Donald Eugene Smith, ed., *South Asian Politics and Religion*. Princeton, NJ: Princeton University Press, 371–397.

Adcock, C. S. 2014. *The Limits of Tolerance: Indian Secularism and the Politics of Religious Freedom*. New York: Oxford University Press.

[21] For a discussion about the early manifestation of tensions between different visions of democracy following the French Revolution see Tomba 2015.

Asad, Talal. 2002. "Muslims and European Identity: Can Europe Reprsent Islam?" In Anthongy Pagden, ed., *The Idea of Europe: From Antiquity to the European Union.* Cambridge: Cambridge University Press, 209–227.

Bakhle, Janaki. 2010a. "Country First? Vinayak Damodar Savarkar and the Writing of Essentials of Hindutva." *Public Culture* 22.1: 149–186.

Bakhle, Janaki. 2010b. "Savarkar (1883–1966), Sedition and Surveillance: The Rule of Law in a Colonial Situation." *Social History* 35.1: 51–75.

Barkey, Karen. 2010. "In the Land of Ottomans: Religion and Politics." In Ira Katznelson and Gareth Stedman-Jones, eds., *Religion and the Political Imagination.* New York: Cambridge University Press, 90–111.

Bayly, Christopher. 2012. *Recovering Liberties: Indian Thought in the Age of Liberalism and Empire.* New York: Cambridge University Press.

Bayly, Christopher and E. F. Biagini. 2008. *Giuseppe Mazzini and the Globalization of Democratic Nationalism, 1830–1920.* New York: Oxford University Press.

Bose, Sugata and Kris Manjapra, eds. 2010. *Cosmopolitan Thought Zones: South Asia and the Global Circulation of Ideas.* New York: Palgrave Macmillan.

Buck-Morss, Susan. 2000. "Hegel and Haiti." *Critical Inquiry* 26.4 (Summer): 821–865.

Chaturvedi, Vinayak. 2010. "Rethinking Knowledge with Action: V.D. Savarkar, the Bhagavad Gita and Histories of Warfare." *Modern Intellectual History* 7.2: 417–435.

Colley, Linda. 1992. "Britishness and Otherness: An Argument." *Journal of British Studies* 31.4: 309–329.

Cooper, Fred and Jane Burbank. 2010. *Empires in World History: Power and the Politics of Difference.* Princeton, NJ: Princeton University Press.

Devji, Faisal. 2013. *Muslim Zion: Pakistan as a Political Idea.* Cambridge, MA: Harvard University Press.

Gilmartin, David. 1991. "Democracy, Nationalism and the Public: A Speculation on Colonial Muslim Politics." *South Asia* 14.1: 123–140.

Gilmartin, David. 1998. "A Magnificent Gift: Muslim Nationalism and the Election Process in Colonial Punjab." *Comparative Studies in Society and History* 40.3 (July): 415–436.

Gilroy, Paul. 1987. *There Ain't No Black in Union Jack: The Cultural Politics of Race and Nation.* Chicago: University of Chicago Press.

Hartung, Jan Peter. 2013. *A System of Life: Mawdudi and the Ideologization of Islam.* London: Hurst.

Iqtidar, Humeira. 2011. *Secularising Islamists? Jamaat-e-Islami and Jamaat-ud-Dawa in Pakistan.* Chicago: University of Chicago Press.

Iqtidar, Humeira. 2017. "How Long Is Life? Neoliberalism and Islamic Piety." *Critical Inquiry* 43.4: 790–812.

Iqtidar, Humeira. 2020. "Theorizing Popular Sovereignty in the Colony: Abul A'la Maududi's 'Theodemocracy.'" *Review of Politics* 82.4: 595–617.

Jalal, Ayesha. 1985. *The Sole Spokesman: Jinnah, the Muslim League, and the Demand for Pakistan.* New York: Cambridge University Press.

Kaviraj, Sudipta. 2005. "On the Enchantment of the State: Indian Thought on the Role of the State in the Narrative of Modernity." *European Journal of Sociology* 46.2: 263–296.

Kaviraj, Sudipta. 2010. "On Thick and Thin Religion: Some Critical Reflections on Secularization Theory." In Ira Katznelson and Gareth Stedman-Jones, eds., *Religion and the Political Imagination.* New York: Cambridge University Press.

Kelly, Paul. 2015. "Liberalism and Nationalism." In Steven Wall, ed., *The Cambridge Companion to Liberalism.* Cambridge: Cambridge University Press.

Kumar, Aishwary. 2018. "In the Void of Faith: *Sunnyata*, Sovereignty, Minority." In Humeira Iqtidar and Tanika Sarkar, eds., *Tolerance, Secularisation and Democratic Politics*. New York: Cambridge University Press.

Mahmood, Saba. 2012. "Religious Freedom, the Minority Question, and Geopolitics in the Middle East." *Comparative Studies in Society and History* 54.2: 418–446.

Maududi, Syed Abul A'ala. 1941. *Nationalism and India*. Lahore: Tarjuman-al-Qur'an.

Maududi, Syed Abul A'ala. 1971. "Main Abul Ala Maududi Hoon" [I Am Abul A'la Maududi]. *Zindagi*, January: 21–30.

Maududi, Syed Abul A'ala. 1999 [1938–41]. *Tehreek-e-Azadi Hind aur Musalman*. Lahore: Islamic Publications.

Maududi, Syed Abul A'ala. 2007 [1930]. *Al Jihad fil Islam*. Lahore: Idara Tarjuman-ul-Quran.

Mazower, Mark. 2009. *No Enchanted Palace: The End of Empire and the Ideological Origins of the United Nations*. Princeton, NJ: Princeton University Press.

Mehta, Uday. 1999. *Empire and Liberalism: A Study in Nineteenth Century British Thought*. Chicago: University of Chicago Press.

Mill, John Stuart. 1861. *Representative Government*. Kitchener: Batoche Books.

Miller, David. 1995. *On Nationality*. Oxford: Oxford University Press.

Miller, David. 2000. *Citizenship and National Identity*. Cambridge: Polity.

Mills, Charles. 2008. "Racial Liberalism." *PMLA* 123.5: 1380–1397.

Misra, M. 1999. "Savarkar and the Discourse of Islam in Pre-independence India." *Journal of Asian History* 33.2: 142–184.

Mufti, Amir. 1995. "Secularism and Minority: Elements of a Critique." *Social Text* 45 (Winter): 75–96.

Nandy, Ashis. 2014. "A Disowned Father of the Nation in India: Vinayak Damodar Savarkar and the Demonic and the Seductive in Indian Nationalism." *Inter-Asia Cultural Studies* 15.1: 91–112.

Nasr, S. V. R. 1996. *Mawdudi and the Making of Islamic Revivalism*. New York: Oxford University Press.

Pagden, Anthony. 2002. *The Idea of Europe*. Cambridge: Cambridge University Press.

Pandey, Gyanendra. 1998. "The Culture of History." In Nicholas Dirks, ed., *In Near Ruins: Cultural Theory at the End of the Century*. Minneapolis: University of Minnesota Press.

Raghuramaraju, A. 2007. "Savarkar and Gandhi: From Politicizing Religion to Spiritualizing Politics." In *Debates in Indian Philosophy: Classical, Colonial, and Contemporary*. New York: Oxford University Press.

Scott, David. 2003. "Culture in Political Theory." *Political Theory* 31.1: 92–115.

Sharma, Jyotirmaya. 2003. *Hindutva: Exploring the Idea of Hindu Nationalism*. New York: HarperCollins.

Spinner-Halev, Jeff. 2005. "Hinduism, Christianity and Liberal Religious Tolerance." *Political Theory* 33.1 (February): 28–57.

Tamir, Yael. 1993. *Liberal Nationalism*. Princeton, NJ: Princeton University Press.

Tejani, Shabnam. 2008. *Indian Secularism: A Social and Intellectual History, 1890–1950*. Bloomington: Indiana University Press.

Tomba, Massimiliano. 2015. "1793: The Neglected Legacy of Insurgent Universality." *History of the Present* 5.2 (Fall): 109–136.

Tully, James. 1995. *Strange Multiplicity: Constitutionalism in an Age of Diversity*. Cambridge: Cambridge University Press.

Valls, Andrew. 2010. "A Liberal Defence of Black Nationalism." *American Political Science Review* 104.3 (August): 469–470.

van der Veer, Peter. 2001. *Imperial Encounters: Religion, Nation, and Empire.* Princeton, NJ: Princeton University Press.

Varouxakis, Georgios. 2002. *Mill on Nationality.* London: Routledge.

Waldron, Jeremy. 1988. "Locke: Toleration and the Rationality of Persecution." In Susan Mendus, ed., *Justifying Toleration: Conceptual and Historical Perspectives.* Cambridge: Cambridge University Press, 61–86.

Zaman, Mohammed Qasim. 2015. "The Sovereignty of God in Modern Islamic Thought." *Journal of Royal Asiatic Society* 25.3 (2015): 389–418.

SECTION II
GENEALOGIES OF STATE AND RELIGION

6

Religious Pluralism and the State in India

Toward a Typology

Rochana Bajpai

6.1. Introduction

How do states negotiate between the claims of multiple social groups? What effects do state policies have on societal plurality? Reflecting on India's historical experience, this chapter delineates and disaggregates a relatively neglected category, that of political pluralism. I argue, first, that historically, India has offered an important example of plurality not just as a *social fact* (see Kaviraj chapter in this volume), in terms of the range of its religious diversity, but also in *policy*, with a multiplicity of state approaches and dispositions toward the accommodation of religious diversity. Unpacking political plurality, I distinguish in a provisional and schematic fashion between hierarchical pluralism, integrationist exclusion, integrationist inclusion, and weak multicultural, strong multicultural, and assimilationist approaches toward religious diversity. Second, if pluralism is understood as a normative category that for clarity's sake we term *pluralist* (Kaviraj chapter, this volume), as denoting broadly approaches that recognize and in some cases respect religious diversity, state approaches in India have differed widely in the extent to which these are pluralist. Political pluralism encompasses a range of dispositions toward socio-religious plurality, ranging from hostility to the celebration of religious difference. Pluralism both institutional and normative is threatened by the hegemony of Hindu nationalism in Indian politics.

The motivations that inform the preliminary exercise in ground-clearing undertaken in this chapter are twofold. First, the influence of postcolonial theory and perspectives has meant that the state is usually seen as an agent of homogenization in relation to societal plurality. In the scholarship on Asia and Africa, state policies and processes are usually seen as rendering religious and social identities more discrete and adversarial than these would otherwise be. In its exploration of political plurality, this chapter pushes back to an extent against such claims. Second, in popular and scholarly opinion, minority claims are often homogenized, aggregated in large monolithic categories (e.g., Muslim), and assumed to be rooted in religious difference. However, given what we know of how state

Rochana Bajpai, *Religious Pluralism and the State in India* In: *Negotiating Democracy and Religious Pluralism*. Edited by: Karen Barkey, Sudipta Kaviraj, and Vatsal Naresh, Oxford University Press. © Oxford University Press 2021.
DOI: 10.1093/oso/9780197530016.003.0007

policies influence the nature of group claims, political plurality at the level of state policy should be reflected in some measure also in the nature of minority claims. This chapter focusses on Muslims, India's preeminent minority since the late nineteenth century.

This chapter departs from existing studies in at least two respects. In the few instances where political scientists have noted the existence of political plurality in India, the focus has been on state policy and its implications for democratic stability. Kanchan Chandra (2005) has notably argued that the recognition by post-independence Indian institutions of multiple and cross-cutting cleavages along lines of language, religion, caste, and tribe has encouraged the politicization of ethnic identities and the proliferation of ethnic parties. Furthermore, this has had positive consequences for institutional stability. For evaluating political pluralism, however, I argue, first, that we need to probe further, to examine the *normative justifications* of state policies, in particular, the form and extent to which these recognize group difference. Second, we need to go *beyond* state policies, to examine the *movements* and demands made of the state on behalf of religious minorities from political and social actors. In this chapter, I explore the nature of claims made on behalf of Muslims in India to inquire whether political plurality extends beyond the level of state policy, to the character of minority claims.

Viewed through such a lens, what does political pluralism in India look like? At one level, the scope of pluralism appears wider, in state policy and minority claims. I argue that state approaches to religious diversity in India have differed not only across time periods, levels of government, areas of policy, and minority groups, but also, importantly, with respect to the *same* group. The Indian constitution itself embodies multiple approaches toward religious minorities, integrationist in some policy areas and multicultural in others. At another level however, on an examination of the normative underpinnings of policies and claims, the scope of pluralism appears narrower. Notably, notwithstanding its political plurality, state policy in India has rarely been pluralist in its political imaginary. In particular, the value of religious diversity for the Indian polity and society as part of a framework of equal citizenship has not been elaborated by policymakers, leaving constitutional policies that protect group difference with a normative deficit.

Some caveats are in order at the outset. This chapter is a preliminary exercise in unpacking political pluralism and delineating its contours, in a broad-brush and schematic fashion. I do not seek to provide here a causal or explanatory account of how the different approaches to dealing with group difference emerged historically in India, nor of why an approach became salient at a particular time. These important questions regarding what makes these categories historically salient require a more extended discussion than is possible here.

6.2. Hierarchical Pluralism

Premodern states in India, as elsewhere, often allowed considerable autonomy to religious minorities in exchange for the recognition of the dominance of the ruling group. In the well-known example of the millet system of the Ottoman Empire, acceptance of the ruler's dominance was the condition for toleration of difference. Broadly speaking, the inclusion of other religions and cultures was based on acknowledging the preeminence of the ruler's religion and symbols of authority.

In precolonial India, the varied state forms across different regions and historical periods were for the most part segmented and constrained, as scholars have noted (Kaviraj 2010; Khilnani 1997). This was the result of, it has been argued, not just a pragmatic concession to the power of local rulers, but also the Hindu principle that society consisting of different social groups is "prior to the state and independent of it." The duty of rulers was to "protect and uphold the respective customs and laws" of self-regulating social groups, a principle adhered to by indigenous as well as foreign rulers who succeeded in ruling over Indian territories for any length of time (Rudolph and Rudolph 2008: 11, 18).

In many respects, hierarchical pluralism was pluralist, accommodating of religious and sociocultural plurality. The precedence of the moral order of society implied that the state would not seek to impose its preferred vision throughout society, but respect the internal rules and practices of social groups so long as taxes and revenues were paid. As Sudipta Kaviraj puts it, "The conceptual language of acting 'on behalf'" of the society as a whole was unavailable to this state" (2010: 13). Furthermore, a compartmentalized social order meant that external groups could be incorporated into what has described as a "circle of circles" by creating a circle of their own, which existed not so much in open communication with the rest, as "in a kind of back-to-back adjacency," "by way of a very peculiar combination of absorption and rejection" (Kaviraj 2010: 15). The caste system exemplified this segmented order of self-regulating groups, with its principle of what Kaviraj terms asymmetric hierarchy, in contrast to the symmetrical hierarchy found in European societies, where a group that was at the top in terms of ritual status, for instance, might be at the middle or bottom in terms of political power and economic holdings in a region.

While a segmented social order was pluralist in terms of the accommodation of socio-religious difference, it was not characterized by equality. With the preeminence of the ruler's religion, and the recognition of some rather than all religions, different religious groups did not have equal status. Different religious groups also did not share a sense of brotherhood with each other (Rudolph and Rudolph 2008: 9), which meant that intergroup relations were not characterized by mutual respect. An asymmetrical hierarchy also reinforced inequality by making it "cognitively more difficult to identify the structure of dominance" (Kaviraj 2010: 12).

Hierarchal pluralism has continued under modern states. The British colonial state's approach to religious diversity in India might be described as hierarchical pluralist. Religious authority was recognized in the realm of family law from the late eighteenth century; religious group membership became the principal route for the inclusion of Indians in colonial representative institutions from the late nineteenth century. In contemporary India, newer forms of hierarchical and segmented pluralism have overlaid older patterns. One instance is the growing residential and occupational segregation of Muslims in many cities. While spatial segregation has long existed in India, with particular religious and caste occupation groups occupying distinct areas in a territory and not welcoming those belonging to other communities (often linked to incompatible food habits, e.g., vegetarianism), this did not preclude cohabitation among elites from different religions in urban areas (Gayer and Jaffrelot 2012). With the ascendancy of Hindu nationalism, older patterns of cohabitation have been replaced in many cities in northern and western India with the formation of enclaves and sometimes ghettoes, propelled by discrimination in the housing market, as well as insecurity experienced after killings in which the state machinery failed to act to protect Muslim lives (Gayer and Jaffrelot 2012: 323).[1] Spatial segmentation represents a form of hierarchical pluralism in which religious diversity is recognized but there is an asymmetric restriction on the choices of individuals belonging to minority groups.

6.3. Integrationist Exclusionary

The transition to a modern democratic state was influenced by the ideals of the Indian nationalist movement, which were articulated in a liberal republican vocabulary comprising notions of secularism, democracy, social justice, national unity, and development that I have detailed elsewhere (Bajpai 2011). The nationalisms that emerged in late nineteenth-century India had to contend from the outset with the claim that India's diversities meant that it was not a nation.[2] The secular nationalist response to this was that India's long history of

[1] Gayer and Jaffrelot distinguish ghettos as characterized by "relative class diversity and the stigmatization and sense of alienation of its residents" (2012: 324), from enclaves, where there is a greater element of self-segregation. Ghetto-like formations are observable in Ahmedabad (Gujarat) as well as Mumbai (Maharashtra) and Jaipur (Rajasthan).
[2] This was expressed famously by John Strachey in 1888, who asserted that national sympathies "should ever extend to India generally . . . is impossible. You might with as much reason and probability look forward to a time when a single nation will have taken the place of the various nations of Europe" (quoted in Guha 2007: xiii).

coexistence of diverse communities reflected a "unity in diversity," and that communal discord was a product of a deliberate colonial "divide and rule" strategy. Central to divide and rule, secular nationalists contended, was the colonial policy of minority representation, with separate electorates, reserved seats, weightage (guaranteed representation for minorities in excess of their enumerated demographic share), and nomination instituted by the British initially for Muslims, and then extended to other religious groups. Accordingly, during the framing of the Indian constitution (1946–50), secular nationalists mostly argued that representative institutions had to be difference-blind as far as possible where religion was concerned. While separate electorates were rejected from the start as a key cause of partition, reserved seats for religious minorities that were included the 1948 draft of the constitution also remained under-supported and came to be withdrawn in 1949 (see Bajpai 2011 for details). Nehru commended their abolition as "a historic turn in our destiny," holding that "doing away with this reservation business . . . shows that we are really sincere about this business of having a secular democracy" (*CAD* 8: 329, 332). The dominant consensus of the time was that the ethnicization of political institutions would lead to intergroup conflict and political instability (on the general point, see eg. McGarry, O'Leary, and Simeon 2008: 45).

In integrationist exclusionary arguments, secular opposition converged with nationalist concerns, which in turn meant that Hindu nationalists often used a liberal, secular language in the Constituent Assembly (see, e.g., Mahavir Tyagi, *CAD* 5: 219). Special representation provisions for minorities were opposed both for violating the separation of religion and state and as divisive of the nation. Secularism would be undermined as these provisions required the recognition of a person's religion in public institutions, and treated individuals differently depending on the community to which they belonged. The overriding apprehensions voiced, however, were regarding national unity, which in turn, encompassed a range of concerns including political stability of the new state, social cohesion among different religious communities, and India's national identity (Bajpai 2011). The different national-unity concerns coalesced here—the "mixing of religion and politics" in the case of separate electorates was thought to have hardened differences between Hindus and Muslims, and resulted in the bloody breakup of the country. And for secular nationalists such as Nehru, the bedrock of India's national identity was to be secular citizenship. Representation provisions on religious lines detracted from becoming Indian, which involved learning to put attachment to India above and beyond belonging to religious, linguistic, caste, or tribal groups. Religion, caste, and other ethno-cultural affiliations were "backward" relics, a hindrance to the task of building a modern nation-state.

While several scholars have noted that secular nationalism converged with Hindu nationalism within the Congress party, it is important to underscore that in theory, an integrationist exclusionary position is *more* pluralist, providing some protections for religious plurality that are not offered by religious majoritarianism. Notably, these include non-discrimination on grounds of religion and equality before the law for religious minorities. This was in evidence during the Constituent Assembly debates, when many secular nationalists who opposed legislative quotas for religious minorities spoke in favor of constitutionalizing rights to religious and linguistic freedom for minorities. For secular nationalists, fundamental rights to equality and freedom for all individuals providing protection for their culture, language, and scripts had been the preferred mechanism for the accommodation of religious differences. During constitution-making, secularism was seen to imply the rights and freedoms of citizens to pursue religion and culture in their "private" individual and associational capacity, as a corollary to their exclusion from the political domain. What scholars have termed moderate secularism (Modood 2010)[3] emphasizing non-discrimination on religious grounds and equal citizenship, together with a national identity defined in civic rather than ethno-cultural terms, was the basis for the inclusion of religious minorities in the Indian nation-state (in the context of Turkey, see Philliou, this volume). In contrast, Hindu nationalists opposed constitutional protections for the rights of religious minorities and cultures (Bajpai 2011).

During constitution-making, several minority representatives articulated integrationist exclusionary arguments, supporting the abolition of legislative quotas for religious minorities (see HC Mookerjee *CAD* 8: 299), and in some cases, arguing for a prohibition on wearing religious markers (see Tajamul Husain *CAD* 7: 819, 871). Muslim leaders have continued to espouse integrationist exclusionary arguments in public debate in independent India. For instance, in the parliamentary debates on the Shah Bano case, several representatives of Muslim background argued against exemptions for Muslims from provisions of the common criminal code, as discriminatory, divisive, and "backward-looking."[4] During election campaigns, Muslim politicians have often sought to caution Muslim voters against religious leaders' interference in politics.[5] In practice, however, in India as elsewhere (e.g., the French headscarf ban),

---

[3] Modood describes as moderate secularism in the context of Western Europe as a pragmatic accommodation with religion. In India, this took the form of a recognition of the importance of religion in people's lives, as well as of the public nature of religious practice.

[4] See, for instance, Saifuddin Ahmad (Asom Gana Parishad), *Lok Sabha Debates* (henceforth *LSD*) 1986 col. 410; Mostafa Bin Quasem (CPI-M), *Rajya Sabha Debates* 1986 col. 311.

[5] Shahnawaz Husain (BJP): "This vote is a worldly thing . . . it is not a matter of religion . . . don't go according to anyone's decree or *fatwa*" (election campaign speech, Bhagalpur, 12.4.14, translated from Urdu). This was in a context in which many Muslim religious leaders gave fatwas or sermons not to vote for the BJP.

integrationist exclusionary arguments have often been used in support of majoritarian assimilationist projects.

6.4. Integrationist Inclusionary

Although scholars see integrationist approaches as difference-blind, as precluding any recognition of religious or social identity in the public sphere (McGarry, O'Leary, and Simeon 2008), a closer examination of the Indian constitution's provisions for quotas for the Scheduled Castes and Scheduled Tribes suggests that these can be inclusionary as well. In constitutionalizing affirmative action in the form of legislative quotas as well as special treatment in government employment and educational institutions for members of historically disadvantaged groups, Indian constitution-makers went beyond the liberal consensus of their time. The Indian constitution of 1950 recognized that non-discrimination and equal opportunity provisions were inadequate for tackling the massive and entrenched inequalities of Indian society, that differential treatment was necessary for groups that were historically disadvantaged along lines of caste and tribe. While inclusionary in recognizing that the national community was not homogenous, and that more than equal treatment was needed, quotas were also integrationist because differential treatment was envisaged as a temporary measure for tackling socioeconomic disabilities and reducing intergroup difference over time, and not as a permanent provision for the recognition of cultural difference.

Indian nationalists rejected quotas as a multicultural right, as a mechanism for protecting distinct group interests, in the case of *all* groups, including the Scheduled Castes and Tribes. In contrast with the late colonial state, which was consociational, quotas were not intended as instruments of self-government, of recognizing a distinct social identity, in the case of any group. In nationalist opinion, special treatment of untouchables was constantly distinguished from that of religious minorities by specifying, for instance, that Scheduled Castes were not a minority but a part of the Hindu community (*CAD* 5: 227–228). Nehru and many others also emphasized that what separated these groups from the majority was not so much religio-cultural difference as socioeconomic inequality (Nehru, *CAD* 8: 331).

Nevertheless, although most Congress members, including Nehru, felt that group quotas detracted from secular nationalist ideals, these were accommodated as necessary for a short period in the Indian context, in the case of the ex-untouchable and tribal groups for the sake of national unity and development. With national development for instance, "catching up" with the industrialized Western world was the desired goal; quotas and other special provisions, it was argued, were needed for some time for those sections of the population "whose present backwardness is only a hindrance to the rapid development of the country" (KT Shah, *CAD* 7: 655). In the case of national unity, the assumption was that vertical leveling would produce horizontal integration, that the reduction of economic disparities would also reduce social division.

Inclusionary integration has been the most influential approach for group-differentiated rights in post-independence India. While intended by constitution-makers for a period of 10 years, legislative quotas for the Scheduled Castes and Scheduled Tribes have been extended every decade since without much debate. These have become a mechanism of group representation to an extent (Galanter 1984), as Dalit and tribal representatives see it as their duty to advocate for their groups. Nevertheless, as representatives are elected by a mixed electorate, and winning elections requires getting support across different ethnic groups, legislative quotas continue to work as an integrative mechanism as well. However, several Dalit leaders feel, as Dr. Ambedkar did in his advocacy of separate electorates, that quotas under joint electorates do not serve as a good mechanism for Dalit representation, for ensuring the election of representatives who are a strong voice for, and accountable to, Dalits.

Over time, affirmative action-type measures, such as educational and employment quotas, and as well as scholarships, have been extended to other disadvantaged ethnic groups, notably the Other Backward Classes (OBCs), including, in many regions, Muslim communities (for details see Bajpai 2011b). Under Prime Minister Manmohan Singh's government (2004–14), there was an attempt to include religious minorities, particularly Muslims, within the ambit of affirmative action. This included the setting up of a Prime Minister's high-level committee (Sachar Committee) to examine the socioeconomic conditions of Muslims, which reported substantial deprivation with regard to assets, income, education, employment, and health, rendering Muslim disadvantage visible for the first time. The prime minister's new 15-point program on minorities sought to earmark 15 percent benefits of a wide range of existing development schemes for members of minority communities. In 2008–9, a new program, the largest for the development of minorities since Independence, sought to identify districts with a concentration of minority population and focus welfare programs in these districts. While the impact of these programs has been limited and hard to ascertain according to the *Post-Sachar Evaluation Committee* report, in recognizing religious identity as a source of exclusion and a criterion for receiving benefits, these targets went beyond color-blind policies. Nevertheless, these policies were not multicultural in the sense of seeking to protect religious difference, but rather sought to reduce the socioeconomic inequalities along religious lines.[6]

---

[6] Some theorists see any recognition of the principle of proportionate representation in public institutions as tending toward multicultural forms of accommodation—see McGarry, O'Leary, and

Several Muslim MPs have also sought to focus government attention on issues of discrimination and disadvantage faced by Muslims and away from multicultural type demands of cultural accommodation. Asaduddin Owaisi of the All India Majli-e-Ittehadul Muslemeen (AIMIM), one of India's best-known Muslim leaders, has been a long-standing advocate of the abolition of the Hajj subsidy for Muslims (removed in 2017 by the Bharatiya Janata Party [BJP] government), calling for its funds to be transferred to more deserving causes such as scholarship schemes for Muslim girls.[7] He has criticized successive national governments for the persistence of discrimination on religious lines in the reservations policy for the Scheduled Castes, which excludes Muslims (currently, Scheduled Caste status and benefits are restricted to Hindus, Sikhs, and Buddhists, although Muslim communities are listed as OBCs in some states).[8] Although the long shadow of Indian partition means that any Muslim assertion tends to be perceived as extremist and separatist, a systematic analysis of Asaduddin Owaisi's speeches shows that the underlying principles invoked are of non-discrimination, equal citizenship, fair equality of opportunity, and secularism (Bajpai and Farooqui 2018). In contrast to the earlier Muslim League's demands, for instance, which focused on the recognition of religious identities through separate Muslim electorates, Owaisi has consistently argued for the *de*-recognition of religion in government policies of affirmative action as well as the functioning of the police forces, which have often targeted Muslims. The demands by Owaisi and other Muslim leaders to end police harassment and violence against Muslims, their frequent detention without trial under false terrorism charges, and torture while in police custody are not multicultural demands. Rather, with the recognition of religious membership serving to identify individuals whose basic rights and liberties are being violated by state agencies, such claims are in an important sense integrationist inclusionary.[9]

Whereas comparative scholarship has tended to categorize integrationist approaches as exclusionary, denying recognition to religious or cultural identity (McGarry, O'Leary, and Simeon 2008), Indian experience suggests that these can be inclusionary as well, with policies recognizing group identities when these overlap with socioeconomic disadvantage, for instance, and minority leaders

---

Simeon 2008: 58. However, while multicultural demands may result from any recognition of the principle of proportionate representation, these do not necessarily form its normative justification.

[7] See, e.g., *LSD*, 13 July 2009.

[8] Other Muslim leaders pressing for reservations include Ali Anwar from Bihar, who has led the demand for affirmative action for *pasmanda* Muslims, lower-caste or backward Muslims in Bihar.

[9] Abusaleh Shariff, a key architect of the Sachar Committee report, cautions: "Day-to-day discrimination, exclusionary practices and feeling of insecurity and the alienation experienced by Muslims who feel like "second class citizens" "may even push them to become reactionary and militant" (2016: 201–202).

demanding the inclusion of specific socio-religious groups in affirmative action schemes, on grounds of non-discrimination and fair equality of opportunity.

6.5. Weak Multiculturalism

In addition to integrationist inclusion, the Indian constitution also proposes another type of accommodationist policy, which might be described provisionally as weak multicultural (Shachar 1998). Unlike many secular constitutions, it recognizes the associational and institutional autonomy of religious groups (as well as tribal and linguistic groups). In a departure from the standard liberal individualist position, groups were recognized as subjects of rights and entitlements (Mahajan 1998: 79–85, 103; Bhargava 2000: 38–39). Demands to restrict religion to the private sphere of individual conscience and belief were rejected; indeed, no hard distinction between the private and public spheres was posited. A broad definition of the right of individuals to freedom of religion was adopted after extensive debate, which included the right to practice religion in public spaces, and even more controversially, the right to "propagate" religion. The latter was vehemently opposed by Hindu opinion in the Constituent Assembly, but in keeping with the demands of Christian representatives, who argued that propagation was fundamental to the Christian faith. Religious denominations were permitted by right to hold property, and the state was allowed to aid educational institutions that imparted religious instruction (including minority institutions), allowing for public funds for support of minority religions and cultures, against the objections of those seeking to restrict the domain of religion (Articles 25, 26 of the Indian constitution). The demands of secularists for a uniform civil code to supplant the different religious laws that governed matters such as marriage and divorce in colonial India were rejected.

While accommodationist with respect to religious freedom, the constitution's overall approach is best described as restricted multicultural. Thus, the right to freedom of religion is subject to other constitutional rights, including those of equality and non-discrimination. State intervention is permitted not just in the interests of public order, morality, and health, as common elsewhere, but also for purposes of social welfare and reform, which constituted a departure to an extent from the colonial state's stance of nonintervention in the religious affairs of its subjects. Further, in keeping with the demand of many secularists and Hindu nationalists, the Indian constitution includes in its non-justiciable Directive Principles a provision for a uniform civil code, opening the door for legal unification in the future.

A restricted multicultural approach toward religious pluralism is also seen in what Al Stepan (2017) termed "co-celebratory recognition for majority and minority religions." Stepan notes that unlike Western European countries, and in common with Muslim-majority Indonesia, the secular state in India historically recognized public holidays for minority religions. Restricted multiculturalism is also to be found in Indian federalism, where six Indian states have non-Hindu majorities,[10] although historically the Indian state has only reluctantly granted territorial autonomy to religious minorities, for fear of separatism. While many Hindu-majority state governments have been oppressive of religious minorities, in a few instances, minority representation has been enhanced where state governments have depended upon the support of minorities. For instance, the creation of the most recent Indian state, Telangana (2014), has benefited the Hyderabad-based Muslim party AIMIM, which has increased its tally of seats in state, municipal, and *panchayat* elections, at a time of declining Muslim representation in parliament and many state assemblies across India.

According to many liberal theorists, restricted multiculturalism is better than strong or maximal multiculturalism, as it offers better protections for individuals and vulnerable groups within minorities, such as women (Kymlicka 1995; Shachar 1998). Indian constitution-makers, however, did not fashion normative resources for the restricted multicultural approach, which remained deficient in relation to the accommodation of religious diversity (Bajpai 2011). How the preservation of religious pluralism was a national good was not elaborated, contributing to a favorable ideological context for the growth of the Hindu Right.

6.6. Strong Multiculturalism

In contrast with weak multiculturalism, where the state reserves the right to curtail the domain of religion, in a strong multicultural approach, the views of the members of the religious community, rather than those of state authorities, are decisive in determining the scope of religion. In post-independence India, a strong or expansive multicultural approach to religious diversity was exemplified in the government legislation on the Shah Bano case (1986).[11] On the one hand, legal plurality achieved greater acceptance, with government spokesmen defending exemptions for followers of Muslim personal law from provisions of a common criminal code on grounds of secularism construed as equal respect for all religions and the rights to religious freedom of groups.[12] Government spokesmen declared

[10] Jammu and Kashmir, Punjab, Nagaland, Meghalaya, Arunachal Pradesh, Mizoram.

[11] For analyses of political discourse in Shah Bano, see Jayal 1999; Parashar 1992; Hasan 1998; Bajpai 2011. On the distinction between strong and weak multiculturalism in the context of state recognition of religious personal laws and the Shah Bano case, see Shachar 1998; Spinner-Halev 2001.

[12] See Eduardo Faleiro, *LSD* 1986 col. 343; also the speech of Ebrahim Sulaiman Sait, *LSD* 1986 cols. 492–493.

secularism as equal respect for all religions dictated deference to the views of Muslims (or as was the case, of their state-recognized representatives) that matters concerning maintenance were an essential part of their religion.

However, given that the state had undertaken reform of Hindu law in the 1950s, the rights to religious freedom were in effect being interpreted differently here in the case of majority and minority communities.[13] Why, normatively speaking, were Muslims different, was not elaborated by policymakers, leaving an impression of unjust minority favoritism. The reasons for the reduced authority of state institutions to intervene in the case of minorities can be several, including avoiding the injustice involved in the imposition of religious law reform on an already oppressed group (Spinner-Halev 2001) and inequalities between majority and minority religions, with the former inevitably supported by the state and society (e.g., Nussbaum 2005).

A common problem with a strong multicultural approach has been that according greater autonomy to religious communities in practice has often meant giving more power to conservative male religious leaders to define community rules, to the detriment of gender equality. In the Shah Bano case as well, the government's approach was seen to have resulted in strengthening the position of the "orthodox sections of the *ulema*" (Hasan 2005: 367–368; also Agnes 2005: 126), bolstering the existing, patriarchal power structures within the community, thereby also reinforcing stereotypes of Muslims as illiberal and obscurantist, preparing favorable ideological ground for the Hindu Right. A strong multicultural position continues to be espoused by a strand of Muslim leadership represented by bodies such as the All India Muslim Personal Law Board, which have argued in favor of practices such as triple talaq. However, Muslim women's organizations, notably the Bharatiya Muslim Mahila Andolan, have pursued a restricted multicultural approach, arguing that triple talaq in a single sitting violates both Quranic and constitutional justice, seeking the intervention of courts and governments in support of their interpretation of Muslim law and proposals for its reform.

6.7. Majoritarian Assimilationist

Assimilationist approaches toward religious pluralism have been an influential strand in India,[14] acquiring new impetus since the ascendancy to power of the

---

[13] Chatterjee notes that the reform of Hindu law in the 1950s created "a serious anomaly in the notion of equal citizenship," a fact noted not only by the Hindu Right but also by progressive opinion at the time (Chatterjee 1998: 361).

[14] These appear in the constitution as well, for instance, in the mention of cow protection in the Directive Principles, and the subsuming of Sikhs, Jains, and Buddhists under Hindu personal law—see Singh 2006.

Hindu nationalist BJP at the national level. In the Hindu nationalist narrative, the historical realization of the Indian nation in a political form was held back by Muslim conquest and, later, the partition of the country in 1947, for which Muslims are held responsible (Brass 2003: 34). Hindu nationalist views are seen to have gained ground in the 1990s as a reaction to the expansion of pluralism-promoting policies, notably in the case of government decisions for exemptions for Muslims (Shah Bano 1986), and for the extension of quotas in government jobs to the OBCs (Mandal 1991).

Like religious nationalisms elsewhere, for instance Sinhala Buddhist nationalism in Sri Lanka, Hindu nationalism in India is fueled by a sense that the majority community is not getting its due share of recognition and resources from the state, reflecting a "minority complex" of victimhood (Tambiah 1986; Hansen 1999). It has sought a greater role for the majority religion in public affairs that is commensurate with Hindu numbers. Protections for minorities in the Indian constitution and multicultural policies are seen as pandering to minorities ("minority appeasement"), with long-standing demands in BJP manifestos for the abolition of special status for the Muslim-majority state of Jammu and Kashmir (enacted in August 2019), and a uniform civil code to replace separate Muslim and Christian personal laws. In India, as in Sri Lanka and other postcolonial countries, the assertion of the majority religion in the public sphere serves as a measure of popular revolt against the liberalism of a secular elite that led movements of independence from European rule and sought to restrain the expression of religion in public affairs.

Like Sunni sectarians in Pakistan (see Ali, this volume), Hindu nationalists in India seek to establish the dominance of their variant of Hindu religion and culture in the Indian polity through acculturation of minorities. In common with religious majoritarianisms elsewhere, the rise of nationalism reflects interest in religion less as a belief system than as a collective demonstration of fervor and of numerical strength in public arenas, with religion often simplified into a few symbols of aggressive manhood seen to offer protection from external and internal threats, exemplified in the militant masculinist makeover of the god-hero Ram.[15] Nationalists have demanded that minorities show respect for Hindu mythical and historical heroes (such as Ram, Shivaji), normative food habits (for instance, not eating beef—most Indian states prohibit cow-slaughter),[16] as well as attitudes toward religion (for instance, opposition to religious conversion, also

[15] The Babri Masjid, regarded by many Hindus to be the birthplace of Lord Ram and as a symbol of Muslim domination, was eventually brought down in 1992, with the Liberhan Commission report finally submitted in 2009 indicting the BJP leadership.

[16] The only exceptions are Kerala, West Bengal, and states in Northeast India.

enacted into law by several Indian states) and Hindu political-theological slogans (e.g., *Bharat Mata ki Jai*).[17] Hindu nationalists regard Islam and Christianity as foreign religions, unlike Sikhism, Jainism, and Buddhism, which are seen as progeny of Hinduism and born on Indian soil. However, most Muslims and Christians are viewed as converts from Hinduism, that is, as former insiders, who therefore ought to be willing to submit to the preeminence of Hindu culture in India. The approach is assimilationist in demanding that religious minorities adopt the culture of the Hindu majority in both their public and private practices (e.g., beef-eating). Conformity with majority Hindu beliefs and practices is enforced through coercion, in the form of laws as well as acts of intimidation and violence against religious and political minorities, as Basu argues (in this volume).

While Hindu nationalist views have long been influential in Indian politics, these have greatly expanded their influence in regions and periods of BJP rule.[18] Laws against cow-slaughter and conversions have been enacted or strengthened by states during the tenure of BJP governments. The period since 2014, when a majority BJP government came to power, has seen rising incidents of violence and murders of minorities and dissidents, emboldening a range of Hindu vigilante groups to take the law into their hands, with the lack of arrests of perpetrators and of condemnation by government leaders creating a climate of impunity, in a context generally marked by weak protections for basic rights and liberties of the vulnerable. Instead, the government has supported initiatives of cultural domination, for instance, demoting public holidays associated with religious minorities.[19] In everyday life, hate speech and demeaning stereotypes of Muslims (as a security threat, Pakistan loyalists, "backward") are rife, encouraged by the pronouncements of government leaders, a pliant news media constantly pushing images of Pakistan as India's geopolitical enemy, and the anonymity offered by social media. In India today, as in Pakistan, we witness the "normalization of violent minoritization, hate, and murder" of minorities under "the hegemonic conditions" of majority (Hindu/Sunni) privilege (see Ali, this volume).

---

[17] Notwithstanding the constitutional right to propagate religion, many Indian states have passed legislation against religious conversion, including Odisha, Rajasthan, Gujarat, Madhya Pradesh, Chhattisgarh, and Himachal Pradesh (so-called Freedom of Religion Acts). Attempts at proselytization by Christian missionaries have been met by deadly violence.

[18] Official data show a rise in incidents of inter-religious violence. On the lynching of Muslims, and the killings of rationalists and journalist critics, see Basu, this volume. There is also an economic dimension to violence and its threat against beef consumption, which results in a loss of income for many poor Muslims who engage in "leather-related trades," even as meat exports appear to have increased under the BJP (Basu).

[19] Since 2014, Christmas has been observed as good governance day in many government offices, schools, and public universities. Official meetings of Supreme Court judges have been held over Easter. Critics have been told that Christmas and Easter remained optional holidays and that the decisions were in accordance with the convenience of the majority, eliding the demotion in the status of these holidays from compulsory to optional status, and the slight felt by many Christians.

Integrationist and assimilationist approaches to religious difference are often conflated. In the Indian case, for instance, many have argued that there is little to separate secular nationalism from Hindu nationalism. Civic nationalisms do tend to have an ethnic core, and it is true, as Sumit Sarkar puts it, that the distinction between secular and Hindu nationalism "can at best claim a certain precision in logic, far less so in practice," which historically saw "enormous overlaps in personnel, assumptions, and symbols" (1998: 360, 363).[20] Nevertheless, significant ideological ground remains between the two, with assimilationist approaches seeking to impose the cultural norms of the majority on minorities, whereas integrationist policies are consistent with maintaining cultural differences (McGarry, O'Leary, and Simeon 2008: 42). These are committed to countering discrimination on the basis of religion in public life, as exemplified in the recent student protests against a discriminatory citizenship law under the banner of constitutional secularism.

6.8. Concluding Remarks

State approaches to religious diversity have generally been discussed in terms of broad categories such as secularism and multiculturalism, concepts that remain useful for comparative normative analysis, but also elide important distinctions within each category that are relevant for the evaluation of pluralism. This chapter has sought to nuance influential characterizations of India as a case either of multicultural accommodation or of integrationist exclusion, and argued that any singular coding of Indian approaches to religious pluralism needs to be qualified. Some broader implications of my argument are as follows.

The first set of implications pertains to our understanding of political plurality. Contrary to influential postcolonial approaches in the scholarship on Asia and Africa, Indian experience suggests that state policies, including those influenced by nationalist ideologies, are not necessarily homogenizing straitjackets that entrench boundaries and differences between religious groups. Scholars have noted that the Indian state recognizes multiple ethnic identities and thereby offers space for ethnic reinvention (Chandra 2005).[21] I have argued that if we probe further, from policies to their underlying justifications on the one hand,

---

[20] As Sarkar notes, secular nationalists typically sought to unite people of all religions living on the territory of India, unlike Hindu nationalists, who held that only "Hindus could be true patriots" and encouraged "hatred or violence" toward other religions (1998: 361–362).

[21] While India is a key example, political plurality is to be found also in several other postcolonial polities, including Turkey and Indonesia, and merits greater exploration in a comparative frame.

and to responses in the form of minority demands on the other, the domain of political plurality expands substantially. Policy plurality in India consists not just in the recognition of multiple groups (e.g., religious, caste, tribal, linguistic in the Indian constitution), or only in different grounds for the recognition of different groups (e.g., religious and caste; see Bajpai 2011), but also in multiple approaches to the recognition of the *same* group. The Indian constitution itself embodies multiple approaches toward religious minorities. It is integrationist exclusionary with respect to the recognition of religious identity in political institutions, re-stricted multicultural in the domains of religious freedom and family laws, with the possibility of integrationist inclusionary approaches of affirmative action in education and jobs (if some religious minorities make the list of socially and educationally "backward" OBCs in some states). Finally, plurality at the level of policy is also mirrored in the demands made for Muslims. The diverse landscape of claims of Muslim MPs and nongovernmental organizations in contemporary India previewed here challenges dominant characterizations of the community as religious or Islamic in any singular, homogenous sense, and suggests religious minorities, like the majority, identify with multiple groups.

A second set of implications pertain to the distinction between political plu-rality and pluralist imaginary elaborated by Sudipta Kaviraj (this volume). I have argued that while India is a leading example of political plurality, state policy has rarely been underpinned by a pluralist political imaginary, with respect for re-ligious diversity within a framework of equal citizenship. Historically, in India, a segmented pluralism has prevailed, where minority groups had autonomy in their practices, but within a hierarchical framework in which the ruling group had greater powers. The growing residential and occupational segregation of Muslims in many Indian cities reflects a continuation of hierarchal pluralism and poses a challenge to pluralist equal citizenship and mutual respect. The majori-tarian nationalist approach of the ruling Hindu Right has sought to reduce po-litical plurality, and is anti-pluralist in its vision. Even the Indian constitution, an exemplary instance of political plurality, is not pluralist in all cases, as some-times suggested. During constitution-making, a normative deficit remained with regard to the protection of cultural difference and minority practices, as I have detailed elsewhere (Bajpai 2011), a result of the convergence of liberal and nationalist concerns. The elaboration of a pluralist vision for India and a multireligious Indian identity that highlights the value of religious diversity for the nation is still awaited, a task for which bottom-up movements in support of the constitution of the kind that India has seen since 2016 seem better suited than top-down policies. Importantly, as the popular protests against the recent citizenship law and government responses suggest, standard liberal individual rights—freedom from arbitrary arrest and detention, of expression, association, belief, lifestyle—are critical for the protection of religious minorities and remain unrealized in India today.

In conclusion, to revisit our category of political pluralism, it has been argued that plurality in state policy allows for the pursuit of "multiple ethnic majorities" (Chandra 2005: 236), prompting ethnic parties to adopt centrist behavior, thereby enhancing democratic stability in India. However, I have sought to suggest that political pluralism offers no easy solutions. As India's recent history suggests, political plurality may not prevent the ascendancy of religious majoritarianism and/or sustain a "centrist equilibrium" in politics. It does not on its own generate pluralist visions, for which popular mobilizations in support of standard liberal rights of equal citizenship and non-discrimination on religious grounds remain crucial.

Acknowledgements

I am grateful to the volume editors Karen Barkey, Sudipta Kaviraj, Vatsal Naresh, and to Uday Mehta for valuable feedback.

References

Agnes, Flavia. 2005. Law and Gender Inequality: The Politics of Women's Rights in India. In Mala Khullar, ed., *Writing the Women's Movement: A Reader*. New Delhi: Zubaan, 113–130.

Bajpai, R. 2011. *Debating Difference: Group Rights and Liberal Democracy in India*. Delhi: Oxford University Press.

Bajpai, R., and Farooqui, A. 2018. Non-extremist outbidding: Muslim leadership in majoritarian India. *Nationalism and Ethnic Politics* 24(3), 276–298.

Bhargava, R. 2000. Democratic vision of a new republic: India, 1950. In F. Frankel et al., eds., *Transforming India: Social and Political Dynamics of Democracy*. Delhi: Oxford University Press, 26–59.

Brass, P. 2003. *The Production of Hindu-Muslim Violence in Contemporary India*. Delhi: Oxford University Press.

Chandra, K. 2005. Ethnic parties and democratic stability. *Perspectives on Politics* 3(2), 235–252.

Chatterjee, P. 1998. Secularism and tolerance. In R. Bhargava, ed., *Secularism and Its Critics*. Delhi: Oxford University Press.

Constituent Assembly Debates. 1950. *Constituent Assembly Debates: Official Report, 1946–1950*, 9 December 1946–24 January 1950, Vols I–XII. New Delhi: Government of India.

Galanter, M. 1984. *Competing Equalities, Law and the Backward Classes in India*. Delhi: Oxford University Press.

Gayer, L., and Jaffrelot, C. 2012. *Muslims in Indian Cities: Trajectories of Marginalisation*. London: Hurst.

Guha, R. 2007. *India after Gandhi: The History of the World's Largest Democracy*. New York: HarperCollins.

Hansen, Thomas Blom. 1999. *The Saffron Wave*. Princeton: Princeton University Press.

Hasan, Z. 1998. Gender politics, legal reform, and the Muslim community in India. In
P. Jeffrey and A. Basu, eds., *Appropriating Gender: Women's Activism and Politicized
Religion in South Asia*. New York: Routledge, 71–88.

Hasan, Z. 2005. Governance and reform of personal law in India. In I. Jaising ed., *Men's
Laws Women's Lives: A Constitutional Perspective on Religion, Common Law and
Culture in South Asia*. New Delhi: Women Unlimited, 353–373.

Jayal, N. G. 1999. *Democracy and the State: Welfare, Secularism, and Development in India*.
Delhi: Oxford University Press.

Kaviraj, S. 2010. *The Trajectories of the Indian State*. Ranikhet: Permanent Black.

Khilnani, S. 1997. *The Idea of India*. London: Hamish Hamilton.

Kymlicka, Will. 1995. *Multicultural Citizenship, A Liberal Theory of Minority Rights*.
Oxford: Clarendon Press.

Lok Sabha Debates. 1986. *Parliamentary Debates, Official Report*. New Delhi: Lok Sabha
Secretariat.

Lok Sabha Debates. 2009. *Parliamentary Debates, Official Report*. New Delhi: Lok Sabha
Secretariat.

Mahajan, G. 1998. *Identities and Rights: Aspects of Liberal Democracy in India*. Delhi:
Oxford University Press.

Mandal Commission Report. 1991 [1980]. *Reservations for Backward Classes: Mandal
Commission Report of the Backward Classes Commission 1980*. New Delhi: Akalank
Publications.

McGarry, J., O'Leary, B., and Simeon, R. 2008. Integration or accommodation? The enduring debate in conflict regulation. In S. Choudhry, ed., *Constitutional Design
for Divided Societies: Integration or Accommodation?* Oxford: Oxford University
Press, 41–88.

Modood, T. 2010. Moderate secularism, religion as identity, and respect for religion.
Political Quarterly 81(1), 4–14.

Nussbaum, M. C. 2005. Religion, culture and sex equality. In I. Jaising, ed., *Men's Laws,
Women's Lives: A Constitutional Perspective on Religion, Common Law and Culture in
South Asia*. New Delhi: Women Unlimited, 109–137.

Parashar, A. 1992. *Women and Family Law Reform in India*. New Delhi: Sage.

Rajya Sabha Debates. 1986. *Parliamentary Debates: Official Report*. New Delhi: Lok Sabha
Secretariat.

Rudolph, S. H., and Rudolph, L. I. 2008. *Explaining Indian Democracy: A Fifty-Year
Perspective, 1956–2006*. New Delhi: Oxford University Press.

Sarkar, S. 1998. *Writing Social History*. Delhi: Oxford University Press.

Shachar, A. 1998. Group identity and women's rights in family law: The perils of multicultural accommodation. *Journal of Political Philosophy* 6(3), 285–305.

Shariff, A. 2016. *Institutionalizing Constitutional Rights: Diversity, Equal Opportunities
and Socio-religious Communities in India*. New Delhi: Oxford University Press.

Singh, Pritam. 2006. Hindu Bias in India's 'Secular' Constitution: Probing Flaws in the
Instruments of Governance. *Third World Quarterly* 26(6), 909–926.

Spinner-Halev, J. 2001. Feminism, multicultural oppression, and the state. *Ethics* 112(1),
84–113.

Stepan, A. 2017. The governance of religious diversity in the public space: Indonesia in
comparative perspective. In A. Triandafyllidou and T. Modood, eds., *The Problem of
Religious Diversity: European Challenges, Asian Approaches*. Edinburgh: Edinburgh
University Press,141–168.

Tambiah, S. J. 1986. *Sri Lanka: Ethnic Fratricide and the Dismantling of Democracy*.
London: Tauris.

7

Is Turkey a Postsecular Society?

Secular Differentiation, Committed Pluralism, and Complementary Learning in Contemporary Turkey

Ateş Altınordu

Within the last decade and a half, the term "postsecular" has become central to debates on religion in many disciplines, including theology (Smith 2004), philosophy (DeVries and Sullivan 2006), literary studies (McLure 2007, Carruthers and Tate 2010), and sociology (Rosati and Stoeckl 2012a). Like many terms that quickly become fashionable in the scholarly world, the postsecular has given rise to a great deal of discussion on its precise meaning (Gorski et al. 2012b), as well as to widespread skepticism about its analytical utility (Calhoun 2011: 78–80, Bader 2012, Beckford 2012, Martin 2016: 14). In social theory and the social sciences, the term has been used alternately to denote a new intellectual paradigm in the study of religion (Keenan 2002, McLennan 2007, Smith 2012) and to describe a new configuration of religion and public life in the contemporary world (Rosati and Stoeckl 2012a). While this growing literature contains multiple strands that conceive the postsecular in different—and sometimes contradictory—ways (Beckford 2012), Habermas's writings on religion and public life (2006, 2008, 2010) constitute a common reference point for most scholars using this concept, whether they adopt or reject the German philosopher's arguments.[1]

This chapter will investigate democratic politics and religious pluralism in contemporary Turkey through the lens of the concept of postsecular society. The first part will reconstruct Habermas's notion of postsecular society as an ideal type and propose concrete criteria by which one can identify postsecular formations—as well as crosscurrents—in a given society. The second part will utilize this framework to investigate relations between religion, state, and civil society in contemporary Turkey, focusing in particular on compulsory religious education in primary and secondary schools, the status of atheism and unbelief in the public realm, and the rise and political suppression of postsecular currents in the course of the Gezi protests of 2013. The conclusion will discuss

---

[1] For a particularly useful collection of essays on Habermas's writings on the postsecular, see Gorski et al. 2012a.

Ateş Altınordu, *Is Turkey a Postsecular Society?* In: *Negotiating Democracy and Religious Pluralism.* Edited by: Karen Barkey, Sudipta Kaviraj, and Vatsal Naresh, Oxford University Press. © Oxford University Press 2021.
DOI: 10.1093/oso/9780197530016.003.0008

the implications of the chapter's findings for future research on democratic politics and religious pluralism.

7.1. Postsecular Societies: An Ideal-Typical Reconstruction

An important critique of the concept of the postsecular has been that its precise meaning is hard to pin down. Beckford (2012) in particular has argued that various scholars use the term to refer to different things and identified six distinctive clusters of ideas associated with it in the scholarly literature. In order to attain definitional clarity in this murky terrain, this section will reconstruct the notion of postsecular society advanced in Habermas's writings as an ideal type and outline a set of tangible criteria through which one can identify postsecular features of a given society.[2]

The meaning of the term "postsecular" depends on the two components of the term—namely, what we mean with "secular," and what kind of a relationship to the secular the prefix "post" denotes (Casanova 2013, Joas 2016: 105–111). José Casanova's (1994: 25–39) threefold distinction of the meanings attributed to "secularization" (and, by implication, to "secular society") by sociologists of religion provides a useful starting point for this work of conceptual clarification.

According to the first meaning of secularization, secular societies are characterized by relatively low rates of religious belief, practice, attendance, and membership. Habermas's writings do not suggest that postsecular societies are marked by rising rates of religiosity. He holds that the adjective "postsecular" applies only to societies "where people's religious ties have steadily or rather quite dramatically lapsed in the post-World War II period" (2008: 17). This assumption rules out the relevance of the concept to most non-European settings—an unnecessary restriction in scope, as I will argue in more detail subsequently.

According to the second meaning of secularization, in secular societies, key social spheres—government, law, education, welfare, economy, science—are differentiated from religion, which, in turn, serves functions specific to itself. Habermas stresses that to qualify as postsecular, a society must remain secular in the sense of maintaining this institutional differentiation between religious and secular spheres. As Rosati and Stoeckl (2012b: 4) emphatically put it, "A postsecular society is not a de-secularized society."

---

[2] Here I follow Max Weber's (2017: 90) classical understanding of the ideal type: "In its conceptual purity, this mental construct (*Gedankenbild*) cannot be found empirically anywhere in reality. It is a *utopia*. Historical research faces the task of determining in each individual case, the extent to which this ideal-construct approximates to or diverges from reality." For the uses of ideal types in empirical social research, see Swedberg 2018.

According to the third meaning of secularization, secular societies are marked by the loss of religion's relevance in public life. Rosati and Stoeckl (2012b: 5) identify deprivatization as the key process that differentiates postsecular societies from secular ones, arguing that religious actors, organizations, arguments, and symbols have a palpable public presence in the former. Yet critics of the concept of postsecular society rightly point out that the assumed privatization of religion in modern societies has never occurred in the first place (Calhoun 2011: 78, Joas 2016: 106). In other words, if secularization as privatization is a myth, then it also does not make sense to talk about postsecularization as deprivatization. David Martin (2016: 85) has expressed strong skepticism about the usefulness of the concept on this ground: "When some commentators speak of 'post-secularity' I merely note they have overlooked the evidence of the persistence of religion on the ground, and ignored its continuous presence in the public debate."

If postsecular societies do not fundamentally differ from secular ones in terms of rates of religiosity, institutional differentiation between religious and secular spheres, or the public presence of religion, should we then dispose of the concept of postsecular society altogether? This is precisely the suggestion made by David Martin (2016: 14), who dismisses the concept as "a construction of the intelligentsia, no doubt useful for obtaining grants, but lacking secure root in the empirical and historical data."

This stance overlooks Habermas's emphatic argument that the defining characteristic of postsecular society is "a change in consciousness" (2008: 20). What distinguishes postsecular societies from secular ones is not a rise in the religiosity of the population, the dedifferentiation of religious and secular spheres, or the return of religion to public life, but a decline in ideological secularism (Casanova 2013: 31). As José Casanova (1994: 30–35) has argued, under the influence of the radical Enlightenment, secularization theory's empirical predictions of religious decline, functional differentiation, and privatization have often doubled as normative prescriptions. The presumed marginalization of religion was thus welcomed as humanity's liberation from cognitive, political, and expressive limitations imposed by religious authority and dogma. Built upon a teleological philosophy of history—moving from superstition, oppression, and self-alienation toward scientific reason, freedom, and human emancipation—this strand of ideological secularism has informed the self-understanding of European societies (Casanova 2006: 85) and—as I emphasize in this chapter—the social and political projects of modernizing elites in postcolonial and postimperial non-Western settings (Nandy 1988, Parla and Davison 2004, Hanioğlu 2011).

Habermas's identification of the distinctive feature of postsecular societies as "a change in consciousness" (2008: 20) refers precisely to the decline of this ideological secularism. As a result of the palpable influence of religion in world politics, religious revivals in various parts of the world, and the vital presence of religious actors in their public spheres, citizens in postsecular societies no longer expect that (1) religious belief, practice, and belonging will eventually disappear from their societies, and (2) religion will be confined to the private sphere and the individual conscience. This postsecular shift in consciousness "robs the secular understanding of the world of any triumphal zest" (Habermas 2008: 20).

As already suggested, Habermas (2008: 17) limits the adjective "postsecular" to European societies (and to Canada, Australia, and New Zealand), which, having experienced a significant decline in religiosity in the postwar period, are now coming to terms with the persistence of religion in their domestic public spheres and international political environment. This scope condition not only excludes the United States—which did not experience a linear decline in religiosity in the postwar period or generally develop a secularist self-understanding—but also most of the "non-Western" world. Given the preceding discussion of the relationship of the postsecular to the secular, however, this limitation of scope appears unnecessarily restrictive.

As already argued, at the core of the concept of the postsecular lies the decline of the secularist consciousness, which predicts and welcomes the decline of religiosity in society and the removal of religion from the public realm as both prerequisites for and outcomes of modernization. This consciousness has indeed been most pervasive in Western Europe, where "a secularist self-understanding . . . shared by European elites and ordinary people alike" has interpreted religious decline "as 'normal' and 'progressive,' that is, as a quasi-normative consequence of being a 'modern' and 'enlightened' European" (Casanova 2006: 66). Yet neither the secularist consciousness Habermas delineates, nor the changes in that consciousness he detects in the present, are unique to European societies. In many non-European settings, political and cultural elites saw secularization as the sine qua non of building a modern state and society, expected that religiosity would decline as a result of modernization, and sought to relegate religion to the private sphere. While not always shared by the masses, this secularist consciousness often found resonance among powerful social actors, including politicians and judges, military officers and civil servants, journalists and lawyers, scientists and teachers in settings from Turkey and the United States to Mexico and Brazil (Davison 1998, Smith 2003, Lomnitz 2016, Nachman 1977).[3] In many of these cases, secularist currents led to limitations on the public presence of religion (Çınar 2005). Moreover, even those who viewed secularization in a negative light accepted some of the underlying assumptions of ideological secularism and came to see themselves as on the losing side of history.

---

[3] On the ideology and policies of Kemalist *laïcité* in Turkey, see Davison 1998. On secularist currents in American law, education, social science, and journalism, see the chapters in Smith 2003. For a discussion of radical secularism in Mexican history, see Lomnitz 2016. On the social and political influence of positivism in Brazil, see Nachman 1977.

Where the once hegemonic status of ideological secularism has come under serious challenge, whether in or outside Europe, the concept of postsecular society promises to be of critical relevance. Scholarly practice seems to agree: a number of empirical studies have already applied this concept to settings such as Turkey (Keyman 2010, Kömeçoğlu 2012, Rosati 2012, 2015) and Russia (Stoeckl 2012), which fall outside the narrow boundaries drawn by Habermas.

The normative thrust of Habermas's writings on religion and public life concerns the ethics of citizenship in postsecular societies (Habermas 2008: 27–29). In postsecular societies, he argues, it is not sufficient that religious and secular citizens merely tolerate each other's presence in the public sphere. They must also recognize each other as worthy participants in public debate and engage in "complementary learning processes." This requires that secular citizens do not dismiss faith communities as "archaic relics of pre-modern societies that continue to exist in the present" and recognize religious citizens as their modern contemporaries capable of reasoned deliberation (Habermas 2006: 15). Moreover, they must be open to the idea that religious traditions offer cognitive, moral, and symbolic resources that can contribute to human welfare and social progress, and willing to acknowledge historical links and explore meaningful overlaps between their moral convictions and the religious traditions in question (Habermas 2006: 15).

Religious citizens, on the other hand, must adopt "a reflexive form of religious consciousness" and come to terms with the religious and philosophical pluralism of modern society by drawing on the resources of their own religious traditions (Habermas 2008: 28). A further requirement must be added to Habermas's framework of postsecular citizenship ethics, if the learning processes are to be truly complementary: just as secular citizens must overcome their secularist prejudices to recognize the rational capacity of religious citizens and appreciate the normative resources of religious traditions, a symmetrical obligation exists for religious citizens to acknowledge that (1) a lack of religious belief or practice does not imply a lack of moral capacity, and (2) many secular traditions and life forms contain deep value commitments.

The following three criteria, then, can be identified as essential characteristics of postsecular societies:

1. **Secular differentiation:** Postsecular societies must be secular in the sense of having institutionalized a substantive degree of differentiation between religious and secular spheres, particularly between religious and political authority. State-imposed religious monopolies, the coupling of citizenship with religious identity, or religious experts with powers to set limits to legislation by popular assemblies all violate the secular differentiation criterion.

2. **Committed pluralism:** As a spontaneous sociological condition, all modern societies are characterized to some degree by religious and world-view pluralism. Postsecularity, however, does not merely refer to the empirical co-presence of religious and secular voices and symbols in the public sphere. It also requires a normative commitment to pluralism on the part of both religious and secular citizens. In order to be able to talk about postsecularity in settings where ideological secularism has been historically dominant, the secularist monopoly over the public realm must have been dismantled and public manifestations of religion must no longer be suppressed or marginalized. On the other hand, we cannot talk about a postsecular society where a dominant religion, backed by political authority, monopolizes the public realm and confines other religions and unbelief to the private sphere.

3. **Complementary learning processes:** Postsecularity requires that religious and secular citizens respect each other's moral and political capacities and cooperate with each other in questions concerning the common affairs and future direction of their society. In other words, a society where religious and secular groups merely tolerate each other and seal themselves off from each other does not qualify as postsecular.

7.2. Is Turkey a Postsecular Society? Promise and Realities

The rest of this chapter will investigate the ways in which religion-society-state relations in contemporary Turkey approximate or diverge from the ideal type of postsecular society. As all aspects of this triangular relationship cannot be addressed within the limits of the chapter, I will focus on three illustrative areas: compulsory religious education in primary and secondary schools, the status of atheism and unbelief in the public realm, and interactions between religious and secular citizens in the course of the Gezi protests of 2013. These three discussions respectively speak to the three criteria of postsecularity outlined in the preceding section: secular differentiation, committed pluralism, and complementary learning processes.

From the foundation of the Turkish republic in the 1920s until the end of the twentieth century, secularist state elites, in collaboration with their allies in civil society, often constrained and occasionally repressed public manifestations of Islam. Since the beginning of the present century, however, this secularist bloc has lost not only its bases of power in state institutions but also its hegemony over public life. The dismantling of the secularist monopoly over the public realm prompted some scholars to hastily declare the rise of a postsecular society in Turkey. As the subsequent analysis will demonstrate, however, this view can only be maintained if one selectively neglects the monopolistic impulses of Sunni Islam in contemporary Turkey.

The dual nature of Kemalist secularism has been extensively discussed by students of Turkish secularism. Kemalist reformers on the one hand sought to eliminate religion from the secular spheres of state, law, and education and confine it to the private sphere; on the other hand, they formulated and promoted an official version of Islam that was supposed to be compatible with modern science and nationalism (Davison 1998). The Directorate of Religious Affairs systematically promoted this officially sanctioned Islam through its immense network of mosques and religious personnel (Gözaydın 2020), while secularist state officials and political actors took action to eliminate unauthorized manifestations of public religion—branded as "reactionary" or "obscurantist" (Parla and Davison 2004: 114)—as they emerged (Kuru 2009).

Kemalist nationalism might be seen as a perfect embodiment of ideological secularism. It contains a "secularist philosophy of history," which associates secularization with modernization and conceives the marginalization of religion as "progressive emancipation" and "maturation" (Casanova 2013: 31–34). Moreover, it promotes an exclusive reliance on science as the solution to all social problems and the precondition of social progress (Parla and Davison 2004: 100–125). Even the dual, paradoxical nature of Kemalist secularism might be seen as rooted in a particular strand of Enlightenment thinking that concedes the social benefits of religion as a source of morality and contentment for "the unthinking masses" and advocates its utilization for social integration and control (Casanova 1994: 32).

Starting in the mid-1980s, Turkey witnessed a proliferation of public Islam. This process manifested itself in the rise of Muslim intellectuals, publications, and civil society organizations on the one hand, and the growing visibility of Islamic symbols and lifestyles—e.g., the prevalence of headscarves among university students, sex-segregated luxury hotels, Islamic banking—on the other. The seminal work of Nilüfer Göle (1996, 1997, 2000, 2002) and case studies conducted by her students (Göle et al. 2000) have extensively explored these public articulations of Islam with cultural, economic, and political modernity.

Kemalist state and civil society actors responded to these manifestations of public Islam with discourses and policies rooted in ideological secularism. The headscarf in particular, which served as the foremost symbol of the Islamic revival, became a central target of secularist policy. When a December 1986 decision of the Higher Education Council declared that university students must wear "modern clothing" at all times, some university administrators prohibited the wearing of headscarves on campus, leading to the reprimands, suspensions, and expulsions of students who refused to comply. A Constitutional Court decision in 1989 overturned legislation that allowed the wearing of headscarves in universities, arguing that the practice "creates an archaic appearance" and "is liable to have drawbacks for the republic and for the principles of reform and laicism." Around the same period, a substantial number of Islamic activists, journalists, writers, and members of Islamic associations and orders were arrested and tried in state security courts on charges of "attempting to change the secular nature of the state" (Altınordu 2010: 532–533).

Turkish state actors began to assert secularism more drastically in response to the electoral rise of Islamic parties in the mid-1990s. The era that came to be known as the "February 28 process" represented a major backlash not only against religious parties, but also against manifestations of public Islam (Altınordu 2016: 157–162). The directives of the military-dominated National Security Council issued in February 1997 called for placing Islamic orders, foundations, schools, student dormitories, and Quran courses under strict state control and preventing the "infiltration" of Islamists into the civil service, the judiciary, and institutions of higher education (Yavuz 2003: 275–276). In the course of the February 28 process, dozens of elected mayors and hundreds of army officers were removed from their posts, and hundreds of local governors and civil servants were subject to official investigation on charges of involvement in "reactionary activities" (Bayramoğlu 2007: 285).

Since then, the tables have turned under successive AKP (Justice and Development Party) governments. The constitutional amendments of 2010, the turnover in bureaucratic, judicial, and military personnel, and the controversial trials of military officers charged with conspiracy against the government have significantly eroded the institutional power of Kemalist secularism in Turkey (Bâli 2012, Cizre 2012). Concurrently, the Kemalist project to maintain a secular monopoly in the public realm has lost steam.

These developments led some scholars to declare that Turkish society had taken a postsecular turn. The late Italian sociologist Massimo Rosati, for instance, characterized "the shift from a Kemalist to a post-Kemalist Turkey" as "the making of a postsecular society" (2015: 175), and commended the displacement of the "Kemalist narrative" by a "neo-Ottoman narrative" as conducive to the rise of a more pluralist "central value system" in Turkish society (2015: 119–174). Another sociologist of religion, Uğur Kömeçoğlu (2012), similarly portrayed growing manifestations of Muslim agency in the Turkish public sphere as a pluralist challenge against the hegemony of secularism, which, he argued, brings the country closer to postsecularity.

Kemalist nationalism undoubtedly posed a significant barrier to the emergence of a postsecular society in Turkey. In their eagerness to identify and embrace manifestations of the postsecular, however, these sociologists have selectively neglected or discounted major challenges to secular differentiation, serious obstacles to religious and worldview pluralism, and the deep political polarization along the religious-secular cleavage that mark post-Kemalist Turkey. If the concept of postsecular society is to have analytical and normative purchase, it must be applied more critically, with an eye to the persistent threat of religious hegemony.

7.2.1. Secular Differentiation

The secularizing reforms of the early Turkish republic resulted in the removal of religious authority from state administration and the abolition of religious courts and legal codes. Furthermore, since 1937, all Turkish constitutions have defined the state as secular (Berkes 1998). This "secular settlement" (Gorski and Altınordu 2008) in the political and legal spheres has been maintained after the shift to competitive party politics in 1950.

There are important ways, however, in which the Turkish state directly intervenes in the religious field. The main government agency regulating the religious sphere, the Directorate of Religious Affairs, supports a vast network of mosques and religious personnel in the Sunni tradition. Thus, it would not be a stretch to talk about Turkey as a case of de facto establishment despite the secularity clause in its constitution. This agency's role in reinforcing the hegemony of Sunni Islam in Turkey has been extensively discussed by scholars of Turkish secularism (e.g., Gözaydın 2020). This section will instead focus on the issue of compulsory religious instruction in primary and secondary schools.

Religion courses were introduced into the curriculum of Turkish elementary schools in 1949, middle schools in 1956, and high schools in 1967. Until 1982, these course were elective; students, regardless of their religious identity, received exemption simply by submitting a petition to the school administration. Religion courses became mandatory for the first time with the constitution of 1982 written under the close supervision of the military junta (Müftügil 2015: 191–192).[4]

The content of these "Religious Culture and Ethics" courses taught continually from the fourth grade through the final year of high school is mostly devoted to Sunni Islam. In both language and substance, the course is designed to teach Sunni history, doctrine, and rituals from the perspective of a believer, with a

---

[4] Article 24 of the Turkish constitution of 1982 states: "Religious and moral education and teaching will be conducted under state supervision and regulation. Religious Culture and Ethics is among the mandatory subjects taught in institutions of primary and secondary education." This historical origin is telling about the political motivation behind the policy: In the aftermath of the coup of 12 September 1980, the Turkish military advocated a strand of religious nationalism dubbed "the Turkish-Islamic synthesis," which aimed to provide a counterforce against leftist currents in Turkish society. Mandatory religious education was introduced as an important means of socializing citizens-in-formation to this new communal identity (Türkmen 2009: 386, Müftügil 2015: 192).

limited amount of information on "other religions" and, more recently, Alevism presented from an outsider's perspective. For nearly four decades, this compulsory course has led to discrimination against non-believers, non-Muslims, and Alevis, the country's largest non-Sunni Muslim minority.

Since the introduction of the mandatory religion course, whether and how non-Muslim students would receive exemption has been a matter of debate (Müftügil 2015). A 1990 memorandum by the Ministry of National Education stated that Christian and Jewish students should be exempt from religion lessons by default. However, another memorandum by the ministry two years later required that all students—Muslim and non-Muslim—take the course, arguing that it was based on a "supradenominational" approach and discussed all major world religions. Notably, the same memorandum instructed teachers to exempt non-Muslim students from those portions of the course that required the memorization of Quranic verses and the practice of the Muslim ritual prayer, acknowledging in practice that the lessons entailed confessional instruction after all (Türkmen 2009: 388). These ambiguous and contradictory decrees resulted in diverse practices across the country, leading to confusion and frustration for non-Muslim students and their parents (Foggo 2014). Furthermore, as the European Court of Human Rights (ECtHR) observed in *Hasan and Eylem Zengin v. Turkey*, exemption methods that obliged parents to disclose their religious convictions to school authorities subjected them to a heavy burden (ECtHR 2008: 20–21).

Buket Türkmen's (2009) analysis of high school Religious Culture and Ethics textbooks shows that these courses present Islam as an indispensable element of Turkish national identity and culture. Moreover, while the textbooks refer to Mohammed as "our prophet" and to the Quran as "our holy book," they depict non-Muslim religions as the belief systems of other societies, thus naturalizing Islam as the default religion of Turkish citizens.

The already palpable emphasis on Sunni Islam in religion courses was further reinforced under the AKP governments that ruled the country after 2002. In 2006, a reform committee set up by the Ministry of National Education added a new unit on the life of Muhammad to the religion syllabus. Moreover, the Sunna, the exemplary words and practices of the Muslim prophet, was given new emphasis as a central reference throughout the textbooks. With these revisions, the chapters on non-Muslim religions were reduced from 9 percent to 6 percent of the syllabus (Türkmen 2009: 391–393).

For the Alevis, compulsory religious education based on Sunni doctrines and rituals represents not only the marginalization but also the assimilation of their faith. The course presents Sunni versions of ritual prayer and fasting as the correct practice and the mosque as the exclusive place of worship for the Muslims, naturalizing Sunni belief and practice as the normative form of Islam in the process.

The landmark case concerning the assimilation of Alevis through compulsory religion courses was a lawsuit filed with the ECtHR in 2004 by Hasan and Eylem Zengin, an Alevi father and his daughter.[5] In its 2007 decision, the court found that religion courses in Turkish primary and secondary schools "cannot be considered to meet the criteria of objectivity and pluralism" and stressed that the course syllabus is "clearly lacking" on the subject of Alevi faith (ECtHR 2008: 19). The judges thus concluded that the Turkish government's religious education policy constitutes a breach of the European Convention on Human Rights, which requires states to "respect the right of parents to ensure such education and teaching in conformity with their own religious and philosophical convictions" (ECtHR 2008: 11, 19). The court required that this infringement on non-Sunni citizens' freedom of conscience be remedied by "bringing the Turkish educational system and domestic legislation into conformity" with the relevant articles of the European Convention.

While no such legislation ensued, experts commissioned by the Ankara Administrative Court in a subsequent case argued that a new Religious Culture and Ethics syllabus that came into effect in March 2005 resolved any problems that may have existed in earlier textbooks. Following this expert opinion, the court determined that textbooks based on the new syllabus, which were adopted in all grades by the fall semester of 2007, represented a "supradenominational approach" (AİHM 2014: 5–8).

Yet the new textbooks soon received criticism on similar grounds. In the case they filed with the ECtHR in February 2011 (*Mansur Yalçın and Others v. Turkey*), the complainants argued that the textbooks introduced Alevism as a "mystical interpretation of Islam" rather than as a distinct confession. Furthermore, the books presented Alevi rituals such as *cem* and *semah* as cultural-traditional phenomena rather than as forms of worship and failed to define the *cemevis* as places of worship.

The Turkish government responded with yet another claim that a new set of textbooks, adopted in the 2011–12 school year, entailed a supradenominational perspective and discussed Alevism in an appropriate manner (AİHM 2014). However, the ECtHR found in its 2014 decision that "the few references to Alevi beliefs and practice that had been included in the textbooks" did not allow Alevi students to avoid "a conflict between the religious instruction provided by the school and their parents' religious or philosophical convictions" (ECtHR 2014: 1–2). The judgment stressed that the problem is structural and insisted that the government must offer appropriate methods of exemption that do not require parents to disclose their religious convictions (AİHM 2014: 38).

---

[5] For a detailed discussion of this and other lawsuits filed by Turkish Alevi complainants with the ECtHR, see Senem Aslan's chapter in this volume.

These two ECtHR decisions, which found Turkey to be in violation of the European Convention, did not lead to structural reforms. On the contrary, top government officials' responses to the judgments showed that they did not take these convictions seriously. The day after the court issued its decision in the Mansur Yalçın case, Prime Minister Davutoğlu remarked: "In Turkey, the Religious Culture and Ethics course is taught in such a way as to tell about all religions. In some countries, students are taken to church and are given practical religious instruction—in certain schools this is taught to all. Now, we cannot disregard all of these practices and accept efforts to project [the religion course] in Turkey as if it were a means of religious oppression" (Milliyet 2014). In a public speech two weeks later, President Erdoğan criticized the ECtHR decision and asked why the compulsory religion course was being questioned while school curricula also include mandatory physics, chemistry, and mathematics courses. He then suggested that making religion classes optional would lead to drug addiction and violence: "This decision is a wrong decision. . . . If you open the mandatory Religious Culture and Ethics course to debate, if you abolish it, most naturally drugs will replace it, they will fill its space. Violence will come, racism will come, and they will fill its place" (Cumhuriyet 2014b).

7.2.2. Committed Pluralism

As already discussed, postsecular societies are marked by the co-presence of religious and secular voices, symbols, and lifestyles in the public realm. More crucially, in postsecular societies, religious and secular citizens must be committed to this pluralism on principle. While the secularist monopolization of the public realm in Turkey—epitomized by the headscarf ban in universities and state institutions—came to an end at the turn of the 21st century,[6] this did not give rise to a postsecular society. Instead, government authorities and religious-conservative citizens exert considerable pressure against the public presence of non-Sunni religions and secular worldviews. The case of atheists, agnostics, and other non-believers is illustrative in this regard.

According to a survey conducted by the Turkish polling company Konda in 2018, about 5 percent of the Turkish population identifies as atheists or non-believers (Konda 2019). Discrimination against—and at times the violent repression of—public atheism in Turkey predates the AKP era. The most tragic of these incidents was the Sivas Massacre of July 1993. The atheist author Aziz

---

[6] The AKP government lifted the ban on wearing the headscarf in universities (2010), civil service (2013), high schools (2014), the judiciary (2015), the police force (2016), and, finally, the military (2017) (The Guardian 2017).

Nesin, who had recently published excerpts from Rushdie's *Satanic Verses* in Turkish, participated in an Alevi cultural festival at the time. An angry mob that gathered after the Friday prayer surrounded the hotel where Nesin and other festival participants took shelter and burned it down under the indifferent gaze of local public authorities. The attack resulted in the death of 35 festival participants (mostly Alevi intellectuals), two hotel workers, and two assailants (Dündar 2015).

The repeated use of the word "atheist" as an epithet by top government officials, however, is a phenomenon of the AKP era. In 2012, after receiving criticism from an opposition party for his remarks on "raising a religious youth," Prime Minister Erdoğan asked rhetorically, "Do you expect us to raise an atheist generation?" (Cumhuriyet 2012). In 2014, Erdoğan attacked university students who had protested against him during an opening as atheists, a status that he identified with terrorism: "I conducted an opening in Ankara on Monday. . . . Despite whom? Despite those leftists. Despite those atheists. These are atheists, these are terrorists" (Dirik 2014). In the campaigns leading to the elections of June 2015 and November 2015, Erdoğan, this time as president, condemned the leaders of the PKK (the Kurdish Worker's Party)—which is listed as a terrorist organization by the Turkish government—as atheists (Radikal 2015a, 2015b). Other prominent AKP deputies followed suit, declaring the PKK to be "an irreligious and atheist organization" (Radikal 2015c).

The discriminatory remarks of government officials in this period were accompanied by the legal harassment of public atheists. Within the last decade, religious activists have systematically pressed charges against authors, editors, cartoonists, publishing houses, and internet users who articulated their atheistic views or expressed skepticism about Islamic beliefs in the public sphere (Ateizm Derneği 2014: 6–7). All of these lawsuits referred to Article 216/3 of the Turkish Penal Code, which states, "Openly insulting the religious values embraced by a section of society is punishable by six months to one year in prison, when the deed is conducive to the disturbance of public peace." In 2013, local criminal courts convicted two openly atheist public figures—Fazıl Say, an internationally renowned Turkish pianist, and Sevan Nişanyan, a Turkish-Armenian author—with reference to this article (Cumhuriyet 2013a, 2013b).[7] Practically functioning as a blasphemy law that exclusively serves Sunni complaints, Article 216 "has been used as a kind of political means to silence, censor, or intimidate different faith groups in Turkey" (Ateizm Derneği 2014: 7).

This wave of discrimination against non-believers prompted the formation of the Atheism Association in 2014. The association aims to provide

---

[7] The Supreme Court of Appeals reversed Say's conviction in 2015 and ordered a retrial of Nişanyan in 2016.

support for Turkish atheists, deists, and agnostics who are reluctant to publicly voice their convictions and offers legal aid to its constituency (Çağlar 2014). It advocates the establishment of crematories for secular funerals, the abolition of Article 216/3 of the Turkish Criminal Code, and the removal of mandatory religion courses from primary and secondary school curricula (Ateizm Derneği 2014, Bora et al. 2015). Within weeks of its foundation, the organization had to step up security measures in its office due to frequent threats of violence (Cumhuriyet 2014a). In January 2015, a court temporarily banned the association's website on the grounds that its "activities are of a nature that disturbs public peace" (Cumhuriyet 2015). Government officials' and legal authorities' discriminatory approach finds strong resonance in Turkish society: according to a major survey conducted in 2011, 64 percent of the Turkish population does not want atheists as neighbors (Bianet 2011).

7.2.3. Complementary Learning

According to Habermas, complementary learning processes between religious and secular citizens—"which the state cannot influence by its own means of law and politics" (2006: 4)—are exclusively a matter of civil society. While postsecular citizenship ethics must be rooted in civil society, the Turkish case shows that government policies and discourse can play a significant role in facilitating or hindering civil interactions between religious and secular citizens. This was clearly demonstrated in the case of Erdoğan's response to the Gezi protests of 2013, the largest antigovernment protests in the history of the Turkish republic. Through a populist discourse pitting a putative secular elite against a religious people, the prime minister sought to exploit the religious-secular cleavage in Turkish society and sabotaged emergent processes of complementary learning between secular and religious citizens.

The Gezi Park protests of 2013 gave rise to profound examples of postsecular citizenship. While the demonstrators largely came from the secular sectors of society, the protests included significant Muslim voices from the beginning, and secular protesters approached the religious practices of pious citizens with careful respect. Within the confines of the park, anarchists, revolutionary Marxists, LGBTQI activists, and Kemalists peacefully coexisted with pious groups performing Friday prayers. Secular demonstrators acknowledged the holy night of Miraç Kandili by voluntarily giving up alcohol for the day and distributing the traditional *kandil* simits in the park. As Göle (2013: 14) observed during the protests, "The Gezi movement is reuniting people across ancient divides by rejecting the politics of polarization and stigmatization. While it is predominantly a secular movement, it is not a movement in favor of authoritarian state secularism and the exclusion of Muslims from sharing the same public spaces."

Some religious groups, such as the Anti-Capitalist Muslims, worked in cooperation with secular associations to organize the demonstrations, while women's rights activists, religious and secular, marched together to condemn reported attacks on women wearing headscarves (Altınordu 2013). In response to the government crackdown on the protests, the Labor and Justice Platform, a social justice-oriented Muslim initiative, and prominent members of Mazlum-Der, a Muslim human rights organization, issued a public statement supporting the protesters. The statement concluded with a plea to pious citizens: "The fact that we have been oppressed in the past does not require that we become oppressors or support oppressors now" (Radikal 2013).

During the month of Ramadan that followed the Gezi Park protests, Anti-Capitalist Muslims organized fast-breaking dinners known as "Tables of the Earth" (Damar 2016). In the course of these dinners, participants sitting on pedestrian streets—including many nonpracticing and non-Muslim individuals—formed long human chains and shared communal meals. The dinners offered an alternative to the lavish Ramadan dinners in luxury hotels preferred by religious-conservative elites on the one hand and the large fast-breaking meals for the poor organized by AKP-controlled municipalities and sponsored by pro-government businesses on the other. Tables of the Earth thus directly challenged the AKP government's monopolization of Islamic discourse and practice and demonstrated "the remarkable interest shown by secular communities towards this 'Islamic political' form of protest" (Damar 2016: 209).

While the Gezi protests thus witnessed the emergence of a postsecular ethics of citizenship, Erdoğan's strategy relied on reinforcing the religious-secular cleavage in society. In a widely watched television interview at the height of the protests, Erdoğan asserted a putative opposition between a secular elite and a religious people and identified his government with the latter: "We and people like us have been oppressed in this country for a long time. . . . Now this group has won 50 percent of the vote. But . . . some people still want to oppress it" (quoted in Altınordu 2013). In his public speeches, Erdoğan repeatedly told apocryphal stories about Gezi protesters consuming alcohol in the historic Dolmabahçe Mosque and violently assaulting a headscarved woman in a central Istanbul neighborhood (Altınordu 2014).

Since then, Erdoğan and other AKP leaders have recurrently invoked the theme of a religious people oppressed by a secular elite to consolidate their religious-conservative base. This populist discourse, which further politicizes religious and secular identities and fosters distrust between religious and secular citizens, has sabotaged emergent processes of complementary learning and constitutes a major obstacle to the entrenchment of a postsecular citizenship ethics in Turkish society.

7.3. Conclusion

Against the skepticism of some sociologists of religion, this chapter sought to demonstrate that the concept of postsecular society is distinctly useful for analyzing the multifaceted relations between religion, society, and the state in empirical settings. Furthermore, as an ideal type, the concept provides a powerful tool for identifying the forces for and against religious pluralism in contemporary societies, including those outside of Europe. This requires, however, that the framework be applied critically, that is, in a way that takes the threat of religious hegemony seriously. Uncritical approaches that selectively stress postsecular formations at the expense of crosscurrents ironically fall into the same trap of teleological thinking as the secularization theories, which the concept of the postsecular was intended to transcend in the first place.

As Habermas has argued, in order to open themselves to complementary learning processes, secular citizens must give up their prejudices against religious communities as relics from a premodern past and take the contributions of religious citizens to public debate seriously. Moreover, they must be perceptive to historical links and actual overlaps between their values and the religious traditions found in their society. Based on the analysis of the Turkish case, this chapter contended that a complementary requirement exists for religious citizens who must give up their frequent association of nonbelief with immorality.

Conservative Turkish politicians' recurrent identification of atheism with moral depravity and the aversion of a majority of the Turkish population to having atheist neighbors show that religious actors often have prejudices about secular citizens that are as deeply entrenched as those held by secular actors about religious citizens. In order to open themselves to complementary learning processes, religious citizens must acknowledge the moral capacities of their secular co-citizens and recognize that many secular traditions and life forms contain deep value commitments.

Finally, the Turkish case illustrates that political authority has a larger impact on complementary learning processes than Habermas has acknowledged. While postsecular citizenship ethics is primarily a matter of civil society and cannot be imposed from above, the state plays a major role in structuring the environment in which religious and secular citizens interact with each other. Thus, government policies and discourses that target either religious or secular citizens as a group and polarize society along the religious-secular divide are likely to derail ongoing complementary learning processes. Where government officials promote a populist discourse relying on the trope of a religious people oppressed by a secular elite, as in contemporary Turkey, they pose a major obstacle to mutual recognition and social cooperation between religious and secular citizens.

Bibliography

Altınordu, Ateş. 2010. "The Politicization of Religion: Political Catholicism and Political Islam in Comparative Perspective." *Politics & Society* 38, no. 4: 517–551.

Altınordu, Ateş. 2013. "Occupy Gezi, beyond the Religious-Secular Cleavage." *The Immanent Frame: Secularism, Religion, and the Public Sphere*, 10 June. http://blogs.ssrc.org/tif/2013/06/10/occupy-gezi-beyond-the-religious-secular-cleavage/.

Altınordu, Ateş. 2014. "The Unprecedented Alliance of Taksim Square." *Oasis* Year 10, no. 19: 23–28.

Altınordu, Ateş. 2016. "The Political Incorporation of Anti-system Religious Parties: The Case of Turkish Islam (1994–2011)." *Qualitative Sociology* 39, no. 2: 147–171.

Ateizm Derneği. 2014. *Türkiye'de İnanç Özgürlüğü Kapsamında Görüş ve Önerilerimiz.* Istanbul.

Avrupa İnsan Hakları Mahkemesi (AİHM). 2014. *Mansur Yalçın ve Diğerleri / Türkiye Davası* (Başvuru no. 21163/11) Karar. Strazburg. 16 September 2014.

Bader, Veit. 2012. "Post-secularism or Liberal-Democratic Constitutionalism?" *Erasmus Law Review* 5, no. 1: 5–26.

Bâli, Aslı Ü. 2012. "The Perils of Judicial Independence: Constitutional Transition and the Turkish Example." *Virginia Journal of International Law* 52, no. 2: 235–320.

Bayramoğlu, Ali. 2007. *28 Şubat: Bir Müdahelenin Güncesi.* Istanbul: İletişim Yayınları.

Beckford, James A. 2012. "SSSR Presidential Address—Public Religions and the Postsecular: Critical Reflections." *Journal for the Scientific Study of Religion* 51, no. 1: 1–19.

Berkes, Niyazi. 1998. *The Development of Secularism in Turkey.* New York: Routledge.

Bianet. 2011. "Türkiye'nin Değer Haritası." http://bianet.org/bianet/toplum/131644-turkiye-nin-deger-haritasi. Accessed 15 October 2019.

Bora, Tanıl, Ömer Laçiner, Barış Özkul, Kerem Ünüvar, and Aybars Yanık. 2015. "Ateizm Derneği üyeleri ile söyleşi: 'Bizler varız ve buradayız demek istiyoruz.'" *Birikim* nos. 314–315 (June–July 2015): 146–158.

Çağlar, Özgün. 2014. "Hiçbir ateist kendini yalnız hissetmeyecek." *Agos*, 14 March. http://www.agos.com.tr/tr/yazi/6657/hicbir-ateist-kendini-yalniz-hissetmeyecek.

Calhoun, Craig. 2011. "Secularism, Citizenship, and the Public Sphere." Pp. 75–91 in Craig Calhoun, Mark Juergensmeyer, and Jonathan VanAntwerpen (eds.), *Rethinking Secularism.* New York: Oxford University Press.

Carruthers, Jo, and Andrew Tate, eds. 2010. *Spiritual Identities: Literature and the Post-secular Imagination.* Bern: Peter Lang.

Casanova, José. 1994. *Public Religions in the Modern World.* Chicago: University of Chicago Press.

Casanova, José. 2006. "Religion, European Secular Identities, and European Integration." Pp. 65–92 in Timothy A. Byrnes and Peter J. Katzenstein (eds.), *Religion in an Expanding Europe.* New York: Cambridge University Press.

Casanova, José. 2013. "Exploring the Postsecular: Three Meanings of 'the Secular' and Their Possible Transcendence." Pp. 27–48 in Craig Calhoun, Eduardo Mendieta, and Jonathan VanAntwerpen (eds.), *Habermas and Religion*. Cambridge: Polity.

Çınar, Alev. 2005. *Modernity, Islam, and Secularism in Turkey: Bodies, Places, and Time*. Minneapolis: University of Minnesota Press.

Cizre, Ümit. 2012. "A New Politics of Engagement: The Turkish Military, Society, and the AKP." Pp. 122–148 in Ahmet T. Kuru and·Alfred Stepan (eds.), *Democracy, Islam, and Secularism in Turkey*. New York: Columbia University Press.

Cumhuriyet. 2012. "'Ateist mi yetiştirecektik.'" 2 February: 1.

Cumhuriyet. 2013a. "Bir utancımız daha oldu. " 16 April: 1.

Cumhuriyet. 2013b. "Nişanyan'a hapis cezası." 23 May: 6.

Cumhuriyet. 2014a. "Ateistlere panik butonu." 5 May. http://www.cumhuriyet.com.tr/haber/turkiye/68179/Ateistlere_panik_butonu.html.

Cumhuriyet. 2014b. "Zorunlu din dersi kalkarsa uyuşturucu gelir." 30 September: 4.

Cumhuriyet. 2015. "Ateizm Derneği'nin internet sitesine yasak." 3 March. http://www.cumhuriyet.com.tr/haber/turkiye/225677/Ateizm_Dernegi_nin_internet_sitesine_yasak.html.

Damar, Erdem. 2016. "Radicalisation of Politics and Production of New Alternatives: Rethinking the Secular/Islamic Divide after the Gezi Park Protests in Turkey." *Journal of Contemporary European Studies* 24, no. 2: 207–222.

Davison, Andrew. 1998. *Secularism and Revivalism in Turkey: A Hermeneutic Reconsideration*. New Haven: Yale University Press.

De Vries, Hent, and Lawrence Eugene Sullivan, eds. 2006. *Political Theologies: Public Religions in a Post-secular World*. New York: Fordham University Press.

Dirik, Hakan. 2014. "Yine 'nefret dili'ni kullandı." *Cumhuriyet*, 1 March: 8.

Dündar, Can. 2015. *O Gün*. Istanbul: Can Yayınları.

European Court of Human Rights (ECtHR). 2008. *Case of Hasan and Eylem Zengin v. Turkey* (Application no. 1448/04) Judgment. Strasbourg. 9 October 2007 (Final).

European Court of Human Rights (ECtHR). 2014. Information Note on the Court's case-law no. 177.

Foggo, Hatice Yıldırım. 2014. "Çocuğa 'Zorunlu' Ayrımcılık." *Radikal İki*, 24 October.

Gorski, Philip S. 2005. "The Return of the Repressed: Religion and the Political Unconscious of Historical Sociology." Pp. 161–188 in Julia Adams, Elisabeth Clemens, and Ann Shola Orloff (eds.), *Remaking Modernity: Politics, History and Sociology*. Durham: Duke University Press.

Gorski, Philip S. 2013. "Beyond the Fact/Value Distinction: Ethical Naturalism and the Social Sciences." *Society* 50, no. 6: 543–553.

Gorski, Philip S., and Ateş Altınordu. 2008. "After Secularization?" *Annual Review of Sociology* 34: 55–85.

Gorski, Philip S., David Kyuman Kim, John Torpey, and Jonathan VanAntwerpen, eds. 2012a. *The Post-Secular in Question: Religion in Contemporary Society*. New York: New York University Press.

Gorski, Philip S., David Kyuman Kim, John Torpey, and Jonathan VanAntwerpen. 2012b. "The Post-Secular in Question." Pp. 1–22 in Philip S. Gorski, David Kyuman Kim, John Torpey, and Jonathan VanAntwerpen (eds.), *The Post-Secular in Question: Religion in Contemporary Society*. New York: New York University Press.

Göle, Nilüfer. 1996. *The Forbidden Modern*. Ann Arbor: University of Michigan Press.

Göle, Nilüfer. 1997. "Secularism and Islamism in Turkey: The Making of Elites and Counter-elites." *Middle East Journal* 51, no. 1: 46–58.

Göle, Nilüfer. 2000. "Snapshots of Islamic Modernities." *Daedalus* 129, no. 1: 91–117.

Göle, Nilüfer. 2002. "Islam in Public: New Visibilities and New Imaginaries." *Public Culture* 14, no. 1: 173–190.

Göle, Nilüfer. 2013. "Gezi—Anatomy of a Public Square Movement." *Insight Turkey* 15, no. 3: 7–14.

Göle, Nilüfer, Kenan Çayır, Defne Suman, Umut Azak, Buket Türkmen, Uğur Kömeçoğlu, Esra Özcan, Mücahit Bilici, and Oğuz Erdur. 2000. *İslamın Yeni Kamusal Yüzleri: İslam ve Kamusal Alan Üzerine Bir Atölye Çalışması.* Istanbul: Metis.

Gözaydın, İştar. 2020. *Diyanet: Türkiye Cumhuriyeti'nde Dinin Tanzimi.* Istanbul: İletişim Yayınları.

The Guardian. 2017. "Turkey Lifts Military Ban on Islamic Headscarf." 22 February. https://www.theguardian.com/world/2017/feb/22/turkey-lifts-military-ban-on-islamic-headscarf.

Habermas, Jürgen. 2006. "Religion in the Public Sphere." Trans. Jeremy Gaines. *European Journal of Philosophy* 14: 1–25.

Habermas, Jürgen. 2008. "Notes on Post-secular Society." *New Perspectives Quarterly* 25, no. 4: 17–29.

Habermas, Jürgen. 2010. *An Awareness of What Is Missing: Faith and Reason in a Post-secular Age.* Cambridge: Polity.

Hanioğlu, Şükrü. 2011. *Atatürk: An Intellectual Biography.* Princeton, NJ: Princeton University Press.

Jacobsohn, Gary Jeffrey. 2003. *The Wheel of Law: India's Secularism in Comparative Constitutional Context.* Princeton, NJ: Princeton University Press.

Joas, Hans. 2016. *Do We Need Religion? On the Experience of Self-Transcendence.* New York: Routledge.

Keenan, William. 2002. "Post-secular Sociology: Effusions of Religion in Late Modern Settings." *European Journal of Social Theory* 5: 279–290.

Keyman, Fuat E. 2010. "Assertive Secularism in Crisis: Modernity, Democracy, and Islam in Turkey." Pp. 143–158 in Linell E. Cady and Elizabeth Shakman Hurd (eds.), *Comparative Secularisms in a Global Age.* New York: Palgrave Macmillan.

Kömeçoğlu, Uğur. 2012. "Multifaceted or Fragmented Public Spheres in Turkey and Iran." Pp. 41–60 in Massimo Rosati and Kristina Stoeckl (eds.), *Multiple Modernities and Postsecular Societies.* Surrey: Ashgate.

Konda. 2019. "10 Yılda Ne Değişti?" https://interaktif.konda.com.tr/tr/HayatTarzlari2018/#7thPage/1. Accessed 15 October 2019.

Kuru, Ahmet. 2009. *Secularism and State Policies toward Religion: The United States, France, and Turkey.* New York: Cambridge University Press.

Lomnitz, Claudio. 2016. "Secularism and the Mexican Revolution." Pp. 97–116 in Akeel Bilgrami (ed.), *Beyond the Secular West.* New York: Columbia University Press.

Martin, David. 2015. "Massimo Rosati and Kristina Stoeckl, Multiple Modernities and Postsecular Societies." *Religion, State & Society* 43, no. 1: 105–108.

Martin, David. 2016. *The Future of Christianity: Reflections on Violence and Democracy, Religion and Secularization.* New York: Routledge.

McLennan, Gregor. 2007. "Towards Postsecular Sociology?" *Sociology* 41, no. 5: 857–870.

McLure, John A. 2007. *Partial Faiths: Postsecular Fiction in the Age of Pynchon and Morrison.* Athens: University of Georgia Press.

Milliyet. 2014. "Davutoğlu'ndan 'zorunlu din dersi' cevabı." 17 September. http://www.milliyet.com.tr/davuoglu-ndan-zorunlu-din-dersi-/siyaset/detay/1941548/default.htm. Accessed 1 February 2016.

Müftügil, Ayşe Seda. 2015. "Education and Religious Minorities in Turkey: The Story behind the Introduction of Compulsory Religion Courses." Pp. 189–204 in Michael Rectenwald, Rochelle Almeida, and George Levine (eds.), *Global Secularisms in a Postsecular Age*. Boston: Walter de Gruyter.

Nachman, Robert. 1977. "Positivism, Modernization, and the Middle Class in Brazil." *Hispanic American Historical Review* 57, no. 1: 1–23.

Nandy, Ashis. 1988. "The Politics of Secularism and the Recovery of Religious Tolerance." *Alternatives* 13, no. 2: 177–194.

Parla, Taha, and Andrew Davison. 2004. *Corporatist Ideology in Kemalist Turkey: Progress or Order?* Syracuse, NY: Syracuse University Press.

Radikal. 2013. "Mazlum-Der'de Gezi Parkı çatlağı." 19 June. http://www.radikal.com.tr/turkiye/mazlum-derde-gezi-parki-catlagi-1138337/. Accessed 1 February 2016.

Radikal. 2015a. "Cumhurbaşkanı Erdoğan Aksaray'da." 28 May. http://www.radikal.com.tr/ankara-haber/cumhurbaskani-erdogan-aksarayda-1368105/. Accessed 1 February 2016.

Radikal. 2015b. "Cumhurbaşkanı Erdoğan: Ülkemde mezhep farkından ateist terör örgütlerini destekleyenler var." 31 July. http://www.radikal.com.tr/politika/cumhurbaskani-erdogan-ulkemde-mezhep-farkindan-ateist-teror-orgutlerini-destekle-1406866/. Accessed 1 February 2016.

Radikal. 2015c. "Ak Parti Genel Başkan Yardımcısı Özdağ." 31 October. http://www.radikal.com.tr/manisa-haber/ak-parti-genel-baskan-yardimcisi-ozdag-1463224/. Accessed 1 February 2016.

Rosati, Massimo. 2012. "The Turkish Laboratory: Local Modernity and the Postsecular in Turkey." Pp. 61–78 in Massimo Rosati and Kristina Stoeckl (eds.), *Multiple Modernities and Postsecular Societies*. Surrey: Ashgate.

Rosati, Massimo. 2015. *The Making of a Postsecular Society: A Durkheimian Approach to Memory, Pluralism and Religion in Turkey*. Surrey: Ashgate.

Rosati, Massimo, and Kristina Stoeckl, eds. 2012a. *Multiple Modernities and Postsecular Societies*. Surrey: Ashgate.

Rosati, Massimo, and Kristina Stoeckl. 2012b. "Introduction." Pp. 1–16 in Massimo Rosati and Kristina Stoeckl (eds.), *Multiple Modernities and Postsecular Societies*. Surrey: Ashgate.

Smith, Christian, ed. 2003. *The Secular Revolution: Power, Interests, and Conflict in the Secularization of American Public Life*. Berkeley: University of California Press.

Smith, James K. A. 2004. *Introducing Radical Orthodoxy: Mapping a Post-secular Theology*. Grand Rapids: Baker Academic.

Smith, James K. A. 2012. "Secular Liturgies and the Prospects for a 'Post-secular' Sociology of Religion." Pp. 135–158 in Philip S. Gorski, David Kyuman Kim, John Torpey, and Jonathan VanAntwerpen (eds.), *The Post-secular in Question*. New York: New York University Press.

Stoeckl, Kristina. 2012. "European Integration and Russian Orthodoxy: Two Multiple Modernities Perspectives." Pp. 97–114 in Massimo Rosati and Kristina Stoeckl (eds.), *Multiple Modernities and Postsecular Societies*. Surrey: Ashgate.

Swedberg, Richard. 2018. "How to Use Max Weber's Ideal Type in Sociological Analysis." *Journal of Classical Sociology* 18, no. 3: 181–196.

Türkmen, Buket. 2009. "A Study of 'Religious Culture and Morality' Textbooks in the Turkish High School Curricula." *Comparative Studies of South Asia, Africa and the Middle East* 29, no. 3: 381–397.

Weber, Max. 2017. *Methodology of Social Sciences*. Translated and edited by Edward A. Shils and Henry A. Finch. New York: Routledge.

Yavuz, M. Hakan. 2003. *Islamic Political Identity in Turkey*. New York: Oxford University Press.

8

The Meaning of Religious Freedom

From Ireland and India to the Islamic Republic of Pakistan

Matthew J. Nelson

8.1. Introduction

Notwithstanding more than 100 years of British colonial rule, constitutional references to religious freedom in postcolonial Pakistan are not rooted in English law. Nor, despite its formation as an "Islamic republic," are they tied to Islamic law. Instead, constitutional references to religious freedom in Pakistan are bound up with an attachment to enumerated fundamental rights—an attachment inspired by the anti-colonial constitutional politics of Catholic-majority Ireland (1922, 1937) and Hindu-majority India (1950). Like Ireland (Article 44(2)) (1937) and India (Articles 25 and 26) (1950)—each recalling France's post-revolutionary Declaration of the Rights of Man (Article 10) (1789)—Pakistan's constitutions (1956, 1962–63, 1973) have consistently noted that each citizen's right to profess and practice his or her religion is guaranteed "subject to public order."[1]

What follows is an account of Pakistan's relationship with this transnational legal formulation. Scholars have long wrestled with questions about the degree to which, or the ways in which, the laws of one country might take root in another. In his early contribution to such debates, Alan Watson (1974) stressed the relative autonomy of legal texts, pointing to instances of textual borrowing stretching from Persia's adaptation of the Babylonian Code to Scotland's understanding of Roman law. Still, Watson was criticized—above all by Pierre Legrand (1997, 2001)—for his failure to appreciate the "cultural embeddedness" of legal norms.[2] Moving beyond legal texts, Legrand insisted that legal transplants often

---

[1] France (1789): "No one shall be disquieted on account of his . . . religious views, provided their manifestation does not disturb the public order established by law"; see also the United Nations' International Convention on Civil and Political Rights (Article 18) (1966): "Freedom to manifest one's religion or beliefs may be subject only to such limitations as are prescribed by law and are necessary to protect public safety, order, [and so on]." (Pakistan accepted the ICCPR in 2010 with reservations regarding Article 18; those reservations were dropped in 2011; see Khan [2015]).

[2] For summaries of the "Watson vs. Legrand" debate, see Cohn (2010); Cairns (2013).

Matthew J. Nelson, *The Meaning of Religious Freedom* In: *Negotiating Democracy and Religious Pluralism*. Edited by: Karen Barkey, Sudipta Kaviraj, and Vatsal Naresh, Oxford University Press. © Oxford University Press 2021. DOI: 10.1093/oso/9780197530016.003.0009

"fail" owing to the presence of intersubjective gaps at the level of legal *meaning* (Berkowitz et al. 2003; Osiatynski 2003; Small 2005; Arvind 2010). To be sure, Watson and Legrand examined private rather than public or constitutional law (Perju 2012: 1306–1311).[3] But, today, much of the literature on constitutional migration and borrowing continues to struggle with "Watson v. Legrand" debates.[4] Particular attention has been paid to the link between migrating texts and what those texts are actually taken to mean.

In this chapter I examine constitutional references to religious freedom as these references migrated from Ireland to India and, then, to Pakistan. Focusing primarily on patterns of migration from India to Pakistan, I note that those who import constitutional clauses often treat those clauses as "empty signifiers" (Laclau 1996)—that is, as texts with several different possible meanings across which political actors, actively pressing for *one* meaning, exploit interpretive ambiguities even as they attempt to crowd out the appearance of alternatives.[5] In effect, I examine political actors who recast their (politically motivated) interpretations of imported constitutional clauses as a single all-encompassing statement "constituting" their own legal landscape. I do not characterize these politically motivated efforts to recast the legal meaning of imported constitutional clauses as a matter of interpretive "failure" (Nelken 2003). Instead, following Ernesto Laclau (1996), I read them as politically embedded appeals to new forms of constitutional and conceptual order (Rosenfeld 2001–3: 72; Cohn 2010: 583). Tracking forms of constitutional migration from India to Pakistan, I argue, the challenge lies in grasping the political dynamics that provide (imported) constitutional clauses with new forms of constitutional meaning.

Pakistan's constitutional references to religious freedom note that, "subject to public order," "every citizen shall have the right to profess, practice, and propagate his religion" (Article 20(a)). Moving beyond individual to group rights, however, they also note that "every religious denomination . . . shall have the right to establish, maintain, and manage its [own] religious institutions" (Article 20(b)) (Constitution 1973). Drawn almost verbatim from Ireland and, then, India (see Section 8.3, below), these clauses have remained largely unchanged for more than 60 years. But, within these clauses, I highlight various ways in which the balance of meaning has changed.

Over time, the meaning of these clauses has pulled away from any protection for peaceful forms of religious profession or practice (Article 20(a)), focusing, instead, on right-wing claims that, however peaceful, *some* forms of religious profession or practice—particularly, but not exclusively, those associated with

---

[3] For scholarship focusing on constitutional law, see Choudhry (2006); Hirschl (2014).
[4] For constitutional migration, see Graziadei (2006); for borrowing and transplants, see Cotterell (2001).
[5] This argument was partly developed in conjunction with Bâli, Mednicoff, and Lerner (2020).

a heterodox minority known as the Ahmadiyya—*offend* Pakistan's Muslim majority (as a "denomination") (Article 20(b)) in ways that provoke private consternation and public rioting. This focus on matters of religious provocation and public rioting has slowly altered the balance of *meaning* within the constitutional clauses that Pakistan initially imported from outside.

This shift in meaning is tied to an expanding appreciation for "public order" inspired by the actions of right-wing religious vigilantes. The politicians and judges who consolidated this new reading of religious freedom simply developed new forms of legal reasoning according to which, for the sake of public order, the rights of otherwise peaceful citizens, recast as religious "provocateurs," could be (and should be) limited. Religious freedom, they noted, was never absolute. Strictly speaking, it was always subject to politically shifting calculations regarding threats to public order.

Moving from Ireland to India and, then, Pakistan, I argue that the meaning of religious freedom was never confined to a seamless transplantation of legal text (Watson); nor was it framed by the inexorable power of culture (Legrand) and, therein, the "inevitable" failure of Irish or Indian meanings in an "Islamic" cultural context like Pakistan. Meanings, I argue, bring together *both* text *and* context (Small 2005; Cohn 2010: 589–590). What follows is, therefore, a historically contextualized account of the Pakistani political forces that underpinned a gradual shift in the meaning of imported constitutional provisions.[6]

8.2. Legal Transplants, Religious Freedom, and the Politics of Constitutional Meaning

The best predictor of any constitutional text lies in the text immediately preceding it (Ginsburg et al. 2010). But, in South Asia, religious freedom is different. As an explicitly enumerated fundamental right, religious freedom is a constitutional element that neither India nor Pakistan inherited from colonial Britain's departing Government of India Act (1935). With reference to religious freedom, both India and Pakistan pulled away from that (proto-constitutional) act in favour of enumerated and enforceable provisions drawn from anti-colonial Ireland.[7]

---

[6] Gary Jacobsohn (2006) compares articulations of "constitutional identity" in Ireland and India; whereas I stress similarities, however, Jacobsohn highlights differences.

[7] At various points, Pakistan's first Constituent Assembly (CA) members noted that they had "adapted" clauses from Iraq, Turkey, and Yugoslavia (B. K. Datta, *CA Debates* 4 October 1950, 80), "borrowed" them from the United States (R. K. Chakraverty, 4 October 1950, 120), "taken" them from Canada (A. K. Brohi, 23 October 1953, 348), and so on.

8.2.1. Legal Transplants

Departing from those who trace the diffusion of foreign laws to impersonal forces like "imperialism" (Beer 1990; Al-Ali 2011) or "globalization" (Tushnet 2009; Dixon and Posner 2011), I focus on particular agents (constitutional "importers") and forms of deliberate borrowing (Cohn 2010: 591). In doing so, I seek to highlight the political circumstances that inspired constitutional drafters, as agents, to import the texts they did—rejecting Britain's traditional aversion to the enumeration of fundamental rights, for instance, when importing religious freedom provisions from a relatively distant jurisdiction like Ireland and, then, a relatively antagonistic neighbor like India, all while avoiding more proximate or parochial references to Islamic jurisprudence or *fiqh*.[8]

Building on the work of Jonathan Miller (2003), who describes the "prestige-oriented" motivations that often underpin transnational legal borrowing, I ask: why did Pakistani constitutional drafters borrow their religious freedom provisions from Ireland and, then, India, rather than a more "prestigious" global power like Britain? Indeed, having adopted India's approach to enumerated fundamental rights in 1956, why did those who rewrote Pakistan's constitution in 1973 (following several wars with India) *retain* the clauses their predecessors chose to import from India years before?[9]

Briefly stated, Pakistan's first Constituent Assembly (1947–54) embraced India's enumeration of fundamental rights owing to mid-twentieth-century considerations of anti-colonial prestige as well as domestic politics. In the first instance, India's enumeration of fundamental rights was read as "prestigious" in a broadly anti-colonial sense, turning away from colonial Britain's aversion to enumerating enforceable rights in ways that also resonated with ongoing transnational efforts to articulate a "universal" enumeration of rights at the UN. Within the UN, both India and Pakistan helped to formulate the Universal Declaration of Human Rights in 1948—including, especially, Article 18 regarding religious freedom (Kelsay 1988; Waltz 2004; Bhagavan 2010).

At the same time, however, moving away from anti-colonial notions of prestige focused on an explicit enumeration of enforceable rights, Pakistan's Constituent Assembly also embraced Indian constitutional provisions regarding religious freedom owing to specific domestic concerns—not only because those provisions promised to place a formal constitutional check on Muslim clerics who, pushing back against the state, claimed that they, and they alone, were entitled to adjudicate religious matters (via *fiqh*), but also, and more explicitly,

---

[8] For Britain's aversion to the enumeration of fundamental rights, see Schonthal (2015); for "Islamic" ideas about religious freedom, see Friedman (2003).

[9] On prestige-oriented motivations, see also Arvind (2010: 82–83).

because those provisions (as "Indian" provisions) promised to address specific concerns articulated by Pakistan's *Hindu* minority.

8.2.2. Religious Freedom

Too often, the source of specific constitutional provisions regarding religious freedom is not examined in any depth—except, perhaps, as a legacy of European colonialism or the emergence of international law. In his article "The Emergence and Structure of Religious Freedom in International Law Reconsidered," Peter Danchin (2007–8) traces the emergence of formal legal protections for religious freedom to complex political patterns rooted in the European Middle Ages, treating the emergence of such protections *outside* of Europe as either (a) nonexistent (in the case of "individual" protections) or (b) derived solely from European intervention—what he calls "projection[s]" of "*jus publicum europaeum* in a wider globalizing world" (2007: 467–468).

With reference to Article 18 of the Universal Declaration of Human Rights, however, Danchin does not acknowledge the role that India and Pakistan played in the process of negotiation or drafting; he simply notes that, in 1948, "most African and Asian states were [still] European colonies" (adding that, in the end, "not all of today's states or religions . . . consented to the final [article]") (2007: 529–530). The anti-colonial politics that prompted both India and Pakistan to play such a prominent role in the UN, with particular reference to religious freedom (Article 18), is not acknowledged at all.

Retaining this focus on "*jus publicum europaeum* in a wider globalizing world," Anthony Gill (2009) examines the motivations that led European Christian merchants to extend formal protections for religious freedom to potential trading partners worldwide (see also Finke 1990: 611). In his book *The Origins of Religious Liberty*, however, Gill limits his argument to merchants who, ostensibly, invented their own religious freedom provisions and then "exported" them, via trading ties, to new territories: the Dutch in the sixteenth century, the English in the seventeenth century, the Americans in the eighteenth century, and so on. There is, as such, no focus on the ways in which key actors might seek to "import" new forms of constitutional protection.

Gill's work succeeds in illuminating the origins of *some* legal protections for religious freedom. But, like Danchin, his work does not illuminate the constitutional experience of states like Pakistan—states that *imported* their religious freedom provisions from *non*-European states (while, at the same time, turning to states like India, *rejecting* those states as key trading partners). In fact, even when scholars have examined deliberate efforts to import religious freedom provisions in anti-colonial or non-European contexts, they have generally focused on simple transfers of text; they have not shown much interest in what "imported" constitutional provisions have actually been taken to *mean*.[10]

Focusing on text alone, Indian and Pakistani clauses regarding religious freedom are often read as a case of transnational convergence targeting "global" (even "liberal") legal norms. But, over time, this focus on traveling text has not provided a persuasive account of legal meaning. In fact, as I will explain, the challenge does not lie in capturing the motivations that underpin a simple transfer of text; the challenge lies in grasping the domestic *political* motivations that lead constitutional importers to produce new forms of legal *meaning* (Rosenfeld and Sajó 2006). What were the domestic political drivers that led "India's" religious freedom provisions to acquire a "Pakistani" meaning?

8.2.3. The Politics of Meaning

Much of the literature regarding constitutional migration and borrowing rests on a series of debates concerning the degree to which constitutional clauses might be transplanted *without* any sacrifice in their meaning (Berkowitz et al. 2003; Osiatynski 2003). These debates often obscure what linguistic social scientists see as an inevitable gap between textual "signifiers" and what they actually "signify" (Saussure 1959; Levi-Strauss 1963). Here, the meaning of a given text is always seen as deeply contextualized: "toleration," for instance, means what it does (for example, in Locke's seventeenth-century England) owing to its location in a much larger web of concepts like "commonwealth," "church," and "reason" (Danchin 2007–8: 489–497). Breaks in this larger web, however, often allow the *same* basic text to enjoy different forms of meaning in different historical or political contexts. Where there is no "commonwealth" or "church," for instance, the meaning of a word like "toleration" (or a phrase like "religious freedom") tends to shift.

My approach to the meaning of traveling constitutional texts builds on these linguistic insights, drawing attention to the relationship between legal text, political context, and *meaning*. As noted previously, I am particularly interested in the work of Ernesto Laclau and his appreciation for the political work performed by "empty signifiers" (see also Said 1983: 226–247). For Laclau (1996: 36), empty signifiers are endowed with a powerful political element: their meaning is always

[10] See Nelson et al. (2020). Like Anthony Gill, Ramazan Kılınç (2014) provides an account of legal origins—in this case, the late twentieth-century origins of formal legal protections for Christian minorities in Turkey. In fact, like Pakistan, which might have been expected to draw its legal provisions from British or Islamic law, Kılınç notes that "Islamists" in Turkey's Justice and Development Party (AKP) chose to avoid both the secular legacy of Kemal Ataturk and the specific parameters of *fiqh* (including *fiqh*-based protections for Christians and Jews as People of the Book) when formulating new legal protections for minorities.

184 GENEALOGIES OF STATE AND RELIGION

contested. In fact, drawing attention to a term like "freedom," historically situated political agents often find themselves wrestling with *many* possible meanings while, at the same time, actively pressing for *one*.[11] The ideological struggles we associate with a concept like "religious freedom" are, thus, merely political struggles over the "filling up" of empty signifiers: the meaning of an empty signifier is never completely vague or inconceivable; it simply "exists in the various forms in which it is actually [i.e., politically] realized" (1996: 44).

In what follows, I do not ask what a right to religious freedom "truly" means. Instead, I ask: how do shifting political permutations help to explain why *this* meaning of religious freedom (linking public order to a limitation on the rights previously enjoyed by heterodox minorities, for instance) came to prevail over *that* one (linking notions of public order to a common defense of peaceful religious practice for all)? How did "Irish" and, then, "Indian" constitutional provisions come to acquire a "Pakistani" meaning? What were the political motivations that drove patterns of legal re-signification over time?[12] Again, the challenge does not lie in a one-dimensional account of traveling text. The challenge lies in grasping the political dynamics that led Pakistan's constitutional actors to produce new strains of legal meaning *within* certain traveling texts.

8.3. Religious Freedom and the Constitution in Pakistan: Background

In 1922, the Irish Provisional Government published a book entitled *Select Constitutions of the World* to inform the constitutional drafters of the Irish Free State. This book contained 18 up-to-date constitutions, including those of the German Reich, the United States of Mexico, and the Russian Socialist Federal Soviet Republic. The same book was republished by B. Shiva Rao in 1934 as a resource for India's Constituent Assembly. And, in 1951, it was paired with a second volume entitled *Constitutions of Eastern Countries* to support the Constituent

---

[11] In this sense, Laclau's "empty signifiers" are not unlike W. B. Gallie's) "essentially contested concepts": both involve actors who compete to define the meaning of a concept seen as "variously describable" depending on the (interchangeable) elements associated with its core features (Gallie 1955–56: 172). Empty signifiers and essentially contested concepts, however, are not identical: whereas Gallie's essentially contested concepts are bound up with actors who acknowledge the presence of a never-ending dispute with ideational rivals, Laclau's signifiers are associated with those who *resist* any such acknowledgement. In Laclau's formulation, those who trade in empty signifiers do not merely contest the meaning of (say, constitutional) concepts; crucially, they also seek to *transcend* "the politics of contestation" by emptying the discursive terrain surrounding a particular concept and, then, filling it up with content believed to stand alone: "the people," "justice," and so on. (These hegemonic claims seek to obscure their status as options within a contested space. Indeed, according to Aletta Norval [2000], those who deal in "empty signifiers" seek to trade on what she describes as myths of "de-contestation" or closure.)

[12] Ran Hirschl (2014) also calls for more attention to the politics of constitutional "borrowing."

Assembly of Pakistan (Ahmad 1951). These books laid the foundation for Pakistan's pattern of adopting and adapting foreign constitutional models.

With reference to religious freedom, the "interim" constitution produced by Pakistan's first Constituent Assembly (CA) in 1954 clearly reflected the influence of Ireland and India. In Ireland (1922), Article 8 noted that "the free profession and practice of religion are, subject to public order, . . . guaranteed to every citizen." This article was retained in the Irish Constitution of 1937 as Article 44(2). In India (1950), Article 25 noted that "subject to public order, . . . all persons are equally entitled to . . . the right freely to profess, practice, and propagate religion." Pakistan simply merged these two examples, noting in Article 10 (after 1973, Article 20(a)) that "the right to profess, practice, and propagate religion [is] guaranteed subject to public order."[13]

In India, Article 26 went on to specify, not merely the rights of individuals, but also those of groups, noting that "subject to public order, . . . every religious denomination or any section thereof shall have the right (a) to establish and maintain institutions for religious . . . purposes; (b) to manage its own affairs in matters of religion; (c) to own and acquire movable and immovable property; and (d) to administer such property in accordance with [the] law." Pakistan's first CA simply reordered these clauses, specifying in Article 11 (after 1973, Article 20(b)) that "subject to public order, . . . every religious denomination or any section thereof shall enjoy freedom in the management of its religious affairs, including the establishment and maintenance of religious . . . institutions and the acquisition of movable and immovable property for that purpose."

Within Pakistan, Hindu CA members hoped to postpone any discussion of these articles until a report from a closely related Committee on Minority Rights had been published. But their colleague, Abdulla-al-Mahmood, deflected their efforts, noting that there was no cause for concern because Pakistan's approach to religious freedom already reflected the approach adopted in Hindu-majority India: "Clause 10 has provided the same thing but on a little wider scale than what has been provided in Clause 35 [sic: 25] of the Indian Constitution," he noted; Clause 11 addresses "the principles . . . incorporated in Clause 26 of the Indian Constitution."[14] When Hindu CA members went on to complain that Pakistan's preambular reference to "the principles of . . . freedom, equality, tolerance, and social justice as enunciated by Islam" should be qualified as "not inconsistent

---

[13] The Indian CA added a clarifying provision noting that "nothing in this article shall . . . prevent the State from making any law . . . regulating or restricting any economic, financial, political, or other secular activity which may be associated with religious practice" (Article 25(2)). Pakistan's first and second CAs incorporated a similar provision noting that "this Article shall not . . . prohibit the making of any law regulating or restricting any activity of a secular nature"; see Tariq Ahmad (2014: 8). In Pakistan, some Hindu members argued for the phrase "activity of a secular nature *associated with religious practice*," but this was rejected (*CA Debates* 6 October 1950, 128).

[14] Abdulla-al-Mahmood, *CA Debates* 4 October 1950, 78.

with the [UN] Charter [of Human Rights]," CA member Sardar Abdur Rab Khan Nishtar returned to the logic underpinning Pakistan's decision to import key fundamental rights provisions from India: "We [Muslims] thought . . . [that our imported] approach towards the rights of [religious] minorities would . . . create a better feeling" after the violence of Partition, he noted, "and they [Hindus] would be considerate towards us also." "Unfortunately," he complained, referring to his colleagues' push for an international check on domestic constitutional references to "the principles of . . . Islam," "they deny . . . us even this much."[15]

Within Pakistan's first CA, Muslim efforts to accommodate their Hindu colleagues with provisions imported from India did not extend much beyond Articles 25 and 26 of the Indian Constitution. For instance, Pakistani Hindus failed to persuade their Muslim colleagues to follow India's constitutional example with respect to (a) avoiding any religious qualifications for the country's head of state and (b) removing separate electorates for Pakistan's religious minorities.[16] Instead, stressing proposals drafted in Karachi (1951) by Muslim religious leaders, many CA members argued that a "Muslim" head of state and a dedicated "Muslim" electorate should be regarded as necessary features of the Islamic democracy they explicitly sought to create.[17]

In the end, Pakistan's first constitution—finally promulgated in 1956—was cut short by a military coup in 1958. But, in the wake of this coup, the so-called Constitution Commission convened by General Ayub Khan to prepare Pakistan's second constitution retained *both* of the articles that Pakistan had previously imported from India—in this case, renumbering Articles 10 and 11 as Articles 10(a) and 10(b) (after 1973, Articles 20(a) and 20(b)). "In the constitution[s] of Eire, India, and the late Constitution [of Pakistan]," noted Ayub's Constitution Commission, "fundamental rights are specific and protected." The question, according to Ayub, was simply whether these rights should be, as in Ireland and India, explicitly enumerated and then "incorporated in the new Constitution" or, turning to Ayub's own preference, whether they should be left, "as in the United Kingdom, to the fundamental good sense of the legislature and the [periodic] operation of the . . . courts."[18]

---

[15] Sardar Abdur Rab Khan Nishtar, *CA Debates* 10 March 1949, 60.

[16] In India, Muslim (minority) CA members argued *for* separate electorates; see Bajpai (2011: ch. 4).

[17] The members of Pakistan's first CA—more than 70 percent of whom belonged to the Pakistan Muslim League led by Muhammad Ali Jinnah—were indirectly elected from among those who prevailed in late-colonial elections across British India (1945–46). After the independence of India and the formation of Pakistan in August 1947, India's CA was split in two (with delegates from Bengal and Punjab being divided between their Indian and Pakistani constituencies). Most of Pakistan's Muslim religious leaders, however, were excluded from the formation of Pakistan's first CA because they did not participate in India's 1945–46 elections. (See Binder 1961: 121–123).

[18] *Report of the Constitution Commission, Pakistan* (1961: 101).

Building on a public-opinion survey with 6,269 respondents, Ayub's Constitution Commission noted that, within Pakistan, the "preponderance" of public opinion (98 percent) favored a constitutional chapter specifically devoted to an "Irish/Indian" enumeration of rights. This preponderance of public opinion, however, was not enough to prevent General Ayub from relegating fundamental rights to a set of non-justiciable "Principles of Law-Making" when his constitution was unveiled in 1962 (Newman 1962: 361–362). Widespread public protests, however, prompted a swift amendment restoring fundamental rights to their original position (as justiciable rights) the following year. In fact, reporting from Islamabad, Ralph Braibanti explained that no feature of Ayub's 1962 constitution "provoked greater opposition than [his] elimination of [fundamental] rights and the power of the courts to enforce them" (1965: 79).

Indeed, when Pakistan's third constitution finally emerged in 1973—following the separation of East Pakistan (as Bangladesh) (1971) and the restoration of civilian rule (1972)—the lessons learned by General Ayub remained firmly intact. The 1973 constitution promulgated by Pakistan's National Assembly under Prime Minister Zulfiqar Ali Bhutto *retained* Pakistan's "imported" religious freedom provisions from Ireland and India, renumbering them as Articles 20(a) and 20(b) (focusing, respectively, on freedoms for "individuals" and "groups").

Even as these articles were renumbered, however, their meanings began to change. This change was closely tied to the influence of two further constitutional provisions stressing Pakistan's "Islamic" character. The first of these two provisions was associated with Pakistan's (preambular) Objectives Resolution, which specified that, throughout Pakistan, "Muslims" should be enabled "to order their lives . . . in accordance with the teachings and requirements of Islam" (even as "adequate provision" was made for minorities "freely to . . . practice their religions"). The second provision, returning to a constitutional formula imported directly from Ireland and India, highlighted what were known as "Directive Principles of State Policy." Within these non-justiciable directive principles, Articles 31 and 36 sought to operationalize Pakistan's Islamic identity while, at the same time, recognizing the "legitimate rights . . . of minorities."[19]

Neither the Objectives Resolution nor the constitution's Directive Principles of State Policy could be enforced in Pakistan's courts. Both were constitutional statements of ideological aspiration or intention. But, alongside enforceable provisions regarding a "Muslim" head of state and a dedicated "Muslim" electorate, these two statements of aspiration and intention provided a formal constitutional platform for later changes in the meaning of Article 20. In effect, they

---

[19] CA member A. K. Brohi noted that "the first experiment [with Directive Principles] . . . was in the constitution of Ireland, which was followed by [its] then sister dominion . . . India," *CA Debates* 23 October 1953, 332.

outlined the constitutional "objectives" and "principles" underpinning later efforts to *shift* the meaning of Pakistan's imported constitutional provisions.

8.4. The Constitutional Politics of Religious Freedom in Pakistan

Initially, some expected a preambular focus on "Islam" to undercut Pakistan's constitutional focus on basic rights (Lau 1996). This concern emerged almost immediately in a context seeking to determine who was (and who was not) a "Muslim" for the purposes of (a) serving as the country's Muslim head of state or (b) voting in Pakistan's provincial "non-Muslim" electorates. Preambular references to "Islam," however, were not enforceable. In fact, it quickly emerged that any effort to define who was (and who was not) a "Muslim" within the terms of Pakistan's constitution would require either formal legal recognition for an *individual's* right to religious self-identification or some type of legal reform clarifying the formal boundaries of Pakistani "Muslims" as a *group*.

Even before Pakistan's interim constitution emerged in 1954, conservative religious activists had sought to clarify the boundaries of Pakistan's Muslim community with reference to the Ahmadiyya. The Ahmadiyya identify themselves as Muslim, but this identity is contested owing to claims made by the group's founder, Mirza Ghulam Ahmad (d. 1908), that he was not merely a religious reformer but a prophet—indeed, a prophet *after* Muhammad. (Muslims typically see Muhammad as the "seal" of prophecy itself.)[20] Leveraging the Ahmadiyya to clarify the boundaries of Pakistan's "Muslim" community, however, some activists argued that Pakistan's Ahmadiyya should be legally defined as "non-Muslims," barred from serving as Pakistan's head of state, and relegated to the country's separate non-Muslim electorates. This view, however, was not reflected in Pakistan's constitution (because, as noted earlier, the activists who articulated this view failed to participate in the elections that underpinned the formation of Pakistan's first CA). Still, key features of their views were not entirely excluded: many advocates simply turned to riots to make their opinions known (*Report of the Court of Inquiry* 1954; Binder 1961; Bokhari, Chapter 11 in this volume).

The political history of this right-wing effort to define the boundaries of Pakistan's "Muslim" community is complex, but in certain respects it begins with the fact that many of the religious activists seeking to formalize a "non-Muslim" identity for Pakistan's Ahmadiyya had opposed the formation of Pakistan itself. As Humeira Iqtidar points out (Chapter 5 in this volume), activists like Abul

---

[20] For an account of Ahmadi beliefs and practices, see Friedman (1989).

Aʿla Maududi opposed Pakistan's formation as an articulation of "territorial nationalism" that threatened to divide a key portion of the global umma (i.e., the worldwide Muslim community) between India and the two wings of Pakistan. Following the creation of Pakistan in 1947, however, many of these religious activists began to pull away from their earlier objections in a bid to rehabilitate their "nationalist" credentials. Specifically, they claimed to articulate what they saw as a key point of religious-cum-political *consensus* within Pakistan's Muslim community, namely that "Muslims" must be distinguished, or at least distinguishable, from "non-Muslims" (see Kazi 2015: 63–64).

In 1952–53, right-wing activists associated with a Deobandi Sunni body known as the Majlis-e-Ahrar-e-Islam (Council of Free Muslims) took to the streets of the Punjab in a series of violent protests demanding that Pakistan's Ahmadiyya be relegated to the country's "non-Muslim" electorate. Their protests came to an end with a declaration of martial law. (In fact, key actors, including Maududi, were charged with treason for their use of violence in defiance of state authority, i.e., for creating "public disorder.") But the army's declaration of martial law did not seek to limit the religious freedom of Pakistan's Ahmadiyya; it merely sought to protect those targeted in the course of the rioting while, at the same time, restoring the writ of the state. The army's declaration of martial law, however, was not confined to matters of religious freedom or public order. It also prompted Pakistan's CA to focus its attention, more intensively, on preventing future military encroachments in the realm of civilian affairs (Nelson 2016).

Unfortunately, this effort to shore up civilian power while, at the same time, limiting executive authority led Pakistan's executive governor-general to *dissolve* Pakistan's CA in 1954. After several months of constitutional wrangling, however, a new CA was formed in 1955 to promulgate Pakistan's first constitution in the spring of 1956. This constitution, however, was subsequently abrogated following the military coup of General Ayub Khan in 1958. Ayub rewrote Pakistan's constitution in 1962. But, as noted above, his "new" constitution, *as amended in 1963*, did not alter the approach to religious freedom that Pakistan had previously imported from India. Instead, owing to widespread demonstrations, Pakistan's second constitution retained a chapter explicitly devoted to the enumeration of enforceable rights, including a right to (individual and group-based) religious freedoms.[21]

---

[21] In 1954 and 1956, this anti-colonial commitment to an explicit enumeration of fundamental rights was still seen as "Irish" or "Indian." By 1962, however, as the Cold War unfolded under Ayub Khan, it was also seen as "American."

8.4.1. Indigenizing Imported Text

This right to religious freedom, however, did not prevent the state from introducing certain limitations when confronted with threats to public order. And, in 1969, the Lahore High Court finally stepped in to clarify Pakistan's transnational approach to "religious freedom" with particular reference to the constitution's clauses concerning "public order." It did so in a high-profile case reviewing a decision by the provincial government of the Punjab to shutter an inflammatory anti-Ahmadi newspaper known as *Chattan* (published by one of the groups that had supported the anti-Ahmadi riots of 1952–53).

The judgment in this case, known as *A.K. Shorish Kashmiri v. West Pakistan*, noted that, even apart from the emergency powers associated with General Ayub Khan's ongoing martial law, the state was constitutionally empowered by the terms of Article 20 to prohibit any derogatory articles of a religious nature that might pose a risk to "public order." In fact, the court adopted a rather conventional reading of the parameters within which a fundamental right to religious freedom is often situated: it simply condemned forms of religious incitement and the work of religious vigilantes who, acting in defiance of state authority, sought to intimidate their fellow citizens and, in doing so, restrict their civil liberties, adding that, in Pakistan, questions regarding *individual* religious liberty were only limited by *group*-based provisions regarding "public office" (e.g., the presidency) or a denomination's right to acquire and administer its own "religious property" (Saeed 2011: 17). The court specifically rejected the view that religious bullies might be permitted to define the parameters of Pakistan's "Muslim" community via vigilante action beyond the realm of constitutionally sanctioned authority.

The demise of Ayub Khan's dictatorship later that year (1969), however, followed by a war with India culminating in the formation of Bangladesh (1971), soon prompted a more focused effort to shore up the power of Pakistan's parliament while, at the same time, promoting a deeper appreciation for the unifying potential associated with articulations of "Muslim" nationalism. Framed to offset persistent concerns about divisive forms of ethnic provincialism, this renewed emphasis on "Muslim" nationalism culminated in two constitutional adjustments that gradually shifted the ways in which the provisions of Article 20 were read.

The first adjustment emerged in Pakistan's third constitution (1973), which included a new schedule (Schedule 3) requiring each new president and prime minister to swear an oath, not only that he or she was a "Muslim," but also, to clarify, that he or she regarded Muhammad as "the last of the Prophets." The second adjustment emerged one year later (1974) in the form of Pakistan's Second Constitutional Amendment. This amendment modified Article 260, regarding constitutional definitions, to clarify that, from the state's perspective, a "Muslim" could only be defined as one who "does not believe in, or recognize as a prophet or religious reformer, any person who claimed or claims to be a prophet . . . after Muhammad."

Politically, these two adjustments targeting Pakistan's Ahmadiyya set in motion a number of changes in the *meaning* of Pakistan's imported constitutional provisions regarding religious freedom. A proper understanding of the ensuing political dynamics, however, requires some appreciation for the *politics* and especially, the political violence, surrounding these two adjustments. In April 1973, almost immediately after the approval of Pakistan's third constitution, the same religious activists who had previously challenged Pakistan's approach to the rights of the Ahmadiyya (e.g., the Majlis-e-Ahrar-e-Islam) reasserted themselves in a series of violent protests and skirmishes (see Qasmi 2014: 176; also Bokhari, Chapter 11 in this volume). Prime Minister Zulfiqar Ali Bhutto did not respond with a further declaration of martial law. (After all, Pakistan had only emerged from its previous martial law one year before.) Instead, Bhutto nominated a judicial commission under Supreme Court justice Khwaja Mohammad Ahmad Samdani as well as a parliamentary Committee of the Whole House—chaired by the speaker of the National Assembly and managed by the attorney general—to decide whether, in light of existing religious freedom provisions, the formal legal status of Pakistan's Ahmadi community (as a "Muslim" or a "non-Muslim" community) should be examined in greater depth.

Initially, Prime Minister Bhutto asked whether the legal status of the Ahmadiyya should be scrutinized by the Supreme Court or Pakistan's Council of Islamic Ideology. But, because there was no claim that Pakistan's existing laws governing the Ahmadiyya were in some sense "un-Islamic," Bhutto turned away from these two bodies—both empowered to review *existing laws*—in favor of a fresh parliamentary inquiry regarding the need for legal reforms. This turn towards parliament was not surprising given the country's recent experience with dictatorship. However, with respect to the evolving meaning of Pakistan's imported constitutional provisions regarding religious freedom, this push in the direction of parliamentary power (and, therein, majoritarian politics) was pivotal. Briefly, right-wing religious activists stepped forward *within* Pakistan's parliament to position themselves as the "protectors" of Pakistan's "Muslim" majority vis-à-vis what they described as Ahmadi "provocations." Inter alia, they sought to shift the onus of responsibility for any violence that might surround community protests *responding* to these "provocations." Whereas, in the past, the Ahmadiyya were cast as the victims of right-wing protesters, those protesters now sought to recast *themselves* as victims—the victims of religious "provocation."

Ultimately, with a nod to some of his erstwhile opponents in the Majlis-e-Ahrar-e-Islam, Bhutto's parliamentary Committee of the Whole House turned its attention to the promulgation of a constitutional amendment targeting the formal definition of a Muslim in Article 260 (Qasmi 2014: 178). The leader of an Ahmadi branch known as the Qadiani was invited to defend his group's "Muslim" identity before the parliamentary committee. But, in doing so, his remarks were not confined to elements of the constitution. Instead, recalling the views articulated by certain Hindus within Pakistan's first CA, he tied his comments to global principles broadly articulated by the UN.

The majority within Pakistan's National Assembly, however, were no longer persuaded by such transnational markers of "prestige." Moving away from *global* standards to *domestic* priorities, many stressed more immediate political concerns. Even apart from increasing ties between Pakistan and Saudi Arabia (which many parliamentarians sought to cultivate as a religiously suitable destination for Pakistan's migrant workers) (Qasmi 2014: 213),[22] for instance, National Assembly members likes Ghulam Ghaus Hazarwi returned to the notion of "denominational" self-governance spelled out in Article 20(b), stressing that improved legal guidance was needed to prevent any "encroachment" on the *group*-based rights of Pakistan's Muslim majority (Qasmi 2014: 189). Hazarwi's domestic political logic is relatively easy to summarize: if Pakistan's Muslim majority was endowed with special rights and privileges—for example, access to a Muslim presidency (as a type of denominational "property")—Hazarwi felt that the state must be empowered to identify who was entitled to these privileges. "The state," he argued, "must be able to . . . identify [both] its Muslim and [its] non-Muslim citizens" (Qasmi 2014: 195).

To accomplish this task of religious identification (read as a task of state-based categorization), Pakistan's Committee of the Whole House led by the attorney general did not believe the state was required to prioritize an individual's right to religious self-identification. With a two-thirds majority in both houses, the attorney general simply noted that Pakistan's parliament was empowered to amend the constitution, even to the point of "limiting" certain constitutional rights (Qasmi 2014: 196; Kazi 2015: 91). Accordingly, Article 260 was amended (unanimously) to ensure that, as noted earlier, a "Muslim" would be defined as one who did not believe in "any person who claimed or claims to be a prophet . . . after Muhammad." Politically situated parliamentarians, if you will, wrestled with the many extant meanings of a key term like "Muslim" while, at the

---

[22] In 1948, Saudi Arabia opposed Pakistan's support for the UDHR (Article 18) (Kelsay 1988; Waltz 2004). And shortly before the anti-Ahmadiyya agitation of April 1973, a Saudi organization known as Rabita Alim-e-Islamia sponsored a conference discussing the redefinition of Ahmadiyya as "non-Muslims" (Qasmi 2014: 175).

THE MEANING OF RELIGIOUS FREEDOM 193

same time—seeking to consolidate a more clearly delineated sense of Muslim nationalism—actively highlighting only *one*.

Within parliament, the attorney general simply clarified that, in its push to define the terms of religious-cum-national solidarity, Pakistan's parliament was empowered to guard against any Ahmadi "encroachment" on Muslim constitutional prerogatives—especially, forms of encroachment associated with what the attorney general called religious "false belonging" (Qasmi 2014: 193, 224). Taking steps to restrict this type of encroachment, the attorney general simply hoped to avert what he described as a form of "tangible material damage" (for instance, diluted Muslim access to the office of the presidency) (Qasmi 2014: 192–193). And, then, by averting this type of material damage, he hoped to prevent any resistance to that damage in the form of public rioting.

8.4.2. Ireland/India as Empty Signifier

Although Pakistan's Second Constitutional Amendment redefined the Ahmadiyya as "non-Muslims" in 1974, the Pakistani judiciary did not immediately jettison its traditional reading of religious freedom. Even one year after the military coup that replaced Prime Minister Zulfiqar Ali Bhutto with General Zia-ul-Haq in 1977, the Lahore High Court decided a case known as *A.R. Mubashir v. A.A. Shah*, noting that, although official recognition of the Ahmadiyya as "Muslims" was now constitutionally barred, their fundamental right to peaceful religious practice was still intact. In effect, the court held that the peaceful religious practices of Pakistan's Ahmadi community (including references to their places of worship as "mosques") were neither a provocation amounting to a public nuisance nor a threat to any group-based right associated with denominational "property." Again, recalling the case of *A.K. Shorish Kashmiri* (1969), the court simply reiterated that the Ahmadiyya could be excluded from "Muslim" matters only when those matters were clearly defined by the terms of constitutional law—for example, matters of "public office" or "property."

At the same time, however, just across the border in India, the Indian Supreme Court had begun to modify its own understanding of group-based religious freedoms, highlighting the power of the state to identify the "essential" practices of any religion and, by extension, any "nonessential" practices that might be subject to legal regulation, restriction, or reform (Ahmad 2014: 13). This "Indian" notion—that states were empowered to regulate the "nonessential" features of any religion (outlined by Mathew John in Chapter 9 in this volume)—was also in place during Pakistan's first CA (1947–54), wherein a provisional article was adopted stipulating that, "subject to regulations," every religious denomination "shall have the right to procure . . . articles which are proved as being essential for worship" (1954: Article 12). But, in Pakistan, this constitutional provision was dropped in 1956, forcing future Pakistani judges to rely on jurisprudence from India (rather than their own constitution) whenever they sought to consider the statutory regulation of any religious practice that might be deemed "nonessential."[23]

Still, Indian and Pakistani judges adopted very different approaches to the notion of "essential" and "nonessential" religious practices. Whereas Indian judges sought to regulate an ever-expanding notion of "nonessential" religious practices, for instance, Pakistani judges chose to stress (a) "essential" Muslim practices (protected from adverse forms of state encroachment) as well as (b) "essential" non-Muslim practices construed as a provocation to public disorder (and, then, legally restricted as such).[24]

During the dictatorship of Pakistan's General Zia ul-Haq (1977–88), for instance, officials faced with yet another round of violent protests by right-wing religious activists stepped in to further restrict the formal parameters of Ahmadi religious freedom.[25] In particular, they stepped in to prevent the Ahmadiyya from using ostensibly "Muslim" words (e.g., *masjid*, or mosque) and "Muslim" practices (e.g., the *azan*, or call to prayer), describing their attachment to such words and practices as a provocative form of "encroachment" on the special religious "property" of Muslims.

This notion that Muslim property might include words like *masjid* as well as peaceful religious practices like the *azan* had already emerged in the parliamentary debates surrounding Pakistan's Second Constitutional Amendment (1974). But, after 1985, Zia provided these ideas with enhanced legal teeth, modifying Section 298 of the Pakistan Penal Code—a colonial law regarding blasphemy (construed as a form of religious insult intended to "wound" religious feelings)— to ensure that, legally, the Ahmadiyya would no longer be permitted to access words like *masjid* or practices like the *azan* insofar as these were recast as a type of religious "property" specifically reserved for "Muslims."[26]

This novel approach to the restriction of religious freedom was soon taken up in a landmark case known as *Zaheeruddin* (1993)—by far the most important case treating Pakistan's imported religious freedom provisions as a basket of "empty signifiers." In this case, a small group of Ahmadiyya urged Pakistan's

---

[23] The Pakistani Supreme Court followed India in arguing that the state should be empowered to regulate any "activity of a secular nature *associated with religious practice*" (see note 14).

[24] On religious freedom restrictions in India, see Osurie (2013); in India, too, public order concerns have been cited to support restrictions on ("nonessential") minority practices said to offend the sentiments of the majority.

[25] On the political and "public order" motivations underpinning Zia's reforms, see Saeed (2011: 88); Kazi (2015: 129).

[26] Ahmed (2009) describes the colonial roots of Pakistan's blasphemy law but does not address the ways in which Pakistan's religious freedom laws (as constitutional laws) were explicitly set *apart* from the British tradition.

Supreme Court to overturn their prior convictions for (a) wearing badges bearing the *kalima* (i.e., the Muslim profession of faith) and (b) celebrating an Ahmadi holiday in the Punjabi district of Jhang (Lau 1994; Mahmud 1995). Turning to Article 20 of Pakistan's Constitution and Section 298 of Pakistan's Penal Code as well as a series of Indian Supreme Court cases regarding "essential" religious practices (Ahmad 2014: 11), however, the Supreme Court of Pakistan upheld their convictions. It upheld their convictions in light of three points directly seeking to empty Pakistan's constitutional provisions regarding religious freedom of their prior meaning while, at the same time, filling them up again with new forms of legal meaning.

First, turning to questions regarding the exclusive "property" of Muslims, the court reframed several Indian and American Supreme Court judgments to argue that "[the] Ahmadis, as non-Muslims, could not use Islamic epithets in public [for example, during their celebrations in Jhang] without violating ... [Pakistani] trademark laws" (Khan 2011: 509). In fact, just as the presidency had been construed as an exclusive form of Muslim "property," the court held that Muslims alone held a proprietary claim to certain religious words and practices.[27]

Second, turning to questions regarding the possibility of further limits on peaceful religious practice, the court drew on a series of Indian Supreme Court judgments to insist that groups seeking to *avoid* any state-based regulation of "essential" religious practices were required to prove, in court, that those practices were, in fact, "essential." Because, according to the court, the Ahmadiyya had *failed* to prove that their celebrations in Jhang were "essential," the court decided that those celebrations could be described as "nonessential" and, then, however peaceful, legally regulated as such (without, in any way, undermining a fundamental right to religious freedom).

Finally, and most importantly, returning to the imported text of Article 20, the court saw Ahmadi religious practices, however peaceful, as angering and offending Pakistan's Sunni Muslim majority. So, to maintain law and order, the court decided that the state was empowered to control them (Khan 2003: 228; 2011: 509).[28] Clearly, this reading of Article 20 dramatically shifted Pakistan's understanding of its own (imported) constitutional provisions. In particular, Pakistan's new reading of Article 20 treated core ("essential") features of Ahmadi religious faith and peaceful religious practice as, prima facie, a provocative threat to public order, allowing for their regulation in a *preemptive* bid to avoid

---

[27] Years later, in Malaysia, the courts adopted a similar view when barring Christians from using Muslim words like "Allah" (see Neo 2014).

[28] The Supreme Court described the Ahmadiyya as "a serious and organized attack on [Islam's] ideological frontiers" that is "bound to give rise to a serious law and order situation" (*Zaheeruddin* 1993: 1765). In particular, the court noted that Muslims cannot be blamed for losing "control" after encountering the "blasphemous" material produced by Mirza Ghulam Ahmad. According to the Supreme Court, this was "like permitting civil war" (1993: 1777).

any violent response.[29] As Fatima Bokhari notes in Chapter 11 of this volume, quoting C. S. Adcock (2016), "Instead of simply responding to hurt feelings," the court gave "strategic value to ... mobilizing wounded religious feelings."

8.4.3. Religious Freedom, Public Order, and (Majoritarian) Parliamentary Power

Recalling Legrand's notions of interpretive "failure" in the realm of legal transplants, Amjad Mahmood Khan (2011) and Tariq Ahmad (2014) have argued that Pakistan's Supreme Court "mistranslated" specific foreign laws: American law, Indian law, and international human rights law. Unfortunately, this assessment merely revives a number of questions about the relationship between legal text, legal meaning, and the larger political contexts within which legal meanings are created. What were the domestic *political* factors that drove Pakistan's judicial reasoning and, thus, its approach to the legal *meaning* of foreign constitutional texts?

Focusing on what she calls "core juridical signifiers" (i.e., fundamental rights), Saadia Saeed (2018) has examined the ways in which Pakistan invested key constitutional principles with new meanings.[30] In particular, she attributes Pakistan's repurposing of constitutional rights to the influence of General Zia-ul-Haq's military dictatorship during the early to mid-1980s. This focus on the influence of General Zia, however, is difficult to reconcile with the historical record— above all, the fact that crucial Supreme Court decisions seeking to *protect* the rights of the Ahmadiyya (e.g., *Mubashir* [1978]) were delivered *after* the coup that brought General Zia to power and, moreover, the fact that key decisions *restricting* the Ahmadiyya (e.g., *Zaheeruddin* [1993]) were delivered after Zia died and Pakistan's 1973 constitution (including its provisions regarding religious freedom) was *restored*. Indeed, Saeed's argument (2011: 4, 22) is difficult to reconcile with the fact that, ultimately, much of the *political* energy driving restrictions on the religious freedom of the Ahmadiyya emerged *before* Zia's military regime via assertions of *parliamentary* power.

---

[29] Here the Pakistan Supreme Court ignored US reasoning noting that, although the state was not empowered to ban the peaceful and essential practices of selected religious groups, it could, for the sake of public order, legally regulate the practices of all religious groups (for example, with an administrative requirement noting that any group engaged in a religious procession would have to obtain a permit for that procession however "essential" it might be). In Pakistan, the court held that the state was entitled to ban, not a particular practice for all religious groups, but almost *all* of the practices employed by a *particular* religious group.

[30] For a similar rereading of US Supreme Court jurisprudence regarding a basic right to free speech in Israel, see Jacobsohn (1993).

Clearly, Zia extended what parliament had begun in 1973 and 1974. But, since 1974, and despite numerous efforts to annul ostensibly religious ordinances promulgated by military dictators like General Ayub (e.g., regarding inheritance) and Zia (e.g., regarding adultery), Pakistani parliamentarians have *not* sought to annul Zia's work in the realm of religious freedom.[31] As Saeed herself points out (2011: 33), quoting former Supreme Court judge Fakhruddin Ebrahim (who served as lead counsel for Pakistan's Ahmadiyya during the early stages of *Zaheeruddin*), the judges who decided *Zaheeruddin* (1993) were not beholden to Zia (d. 1988). As common *political* actors, she notes, they were simply "afraid . . . of becoming unpopular" (see also Mahmud 1995: 83, 96).

Martin Lau (2006) is known for his account of "Islamization" within Pakistan's superior judiciary. As an explanation for Pakistani efforts to fill up imported constitutional provisions regarding religious freedom with new meaning, however, Lau's focus on religious reasoning in the superior judiciary is difficult to reconcile with the fact that religious reasoning was notably absent in several key decisions: *Kashmiri* (1969), *Mubashir* (1978), *Mujibur Rahman* (1988), and *Zaheeruddin* (1993). As noted earlier, judgments like *Zaheeruddin* actively avoided "Islamic" references in favor of "Indian" or "American" references.[32] Indeed, as Anser Aftab Kazi has pointed out (2015: 123, 126–127), the jurisprudence in *Zaheeruddin* clearly shows that religious freedom was "successfully translated into, and proscribed within," a nonreligious "Liberal-Legal [idiom]."

Ali Usman Qasmi (2014) does not trace the shifting meaning of Pakistan's religious freedom provisions to the work of military dictators or superior court judges. Instead, he focuses on the interventions of religious parties in the context of Pakistan's parliament. But, again, Qasmi's argument is difficult to reconcile with the fact that, inside Pakistan's parliament, the religious actors he highlights were greatly outnumbered by those from secular parties like the Pakistan People's Party (PPP) and the Pakistan Muslim League (PML)—not only in the PPP-led government of 1973–74 (13 percent religious parties in parliament), but also in the wake of every general election since then: 1988, 1990, 1993, 1997, 2008, 2013, and 2018.

What accounts for Pakistan's rereading of its imported religious freedom provisions is, thus, not the "Islamizing" dictatorship of General Zia, the "religious" reasoning of its courts, or the special power of "Islamist" parties in

---

[31] When Prime Minister Benazir Bhutto suggested blasphemy law amendments in 1994 (e.g., imprisonment for false allegations), her proposals were defeated. When parliamentarian Sherry Rehman called for similar reforms after the assassination of Governor Salman Taseer (who did the same in 2011), she faced death threats. Even today, Zia's reforms remain intact. (In 2015, however, Pakistan's Supreme Court upheld the execution of Salman Taseer's assassin in a landmark judgment criticizing vigilante violence; see *Mumtaz Qadri v State* [2015].)

[32] For a similar account of the Federal Shariat Court judgment in *Mujibur Rahman v Pakistan* (1988) PLD (SC) 167, see Kazi (2015: 111, 113).

parliament. What accounts for Pakistan's revised approach is a much wider pattern in which enumerated fundamental rights imported from India were paired with (a) right-wing religious protests and, then, (b) within Pakistan's National Assembly, an increasingly narrow framing of "Muslim" majoritarian power.

8.5. Conclusion

For those with an interest in constitutional borrowing, mapping textual transfers is not enough. On the contrary, the *meaning* of a borrowed constitutional provision only emerges with reference to a particular *political* context. The challenge, I argue, lies in tracking the political motivations of those who import and, then, actively reinterpret foreign constitutional texts.

In Pakistan, it was not the influence of "religious" parties in parliament, an increasingly "religious" orientation within the superior courts, or the promulgation of ostensibly "religious" laws by General Zia-ul-Haq that reframed the meaning of religious freedom provisions initially imported from India. What reframed the meaning of those provisions was actually broad-based and remarkably enduring political sense that appeasing right-wing vigilantes with a more restricted legal framing of "Muslim" identity might end their periodic bouts of rioting. The religious freedom clauses that Pakistan imported from India never sought to treat a fundamental right to religious freedom as absolute. From the outset, those clauses noted that formal constitutional protections for religious freedom were always subordinated to politically contingent concerns regarding "public order." Within Pakistan, that focus was simply refashioned, *politically*, over time—moving away from right-wing vigilantes as the most important driver of public disorder toward a more explicit focus on the "provocations" associated with (otherwise peaceful) Ahmadi religious beliefs and practices. This is the conceptual, political, and formal legal shift that ultimately allowed Pakistan to limit religious freedom as a fundamental constitutional right.

Drawing inspiration from the anti-colonial politics of Ireland and India more than "prestigious" European powers like Britain, Pakistan clearly illustrates the ways in which explicit textual transplants are subject to an ongoing "politics" of conceptual re-signification. Over time, in different ways, Pakistani politicians, judges, and executive officials found ways to accommodate right-wing patterns of religious-cum-political agitation. Above all, they reversed the onus of responsibility surrounding periodic episodes of vigilante violence, arguing that, in Pakistan, parliament was fully empowered to limit the rights of "peaceful" religious practitioners—practitioners who might be recast, even *preemptively*, as religious "provocateurs" and, thus, as a primary impetus for "public disorder."

In debates regarding the status of foreign law in the United States, the late Supreme Court justice Antonin Scalia famously noted that American judges must rely on "the standards of decency of American society—not the standards . . . of the world [or of] . . . other countries" (Chaudhry 2006: 7). In Pakistan, the same view prevailed: not only (following Scalia) with respect to "domestic" laws, but also with respect to Pakistan's *domestic* reading of imported *foreign* laws. Treating imported constitutional provisions regarding religious freedom as a constitutional "empty signifier," Pakistan simply found new ways to have Alan Watson's (1974) textual cake while, at the same time, following Pierre Legrand (2001), eating that cake in specifically Pakistani way.

Acknowledgments

The editors are grateful to Cambridge University Press and the *Journal of Asian Studies* for allowing Nelson to draw on his article "Constitutional Migration and the Meaning of Religious Freedom: From Ireland and India to the Islamic Republic of Pakistan," *Journal of Asian Studies* 79, no. 1 (2020): 129–154.

References

Abdul Rehman Mubashir v. Amir Ali Shah (1978) PLD (Lah.) 113.

Adcock, C. S. 2016. "Violence, Passion and the Law: A Brief History of Section 295-A and Its Antecedents." *Journal of American Academy of Religion* 84:2, 337–351.

Ahmad, Mohammad Bosheer. 1951. *Constitutions of Eastern Countries*. Select Constitutions of the World, vol. 1. Karachi: Governor-General's Press and Publications.

Ahmad, Tariq. 2014. "Defining Religion: The Use (or Misuse) of the 'Essential Practices Doctrine' in *Zaheer-ud-Din*." Unpublished manuscript.

Ahmed, Asad Ali. 2009. "Specters of Macaulay: Blasphemy, the Indian Penal Code, and Pakistan's Postcolonial Predicament." In *Censorship in South Asia*, R. Kaur and W. Mazzarella, eds. Bloomington: Indiana University Press, 172–205.

A.K. Shorish Kashmiri v. West Pakistan (1969) PLD (Lah.) 289 (Pak.).

Al-Ali, Zaid. 2011. "Constitutional Drafting and External Influence." In *Comparative Constitutional Law*, Tom Ginsburg and Rosalind Dixon, eds. Northampton, MA: Edward Elgar, 77–95.

Arvind, T. T. 2010. "The 'Transplantation Effect' in Harmonization." *International and Comparative Law Quarterly* 59:1, 65–88.

Bajpai, Rochana. 2011. *Debating Difference: Group Rights and Liberal Democracy in India*. Delhi: Oxford University Press.

Beer, Lawrence. 1990. "Constitutionalism and Rights in Japan and Korea." In *Constitutionalism and Rights: The Influence of the United States Constitution Abroad*, L. Henkin and A. Rosenthal, eds. New York: Columbia University Press, 225–259.

Berkowitz, Daniel, Katharina Pistor, and Jean-François Richard. 2003. "The Transplant Effect." *American Journal of Comparative Law* 51, 163–203.

Bhagavan, Manu. 2010. "A New Hope: India, the United Nations, and the Making of the Universal Declaration of Human Rights." *Modern Asian Studies* 44:2, 311–347.

Binder, Leonard. 1961. *Religion and Politics in Pakistan.* New York: Columbia University Press.

Braibanti, Ralph. 1965. "Pakistan: Constitutional Issues in 1964." *Asian Survey* 5:2, 79–87.

Cairns, John. 2013. "Watson, Walton, and the History of Legal Transplants." *Georgia Journal of International and Comparative Law* 41, 637.

Choudhry, Sujit. 2006. *The Migration of Constitutional Ideas.* New York: Cambridge University Press.

Cohn, Margit. 2010. "Legal Transplant Chronicles: The Evolution of Unreasonableness and Proportionality Review of the Administration in the United Kingdom." *American Journal of Comparative Law* 58:3, 583–629.

Cotterell, Roger. 2001. "Is There a Logic of Legal Transplants." In *Adapting Legal Cultures,* D. Nelken and J. Feest, eds. London: Hart, 71–92.

Danchin, Peter. 2007-8. "The Emergence and Structure of Religious Freedom in International Law Reconsidered." *Journal of Law and Religion* 23:2, 455–534.

Dixon, Rosalind and Eric Posner. 2011. "The Limits of Constitutional Convergence." *Chicago Journal of International Law* 11, 399.

Finke, Roger. 1990. "Religious Deregulation: Origins and Consequences." *Journal of Church and State* 32:3, 609–626.

Friedman, Yohannan. 1989. *Prophecy Continuous: Aspects of Ahmadi Religious Thought and Its Medieval Background.* Berkeley: University of California Press.

Friedman, Yohannan. 2003. *Tolerance and Coercion in Islam: Interfaith Relations in the Muslim Tradition.* New York: Cambridge University Press.

Gill, Anthony. 2009. *The Political Origins of Religious Liberty.* New York: Cambridge University Press.

Ginsburg, Tom, James Melton, and Zachary Elkins. 2010. *The Endurance of National Constitutions.* Chicago: University of Chicago Press.

Graziadei, Michele. 2006. "Comparative Law as the Study of Transplants and Receptions." In *Oxford Handbook of Comparative Law,* M. Reimann and R. Zimmermann, eds. Oxford: Oxford University Press, 441–476.

Hirschl, Ran. 2014. *Comparative Matters: The Renaissance of Comparative Constitutional Law.* Oxford: Oxford University Press.

Jacobsohn, Gary. 1993. *Apple of Gold: Constitutionalism in Israel and the United States.* Princeton, NJ: Princeton University Press.

Jacobsohn, Gary. 2006. "Constitutional Identity." *Review of Politics* 68:3, 361–397.

Kazi, Anser Aftab. 2015. *The Politics of Blasphemy: Religion and Public Reasoning in Pakistan.* Cambridge University: DPhil thesis.

Kelsay, John. 1988. "Saudi Arabia, Pakistan, and the Universal Declaration of Human Rights." In *Human Rights and the Conflicts of Culture: Western and Islamic Perspectives on Religious Liberty,* D. Little, J. Kelsay, and A. Sachedina, eds. Columbia: University of South Carolina Press, 33–52.

Khan, Amjad Mahmood. 2003. "Persecution of the Ahmadiyya Community in Pakistan: An Analysis under International Law and International Relations." *Harvard Human Rights Journal* 16.

Khan, Amjad Mahmood. 2011. "Misuse and Abuse of Legal Argument by Analogy in Transjudicial Communication: The Case of Zaheeruddin v State." *Richmond Journal of Global Law and Business* 10:4, 497–523.

Khan, Amjad Mahmood. 2015. "Pakistan's Anti-blasphemy Laws and the Illegitimate Use of the 'Law, Public Order, and Morality' Limitation on Constitutional Rights." *Review of Faith and International Affairs* 13:1, 13–22.

Kılınç, Ramazan. 2014. "International Pressure, Domestic Politics, and the Dynamics of Religious Freedom: Evidence from Turkey." *Comparative Politics* 46:2, 127–145.

Laclau, Ernesto. 1996. "Why Do Empty Signifiers Matter to Politics." In *Emancipation(s)*. New York: Verso, 36–46.

Lau, Martin. 1994. "The Case of Zaheeruddin v The State and Its Impact on the Fundamental Right to Freedom of Religion." *Center for Islamic and Middle Eastern Law (SOAS) Yearbook* vol. 1, 1. https://www.soas.ac.uk/cimel/materials/intro.html

Lau, Martin. 2006. *The Role of Islam in the Legal System of Pakistan* (Leiden: Nijhoff).

Legrand, Pierre. 1997. "The Impossibility of Legal Transplants." *Maastricht Journal of European and Comparative Law* 4, 111.

Legrand, Pierre. 2001. "What 'Legal Transplants'?" In *Adapting Legal Cultures*, D. Nelken and J. Feest, eds. Oxford: Hart, 55–70.

Lévi-Strauss, Claude. 1963. *Structural Anthropology.* New York: Basic Books.

Mahmud, Tayyab. 1995. "Freedom of Religion and Religious Minorities in Pakistan: A Study of Judicial Practice." *Fordham International Law Journal* 19:1, 40–100.

Miller, Jonathan. 2003. "A Typology of Legal Transplants: Using Sociology, Legal History, and Argentine Examples to Explain the Transplant Process." *American Journal of Comparative Law* 51:4, 839–885.

Mumtaz Qadri v. State (2015) Crim. Appeal 210.

Nelken, David. 2003. "Comparativists and Transferability." In *Comparative Legal Studies: Traditions and Transitions*, Pierre Legrand and Roderick Munday, eds. Cambridge: Cambridge University Press, 437–466.

Nelson, Matthew J. 2016. "Islamic Law in an Islamic State: What Role for Parliament?" In *Constitution-Writing, Religion, and Democracy*, A. Bali and H. Lerner, eds. New York: Cambridge University Press, 235–263.

Nelson, Matthew J., Aslı Bâli, Hanna Lerner, and David Mednicoff. 2020. "From Foreign Text to Local Meaning: The Politics of Religious Exclusion in Transnational Constitutional Borrowing." *Law and Social Inquiry* 45:4, 935–964.

Neo, Jaclyn. 2014. "What's in a Name? Malaysia's 'Allah' Controversy and the Judicial Intertwining of Religious and Ethnic Identity." *International Journal of Constitutional Law* 12:3, 751–768.

Newman, K. J. 1962. "The Constitutional Evolution of Pakistan." *International Affairs* 38:3, 353–364.

Norval, Alleta. 2000. "The Things We Do with Words: Contemporary Approaches to the Analysis of Ideology." *British Journal of Political Science* 30:2, 313–346.

Osiatynski, Wiktor. 2003. "Paradoxes of Constitutional Borrowing." *International Journal of Comparative Law* 1, 244.

Osurie, Goldie. 2013. *Religious Freedom in India: Sovereignty and (Anti) Conversion.* London: Routledge.

Perju, Vlad. 2012. "Constitutional Transplants, Borrowing, and Migrations." In *Oxford Handbook on Comparative Constitutional Law*, M. Rosenfeld and A. Sajó, eds. Oxford: Oxford University Press, 1304–1326.

Qasmi, Ali Usman. 2014. *The Ahmadis and the Politics of Religious Exclusion in Pakistan.* London: Anthem.

Rao, B. Shiva, ed. 1934. *Select Constitutions of the World.* Madras: Madras Law Journal Press.

Report of the Court of Inquiry (Punjab Disturbances of 1953). 1954. Lahore: Government Printing.

Rosenfeld, Michel. 2001–3. "Constitutional Migration and the Bounds of Comparative Analysis." *NYU Annual Survey of American Law* 58, 67–83.

Rosenfeld, Michael and András Sajó. 2006. "Spreading Liberal Constitutionalism: An Inquiry into the Fate of Free Speech in New Democracies." In *The Migration of Constitutional Ideas*, S. Choudhry, ed. Cambridge: Cambridge University Press, 142–177.

Saeed, Sadia. 2011. "The Nation and Its Heretics: Courts, State Authority, and Minority Rights in Pakistan." http://web.law.columbia.edu/sites/default/files/microsites/law-culture/files/2011-files/Nation%26Heretics_SAEED.pdf.

Saeed, Sadia. 2018. *Politics of Desecularization: Law and the Minority Question in Pakistan.* Cambridge: Cambridge University Press.

Said, Edward. 1983. *The World, the Text, and the Critic.* Cambridge, MA: Harvard University Press.

Saussure, Ferdinand. 1959. *Course in General Linguistics.* New York: Philosophical Library.

Schonthal, Benjamin. 2015. "Ceylon/Sri Lanka: The Politics of Religious Freedom and the End of Empire." In *Politics of Religious Freedom*, Winnifred Fallers Sullivan, Elizabeth Shakman Hurd, Saba Mahmood, and Peter G. Danchin, eds. Chicago: University of Chicago Press, 149–157.

Select Constitutions of the World (Prepared for Presentation to Dáil Eireann by Order of the Irish Provisional Government). 1922. Dublin: Constitution Committee.

Small, Richard. 2005. "Towards a Theory of Contextual Transplants." *Emory International Law Review* 19:3, 1431–1455.

Tushnet, Mark. 2009. "The Inevitable Globalization of Constitutional Law." *Virginia Journal of International Law* 49, 985.

Waltz, Susan. 2004. "Universal Human Rights: The Contribution of Muslim States." *Human Rights Quarterly* 26:4, 799–844.

Watson, Alan. 1974. *Legal Transplants: An Approach to Comparative Law.* Edinburgh: Scottish Academic Press.

Zaheeruddin v. The State (1993) 26 SCMR (SC) 1718.

9

The Limits of Pluralism

A Perspective on Religious Freedom in Indian Constitutional Law

Mathew John

9.1. Introduction

Almost at all times in the history of independent India, its broadly liberal and secular constitutional state has been called on to resolve disputes, both over religious practices and between various religious groups. Disputes over practices like temple entry, animal sacrifice, ritual suicide, and meat-eating, as well as events that have defined the course of Indian history like the Shah Bano controversy and the Babri Masjid demolition, have all required India's secular constitutional state and especially its judiciary to play a central role in resolving religious and cultural conflict. At one level of constitutional practice these examples of religious disputes are merely specific instances that illustrate the challenge of defending the normative ideals of religious liberty, free expression, and equal citizenship that are guaranteed by the Constitution. However, the defenses of norms in courts are also instances and sites at which the reach and span of sovereign power over religious and social practices are negotiated at the interface of state and society. It is this negotiation that forms the core concern of this chapter. Accordingly, by elaborating the modes through which religion is framed, patterned, and characterized by Indian constitutional law, this chapter will argue that the conceptual and epistemic frames of Indian constitutionalism have operated to constrain rather than expand the range of religious pluralism and liberty. In addition, the chapter also attempts to outline an alternative interpretative orientation through which Indian constitutional law might defend religious pluralism and freedom while also granting the state power to act against religion when it fundamentally undermines the bonds of political solidarity.

Mathew John, *The Limits of Pluralism* In: *Negotiating Democracy and Religious Pluralism*. Edited by: Karen Barkey, Sudipta Kaviraj, and Vatsal Naresh, Oxford University Press. © Oxford University Press 2021.
DOI: 10.1093/oso/9780197530016.003.0010

9.2. Framing Religious Freedom in the Indian Constitution

Historically, the contours of religious freedom in Indian constitutional law have been defined by what seemed to be a will to constrain the overdetermination of everyday life by religious practices. In an extremely well-worn description of this problem, B. R. Ambedkar's accounts for the challenge of religion in the following manner when intervening on the impending reform of religious personal laws in the Constituent Assembly:

> *The religious conceptions in this country are so vast that they cover every aspect of life, from birth to death.* There is nothing which is not religion and if personal law is to be saved, I am sure about it that in social matters we will come to a standstill. . . . There is nothing extraordinary in saying that *we ought to strive hereafter to limit the definition of religion in such a manner that we shall not extend beyond beliefs and such rituals as may be connected with ceremonials which are essentially religious.* . . . I personally do not understand why religion should be given this vast, expansive jurisdiction so as to cover the whole of life and to prevent the legislature from encroaching upon that field. (Constituent Assembly Debates 1999: 781, emphasis added)

That is, religion in India would have to be reformed, and the reformer's search for beliefs and practices that Ambedkar calls "essentially religious" would form an important aspect of state regulation of religious freedom in Indian constitutional law. But how would the "essentially religious" aspects of a community's practices be defined and delimited?

Perhaps the best place to begin the task of contouring state regulation of religion in India is the Indian Constituent Assembly. In what was perhaps the Assembly's earliest attempt to draft a clause on religious freedom, its Fundamental Rights Sub-Committee[1] placed for consideration a draft clause on religious freedom presented to it by K. M. Munshi granting all persons equal rights to freedom of conscience and the right to freely practice religion. This draft right was subject to the maintenance of public order, morality, or health. A clarifying clause stated that "the right to profess and *practice* religion shall not include economic, financial, political or other secular activities associated with religious worship" (Rao 1966: 122, 140, emphasis added). However, despite the significant

---

[1] The Indian Constituent Assembly was advised by an advisory committee set up under the Cabinet Mission Statement. In turn the advisory committee constituted sub-committees on various aspects of constitutional governance. A considerable part of the structure and design of religious freedom took shape in the deliberations of this committee process, especially in the sub-committees on fundamental rights and on minority rights.

role envisaged in this provision for state regulation, it was instantly subjected to strong and sustained opposition by the social reformers in the Assembly.

Speaking for the reformist position, Rajkumari Amrit Kaur expressed apprehensions about Munshi's clause "inasmuch as it might invalidate legislation against anti-social customs which might have the sanction of religion" (Rao 1966: 122). To facilitate such legislation Rajkumari Amrit Kaur thought it appropriate to limit religious freedom by conceiving of it narrowly to include only the right to conscience and worship and not the right to religious practice (Rao 1966: 146–7). Thus when the Minorities' Committee of the Assembly suggested that a prospective right of religious freedom must protect "religious practice," it was once again opposed by Amrit Kaur who feared, perhaps mistakenly, that such rights

> would not only be a bar to future social legislation but would even invalidate past legislation such as the Widow Remarriage Act, the Sarda Act or even the law abolishing Sati. Everyone is aware how many evil practices, which one would like to abolish, are carried on in the name of religion, e.g., purdah, polygamy, caste disabilities, animal sacrifice, dedication of girls to temples, to mention a few. (Rao 1966: 213)

Amrit Kaur's concerns were not unusual, and her arguments for constraining religious practice formed an important part of the regulatory imagination that sought to narrow religion to its essential core.

The ambition of religious reformers such as Amrit Kaur was driven by the entirely legitimate aim of eradicating unethical practices that were understood to be associated primarily though not exclusively with the Hindu religion. However, as Shyama Prasad Mookherjee and others pointed out, a sweeping reform agenda that sought to target and restrict religious practices would impose potentially unjustifiable burdens on the Indian religious traditions that as a matter of fact emphasized *practices* over worship. Consequently, Mookherjee suggested that the Assembly provide a significantly greater leeway for practices, permitting reform of religious practices only in exceptional circumstances. It was accordingly decided that a more comprehensive provision would be drafted in which practices would be included as part of the right to freedom but one that also empowered the legislature to reform religious practices as a separate proviso. (Rao 1966: 265–67)[2] In other words appropriate provisions to guarantee religious freedom were crafted by balancing India's plural traditions of religious practice and the need for a strong state that could intervene against the ethically

---

[2] This was suggested by C. Rajagopalachari in response to the issues raised by the debate (Ibid. 265–267).

unjustifiable practices found nested in that plurality. An appropriately redrafted clause was subsequently debated in the Constituent Assembly and adopted as Article 25 of the contemporary Constitution.

Religious freedom is also dealt with in the India Constitution in three other provisions besides Article 25. However, as it is the central constitutional provision that frames the character of the right to religious freedom, this chapter is primarily concerned with the interpretation of Article 25 and to a limited extent Article 26, which deals with the right of religious denominations to manage their affairs in matters of religion. Article 25 of the Constitution grants all persons the right to practice, profess, and propagate religion while simultaneously also permitting the state to regulate and reform aspects of religious practice. In its detail one part of Article 25 is structured like a standard liberal freedom where the state is required not to interfere in the individual's right to practice, profess, and propagate religion in a manner that is consistent with the similar rights of others (Article 25(1)). However, the Constitution also includes an altogether different kind of restraint on religious practice that permits the state to restrain religious freedom by subjecting it to the power to "regulate or restrict economic, financial, political or other secular activity which may be associated with religious practice" (Article 25(a)) or "provide for social welfare and reform or the throwing open of Hindu religious institutions of a public character to all classes and sections of Hindus" (Article 25(2)(b)). It is these explicitly interventionist and reforming provisions that have determined the shape and form that religious freedom has taken in Indian constitutional practice.

The explicit grant of state power in the Indian Constitution to regulate and reform religion necessarily calls for some kind of balancing between its interventionist and reforming power, and the regard it is obliged to show toward the freedom to practice religion that is simultaneously also protected by the Constitution. In striking this balance in constitutional adjudication, courts have followed the historical trajectory charted by Ambedkar and others in the Constituent Assembly by extending protection to a core set of essential religious practices, leaving all other peripheral and "secular" practices open to active state regulation. Consequently, by examining the manner in which the essential core of a religious tradition has been delimited and demarcated by courts, this chapter will illustrate the form in which courts have shaped religious practice.

9.3. The Search for the Essential Truth of Religious Practices

In one of the earliest and definitive decisions on the determination of essential religious practices, the Supreme Court was called on to delivered judgment on the constitutional validity of the Madras Hindu Religious and Charitable

Endowments Act 1951. Popularly called the *Shirur Mutt* case (MANU/SC/0136/1954) after the religious institution that challenged this statute, the case considered claims of the appellant that the power granted to the government to take over mismanaged Hindu religious institutions as a trustee violated the freedom of religious groups to manage religious institutions as permitted by Article 25(1) and Article 26(b) of the Constitution.

Countering the claims of the appellants, the state contended that it had the broadest powers of regulating "secular" aspects related to a religious tradition under Article 25(2)(a) and that the petitioner's right to religious freedom did not extend beyond the relationship between a believer and his deity—an argument not unlike those made by the likes of Amrit Kaur to assert the power of the state to reform socially unjust practices. A stretched reading of Article 25(2) could suggest that the state was vested with vast powers to regulate and reform religious practice as long as it did not completely extinguish the right to religious freedom. However, the court categorically refused to accept this contention that sought to limit religious freedom solely to the relationship of conscience between believers and their deities.

In keeping with the debates in the Constituent Assembly, the court instead attempted to devise an adjudicative test or framework to balance traditions of religious practice and the power of the state to reform and manage religion. Accordingly it held that

> what constitutes the essential part of a religion is primarily to be *ascertained with reference to the doctrines of that religion itself*. If the tenets of any religious sect of the Hindus prescribe that offerings of food should be given to the idol at particular hours of the day, that periodical ceremonies should be performed in a certain way at certain periods of the year or that there should be daily recital of sacred texts or oblations to the sacred fire, all these would be regarded as parts of religion and the mere fact that they involve expenditure of money or employment of priests and servants or the use of marketable commodities would not make them secular activities partaking of a commercial or economic character; all of them are religious practices and should be regarded as matters of religion. (*Shirur Mutt* case: para 20, emphasis added)

In other words, the court stressed that the essential core of a religion had to reflect those doctrines and practices that a community *subjectively* viewed to be essential to their religion. However, in what manner would the court arrive at a subjectively satisfactory account of essential religious beliefs and practices?

It is important to note that it is the court or perhaps another organ of state that would have to ultimately make a "subjectively" sympathetic determination about whether the claims of a community form part of the core of its religious tradition. However, the criterion for the subjective determination of essential practices has never been particularly clear. Perhaps as a consequence, Indian courts have over the years performed something akin to a theological function in sifting between different kinds of religious claims, establishing some while denying others. Thus the Supreme Court has held that the sacrifice of cows did not constitute an essential part of the Islamic faith (*All India Reporter* [*AIR*] 1958 SC 731); overruled Muslim claims that prayer in a mosque was crucial to the Islamic faith (*Supreme Court Cases* [SCC] 6 SCC 360); refused to accept traditional rights of the Tilkayats of the Shrinathji temple at Nathdwara, which was taken from them by the Nathdwara Temple Act, 1959 (*AIR* 1963 SC 1638); stipulated that the *tandava* dance was not a significant part of the Anand Margi community (*AIR* 1984 SC 51); declared that the followers of Aurobindo did not constitute a distinct religion (1983 SC 1); and so on. As in any hermeneutic exercise there are many equally valid candidates that could claim to embody essential religious truth, leaving the court open to the charge that its determinations of essential religious practices are entirely ad hoc (Dhavan 1987: 209).

The charges of ad hocism difficult are to shrug away. Nonetheless, it is possible to discern a conceptual pattern in the judicial characterization of essential religion by extrapolating two inchoately articulated conceptions of religious practice from the *Shirur Mutt* case. The *first* of these draws on an intuitive sociology of Indian religions and emphasizes the importance of *practice*, as already highlighted in the debates of the Constituent Assembly. This intuitive sociological account of religion is also tied into a second conceptualization of religion. In the words of the court,

> There are well known religions in India like Buddhism and Jainism which do not believe in God or in any Intelligent First Cause. *A religion undoubtedly has its basis in a system of beliefs or doctrines* which are regarded by those who profess that religion as conducive to their spiritual well being, but it would not be correct to say that religion is nothing else but a doctrine or belief. A religion may not only lay down a code of ethical rules for its followers to accept, it might prescribe rituals and observances, ceremonies and modes of worship which are regarded as integral parts of religion, and these forms and observances might extend even to matters of food and dress. (*Shirur Mutt* case: para. 19, emphasis added)

Thus, though the court places considerable emphasis on practice and ritual as distinctive markers of religion, it seems to believe that a religion and its practices are *founded in doctrine*, which is a second frame that the court employs to characterize religion.

In extrapolating practice as a defining feature of the sociology of Indian religious experience from *Shirur Mutt*, it is important to note that even doctrinal accounts of religion can lay considerable emphasis on practice. Thus, in speaking of practice, Indian courts (including in *Shirur Mutt*) have emphasized the centrality of practice and have on occasion drawn on the Australian judgment *Adelaide Company of Jehovah's Witnesses Inc. v. Commonwealth*, in which it was stated that

> there are those who regard religion as constituting principally a system of beliefs or statements of doctrine. So viewed religion may either be true or false. Others are more inclined to regard religion as prescribing a mode of conduct. So viewed religion may be good or bad. There are others who pay greater attention to religion as involving some prescribed form of ritual or religious observance. (67 Commonwealth Law Reports (C.L.R.) 116, 1943, 123)

Drawing on these comments, Indian courts and commentators have gone on to presume that the dominant conception of religion endorsed by the court in the *Shirur Mutt* case is one that emphasizes practice. Indian courts have indeed used this decision to distinguish between the narrower protection of belief and conscience from the broader protection of religious practice (Mehta 2008a: 322). However, there is a relatively under examined and perhaps more significant aspect of the conception of religious practice that could be read into and from *Shirur Mutt*.

Pratap Bhanu Mehta illustrates this conception of religious practice by drawing out different senses of being religious from two important figures in Roman antiquity. Drawing from Cicero's *De Natura Deorum*, Mehta highlights how Cicero asserts that

> *religion has been* dissociated from superstition not only by philosophers but by our own ancestors as well. I may mention as to these two terms that men who used to spend whole days in prayer and sacrifice in order that their children might survive them (*essent superstites*), were called *superstitiosus*, a title which afterwards extended more widely, while such as heedfully repeated and, as it were, "regathered" (*relegerent*) everything that formed a part of divine worship, were named *religiosus* from *relegere*, in the same way that *elegans* is derived from *eligere*, *diligens* from *diligere*, and *intellegens* from *intellegere*, for in all these words the force of *legere* is the same as in *religiosus*. It was in this way that with the words *superstitiosus* and *religiosus*, the one became the designation of a fault, the other of an excellence. (Mehta 2008b: 67)

Mehta contrasts Cicero with Lactantius, a Christian who took issue with this characterization of religion three centuries later. According to Lactantius, religion is a bond of piety that ties man to God. Countering Cicero's account of religion, he argued that

> the word is not as Cicero interpreted it from "re-reading," or "choosing again" (*relegendo*). . . . We can know from the matter itself how inept this interpretation is. For if superstition and religion are engaged in worshipping the same gods, there is little or rather no difference . . . because religion is a worship of the true; superstition of the false. And it is important, really, why you worship, not how you worship, or what you pray for. . . . We have said that *the name of religion is taken from the bond of piety, because God has bound and fastened man to Himself of piety, since it is necessary for us to serve Him as Lord and obey Him as father. . . . They are superstitious who worship many and false gods; but we, who supplicate the one true God, are religious.* (Mehta 2008b: 67–8)

Consequently, there are three different sensibilities that could be drawn from Mehta's discussion of religiosity: first, religion as the devotion to regathering and repetition of what is excellent or valued in a tradition; second, religion as a commitment to superstitious, excessive, or absurd practice; and third, religion as commitment to true theology or doctrine. For Cicero, religion is a way of life or a set of inherited and excellent practices. The only reason for its practice is pre-existing practice whose repetition regathers the sense of an ongoing and valued tradition. That is, the significance of practice is nothing but repetition such that it can recreate all that is valuable in a social and cultural milieu, with superstition or excessiveness being the contrasting value against which it acquires salience. Significantly, the truth or falsity of belief or doctrine is unimportant to Cicero's conception of religion, while it is the basis of Lactantius's conception of his religion.

Mehta glosses over the significance of the distinctions between these different conceptions of religion.[3] However, it is the hypothesis of this chapter that the question of religious "practice" in Indian constitutional debates has operated to transform religion understood as valued practice into religion founded in doctrine. In other words, Indian constitutional practice is structurally organized to reform, reformulate, or perhaps even make over religion experienced by a wide range of Indian cultural traditions as plural forms of ritual practice and ethical striving, into religion founded in true or foundational doctrine. Justice Mukherjea's commitment to a subjective determination of essential religion

---

[3] For a more elaborate discussion of the distinctions Mehta makes it is useful to note the more elaborately argued position by Balagangadhara (2005) on the role that the Christian idea of *religio* played in the transformation of the Roman *traditio*.

allowed for a limited recognition of religious experience embodied in practice. However, as decisions such as the *Shirur Mutt* case had no clear conception of practice as a key cog in an ongoing religious tradition, subsequent decisions were unable to defend practice in the face of a reformist court less sympathetic to the subjective determination of essential religious practices. In turn this led to more intrusive demands on religious practice that require elaboration.

9.4. The Eclipse of Traditional Religion in Indian Constitutional Adjudication

In years following the *Shirur Mutt* case and against the background of a con-stitutional scheme that permitted fundamental social change, reformist state claims over religious practice only increased.[4] And under the stewardship of Chief Justice Gajendragadkar the Supreme Court fundamentally reworked the essential practices test to altogether eviscerate the subjective element from the determination of essential practices. What was left of the essential practices test made even sharper demands on traditional practices. Ronojoy Sen describes this development in relation to the Hindu traditions as judicial rationalization, or a technique of interpreting religious experience by reforming or collapsing the practices from everyday Hinduism into those of the Vedic or the high Hindu traditions (Sen 2009: 86). While this chapter draws on the broad contours of Sen's description, it goes one step further to argue that the process of rationalization, going hand in hand with the expansion of judicial and state power over religion, applies to all religious traditions whether it be high Hinduism (*AIR* 1966 SC 1119), everyday Hinduism (1984 SC 51), or indeed any other religious tradition (MANU/SC/0072/1962). The path of judicial precedent leading toward greater rationalization of religion is well described in the legal scholarship and especially in the work of Ronojoy Sen (2010). Therefore, this section only illustrates a par-ticularly stark form of rationalization of religious practice, the manner in which it transforms traditions of religious practice, and its implications for religious pluralism. This dimension of religious rationalization is examined through the much-studied case of *Sastri Yagnapurshdasji v. Muldas Bhudardas* Vaishya (*AIR* 1966 SC 1119).

In this case the Satsangis, or followers of Swaminarayan, a nineteenth-century social reformer, claimed immunity from the provisions of a temple entry statute, the Bombay Hindu Places of Public Worship (Entry-Authorisation)

---

[4] This is in keeping with a constitutional model that was committed to the control of all rival social and cultural centers of power. See, e.g., Mehta 2010.

Act 1956. Like all other mid-century temple entry legislations in India, the statute barred Hindu temples of a public character from refusing entry to any class or section of Hindus on the ground that they belonged to an untouchable caste or community.

Arguing for their traditional and perhaps essential religious freedoms, the Satsangis claimed they were not bound by the temple entry statute because they were a religious sect entirely distinct from the Hindu religion. They argued that though they could be considered socially and culturally Hindu, they were not part of the Hindu "religion" because

> Swaminarayan, the founder of the sect, considered himself as the Supreme God, and as such, the sect that believes in the divinity of Swaminarayan cannot be assimilated with the followers of Hindu religion. It was also urged that the temples in suit had been established for the worship of Swaminarayan him-self and not for the worship of the traditional Hindu idols. . . . It was further contended that the sect propagated the ideal that worship of any God other than Swaminarayan would be a betrayal of his faith, and lastly, that the Acharyas who had been appointed by Swaminarayan adopted a procedure of "Initiation" (*diksha*) which showed that on initiation, the devotee became a Satsangi and assumed a distinct and separate character as a follower of the sect. (*AIR* 1966 SC 1123)

That is, the Satsangis offered a subjective, traditional, and practice-based ac-count of what made them into a distinct religious community with practices they viewed as distinct from the Hindu "religion." However, it was not clear whether and how this description of their practices set them apart from the Hindu "religion." What was the Hindu religion from which the Satsangis claimed distinctness?

Delivering the unanimous opinion of the Supreme Court, Justice Gajendragadkar disallowed the Satsangi claims, pronounced them "Hindu," and subjected them to the demands of the temple entry statute. However, there was an irresolvable contradiction in Justice Gajendragadkar's account of the Hindu religion. On the one hand he argued that the Hindu religion

> does not claim any one prophet; it does not worship any one God; it does not subscribe to any one dogma; it does not believe in any one philosophic con-cept; it does not follow any one set of religious rites or performances; in fact, it does not appear to satisfy the narrow traditional features of any religion or creed. It may broadly be described as a way of life and nothing more. (*AIR* 1966 SC 1128)

This account of the Hindu religion might perhaps seem far too vague and broad to refer to any well-defined or discrete entity. However, despite its fuzziness, this is not an uncommon way to describe the "Hindu" traditions or even a broader form of sub-continental civilizational religiosity. Therefore, it could be argued that Justice Gajendragadkar draws on intuitive sociology of sub-continental religiosity to characterize the Hindu religion as non-doctrinal traditions of practice that define the Indian sociocultural milieu. In addition, it is also important to note that this characterization of religiosity also comports with Mehta's conception of religion as forms of traditional practice or striving.

On the other hand, however, Justice Gajendragadkar's opinion in the Satsangi case also advanced a much more formalist, reductive definition of the Hindu religion. Drawing significantly from the writing of Dr. S. Radhakrishnan and other modern commentators on the "Hindu" traditions, Justice Gajendragadkar went on to note that the wide variety of practices and philosophical reflections found in the tradition were nevertheless held together by a common philosophy of monistic idealism. That is:

> Beneath the diversity of philosophic thoughts, concepts and ideas expressed by Hindu philosophers . . . lie certain broad concepts which can be treated as basic. The first amongst these basic concepts is the acceptance of the Veda as the highest authority in religious and philosophic matters. (*AIR* 1966 SC 1130)

In this way, Justice Gajendragadkar defined the Hindu religion, not in traditional and civilizational terms with intuitive sociological appeal, but in terms of ideas such as rebirth and predestination that he likened to doctrine. It is this doctrinal account of Hinduism that he ultimately used to refute the Swaminarayans' claim that they were sufficiently distinct from Hinduism as to constitute a separate religion—a claim that he dismissed as simply a product of "superstition, ignorance and complete misunderstanding of the *true teachings* of Hindu religion and of the real significance of the tenets and philosophy taught by Swaminarayan himself" (*AIR* 1966 SC: 1135, emphasis added).

This dismissal of the Swaminarayans' claims to their religion is significant because it reveals the manner in which the court resolved the problem of Hindu religiosity in determining what was essentially religious in the Swaminarayan tradition. That is, even though it seems to have recognized the sociological reality of the plural traditions and practices of Hindu religiosity, it nonetheless felt compelled to absorb, rationalize, or reform those traditions into a doctrinal account sanctioned or drawn up from the interpretative framework of the essential practices test. It is this judicial reformulation or re-description of religious practice founded in doctrine that captures the process of rationalization that Ronojoy Sen (2010) describes as defining the Indian Supreme Court's approach to religious freedom. Additionally, it is in this manner that the interpretative framework of the essential practices test operates to reformulate religious traditions experienced and lived out as valued practices into religions founded in doctrinal truth.

As we have noticed in this chapter, the protection of traditional practice-based religiosity has constituted an important aspect of the challenge of protecting religious expression in India at least from the time when the Constitution was drafted. However, it is precisely this aspect of religious experience lived as practice that has been collapsed into a conception of religion founded in doctrinal truth when operationalized by the search for essential practices. This is true not just of the Swaminarayan case but in many other cases as well. (See, e.g., discussion in section 9.3.) However, the Satsangis' assertion of their traditional religious practices suggests that judicial rationalization has not been able to collapse the widespread social presence of these traditions into the institutionally hegemonic conception of religion understood as essential doctrine. That is, the semantic power of the essential practices test understood as essential doctrines does not necessarily coincide with social understanding of religion, which continues in many respects to be defined by a commitment to practice rather than doctrine. Consequently, if traditional forms of religious practice constitute a significant dimension of religious expression in India, then the legal demand for the rationalization of religious practice, as exemplified in the Satsangi case, could be understood to be a process that seriously constrains the expression of the plurality that makes up those traditions of religious practice. In turn it could even be read to be a framework of state power that is not in a position to exercise legitimate authority over religion.

Of course, the suggestion that the Indian state and especially its judiciary are unable to legitimately exercise authority over religion does not imply that the regulation of practices like temple entry is per se illegitimate. On the contrary, the suggestion of a legitimacy deficit is entirely consistent with the power of the state to intervene and regulate objectionable religious practices. However, constitutional democracy obliges states to wield power in a manner that can be legitimately justified to the groups whose religious practices are abridged. And it is in this respect that the rationalization or doctrinalization of religious practice produced by the constitutional delimitation of religion is both constraining of the plurality that defines religious experience in India, as much as it dents the legitimacy of state power exercised over religious practice. Consequently, it is with some preliminary speculation on alternative forms of conceiving state power over religion that this chapter will draw its (practice constraining) account of religious regulation to a close.

9.5. Rethinking the Essential Practices Test

The problem posed by the search for essential religion by the Indian state as it has been outlined so far is the manner in which it reformulates, delimits, and constrains religion expressed as plural traditions of practice into religion understood as essence or doctrine. However, plurality and diversity of religious practice are not ends in themselves and are not unqualified values. That is, there may be much that is ethically untenable or otherwise worthy of regulation in such religious practices that makes the exercise of state power over them entirely legitimate. If that is the case, then how might it be possible to think beyond the limitations of characterizing religion as essential doctrines, as it has been deployed by Indian courts, while also allowing for state intervention where appropriate? Alternatively, how might it be possible to facilitate state regulation of religion in a manner that is also consistent with the practice-based and plural forms of religiosity?

One response to this question might be to argue that even if religion was defined narrowly to include only religious doctrines, it might hypothetically be possible to defend such practices as a species of free expression more broadly (Neo 2018: 579). However, this has not been a form of defending religious freedom that has acquired traction in India and will not be considered in further detail in this chapter. Another possibility turns on relegating issues pertaining to the delimitation of religion to the background by emphasizing other constitutional provisions that permit the regulation of religion on grounds of public order morality and so on. Making a case for more robust use of such provisions where applicable is perhaps one way to reduce the emphasis on essential doctrines in the constitutional regulation of religion. However, even such cases carry the presumption that the object of regulation is a religious community or practice. And in instances like the Satsangi case, where the claim brought before the court turns on delimiting the area of religious experience, there may be no getting away from the task of defining what constitutes religious experience and what lies outside it. Consequently, there is no escaping the question of delimiting religion. And if this is so, then how might religion be delimited without constraining religious practice to essential doctrines as noticed in the adjudicatory techniques of the Indian Supreme Court? The concluding section of this chapter explores this question by discussing a carefully argued review of India's constitutional adjudication of religious freedom by Gautam Bhatia where he has attempted to dislodge essential practices as a tool to demarcate religion and religious freedom (Bhatia 2016: 351).

9.5.1. Beyond Essential Practices

Drawing on the formal structure of Articles 25 and 26 and on the normative arguments adopted by courts, Bhatia identifies objections that could displace the search for essential practices and doctrines in constitutional adjudication. These objections include, first, that essential practices test cannot be defended as being consistent with the formal structure of Articles 25 and 26 or the historical debates that have informed these provisions. Second, in the long history of judicial adjudication of religious questions on the basis of essential practices, the court has paid insufficient attention to detailing the nature of the test itself. Third, the test destroys the balance between religious autonomy and state intervention by granting far too much salience to the latter, especially after the reformist orientation given to the court by Justice Gajendragadkar. And last, essential practices are often justified on consequentialist grounds that might not on further scrutiny always hold true.

These objections make up the scaffolding that hold up Bhatia's case against the essential practices test. As is apparent, these objections to essential practices test are framed by the manner in which the essential practices are legally organized and the extent to which the test is consistent with the normative constitutional scheme envisaged for the regulation of religion. The present chapter, on the other hand, is organized quite differently in its emphasis on the form in which the essential practices test characterizes religion and its inability to recognize different forms of religiosity, especially traditional religiosity. Even so, Bhatia's objections to the essential practices doctrine offer a useful foil to outline the form in which the state might legitimately organize its approach the regulation of religious practice and especially traditional religious practice.

Returning to Bhatia's objections to the essential practices approach, this chapter has no quarrel with the latter three objections, which could easily operate to supplement the account here. On the other hand, the first objection requires to be taken more seriously, as it has been the basis of state regulation of religious freedom, and as the regulation and reform of religion requires some distinction between the sphere of religious freedom and that of state regulation. Therefore, engaging Bhatia's concern that there is no legal and constitutional basis for the use of the essential practices test, this chapter argues that it is founded on a formal, technical, and ultimately incorrect reading of the state's power to intervene in matters of religion in Article 25(2) and Article 26(b).

At the heart of Bhatia's objection to the use of the essential practices test is the argument that the text of the Constitution only allows courts to determine the distinction between the "religious" and the "secular" domains in their protection of religious freedom. That is, it is argued that the constitutional scheme does not permit courts to determine what is "essential *to* a religion." This position follows an examination of the text of Article 25(2(a), which permits the state to intervene in "economic, financial, political or *secular* activity associated with religious practice" (emphasis added). Further, Article 26(b) permits religious communities to "manage their own affairs in matters of religion" subject to considerations of public order, morality, and health. By implication Bhatia argues that these provisions permit state intervention in secular matters while protecting, as Ambedkar also argued, what is "essentially religious" activity. Therefore, Bhatia distinguishes the phrase "essentially religious" activity from practice "essential *to* religion," on the assumption that the latter phrase requires a normative or an authoritative internal view of what is religious to a particular religious tradition. Consequently, drawing on Ambedkar's address to the Assembly and the text of the Constitution, Bhatia argues that there is no constitutional mandate permitting courts to make this internal determination of what is essential to a particular religious tradition.

Nonetheless he argues that through a mistaken reading of the constitutional text, the Supreme Court drew itself into the determination of what was essential to *particular* religious traditions. In turn, this power was expanded enormously by the Supreme Court under the stewardship of Justice Gajendragadkar, allowing the court to dismiss religious practice as mere superstition. Whatever the propriety of such judicial determinations of religion, Bhatia's contention that the court should reject the enquiry into what is *essential to a religion* because it violates the formal structure of Article 25 presumes that there is an Archimedean point from which it is possible to separate out the essentially religious from the secular. However, if one takes traditional religiosity seriously, then there are many forms of religious experience and practice that cannot be determined or ascertained except in their particularity. That is, even if we used Bhatia's preferred phrase "essentially religious" to identify what is constitutionally protected in a traditional religious practice, such identification could only be possible by inquiring into what is "essential to" that particular tradition. Thus, in the case of the Satsangis, ascertaining whether the practices they sought to defend as essentially religious could only be identified by determining what is "essential to" their tradition.

Consequently, semantic reordering of phrases like "essential to" and "essentially religious" are unlikely to supply reasons to dislodge the salience of the search for essential doctrines. Quite to the contrary, what is required is a form of delimiting religion that is sufficiently sensitive to various forms of religious practice and especially traditional religious practices, as has been suggested in this chapter. As a corollary, it is also important to note how state power has been exercised to edge out a plurality of religious experience and to fashion and demarcate religion as broadly as possible. In turn this requires a degree of judiciousness and restraint in the exercise of state power that permits the right of religious traditions to define the scope of their religious freedoms broadly even as it empowers the state to intervene in and regulate those practices in constitutionally appropriate ways. An outline of this judicious and restrained constitutional ethic for intervention in religious practice is considered in more detail in the following section.

9.5.2. Reorganization of State Intervention in Religious Practice

Having cleared away the essential practices test in his fashion, Bhatia is also concerned with the form that state intervention should assume in determining the shape of religious freedom in the Indian Constitution. Accordingly, he frames the challenge of state intervention in matters related to religious freedom by drawing on Ambedkar's assessment that religion overdetermined social life, making it important to restrict religious practice to the "essentially religious" to protect basic human freedoms, especially the freedoms of individuals and dissenters. This leads Bhatia to argue that religious liberty in the Indian Constitution is designed to protect the individual from the oppressive bonds of collective social life and communal religiosity (Bhatia 2016: 270–1). Further Bhatia also ties Article 25(2) to the broader transformative vision of Indian constitutionalism, which he also views to be tied to a radical conception of equality as envisioned by the Constitution. Thus, other provisions of the Constitution, like Article 17 (prohibiting untouchability), Article 15(2) (prohibiting discrimination in the access to public spaces), Article 23 (prohibiting forced labor), and other provisions that articulate the broader social transformative vision of Indian constitutionalism, are also identified as being tied to this constitutional vision for a radical equality (Bhatia 2016: 270–1).

It is certainly true, as Bhatia suggests, that religion's grip over everyday life was an important background concern that shaped state control over religious freedom in Indian constitutional law. However, as this chapter has pointed out, protecting traditional forms of religious practice was equally a concern that engaged the Assembly and has been a challenge that has been repeatedly raised before courts. Thus, the characterization of the problem of religious liberty merely as a liberation from the oppressive bonds of community would be too reductionist even if it might be entirely accurate to say that when state intervention is called for, it ought to be directed in significant measure by the Constitution's transformational vision for an equal society. In other words, the Constitution could also read to be a charter for the defense of India's plural, traditional, and perhaps even illiberal religious traditions as much as it is a measured and restrained charter for the limiting the excesses of those traditions as they impinged on shared collective values.

Having re-characterized the problem of religious freedom through Bhatia's account of essential practices, we may now consider the orientation that must direct state regulation of religion in a manner consistent with the plural and especially traditional forms of religious practice as highlighted by this chapter. Primarily, the approach to state intervention in religious practice that this chapter points toward is one that implies that the Constitution's vision for radical equality and social change must also be alive to the variety of religious forms, especially traditional religious forms, that it seeks to regulate and on occasion reform. On the other hand, Bhatia's framework, which represents an important contemporary strand on the constitutional government of religion, seems to emphasize the enabling role given to the state to secure a radical equality and the transformation of Indian society. In contrast, this chapter moderates Bhatia's account by suggesting a tempered exercise of state power over religion enabled by Article 25 as well as provisions such as those addressing untouchability (Article 17) and equality (Articles 14, 15, 23, etc.). The implications of this shift in orientation toward state power exercised on religion for constitutional interpretation is a matter for another occasion. However, it is by being alive to the existing form in which the Indian constitutional state governs religious practice that an alternative and more permissive interpretative approach to religious freedom and especially to religious pluralism might be made possible.

9.6. Conclusion

To summarize by way of a conclusion, this chapter has elaborated the epistemic framework of the essential practices test that has structured the operation of religious freedom in Indian constitutional law to constrain rather than expand India's plural traditions of religious practice. In particular, it has argued that the essential practices test that the courts have devised to structure the bounds of religious freedom has operated to transform and perhaps even distort traditional religiosity into doctrinal religion. As the chapter has pointed out in the Satsangi case, this can impose a significant and even illegitimate burden on religious practices by alienating them from a background of religious plurality. Of course, a defense of the plural traditions of religious practice cannot not mean a carte blanche for religious practice within those traditions. That is, it cannot but be the case that the contours of religious practice in modern states are deeply influenced if not shaped by the exercise of state power. Accordingly, through a critique of Gautam Bhatia's detailed discussion of essential practices, the chapter points to the contours along which the state power to regulate and reform religion would have to be reorganized to accommodate India's plural traditions of religious practice. Consequently, the detailing of the interpretative specificities through which the Indian constitutional framework would be able to achieve this object is the task that awaits the legal defense of India's plural traditions of religious practice.

References

Scholarly Books and Articles

Constituent Assembly Debates: Official Report. 1999. Vol 7. Lok Sabha Secretariat.

Balagangadhara, S. N. 2005. The Heathen in His Blindness: Asia, the West, and the Dynamic of Religion. 2nd ed. New Delhi: Manohar.

Bhatia, Gautam. 2016. Freedom from Community: Individual Rights, Group Life, State Authority and Religious Freedom under the Indian Constitution. Global Constitutionalism 5(3), 351–382.

Dhavan, R. 1987. Religious Freedom in India. American Journal of Comparative Law 35, 209–254.

Mehta, P. B. 2008a. Passion and Constraint: Courts and the Regulation of Religious Meaning. In R. Bhargava, ed., Politics and Ethics of the Indian Constitution. Oxford: Oxford University Press.

Mehta, P. B. 2008b. On the Possibility of Religious Pluralism. In T. Banchoff, ed., Religious Pluralism, Globalization, and World Politics. Oxford: Oxford University Press.

Mehta, U. S. 2010. Constitutionalism. In N. G. Jayal and P. B. Mehta, eds., The Oxford Companion to Politics in India. Oxford: Oxford University Press.

Neo, Jaclyn L. 2018. Definitional Imbroglios: A Critique of the Definition of Religion and Essential Practice Tests in Religious Freedom Adjudication. International Journal of Constitutional Law 16(2), 574 https://doi.org/10.1093/icon/moy055.

Rao, B Shiva. (ed). 1966. The Framing of India's Constitution, vol. 2. Delhi: Indian Institute of Public Administration.

Sen, R. 2009. The Indian Supreme Court and the Quest for a "Rational" Hinduism. South Asian History and Culture 1(1), 86.

Sen, R. 2010. Articles of Faith: Religion, Secularism and Indian Supreme Court. Oxford: Oxford University Press.

Legal cases

Adelaide Company of Jehovah's Witnesses Inc. v. Commonwealth. 67 C.L.R. 116, 1943, 123.

The Commissioner Hindu Religious Endowments, Madras v. Sri Laxmindra Thirtha Swamiar of Shirur Mutt. MANU/SC/0136/1954.

Ismail Faruqui v. UOI (1994). 6 SCC 360.

Jagdishwaranand v. Police Commissioner, Calcutta. AIR 1984 SC 51.

M.H. Qureshi v. State of Bihar. AIR 1958 SC 731.

S.P. Mittal v. Union of India. AIR 1983 SC 1.

Sardar Syedna Taher Saifuddin Saheb v. The State of Bombay. MANU/SC/0072/1962.

Sastri Yagnapurshdasji v. Muldas Bhudardas Vaishya. AIR 1966 SC 1119.

Tilkayat Shri Govindlalji Maharaj v. State of Rajastan. AIR 1963 SC 1638.

10

Plurality and Pluralism

Democracy, Religious Difference, and Political Imagination

Sudipta Kaviraj

10.1. The Historical Sociology of Plurality

To make my argument, I need to set up a clear distinction between the two crucial terms in our collective discussion. By plurality I mean the brute fact of existing differences between religious groups.[1] In the Indian context, this indicates the differences between, primarily, Hindus, Muslims, Christians, and Sikhs. But even at this level, plurality is not a simple question. For example, religious faiths like Buddhism, Jainism, and so on emerged out of internal differentiation of the Hindu religion—in different ways at different points in time. The doctrinal contents of these religious faiths are distinct from each other, and their relations with Hinduism have been separate and varied through the long histories of such difference. The contrast between the historical trajectories of Buddhism and Jainism is an interesting case: though their doctrinal beliefs are in some respects quite similar, and both faiths evolved monastic orders in contrast to the unorganized character of Hindu Brahminic society, the eventual historical fates of these two faiths were entirely divergent. Buddhism expanded its influence over wide areas and segments of society in ancient India, and carried on an intense intellectual and institutional conflict with Hindu orthodoxy for nearly a millennium. After the tenth century, Buddhism went through a decisive, irreversible decline. Jainism, by contrast, maintained both its distinctiveness from Brahminical Hinduism and its capacity for intellectual and social exchange. Sikhism emerged as one of the major lines of the bhakti rethinking of religious life in late medieval India. Remarkably, while other, doctrinally comparable strands of bhakti rethinking—like Bengali Vaishnavism—did not institutionally separate themselves off from Hindu religion, Sikhism developed an unmistakable distinctness. Still, its social relations with Hindu faith remained intimate and complex. In

[1] Interestingly, behind this obvious meaning of the term "plurality," we can also glimpse the American meaning of the term—indicating an arithmetic simple majority in the result of an election.

Sudipta Kaviraj, *Plurality and Pluralism* In: *Negotiating Democracy and Religious Pluralism*. Edited by: Karen Barkey, Sudipta Kaviraj, and Vatsal Naresh, Oxford University Press. © Oxford University Press 2021.
DOI: 10.1093/oso/9780197530016.003.0011

Punjab, the main region of the practice of Sikhism, it is possible for people in the same family to practice Sikh and conventional Hindu faith, for Sikhs and Hindus to intermarry, and also for Sikhs to have a keen sense of their identity even when dispensed with its highly significant external marks.[2] Plurality itself—the descriptive differences between different religious groups or their faiths—has to be defined with some refinement and precision. Two things are undeniably clear at this level: first, Indian society is marked by a plurality of distinct faiths; and second, these faiths are unequally distributed in numbers. Hinduism,[3] at least in modern times, is the religion of a vast numerical majority of Indians; other faith communities are much smaller. Since part of our analysis is historical,[4] it has to be stressed that the partition of India after the end of colonialism affected this numerical distribution significantly. Before partition, Muslims constituted about 30 percent of the total population of undivided India, and a majority in several regions. With the creation of Pakistan, the Muslim population came down to around 12 percent—a precipitous decline in the force of numbers.[5]

Some other features must be kept in mind in the descriptive understanding of religious plurality in India. All religions have their sociological peculiarities: one of the most obvious features of Hinduism is its extreme internal doctrinal diversity. Admittedly, most large religious faiths exhibit internal divisions of doctrine and organization. Islam has divisions between Sunni and Shia, Christianity is riven between Orthodox, Catholics, and Protestants, Buddhists have the Hinayana, Mahayana, and Theravada distinctions. But Hindus are a loose congeries of sects whose objects of worship and observances are at times sharply different.[6] Vaisnavas,[7] Saivas, and Saktas worship different gods, and though it is possible to make an arcane philosophical argument that all Hindus view these different deities as discretely satisfactory forms of an infinite and intellectually unencompassable God, that cannot override the reality of sectarian diversity. An important consequence of this is that Hindus have not historically behaved as a single worship community, and therefore it is not easy to produce among them

---

[2] Conventionally, the Sikh religion used external physical marks—most distinctively the turban.

[3] I am skirting the interesting historical question of when Hindus began to view themselves as a single religious group. Hindu nationalists strain to make the argument that this self-identification began in ancient times (Savarkar 2009). Modernist historians generally held that it was a relatively modern development—influenced by acquaintance with Semitic religions like Islam and Christianity, and by modern conditions of political life. Recent research has suggested that trends toward a unified conception of Hinduism began somewhat earlier—driven by the philosophical influence of the school of Advaita Vedanta (Nicholson 2010).

[4] These historical questions have been discussed in greater detail in two papers: Kaviraj 2014 and Kaviraj 2016.

[5] This of course does not take into account other qualitative social factors—like wealth distribution, education, spatial concentration.

[6] For an interesting discussion of this aspect of Hinduism, see Stietencron 1993.

[7] Sometimes, different subgroups among Vaisnavas will worship different iconic images of Vishnu.

an effortless self-perception of being a majority group. Since these communities are relatively smaller, as long as the primary self-perception of their members is of being a Vaisnava or a Saiva, it is not much different from being a Sikh or a Shia—like one island in an archipelago rather than a massive mainland with a few satellites. Sociological brute facts are mediated into political action through self-perceptions. This peculiarity is accentuated by the regional and linguistic diversities within Hinduism. Bengali Vaishnavism, as the name shows, has a linguistic regional self-identification besides its theological doctrinal determinants. Therefore, although there are great similarities in theological precepts between them and the Vallabhite Pushtimargis, it is unlikely that the two groups would view themselves as parts of a vast all-India Vaisnavite consolidation. There is hardly any evidence that they view themselves as a single entity in social conduct, far less in political action. Elsewhere I have called this feature of multiple axes of diversity a convexity of social identification.[8] Consequently, it is common for Hindus to view themselves as belonging to a community among communities, rather than as an obvious majority religious faith. Indeed, the very fact that Hindu majoritarian politicians have had to make such an effort to convince their fellow Hindus that they should see themselves as "fellow Hindus" and nothing else is testament to the power of this combination of diversity and convexity.

Political effectivity of a religious group depends on a multiplicity of factors, not just numbers. Other, more complex and subtle factors have to mediate the presence and significance of this number to the group itself, for it to be capable of acting upon this perception. In thinking about the political conduct of Indian Muslims after independence, this is an important fact to keep in mind. A reduction from 30 to 12 percent is a precipitous decline—likely to be reflected in the community's perception of its relative political effectiveness and electoral power. This diminution was further reinforced by the fact that the Muslims in post-partition India were reduced in two other ways. They lost a large part of the community's social and professional elite—who migrated in large numbers to Pakistan. Second, the creation of Pakistan deprived Indian Muslims of the immense political force of numerical concentration, except in the Kashmir valley: the powerful argument in a generalized politics of numbers, that although a community might be a minority counted nationally, it constitutes a majority in specific regions. Political efficacy is a complex product of numbers assisted by wealth, professional expertise, political leadership, and collective self-perception. When we say we analyze the politics of numbers, these other sociological features of communities are definitionally folded into them. The reduction of the Muslim community in India is therefore far deeper than what appears if we take a simple, shallow count in numbers alone.

[8] Kaviraj 2013.

10.2. The History of Pluralism

I take pluralism to be a doctrine or political imaginary. It is not inevitable that a society featuring sociological plurality of religious groups will spontaneously give rise to doctrines of pluralism—which I regard as a cognitive and ethical attitude that accepts and in some instances "respects" diversity—in the sense of recognizing as a corollary of this diversity an ethical right of all religious faiths to pursue their own ideas and observances, and finally, regarding this diversity as a "good thing." A disposition toward pluralism can exist in two forms. It can mean, in the first form, allowing all faith-groups to practice their religious life without hindrance from other faiths or from the state. In the second form, it might go further and even consider the existence of different paths of faith—and a society characterized by religious plurality—better than the experience of living in society that is religiously entirely monocultural. For the sake of clarity, we could give these two dispositions separate names: pluralist and cosmopolitan. The first does not necessarily place any value in other religious paths than one's own; the second, more generously, places value in other ways of worshipping God, and considers the existence of these plural paths sources of ethical, philosophical, and aesthetic value. In that sense, the second view accepts finiteness of its own reach for God, and considers other paths to be valuable. Sometimes the trouble with discourses about religious toleration is that these distinctions are not made with sufficient clarity. The term "toleration" often covers both meanings: but it is essential to see their analytical distinction.

After independence, the nationalist political elite faced the task of creating a new constitutional order. At such points in history, elites have to contend with their society's actual prior history and the initial conditions they create for establishment of new political institutions. The enterprise of modern history writing was introduced to India by imperial British authors like James Mill, followed by a long line of historians who presented premodern Indian religious history as an incessant struggle between the Hindu and Muslim faiths that was moderated only by the calming influence of British colonial sovereignty.[9] Nationalist historians often responded to this history by painting a picture of undisturbed tranquility and fraternity, disrupted by malignant colonial schemes of "divide and rule." Modern historical research offers a more complex picture. Political power—especially in northern India—was often controlled by Islamic dynasties, but that did not lead to a condition of religious war between the followers of the two faiths. Sectarian conflicts and rivalries were common both among the Hindus and among Muslims;[10] but religious difference did not

---

[9] Mill 1826.

[10] An interesting picture of these rivalries is offered by a premodern text, *Dabistan-i-Mahazib* (Troyer 1843).

degenerate into religious civil war comparable to early modern European history. European authors were influenced by religious strife in their own history in reading those of others. As the actual history of relations between the two major religious communities was understandably checkered, it was always possible for historical interpreters to select elements and construct a "history" and an accompanying social memory according to the historians' ideological preference. As British authors wrote the first "modern" histories of India, the early historical accounts tended to be focused on the presumed conflict between two contending faiths. In this kind of historical writing, the empirics of Indian history were mediated through a history of secularism that the modern West had given itself—in which tolerance in the face of religious diversity was an exclusive achievement of European modernity. In face of this meta-history underlying all history, empirical evidence was powerless. Such colonial histories, starting from James Mill, declared religious plurality an unresolved curse that premodern Indian institutions were incapable of overcoming. Arrival of British colonial institutions and their design of religious neutrality created conditions for "rule of law" and religious peace for the first time—precisely because the British could play the role of an impartial third party, external to the warring faiths. Rise of political tension between the two communities in response to the enticements of representative politics, particularly of communal representation, was blamed on long-standing enmity between the two religious groups locked in a mortal struggle since the arrival of Islam.[11] It is remarkable how heavily nationalist histories developed by both Hindu and Muslim nationalists drew from the first, colonial, orientalist one. Islamic separatist nationalism, from the second half of the nineteenth century, often drew on this image of long-term conflict—claiming that Muslims for centuries had ruled over Hindu subjects, to raise anxieties of being reduced now to a representational minority.[12] On the Hindu side, writings of V. D. Savarkar, especially his short work *The Essentials of Hindutva*, gave the earlier orientalist history a new nationalistic spin to assert a forceful connection between this history of incessant contention and a demand for the rise of a Hindu nation.[13] In the decades preceding the actual event of partition, this idea was simplified and strategically mobilized in Jinnah's "two nation theory,"[14] as a justification for the creation of two successor states to British India, instead of one. The two inimical political practices of Hindu and Muslim nationalism, in effect, not merely shared an understanding of the

[11] Typically, even the question of arrival of Islam can be contentious: did Islam arrive with merchant and trading communities in South India or through military incursions in the North Western part of the subcontinent?
[12] Khan 1984; Jinnah 1940.
[13] Savarkar 2009.
[14] Jinnah 1940.

premodern past, but also concurred in the colonial and orientalist narrative of medieval religious life.

Opposed to these interpretations of Indian history was an alternative narrative of mutual understanding elaborated by pluralist nationalists like Gandhi, Tagore, Azad, and Nehru.[15] Their central idea—that there was a logic of Indian history that consisted in the continual absorption of new elements into an increasingly complex unity—had origins in social thought in the nineteenth century in the works of earlier authors like Bhudev Mukhopadhyay.[16] This strand contested the orientalist reading of eternal conflict between the two faiths, and pointed to the evidence of the creation of a "composite culture" by merger and parallel existence of two religious communities and their adjacent, and often interactive intellectual and artistic, cultures. As anti-imperialist sentiments crystallized, at times this strand blamed Hindu-Muslim conflicts entirely on imperialist designs of "divide and rule," and often painted a romanticized image of idyllic premodern accommodation. This showed that there was, at least in the last phase of British rule, a direct connection between the nature of political nationalism and a directly related version of history. The politics of history was central to the story of nationalism and its internal conflicts.

10.3. Pluralism and the Constitutional Settlement

At the time of independence, the two conflicting histories in a sense won victories on two sides of the border. But the creation and separation of Pakistan meant that the field of historical contestation was simplified, and the conflict inside India now was between the pluralist and the Hindu-nationalist narratives of the past. The elections of 1951–52, a year after the formal adoption of the constitution, was seen as a ratification of a new vision of the past and future, because the constitutional arrangements drew heavily upon not merely the prior legal structures of British colonial law, but also social traditions of religious accommodation—with one major difference. Accommodation between communities was left in premodern times to political skills of rulers, and generally adapted to varied local conditions, not codified into formal, fixed, legal rules that are permanent and unadaptable. Essentially identical principles, when turned into the structure of constitutional legality, get profoundly altered in their functioning and can produce unintended consequences. The Indian constitution is a marvel of innovative adaptation of liberal principles to the conditions of a society

---

[15] Gandhi 1908/2009; Tagore 1917; Nehru 1946.
[16] Mukhopadhyay 1892/1991.

entirely different from Western Europe.[17] Founders of the constitution crafted a fine balance between the individualist conferment of rights and unfamiliar demands of community-based requirements of fairness that the Indian context required. Improvising upon constitutional rules they had learned from the Western legal orders, they installed two major instances of rights conferred on communities. Alongside the standard list of fundamental rights enjoyed by individual citizens, found in most Western constitutions, the constitution reserved legislative seats, admission to educational institutions, and government employment for the erstwhile untouchable castes and tribal populations—roughly in proportion to their numbers in the population.[18] Comparable reservations were not provided for segments inside other religious communities—like Islam and Christianity—who suffered from quite similar caste-based or caste-like disabilities. Second, religious minorities were given special community-based rights to preserve their cultural heritage through educational institutions.[19] The majority community was not given similar rights. The remarkable thing about these constitutional provisions was that the political elite defended these legal devices frontally on the ground that only minority culture could be threatened in this way, not the cultural practices of the majority. They also forcefully defended the idea that India's claim to have a secular polity depended critically on the reassurance of the Muslims after the trauma of partition. These legal provisions not merely professed the constitutional principle of pluralism in the face of sociological plurality, but also acknowledged the asymmetrical nature of these differences.[20] In the constitutional settlement, plurality was acknowledged; and a powerful theoretical argument was advanced that the best response to historical plurality was political pluralism. The purpose of constitutional construction was to make sure that minorities or historically dispossessed social groups did not suffer discrimination and exclusion—which could happen easily through an easy and unmindful installation of a simple rule of formal legal equality. Some groups required unequal protection and support even in order to take up the legal offer of equality. From the point of view of historical sociology, the interesting fact is that although the constitution conceived of politics in terms of individual rights and economically defined group interest, it inaugurated or indirectly elicited, by its own provisions, a kind of political use of identity.

---

[17] For the distinctiveness of Indian secularism, see Bhargava 2010 and, on the imaginative processes that went into constitution-making, Khosla 2020.

[18] Bajpai 2013.

[19] Constitution of India, Articles 29, 30.

[20] Evidently, the constitution framers worked on the assumption that caste discrimination and untouchability were specific to Hindu society. However, there is widespread evidence of similar practices among Muslims and Christians—which remained unaddressed, in a legally anomalous design.

10.4. Formation of Aggregative Identities

The constitutional settlement therefore mixed the two principles of identity-based rights in specific cases, and entirely identity-independent ones generally. More than the legal and ethical complications created by this mixing move, in effect the constitution sent mixed signals about the use of identity in politics and its prohibition. In general, the constitutional settlement seemed to deplore, and dissuade people from using, identity-based politics; in some exceptional cases, however, it not merely allowed but seemed to encourage them. There has been considerable discussion about the legal and ethical justification of this legal mixture; but the sociological effects of identity recognition in the constitution has been given far less serious attention. Consideration of the internal sociological structure of the Hindu religion—that is, giving attention to segmentary group identities within which Hindus lived, and on which they could be presumably expected to act—would have highlighted two types of internal divisions—one of which the constitution emphasized, and the other completely ignored. Hindu worship practices are not united: Hindus do not worship a single deity. They worship many, and each sect—like Saivas, Vaisnavas, or Saktas—are organized internally and recognized externally as distinct worship communities. The constitution entirely ignored these sect divisions and treated Hindus as a single religious group in this respect. Hindus are also divided internally in terms of castes: by contrast, the constitution accorded great significance to this form of social diversity. These reservation provisions in the constitution produced an immediate sociological effect in democratic electoral mobilization.[21]

To understand that effect, we have to start by recalling the segmentary structure of castes—the fundamental organization of personal experience and collective life in premodern Hindu society. The structure of castes is cellular—organizing human beings into hereditary occupational groups in a series of small subdivisions of sociality. Additionally, caste hierarchies are regionally divergent. Similar castes often exist in neighboring regions; but they might occupy different specific positions in the local caste hierarchy. Even economically comparable castes would not, in the traditional grammar of caste practice, interact in marriage or commensality. The logic of caste is twofold: it is not merely *hierarchical*, but also, equally importantly, *segmentary*. In actual social practice the segmentariness of caste is written over and accentuated by other kinds of division—of region, language, sub-caste, and so on. The consequence of this logic of segmentation is an extreme scale-reduction of agentive groups in terms

---

[21] Of course, this entirely avoided dealing with caste among other faiths. But this was a matter of some complexity. Recognition of caste would have benefited the disadvantaged sections, but might have offended Muslim and Christian elites.

of which actual social individuals recognize themselves and others who are like themselves, and politically act upon the world.

To take an illustration, although the Hindu sect called Vaisnavas can abstractly form a vast body of devotees who could be found in large numbers in nearly all parts of India, this abstract group is in actual terms divided in several ways. Theologically and doctrinally, they are divided between several powerful subsects like the Pushtimargis from the South and the North and the Gaudiya Vaisnavas in Bengal and Orissa. Bengali Vaisnavas themselves are deeply divided between the "normal" householder practitioners of its beliefs and more dissident elements like the "sahajiyas" who might have entirely heterodox beliefs and practices about sexuality and non-marital companionate relationships— which the householders consider degenerate and loathsome. Though it is logically possible and in some ways reasonable to think of Vaisnavas globally as a group, in actual fact they never work in unison for political ends, except at times as regional sects. Caste stratification further segments these religious groups into social communities based on marital and commensal interchange. Caste-structures are generally regionally variant. An identically named caste can be found in two neighboring or non-adjacent areas, but these might occupy a different place and rank in the specific order of caste in the two regions. The caste of Kayasthas is found in Bengal and in adjacent regions like Uttar Pradesh and Bihar, but their relative positions inside the regional hierarchy tend to be different, making it difficult for the Kayasthas of Bengal, Bihar, and UP to make common political cause. The essential truth about the traditional order of caste is its segmentation—which means not merely the occupational and social separation of each of these cells from others, but, also their self-recognition as different groups, and in their consequent capacity for collective action essential for political life. My central point is that question of identity is central to the operation of caste as a social order and given its potency as a social collectivity, in democracy as a political system—but these use identity in exactly opposite ways. The *traditional* grammar of caste confines identity into small segments, and limits collective action to very small scale.[22] Success in democratic electoral mobilization is based on collective action by ever larger numbers. The logic of traditional caste is segmentary; the logic of modern democracy is aggregative.

This general picture needs to be modified in some significant ways. Upper castes—especially Brahmins—are to be found everywhere, in all regions. As the upper castes—the Brahmins, the Vaidyas in Bengal, and Kayasthas in north India—were traditional possessors of literacy, large sections from these groups

---

[22] M. N. Srinivas (1962), a leading sociologist of the contemporary caste system, famously used the term "monster castes" to characterize the vast caste coalitions brought into play by electoral politics: these were monstrous in two senses: first, these were vast numerical groups, but also these were monstrous because these transgressed the conventional segmentary logic of the caste order.

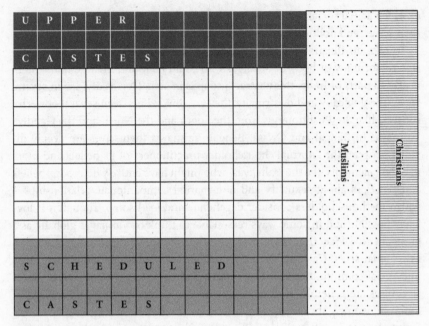

Figure 1 The Structure of Hindu Social Order

could easily transfer their skills through acquisition of English to modern education. During British colonial rule, this created a common modern professional culture among them often overriding their traditionally segmentary caste identities. In social conduct like marriage they might stay within their caste groups, but for political action they often realized the existence of overarching common interests. Much before the emergence of modern democratic politics, educated upper-caste groups learned the techniques of modern aggregative political action. In the later stages of British rule, limited representative institutions were introduced, and these educated upper-caste groups quickly saw the initial advantages of political aggregation. Often they formed region-wide caste associations to mobilize the power of large numbers.[23] Later, such organization spread to lower castes as well. But what marked the political conduct of the educated upper castes was their modernist understanding of common material and professional interests straddling even regional caste-based mobilizations.

Given this historical-sociological structure—a sociological structure that was cellular and marked by uneven degrees of consciousness of common interests and possibilities of collective action—democratic government, if read sociologically, yielded the expected type of results. Figure 1 is considerably simplified

[23] Rudolph and Rudolph 1967; Kothari 1970.

in one respect: it simply offers a stylized picture of the Hindu social order, but omits the representation of the social communities of other religious faiths—like the Muslims and Christians. We do not need here an analysis of the presence of castes within Islam and Christianity in India. But if we convert the sociological basis of Congress electoral dominance in the first two decades of Indian democracy, it is evident that its electoral supremacy was created by a surprising coalition of social forces. It is hardly surprising that the leadership of the Congress—like all other political parties including the Leftists—came primarily from upper, educated, and propertied castes that almost entirely coincided with the modern *class* elites. This elite managed to exercise their influence on their class and caste communities to get this band of the sociological structure to vote primarily for the Congress party. Understandably, because of their anxiety and insecurity after partition, the minorities, especially the Muslims, also tended to vote for the government party as a bloc. But the most interesting and peculiarly modern phenomenon was that at the lower end of the structure; the lowest—former untouchable—castes also voted as an *aggregative* bloc for the Congress party. This aggregative maneuver—which had decisive long-term effects on Indian political life—was less a result of direct electoral mobilization by the Congress party than a consequence of an apparently apolitical constitutional provision. To confer affirmative action benefits on the lowest strata of the traditional caste order through reservations, the Constitution invented a simple legal device—listing the former untouchable castes in the Seventh Schedule of the Constitution, and naming them—collectively—the scheduled castes.[24] There were two entirely unprecedented features in this legal move. First, it treated these disparate castes, for legal purposes, as a single collective entity; and second, it invented a neutral legal collective-aggregative name for them that replaced, at least for legal discourse, their segmentary caste names—like Paraiyas (Tamilnad), Madigas (Andhra), Mahars (Maharashtra), or Namashudras (West Bengal). In legal and subsequently political discourse, the category scheduled caste was soon established as common language because it avoided the use of the deeply derogatory names used before. But the sociopolitical effects of this common naming went much deeper. According to the conventional grammar of caste practice, these distinct untouchable castes from different regions would not have seen themselves as belonging to a superordinant collective entity. Namashudras, for instance, were found only in West Bengal, Malas and Madigas in Andhra Pradesh; and in the conventional, pre-constitutional social universe, there was no question of their regarding each other as belonging to the same caste-group, though

---

[24] This was done in part to invent a new caste-neutral legal language that did not refer to them as "untouchable," which was considered derogatory, or by Gandhi's term "Harijan," which many found patronizing.

it was of course possible to view their common mistreatment as untouchables as "comparable." But "comparability" presupposes distinctness: an entity cannot be compared with itself. The device of constitutional listing was not meant to have a political electoral effect, but simply to enable accurate legal identification of beneficiaries of reservation. Undoubtedly, reservation provisions had a significant effect on the dynamics of social reproduction of castes by creating a new middle class from the lowest caste groups, especially in state bureaucracy. It also had an immensely significant unintended effect on electoral politics. The simple fact of naming—assigning a collective appellation to these disparate cellular groups—conjured up an ungrammatical new political collectivity. Paradoxically, the constitution ushered in the first profound move toward aggregation in Indian electoral politics. As people belonging to these castes began to be mobilized by their national leaders—like Jagjivan Ram, longtime scheduled caste leader of the Congress—for the first time in history a segmentary cellular group abandoned the logic of caste life to adopt aggregative techniques of modern democracy. Over three decades Congress exercised its electoral hegemony over the Indian electoral system through a Disraeliesque coalition of the uppermost and the lowest strata of the Hindu caste order, alongside the solid support of minorities. This combination yielded a winning sociological coalition for three general elections (Figure 1).

This sociological model serves to explain the dynamics of electoral politics from independence to the eve of the fourth general elections in 1967. In the sudden reversal the Congress suffered in the fourth general elections of 1967 there was evidence that this structure of a winning sociological coalition was starting to fail. Some economically defined groups from the upper castes—like rich farmer castes of Northern Indian states like UP and Haryana—began to show signs of deep disillusionment with Congress policies toward agriculture and defected from the upper-caste consolidation at the top of the structure, rendering this bloc inadequate for continuing electoral dominance. Parties like the BKD (Bharatiya Kranti Dal), founded by the veteran Congress farmers' leader from UP Charan Singh, attempted to create a different kind of rural consolidation of peasant groups on the basis of common disgruntlements over agrarian policy—mobilizing a farmers' coalition. These parties targeted their policies and mobilizing efforts at farmers and peasants seeking a broad coalition of rural groups. In the 1920s and 1930s Socialist politicians organized highly successful peasant movements on the basis of a class differentiation within the peasantry— successfully aligning the small peasants and landless agricultural workers into a leftist radical force, joining their political fate with the working class, primarily mobilized by their allies, the Communists. The farmers' mobilization of the 1970s was a countermovement involving largely the same social groups, but with a profound alteration of their political imaginary: instead of making common cause with the working class in the cities on the basis of poverty, this new politics found a language of common cause among *all* peasant strata from the richest farmers to the poorest landless laborers—in a rural united front—alleging that the Nehruvian obsession with industrialization had utterly ignored the interests of the "countryside"—where most Indians lived. This was a move from an economic perspective based on class to another grounded in common interests of a whole "sector" of the economy, "the countryside"—irrespective of internal differentiation—based on a different technique of perceiving and forming group interest. But the implicit caste dimension of this mobilization is important to observe, because this was to facilitate a different interest conglomeration in the next decade. Charan Singh's new electoral agglomeration, though based on the collective interests of all groups in the neglected rural economy, implicitly integrated all rural caste groups—from the landholding castes like Thakurs, Jats, and Rajputs to the poorer peasant and artisanal castes engaged in petty production and lower-level occupations in both economic and ritual terms. This interlude of electoral mobilization of "farmer parties" across northern India, though initially based on perceived economic grievance, coincided with an underlying caste coalition of most agricultural castes since occupation and caste coincided closely in the rural economy. Upper-caste groups like Brahmins and Kayasthas who were the historical repositories of high literacy tended to gravitate to opportunities in the urban and professional economic sectors, leaving the famer castes to emerge as the new leaders of rural society (Figure 2).

However, this period of rural interest mobilization was relatively short. By the mid-1970s, especially after the 1977 elections unfroze democratic politics after the Emergency, a new democratic imaginary took shape that grounded demands for development and against disadvantage primarily on caste identities. This profound change was aligned to another feature in the fundamental transformation of the language of political discourse—the taken-for-granted underlying ideas in terms of which political actors judged cases of discrimination, injustice, collective assertion, and self-esteem. A profound transformation in this underlying conceptual language marked the gradual fading of the socialist concern about poverty and economic indigence, and its replacement by a radical liberal one focused on discrimination and indignity. It is remarkable how decisively the wrongs of poverty and "backwardness" were replaced in Indian political discourse by those of disrespect and affront. This shift produced an amazing alchemy dissolving poverty-related arguments for development, and replaced them for nearly half a century with expanding wars of caste-based affront. Parties based on peasant or rural grievance like the Bharatiya Kranti Dal—which indirectly used caste loyalties for electoral mobilization—were replaced by ones directly based on electoralized castes—like the Bahujan Samaj Party of UP. In the sociological dynamics of electoral politics, successful mobilization

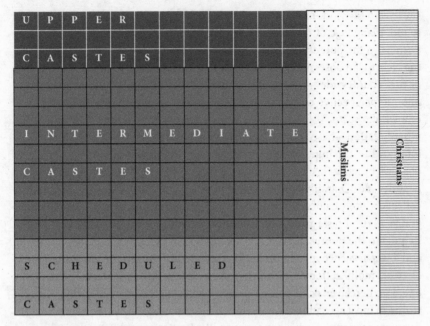

Figure 2 Mobilizing Intermediate Castes

of the SCs could be an extremely effective force—as it proved in cases like UP, where because of the fragmentation of other caste votes between several political parties, the BSP secured a formidable advantage. But the basic fact of elective arithmetic was that the caste system was so segmented that even with the appearance of modern electoralized caste blocs none of these "monster castes" could secure an unambiguous majority. Each bloc had some specific advantages, not others. The bloc of SCs certainly had the power of numbers in some states where they constituted higher than 20 percent of the total electorate, but this constituency tended to be economically poor. The bloc of upper castes had usually great advantages in education, strategic placements in the structure of modern professions, and income, but their numbers were not critically large. For a time, the central bloc of "lower castes"—constitutionally designated as other backward classes (OBCs)—enjoyed an advantage of large numbers, and considerable economic strength, as many of these included landed castes—called "dominant" by modern sociologists[25]—which had been beneficiaries of agricultural growth and reservation of government jobs. But none of these groups had an indisputable

---

[25] Modern sociologists like M. N. Srinivas (1987) and Andre Beteille (1965) argued that the focus of analysis should be the "dominant castes" who controlled land and political power, not the castes high in terms of ritual purity. Srinivas (1987); Beteille (1965); against the purity argument advanced by Dumont (1970).

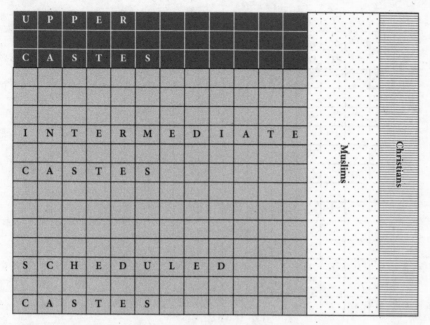

Figure 3 The possibility of an "oppressed majority"

preponderance in numbers and votes. Consequently, after the mid-1970s, electoral politics became a vast cauldron of coalitional experiments in identity—with parties engaged in a war of all against all seeking an identity that would yield an invincible identity majority.

In the electoral politics of UP two of these experiments were tried out. The first was contained in the naming of the BSP itself. Bahujan Samaj meant in Hindi the "society of the large majority"—which was an invocation of a combination—suggestive in theory but elusive in practice—of the two lower-caste blocs—the scheduled castes aligned to the newly mobilized bloc of intermediate castes—represented in UP by Mulayam Singh Yadav's Samajwadi Party, and in neighboring Bihar by Rashtriya Janata Dal, led by Lallu Prasad Yadav. If realized, that combination would have looked like Figure 3. If stabilized, this would have been an unbeatable electoral bloc.

10.5. Competing Identity Coalitions

This could have two alternative formations—with the group led by BSP leaders from the scheduled castes, or by the intermediate castes from the OBCs. For nearly three decades electoral politics in UP was dominated by these two potential

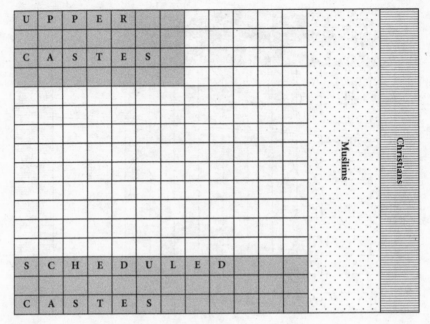

Figure 4 The BSP's co-optation mobilization

blocs. Leadership rivalry between these groups was so intense as to make such a coalition of identities impossible. Usually, the OBC bloc in the Samajwadi Party struck electoral adjustments with the Congress on the ground that these were "secular" parties and enjoyed the support of the large Muslim community. Because of its decisive weakening in the state, the Congress party ordinarily accepted this arrangement, conceding strategic dominance to Samajwadi leaders. The hypothetical electoral bloc of Figure 3 actually never materialized.

Frustrated by the unrealizability of this coalition, the BSP for some periods attempted an entirely counterintuitive electoral combine with the BJP, whose voter support emerged primarily from a part of the upper-caste bloc (Figure 4).

10.6. Transactional Character of Identity Politics

What is often forgotten in the practice of electoral politics and, more surprisingly, in academic examination is the inevitably transactional nature of identity moves. However, I use "transactional" in a special sense. I do not mean the usual bargaining of seats and portfolios that parties routinely engage in. I mean a sociopsychological process of reciprocal affirmation of identity. This is to remind us of the simple fact that since identities are often mutually and transactionally established—that is, one identity is based on its differentiation or opposition to other identities in a differential system—making a political move on the basis of one identity immediately produces an incitement for a mirroring countermove on the opposite sides. It is hard to create a general situation of political actions in which one identity would be mobilized without an effect on others. Sometimes the effect is one of imitation: if an identity move by one group is seen as politically effective, it is likely to be imitated by others simply because of the demonstrative power of political success. In other cases, the identities are so structured in mutual opposition in the social world that any move by one side results in a potential cost to the other side, and immediately encourages the other to act. The most interesting example of this kind was the extension of educational and employment reservation from the scheduled castes—the lowest in caste hierarchy—to cover the other backward classes that correspond roughly to the groups who would self-identify in the second phase of Indian democratic history as intermediate castes. Compared to the upper castes, these groups certainly suffered relative historical disadvantage—in education and preparation for modern professions. But in fact this was an internally heterogeneous and economically complex congeries of caste groups: some of them were quite similar to the SCs in social and economic disadvantage, while others were the "dominant" landholding castes in the countryside who had benefited initially from legal land reforms that removed the power of colonial absentee landlords, and subsequently from economic transformations of the wheat-based green revolution. Paradoxically, the new assertiveness of these intermediate castes stemmed partly from their new economic strength, and greater representation in the panchayat system of local government and consequent social assertion. Their greater representation in state legislatures was linked to the substantial rise in agricultural income of the rich peasantry. Ironically, it was their economic advance that set them on the path of demanding greater "backwardness"—because that opened the path to constitutional reservation of government jobs similar to the SCs. This would enable them to extend their existing economic power in the countryside to bureaucratic and legislative power at administrative centers of state and central government. Research into the short history in political office of intermediate-caste political parties shows a trend entirely consistent with this ironic invocation of entitlement to "backwardness." The rise to high office of some of the leading intermediate-caste politicians was supported by farmers and contractors from these caste groups that already wielded considerable power over rural society; and after their ascension to office, these groups were also the primary financial beneficiaries of government contracts and associated benefits. Economic benefits widely distributed across the entire caste were relatively few. Symbolic assertion of identity—like naming of roads and parks, and building of statues—which are primarily non-economic "benefits," were common and popular. Recent research also shows how the shift of the central theme of political discourse from "development," which was generally understood in economic terms, to "empowerment," which was mainly seen as a symbolic collective ennoblement of the entire community through the rise of their representative leaders, immunized these politicians from developmental criticisms.[26] They may not have brought roads and schools to their neighborhoods, but they brought an intangibly luminous collective prestige. The coalitional bloc that these politicians shaped was also based on the ungrammatical, electoralized idea of the "intermediate castes." They were innovative pioneers in their reading of the logic of electoral arithmetic, because they were the first wholly caste-oriented politicians, unlike Charan Singh, whose thinking was dualistic, using both economic and caste logics.[27] These politicians were the first to grasp the historical fact that while upper castes had traditionally acted aggregatively, and SCs had begun to do so after the constitution conferred a collective appellation on them, the castes in the middle continued to act following the segmentary principles of premodern, pre-electoral caste system, and were constantly outplayed in the incessant aggregative contest of electoral politics. Not surprisingly, once they began to mobilize electoral coalitions on this basis, they reaped immense benefits in initial stages. It is a general truth of political strategy that unexpected first moves are heavily rewarded; when other, competing players deploy similar moves or countermoves, they begin to yield diminishing returns. Sociologically, the weak point of this strategy of intermediate-caste politicians like Mulayam Singh Yadav or Lallu Prasad Yadav was the unwillingness of the SC politicians like Kanshi Ram and later Mayawati to accept their lead and create a truly wide low-caste coalition that could have mobilized overwhelming numbers—if united (see Figure 3). In real social life, the OBC and SC groups lived in adjacency and contention in local rural communities; and SC communities often viewed the OBCs as their more immediate oppressors and fiercer electoral competitors. Upper-caste professionals did not engage in everyday contentions of village life—for local assets and prestige. They exercised a more abstract and distant *structural* domination over the social formation. The imaginary coalition of "social justice" pursued by Communists, Socialists, and Congress reformists was fatally and finally fragmented—destroyed beyond immediate repair. Enthusiasts for this kind of identity politics had no sympathy to spare for other groups of neighborly poor—people of other backward castes, not to speak of individuals from upper castes who may have fallen into poverty through the functioning of an increasingly merciless neoliberal economy.[28]

[26] Witsoe 2013.

[27] Singh 1978.

[28] Ironically, the recent extension of reservation to economically poor individuals from upper castes responds to this issue.

The sequential rise of these forms of identity politics, and their critical sub-stitution of a discourse of distributive justice, was accompanied by other highly significant changes in social life. Initially, such alignments resulted in the election of legislators from these social groups, a form of direct representation; after a time, politicians of the intermediate castes initiated far-reaching legislation affecting the access to state resources in education and employment.[29] Early legislation in the 1950s in states like Tamil Nadu had resulted in large-scale migration of upper-caste groups like Brahmins from some South Indian states, as their access to government employment—the most coveted form of modern employment—was restricted.[30] Because of their higher educational access, individuals from these groups could move into jobs in the private sector in metropolitan centers like Mumbai, Delhi, or Kolkata or in the technological segments of large state sector enterprises. Legislation on expanding reservation to the OBCs passed by the central government in 1990 increased reservation in education—in highly prized educational institutions like medical colleges—to just below 50 percent. Legislations extending reservations hurt interests of upper-caste groups.[31] Since there were no explicit high-caste parties, these disgruntled groups were obliged to find other electoral means to advance their group interests. Agitations by upper-caste student groups that broke out after the government adoption of the Mandal recommendations tended to align the BJP rather than the Congress with these groups. In general, in India social experience of economic change has followed the line of Pareto improvements: deprived groups have slowly benefited without negatively affecting the conditions of dominant groups. This had kept the political costs of redistribution in terms of conflict remarkably low. Expansion of reservation by the Mandal legislation in the 1980s was seen as a direct reduction of benefits for dominant groups; the only prior instance was the expropriation of zamindari property immediately after independence. State action usually did not have much direct impact on economic lives of people. Education and job reservations for the SCs had a fairly limited impact, because, in professional occupations that required minimal education qualifications, quite often the existing openings were not taken up because of the want of qualified SC candidates. Often such jobs reverted to the "general" category and were actually filled by upper-caste appointees. The actual effect of SC reservation was not felt by other groups as a serious shrinkage of their own occupational opportunities. Expansion of reservations under the Mandal recommendations had a much sharper effect on the perception of dominant groups, shifting greater support to the BJP. Ordinarily, upper-caste caste

[29] For an historical account of caste politics, see Jaffrelot 2003.
[30] Varshney 2000.
[31] Mitra 1987.

affiliation in politics was not explicitly argued or acknowledged by BJP leaders or their social constituencies. But clearly BJP increasingly emerged as the party that offered a comprehensive challenge to the historical policies of the Congress on secularism and "socialism." Mandal Commission reservations were widely seen as constituent parts of a policy-complex that advanced the causes of lower castes and minorities at the expense of conventionally dominant groups in Hindu society. And because of their association with the principle of social justice, expansion of reservation could be interpreted as a constituent part of the Congress ethos of "socialism." This caused a subtle process of substitution: while increased reservations could not be opposed openly, some groups found a way of indirect opposition by candidly supporting the BJP's criticisms of minority appeasement into which dissatisfactions of upper-caste groups were folded inexplicitly.

10.7. Democracy and Hindu Identity

The rise of the BJP is generally interpreted by its critics as the emergence of an antidemocratic political force. Seen from this sociological perspective, the rise of the BJP in the 1980s bore a strong connection with the logic of electoral democracy. After independence, the initial demands of Hindu nationalist political parties were often directly opposed to liberal democratic ideals[32]—like the justification of a Hindu state.[33] Electoral statistics clearly reveal that social support for the Jana Sangh and the early BJP came primarily from identifiable economic groups like small traders and government employees in North India—for example, in Delhi municipal elections Hindu parties were electorally successful for a long time.[34] The later rise of the BJP into a national force seems to bear a more causal connection with the logic of electoral aggregation in two separate forms. First, of course, the greatest putative identity majority—which, once established, would become numerically invincible—would be a Hindu majority. That would obviously have to override internal differentiation of the caste structure and include both intermediate and scheduled castes. Frustration among the upper castes after the extension of reservations inclined these groups to align with the BJP. But more significantly, electoral mobilization of identities tends to have an effect of mobilizing all possible putative identities in search of the invincible

---

[32] Hindu nationalist political formations were active before independence—for example, the Hindu Mahasabha. In 1948, a political party—Ram Rajya Parishad—was founded. The Rashtriya Swayamsevak Sangh was a non-political, cultural organization. But in 1951 its supporters established the Bharatiya Jana Sangh, and the Ram Rajya Parishad later merged into the Jana Sangh.

[33] Madhok 1982.

[34] Baxter 1969; Graham 1990.

majority—a group or a coalition so large in numbers that, if united, it simply cannot be electorally defeated. The search for a Hindu electoral majority rather than a Hindu state is deeply connected to this logic of democratic aggregation, and the general replacement of arguments for social justice by assertions of aggrieved identity.

Since the 1980s the electoral strategy of the BJP has aimed at an identity consolidation of all Hindus that will drown out and erase all internal distinctions of sect, caste, language, region: if securely established, it would be impossible for any other potential identity mobilization to defeat this majority bloc (Figure 4a). In reality, the electoral mobilizations of the BJP, even at its most successful, have been more limited. Intermediate castes—particularly in states like UP, where there is now a long legacy of caste-based politics—have generally rejected the BJP's advance till the general election of 2014. Scheduled-caste groups have behaved in many different ways across the country. Though both South India and some parts of the North—like UP, Bihar, and Haryana—have established strong patterns of caste politics, their nature is quite different: and crucially, as in the case of farmers/peasants, SC groups have not produced a mobilization across the entire country. BSP or SP—so powerful in UP—has little traction in South India. Because of the fragmented character of SC party mobilization, using local conflicts

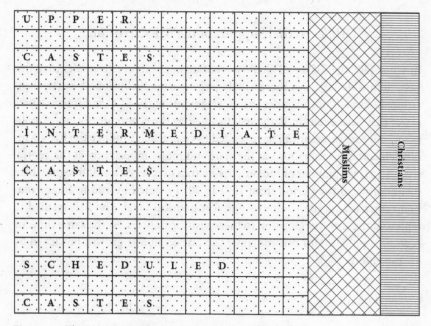

Figure 4a The putative structure of Hindu majoritarianism

and grievances, the BJP has been able to draw significant support from SC groups in specific states. In many parts of traditional India, upper-caste support for the Congress obstructed the BJP's advance among these groups, until the enactment of the Mandal reservations. Finally, the pluralist nationalist imaginary that anchored the Nehruvian settlement slowly began to be undermined due to its cynical manipulation by Congress politicians, accompanied by accusations of unbridled corruption. Decline of the Nehruvian pluralist interpretation of Indian nationalism created an imaginative vacuum that the BJP sought to supplant with an aggressive sense of a rising Hindu political community. Its propaganda sought to make pluralism appear as a weak concession to the problems of plurality—which can lead to political incoherence. Continuous economic growth over two decades has also created a sense that India can emerge as a leading power that requires a suitable accompaniment of more assertive political nationalism. Electoral results in reality do not support the idea that the party has achieved this putative electorally invincible Hindu nation. In its best results in the 2019 elections, the BJP's share of votes was 37.3 percent, but, because of the plurality rule, its seat share was magnified to 55 percent. A real triumph of this imagination of India demands a complete disappearance of caste consciousness, as its original theorist, V. D. Savarkar, suggested in his definition of political Hindutva.[35]

10.8. Actual Support of the BJP Coalition

In actual fact, the BJP's real identity coalition has been much smaller than this vast, invincible bloc. An increasingly large, partly disillusioned, partly aspirational segment of the upper castes, fragments of the SCs, and intermediate castes that have been similarly disillusioned by the economically empty politics of pure representation, have tended to coalesce to produce the BJP's winning electoral combinations at the state and more importantly at the central level. To a large number of Indians, the politics of reservation and regionalism that dominated the period from 1991 to 2014 seemed to lead to fragmentation rather than a high-minded pluralist political ideal. The BJP seemed to represent the surest opposition to these historic policies. At the same time, its economic policies did not endanger the fast economic growth produced by liberalization.

[35] Savarkar 2009.

10.9. The Historical Dialectic of Plurality and Pluralism

To understand the recent political history of the relation between the democratic political form and the sociological structure of religious diversity—democracy and religious pluralism—it is essential to refer to the specificities of the Indian case. Sociologically, Indian society has been historically marked by a double plurality—not merely a plurality of major world religions—Hinduism, Islam, and Christianity—but, because of the structure of caste and regionality, by further forms of internal cross-cutting plurality. This deep sociological diversity—a plural form of plurality—has prevented conflict between these vast religious communities mobilized as single agential blocs. The common idea of a peculiar tolerance of Hindu religion[36] is based on a real sociological feature of this religion: due to its internal diversity of numerous sects, and absence of a form of common worship, Hindu theology developed some intellectual arguments that were "internally" pluralist, advocating toleration among its different paths.

Intellectually, such arguments could be extended to other "external" paths like Buddhism and Jainism; and in some instances, to other "external" paths like Islam and Christianity. Political theorists like Ashis Nandy argued forcefully that the accommodation found in the real world between individuals and groups belonging to different religious communities was more because of this historical logic of "religious toleration" that all three primary religions interactively developed, than the persuasive powers of modern secularism.[37] If this reading of India's long history is correct, it prompts a surprising conclusion—which was clearly implied by Nandy's unsettling proposition. In that case, secularist modernism and Hindu nationalism—both decidedly modern political doctrines—are likely to go against this historical legacy on which the post-independence Indian state, as much as the Mughal Empire, was based. The logic of Hinduism as it historically evolved goes against the modern proposals of political Hindutva.[38]

People with strong Hindu religious beliefs might come to view these homogenizing attempts at compulsory erasure of social diversity as unacceptable and offensive on traditional religious grounds. If Hindus allow the pluralist historical spirit of their religious legacy to be edited out by the entirely modern uniformist nationalism of Hindutva, it will be hard to preserve the pluralist institutions of Indian democracy from a corresponding exclusionary revision. Ironically, the future of Indian democracy might be settled by the outcome of the conflict between old and new Hinduism—rhetorically, between Hinduism and Hindutva.[39]

---

[36] For more detailed arguments on these theological principles, see Kaviraj 2014.

[37] Nandy 1988.

[38] Interestingly, this argument is explicitly advanced by modern critics like Nandy (1988); but it is also implied by Savarkar's own line of reasoning, see Savarkar 2009.

[39] Ashis Nandy (1988) in particular has advanced this argument for some time.

244 GENEALOGIES OF STATE AND RELIGION

It is an elementary principle of political theory that stable democracies tend to reduce violent conflicts, because their institutional design ensures that no social group loses permanently, feels perpetually exiled from power, or perpetually targeted by the apparatuses of the state. Indian democratic politics has, since the 1970s, seen a steady rise in use of violence by political parties in office against their perceived opponents. In some instances, violent groups have attacked ordinary members of specific communities, and state apparatuses like the bureaucracy and the police have remained indifferent. There are two types of instances that demonstrate such rise of tolerated levels of violence.[40] In cases like Kashmir, or the states of the North East, violent political conflict eventually led to the deployment of the army to deal with long-standing armed militancy. Ordinary democratic political life cannot function in a surrounding context of such violent exchange. Apart from these cases, in many instances, state apparatuses have allowed large-scale violence against specific social groups. Two episodes of large-scale political massacre—of Sikhs in Delhi in 1984, and of Muslims in Gujarat in 2002—occurred unobstructed by the state apparatuses of democratically elected governments. In the forty years of continual rule by the Communist Party of India–Marxist (CPI(M)) in West Bengal numerous incidents of violence occurred against political opponents in which the state apparatus of the police allowed government supporters to massacre opponents—the last two events in 2015 ultimately leading to that party's defeat.[41] There was a troubling defense of CPI(M) violence by the invocation of remote and irrelevant "revolutionary" examples drawn from nineteenth-century French history. Paradoxically, such apparently "radical" arguments make a justificatory preparation for violence by other contending groups,[42] fashioning arguments for their ready use once they come to wield political authority.

In the last decade in particular Indian political life has encountered a new kind of violence, with deep and troubling implications for the democratic disavowal of violence as an instrument in political conflicts. Some strands of Hindu nationalism had always extolled a cult of violence—from the worship of Goddess Kali by Bengali terrorists to the practice of paramilitary discipline by members of the Rashtriya Swayamsevak Sangh (RSS). If the paramilitary element was a symbolic response to the organized power the British colonial state, it became entirely purposeless in independent India, except as a tool of menace against religious minorities. I am not interested here in the long history of the rhetoric of violence associated with Hindu nationalism—particularly with the RSS and

---

[40] Such large-scale incidents happened in case of the riots against Sikhs in Delhi under Congress rule, against Muslims in Gujarat under the Modi government of the BJP, and against opposition groups in West Bengal under the government of the CPI(M).

[41] These were the widely reported incidents in Singur and Nandigram.

[42] Like the Trinamool Congress which succeeded the CPI(M) in West Bengal.

the Shiv Sena in Mumbai.[43] I am concerned more with the insidious connec-tion between electoral power of democracy and mobilization of violence against opponents in recent times. Despite the apparent civility of BJP's electoral party leaders, it is notable that the re-emergence of Hindu nationalism as a major po-litical force in the 1980s was associated with incendiary demands for destruc-tion of mosques allegedly constructed in medieval times over demolished Hindu temples in highly significant locations like Ayodhya and Benaras, and a com-plex mobilization of ancillary organizations like the Vishwa Hindu Parishad or the Bajrang Dal that do not follow a primarily electoral purpose, and therefore could be relatively unburdened by the democratic commitment to rejection of violence. L. K. Advani's *rath yatra* in 1990 made direct incitement toward the de-struction of mosques and building temples in their place, though more recently L. K. Advani seems to have learned moderation. Although it can be reasonably claimed that there are fissures inside the BJP itself between a more moderate section—represented now by leaders like Advani and Arun Shourie—and a more extreme one—led by Narendra Modi, Amit Shah, and Yogi Adityanath—besides the serious difference in commitment between the BJP as a political party and non-electoral groups like the VHP and Bajrang Dal, for an understanding of the relation between democracy and violence, they seem to work a division of labor.

For many clear reasons the political party would be wary of creating an atmos-phere of permanent menace of violence—which is unlikely to appeal strongly to either ordinary voters or to international and national business. Additionally, the BJP has often been yoked in coalitions to other parties that do not share their fierce anti-Muslim agenda, and could not pursue its separate aims unilaterally. At the time of the destruction of the Babri mosque in Ayodhya, a Congress gov-ernment was in power at the center, but a BJP government in the state of Uttar Pradesh, and the report of the Liberhan Commission suggests that crucially placed government functionaries were instructed not to interfere with the acts of the mob. Despite the ideological divergences between political groups, it appears that political parties have perfected a technique of formally accepting their com-mitment against violence and circumventing it by using a complex process lying at the heart of group action in politics. A collective act requires a whole range or stacking of enabling conditions, all of which are involved in the agency of that particular action, though these enabling conditions are placed at different agen-tial removes from the immediacy of the act itself. But in most of these cases, the facts of the political world are arranged carefully in such a way that responsi-bility or actual culpable agency is fragmented and distributed across a substan-tial number of people all of whom can nonetheless be regarded as its agents in

---

[43] There are several academic studies of the RSS that illustrate its fascination with violent ac-tion: see, e.g. Basu et al. 1993.

some sense. The violent act itself is first of all fragmented, though its perpetrators are undeniably linked to the result. We witness this kind of arrangement of agentiality in ordinary occurrences like thrashing common thieves in railway stations. If the person dies in the collective beating, and the beating is "collectively" done by hundreds of individuals, every single one responsible can clear his conscience by thinking that his own kicks could never have killed the man; the occurrence was a regrettable and excessive doing of others. If the case comes to court, the judge will face the invidious task of deciding that—if a murder is punishable by a life term, and if all the hundred culpable people are caught—he will have to administer a hundred life sentences—leading to an obvious disproportion between crime and punishment.[44] At a second remove, the incident could take place because of policemen who were absent—who must therefore bear a more unascertainable negative responsibility. Such absence would be linked to their bureaucratic superiors who were not supposed to be present at the scene, and their political handlers who bear at most a distant formal responsibility like the liability taken by an ethical railway minister who resigns from his post because of a bad rail accident. Serious analysis would reveal a series of connections to an act of violence that become less clearly attributable to a personal agent at every single remove. Politicians acquire a commonsensical perception of such ambiguities and often realize the dark opportunity for using violence to assist their objectives. A most significant recent instance of such dispersion of agential responsibility was the massacre of Muslim citizens in the state of Gujarat, when Narendra Modi, the present prime minister, was its chief executive. That event has a whole literature to itself; but I want to draw attention to more recent trends that have appeared after the last general elections.

When political parties that purport to represent identity majorities like Hindus in India come to office, this sets off a trend that is deeply troubling for the functioning of democracy and especially the constitutive rule of rejection of violent means. On 25 September 2015, after the new BJP government came to power, a Hindu mob lynched a Muslim villager on suspicion of eating beef in a town near Delhi. Subsequently, shadowy groups like the Hindu Sena in Delhi stormed a government restaurant to check if beef was served. Scores of people were killed by vigilante groups who decided to stop the transport of cows for slaughter.[45] Incidents like these require analysis because they all illustrate this structure of stretched and dispersed agentiality, making acts of violence empirically more probable, and legally harder to prosecute. They produce spectral events without agents, acts with no one to bear responsibility.[46] Extreme groups,

---

[44] A judicial case of this kind was reported in case of violence at an Egyptian football match.

[45] For more detailed analysis of such trends, see Amrita Basu's chapter in this volume.

[46] Though in some cases, the sense of impunity encouraged some perpetrators to post videos on the internet and pose as warriors of their community.

sometimes relatively small, feel empowered by the fact that a party of similar beliefs controls the government; they are encouraged by vaguer incendiary rhetoric of political leaders and undertake acts of violence and atrocity. Politicians in power usually remain reticent or offer ambiguous denunciations—for fear that they will lose the support of far larger and vaguer groups of their supporters, if they denounce these acts more clearly. Sometimes politicians offer direct justifications by trivializing the incident;[47] or disavowing their connection to the actors. Eventually, even though political parties do not directly plan violence, or feel embarrassed by their occurrence, they do not use their power to enforce restraint. That means that often the tail wags the dog. Small extreme groups could in a way overcommit much larger groups and institutionally responsible agents, and start a logic of worsening violence.

In many parts of India, there is an observable rise in the level of political violence; and what is particularly alarming is the willingness of intellectual groups to provide justification for the acts of their preferred political parties, corroding one of the fundamental barriers that democratic institutions provide against a life of everyday violence.

If rejection and reduction of violence in settling political conflicts is one of the primary conditions of a functioning democracy, there are reasons to feel troubled about the present state of democracy in India. Its map of violence is disturbingly large. Not merely are specific territorial regions marked by high levels of violence—both by the state and by nonstate actors; within states that are not marked by regional insurgencies, there is a creeping rise in the levels of everyday violence, and use of force against critics of incumbent governments that threaten one of the basic principles of a democratic polity.

References

Bajpai, R. 2013. *Debating Difference: Group Rights and Liberal Democracy in India*. Oxford University Press, Delhi.
Basu, T., et al. 1993. *Khaki Shorts and Saffron Flags*. Orient Longman, New Delhi.
Baxter, C. 1969. *Jana Sangh*. University of Pennsylvania Press, Philadelphia.
Beteille, A. 1965. *Caste, Class and Power*. University of California Press, Berkeley.
Bhargava, R. 2010. *The Promise of India's Secular Democracy*. Oxford University Press, Delhi.
Bilgrami, A., ed. 2016. *Beyond the Secular West*. Columbia University Press, New York.
Dumont, L. 1970. *Homo Hierarchicus*. University of Chicago Press, Chicago.
Gandhi, M. K. 1908/2009. *Hind Swaraj*. Cambridge University Press, New York.

[47] A BJP leader was reported to have said that that was not the only death that occurred in India that night.

Graham, B. 1990. *Hindu Nationalism and Indian Politics*. Cambridge University Press, Cambridge.

Jaffrelot, C. 2003. *India's Silent Revolution*. Columbia University Press, New York.

Jinnah, M. 1940. A. *Speech to Annual Session of Muslim League*.

Kaviraj, S. 2013. "The Empire of Democracy." In I. Katznelson and P. Chatterjee, eds., *Anxieties of Democracy*. Oxford University Press, Delhi.

Kaviraj, S. 2014. "Modernity, State and Toleration in Indian History: Exploring Accommodations and Partitions." In A. Stepan and C. Taylor, eds., *Boundaries of Toleration*. Columbia University Press, New York.

Kaviraj, S. 2016. "Disenchantment Deferred." In A. Bilgrami, ed., *Beyond the Secular West*. Columbia University Press, New York.

Khan, S. 1984. A. *The Present State of Indian Politics: Speeches and Letters*. Sang I Meel Publishers, Lahore.

Khosla, Madhav. 2020. *India's Founding Moment*. Harvard University Press, Cambridge, Mass.

Kothari, R., ed. 1970. *Caste in Indian Politics*. Orient Longman, Delhi.

Kung, H., ed. 1993. *Christianity and World Religions*. Orbis, Maryknoll, NY.

Madhok, B. 1982. *Rationale for Hindu State*. Indian Book Gallery, Delhi.

Mill, J. 1826. *The History of British India*. Baldwin, Cradock and Joy, London.

Mitra, S. 1987. "The Perils of Promoting Equality: The Latent Significance of the Anti-reservation Movement in India." *Journal of Commonwealth and Comparative Politics* 25, no. 3, 292–312.

Mukhopadhyay, B. 1892/1991. *Samajik Prabandha*. Pashchim Banga Pustak Parshad, Kolkata.

Nandy, A. 1988. "Politics of Secularism and the Recovery of Religious Tolerance." *Alternatives* 13, 177–184.

Nehru, J. 1946. *The Discovery of India*. John Day, New York.

Nicolson, A. 2010. *Unifying Hinduism*. Columbia University Press, New York.

Rudolph, L. I. and S. H. Rudolph. 1967. *The Modernity of Tradition*. University of Chicago Press, Chicago.

Savarkar, V. 1923/2009. D. *Hindutva: Who Is a Hindu? [Essentials of Hindutva]*. Hindi Sahitya Sadan, New Delhi.

Singh, C. 1978. *India's Economic Policy: The Gandhian Blueprint*. Vikas Publishing House, New Delhi.

Srinivas, M. N. 1962. *Caste in Modern India and Other Essays*. Asia Publishing House, New York.

Srinivas, M. N. 1987. *The Dominant Caste and Other Essays*. Oxford University Press, Delhi.

Tagore, R. 1917. *Nationalism*. Macmillan, New York.

Troyer, A., trans. 1843. *The Dabistan or The School of Manners*. Allen, London.

Varshney, A. 2000. "Is India Becoming More Democratic?" *Journal of Asian Studies* 59, no. 1, 3–25.

Von Stietencron, H. 1993. "Hinduism." In H. Kung, ed., *Christianity and World Religions*. Orbis, Maryknoll, NY.

Witsoe, J. 2013. *Democracy against Development*, University of Chicago Press, Chicago.

SECTION III
VIOLENCE AND DOMINATION

11

Pakistan's Blasphemy Laws versus Religious Pluralism

Fatima Y. Bokhari

> You are free; you are free to go to your temples, you are free to go
> to your mosques or to any other place of worship in this State of
> Pakistan. You may belong to any religion or caste or creed—that has
> nothing to do with the business of the State.
>
> —Muhammad Ali Jinnah, address to the first Constituent Assembly
> on 11 August 1947[1]

11.1. Introduction

Traditional discourse surrounding blasphemy laws has often explored their compatibility with laws protecting freedom of expression and speech; do states have the right to curtail freedom of expression and speech by preventing individuals from speaking against religion, if it upsets the religious sensibilities of their own or other religious communities? It is not the subject of this chapter to add to this query. The primary focus of this chapter is on the relationship between the right to freely practice one's religion and the nature and practice of blasphemy laws. Do blasphemy laws enhance or curtail freedom of religion? Can an argument be made in support of blasphemy laws for contributing to religious freedom, and if yes, under what preconditions? Using Pakistan as a case study, this chapter explores the relationship between legal pluralism and religious pluralism.

The context of Pakistan provides unique insights into the challenges of navigating a space for religious pluralism in a state established on a religious identity, comprising a clear religious majority, and yet retaining considerable religious and other diversity (ethnicities, languages, sects, etc.) within. Moreover,

---

[1] Quaid-e-Azam Mohammad Ali Jinnah, *Speeches as Governor General of Pakistan 1947–1948*, 1962, pp. 8–9; see also Hamid Khan, *Constitutional and Political History of Pakistan* (New York: Oxford University Press, 2001), 75–76.

Fatima Y. Bokhari, *Pakistan's Blasphemy Laws versus Religious Pluralism* In: *Negotiating Democracy and Religious Pluralism*. Edited by: Karen Barkey, Sudipta Kaviraj, and Vatsal Naresh, Oxford University Press.
© Oxford University Press 2021. DOI: 10.1093/oso/9780197530016.003.0012

Pakistan's ideological basis, coupled with its experience of disrupted democratic governance by long periods of dictatorial rule, enables a distinct understanding of the role of a democracy (and the politics that impacts its form and substance) in the definition and protection of fundamental freedoms, including freedom of religion.

In the first section, this chapter seeks to assess the basis of blasphemy laws within the framework of legal and religious pluralism. It argues that while there may be an argument in support of blasphemy laws as a means to protect the freedom of religion of diverse religious communities, in particular minority religious communities within a state, in order to serve the purpose of religious pluralism, any such law would need to be generally applicable, non discriminatory, and include inbuilt safeguards against false accusations through requirement of intent and other pre requisites for prosecution. Despite the theoretical protection such a law may provide, using examples of religious minorities in Europe, the chapter tilts toward the idea that in practice religious rights, especially those of religious minorities, have rarely been protected through the use of blasphemy laws, and protection remains subject to interests of national politics and the religious conceptions of the majority (however defined) in a state.

In the subsequent sections, the chapter uses the case study of Pakistan to highlight the harms of blasphemy laws that no do not meet these preconditions and instead cater to a majority conception of religion and religious identity of the state. Through a historical analysis of the evolution of blasphemy laws in Pakistan, the chapter further explores the complex relationship between national politics and religious rights.

11.2. Definitional Elements: Aims of Legal and Religious Pluralism in the Context of Blasphemy Laws

11.2.1. The Right to Practice One's Religion Freely: Legal Pluralism and Religious Pluralism

Legal pluralism, defined broadly as "presence within a social field of more than one legal order" or, more specifically for this chapter, a legal system in which "different bodies of law apply to different groups in the population . . . defined by ethnicity, religion, nationality or geography," [2] has been

---

[2] The author draws a distinction between a strong and weak conception of legal pluralism. See John Griffiths, "What Is Legal Pluralism?," *Journal of Legal Pluralism and Unofficial Law* 32, no. 24 (1986): 5; see also Sherman A. Jackson, "*Legal Pluralism between Islam and the Nation-State: Romantic Medievalism or Pragmatic Modernity?,*" Fordham International Law Journal 30: 2.

seen as a valuable arrangement for a fuller realization of individual rights. The underlying premise of legal pluralism is a factual acknowledgment of diversity within communities in any given state. These can be a result of pragmatic reasons, that is, for ensuring peaceful coexistence between different religious groups. Moreover, such a pluralistic legal system can ensure that a majority's conception of law is not imposed on a religious minority in a state, or alternatively prevent a majority from feeling threatened by a distinct minority. The latter can be seen as a value- based reason . The two, however, often need not be mutually exclusive.

Legal pluralism catering to a religious diversity in countries has been seen as an important tool in enabling individuals to practice their religion freely, and manage their affairs in accordance with their religious tenets. This right has also been recognized in the Constitution of Pakistan, which in Chapter 1 enshrines freedom of religion, and the freedom to practice one's religion without discrimination as a fundamental right.[3]

Several countries provide for "special" or "personal" laws that deal distinctly with specific religions, usually in matters pertaining to marriage, divorce, and succession, although secular laws often exist that these communities can appeal to, if they choose. Legal pluralism as such can be seen as catering to religious pluralism.

However, it is also important to note that legal pluralism in action may manifest itself in many different ways. For example, special laws may exist only for some communities and not others, leading to discrimination; special or personal laws may in practice serve to oppress some communities, or in other cases suppress voices of dissent within communities. Accordingly, legal pluralism may or may not be conducive to religious pluralism in all circumstances. However, for the purposes of explaining legal pluralism, it is presumed that the inherent purpose of the concept is *not* to enable states to use this as a tool to suppress specific communities, even though that can be and certainly has been the case, as we will see later in the example of Pakistan.

---

[3] Article 20 guarantees every "citizen's freedom to profess, practice and propagate his religion" and gives "every religious denomination . . . and every sect . . . the right to establish, maintain and manage its religious institutions." In addition, under Article 21, a religious community cannot be forced to pay any special taxes "which are to be spent on the propagation or maintenance of any religion other than his [or her] own." Article 22 safeguards members of religious communities from having to engage in religious practices that are not their own; all religious institutions are to be treated equally in relation to any tax exemptions provided for by the s tate; and religious communities cannot be prevented from "providing religious instruction for pupils of that community or denomination in any educational institution maintained wholly by that community or denomination ." S ee Article 20, "Freedom to Profess religion and to manage religious institutions" of the Constitution of Pakistan, 1973; Article 22, "Safeguards as to educational institutions in respect of religion, etc.", Constitution of Pakistan, 1973.

11.2.2. Contextualizing Blasphemy Laws

Several countries around the world retain blasphemy laws, according to a research by Pew Research Center , which terms these laws as "restrictions on religion."[4] Canada, for example, punishes blasphemous libel applying to all religions under its criminal code.[5] In Europe, several countries, including EU member states, such as Spain, Italy, and Finland, retain blasphemy laws within their criminal codes, to name only a few, while others, such as Denmark and the United Kingdom (UK), have recently abolished long-standing blasphemy laws. Denmark abolished its blasphemy law only in June 2017,[6] and the UK did so in 2008.[7] Other countries, such as Australia, have transitioned from blasphemy laws to new offen ses known as "religious vilification laws," which penalize speech that "incites hatred against, serious contempt for, or revulsion or severe ridicule" of persons on the basis of their "religious belief or activity"; [8] this has changed the law from offense against one established religion into an offense against all. (Neither reliance on blasphemy laws nor the substance and application of these laws is uniform in the various countries that retain these laws; nonetheless retention of these laws on the books enables these countries to be included in the debate on the raison d' état for these laws.)

Do blasphemy laws have an important role to play within a multi cultural society and in upholding religious freedom, especially in countries with a minority religious community? At the outset, the answer would depend on whether blasphemy laws in any given country protect the interests of all religious communities or only religious minorities—or exist only in support of the dominant religion . For example, in Pakistan, specific blasphemy provisions apply exclusively in favor of the dominant religion. Similarly, UK's former blasphemy laws applied only to cases in which the blasphemy was committed against Christianity under the Church of England, excluding

[4] Pew Research Center, January 2014, "Religious Hostilities Reach Six Year High." See the full report at http://www.pewforum.org/files/2014/01/RestrictionsV-full-report.pdf.

[5] Section 296 of the Canadian Criminal Code: "1) Everyone who publishes a blasphemous libel is guilty of an indictable offence and liable to imprisonment for a term not exceeding two years. 2) It is a question of fact whether or not any matter that is published is a blasphemous libel. 3) No person shall be convicted of an offence under this section for expressing in good faith and conveyed in decent language, an opinion on a religious subject."

[6] "Denmark Scraps 334-Year-Old Blasphemy Law," *The Guardian*, 2 June 2017, https://www.theguardian.com/world/2017/jun/02/denmark-scraps-334-year-old-blasphemy-law.

[7] The UK abolished the common-law offenses of blasphemy and blasphemous libel by amendment to the Criminal Justice and Immigration Act 2008. See further at http://www.legislation.gov.uk/ukpga/2008/4/contents#pt12-l1g153.

[8] Racial and Religious Tolerance Act 2001. See Jeremy Patrick, "The Curious Persistence of Blasphemy," *Fla. J. Int'l L.* 23 (2011): 195–198.

other sects.[9] Taking the example of the UK, it can be argued that blasphemy provisions in the UK could not have catered to religious diversity or pluralism in any way, as the law only protected sentiments of Christians as per the Church of England, who constituted the religious majority.

Denmark until this year had, like Canada and India,[10] generally applicable blasphemy laws. It may be argued that in such circumstances blasphemy laws may be used to protect religious minorities—in principle. For example, with reference to the Danish c artoons controversy and the failure of the Danish authorities to consider the case as blasphemy under Danish law, Stephanie Lagouette argued that blasphemy laws should have been used to protect the European Muslim community. She draws the analogy with the historically recognized need to punish anti-S em itic propaganda by Nazis against Jews under Denmark's blasphemy laws.[11] The Danish c ourts, however, interpreted the cartoons that outraged the Muslim community as "not sufficiently offensive" under the existing laws.

It is also interesting to note that the repeal of the blasphemy law in Denmark was achieved by a case in which blasphemy was committed against the minority religion. An individual was charged under the blasphemy law for posting a video on Facebook, titled "Yes to freedom—No to Islam," in which he was seen burning the Quran. This case was dropped after the legislation itself was repealed. The Danish MPs stated that they "do not believe that there should be special rules protecting religions against expressions." [12] While it may be a coincidence, the specific circumstances of the case lend support to the earlier trend in Denmark, that the blasphemy law was unable to provide protection to the sentiments of the religious minority, the Muslim community in Denmark.

The preceding examples from Denmark suggest that blasphemy laws and their utilization depend on the political will and interests of the majority. Consequently any safeguards that such laws aim to put in place for religious minorities remain

---

[9] Peter Cumper, "The United Kingdom and the U.N. Declaration on the Elimination of Intolerance and Discrimination Based on Religion or Belief," *Emory Int'l Rev* 21 (2007): 14.

[10] Chapter 15 of the Indian Penal Code deals with offenses against religion. These include S ection 295, Injuring or defiling place of worship with intent to insult the religion of any class; 295A, Deliberate and Malicious acts, intended to outrage religious feelings of any class by insulting its religion or religious beliefs; 296, Disturbing religious assembly; 297, Tres passing on Burial Places, etc.; 298, Uttering words etc. with deliberate intent to wound the religious feelings of any person.

[11] Stephanie Lagouette, "The Cartoon Controversy in Context: Analysing the Decision Not to Prosecute under Danish Law," *Brook J Int'l L* 33 (2007): 397 . Denmark has prosecuted Nazi s under its blasphemy laws, although the law has remained unused since 1930 s. See Rebecca Ross, "Blasphemy and the Modern 'Secular' State," *Appeal* 17 (2012): 3– 19.

[12] "Quran-Burner Trial Dropped after Danish Parliament Revokes Centuries-Old Blasphemy Law," *The Independent* , 3 June 2017, at http://www.independent.co.uk/news/world/europe/quran-burner-denmark-facebook-blasphemy-laws-repeal-a7771041.html.

underutilized at best and a sham at worst. However, at least in principle, blasphemy laws that do not discriminate between different religions and religious communities could arguably assert a verbal legitimacy, and in theory claim to preserve religious freedom of minorities , however na, ve this claim may be in practice.[13]

Contrary to this, blasphemy laws that cater to one majority religion[14] are inherently incompatible with the aims of religious pluralism and in effect hinder religious freedoms of minorities. Peter Cumper has noted that blasphemy laws in many countries were historically instituted to persecute religious minorities, such as Catholics,[15] and present- day push back against repealing blasphemy laws in countries such as Ireland has come from the religious majority, as opposed to any religious minority.[16] In most jurisdictions across the globe, political power is still concentrated in members of the dominant religion, which has the potential to make generally applicable laws target specific communities. These can be in the form of beef bans in India and headscarf bans in several countries across Europe. In such an environment, even blasphemy laws, despite being specifically and exclusively unused against minorities at present, are likely to still remain potential tools for misuse against religious and other minorities when politics deems fit. However, that remains a subject of a larger inquiry distinct from our present purposes.

The next section, on Pakistan, details the impact of such blasphemy laws on religious minorities within the country; it also provides useful lessons on how such laws can be used by the state to more narrowly define its religious identity creating religious minorities within the dominant religion as well. Punishing deviance resulting from differences in sect, culture, ethnicity, and other such variables, which do not fit well within the state- supported conception of Islam and national politics of the time, can further limit the scope of religious pluralism in practice.

[13] This does not mean that blasphemy laws need necessarily be structured as criminal offen ses, or mandate severe punishments such as death and life imprisonment, as is the case in many countries—that debate is distinct and not the subject of this chapter, for obvious reasons of limitations of space and scope. More general criticisms of blasphemy laws, as more inclined by design to be capable of abuse, will be considered in the context of Pakistan in *section 11.2* of this chapter.

[14] By majority religion here I refer to the religion of the majority of the population in the given country—that would be Islam in Pakistan, Hinduism in India, and Christianity in the United Kingdom, for instance. The notion of majority can include further aspects, such as dominant sect , e.g., Shia Islam in Iran or Sunni or Wahhabi schools of thought in other states.

[15] Cumper, " United Kingdom ," 14 .

[16] Kathryn A . O'Brien , "Ireland's Secular Revolution: The Waning Influence of the Catholic Church and the Future of Ireland's Blasphemy Law," *Conn J Intl'L* 18 (2002): 430 . See Ross, "Blasphemy ."

11.3. Historical Analysis: Evolution of Blasphemy Laws in Pakistan

11.3.1. Colonial Origins

The blasphemy laws in Pakistan trace their origin back to the British colonial era, during which these laws were introduced as a result of severe communal rioting among the diverse religious groups within India. "Offences against religion" were incorporated in the Indian Penal Code 1860 (295, 296,[17] 298,[18] and then later, 295A[19]) that were applicable to each religious community within the state, designating specific punishments in the case of any citizen deliberately disrespecting any religion through the means of inappropriate language and gestures, destruction or defilement of any place of worship, and disturbance to a religious assembly.[20] The ostensible intent behind these laws was to enable peaceful co existence among the various religious communities then in India, especially given the sensitivity of religious issues. It has also been stated that, given the Hindu majority in British India, these laws were envisioned to afford protection to minority religions (including Islam) and the religious rights of these communities.[21] Moreover, in British India in many large areas, Muslims

---

[17] Section 296 reads, "Whoever voluntarily causes disturbance to any assembly lawfully engaged in the performance of religious worship, or religious ceremonies, shall be punished with imprisonment of either description for a term which may extend to one year, or with fine, or with both."

[18] Section 298 IPC , "Uttering words, etc. with deliberate intent to wound religious feelings": "Whoever, with any deliberate intention of wounding the religious feelings of any person, utters any word or makes any sound in the hearing of that or makes any gesture in the sight of that person or places any object in the sight of that person, shall be punished with imprisonment of either description for a term which may extend to one year, or with fine, or with both."

[19] Introduced in 1927, following a rise in tensions between Muslim and Hindu communities after the publication of an anonymous pamphlet on the life of the Prophet, the provision criminalized "deliberate and malicious acts intended to outrage religious feelings of any class by insulting religion or religious believers ."

[20] Center for Research and Security Studies , "Blasphemy Laws in Pakistan: A Historical Overview" (2014), 9, http://www.csi-int.org/fileadmin/Files/pdf/2014/blasphemylawsinpakistan.pdf.

[21] Bilal Hayee, "Blasphemy Laws and Pakistan's Human Rights Obligations," *U. Notre Dame Austl. L. Rev.* 14 (2012): 29–30. See also Farhana A. Nazir, "A Study of the Evolution of Legislation on Offences Relating to Religion in British India and Their Implications in Contemporary Pakistan," thesis, University of Edinburgh, December 2013, p. 12 . The author states that "Macaulay's designation of Chapter XV of ' offences against religion' shows his concern to foster multicultural understanding by attempting to ensure that the laws imposed by the colonial power matched the expectation of its colonial subjects. Therefore, in the context of religious diversity, the law's major objective was to bring harmony among religious communities and to control religious conflicts, which occurred through 'the differences among communities of feeling.' This aim encouraged the legislature to protect religious places, worship, or objects including all funeral rites and to prevent religious discussions from causing violence." See also (cited by Nazir) Wing-Cheong Chan , Barry Wright, and Stanley Yeo, eds., *Codification, Macaulay and the Indian Penal Code* (New York: Routledge,

were the majority population, and such a law could be also required to restrain both religious groups.

As Asad Ali Ahmed argues, " These laws enabled the colonial state to assume the role of a rational and natural arbiter of supposedly endemic and inevitable religious conflicts . " [22] Kaviraj notes that this view the state's role is due in part to British authors' writing the first "modern" histories of India, which stipulated, among other things, that the " a rrival of British colonial institutions of religious neutrality created conditions for 'the rule of law' and religious peace for the first time—precisely because the British could play the role of an impartial third party eternal to the warring faiths." [23] However, some doubts may be cast on the supposed neutrality of the colonial state.

By instituting criminal laws to manage violence caused by religious offenses in colonial India, in many ways the colonial s tate laid the groundwork for what was later to transpire in both India and Pakistan. For example, Section 295A of the Indian Penal Code of 1860, as phrased and constituted, required proof that sentiments of a class of citizens had been outraged, and it has been argued that, as opposed to necessarily "reflecting primordial religious attachments, the cases before the colonial courts were not only enabled by the law but largely constituted by it." [24] The laws retained this characteristic despite the departure of the colonial administration ; as Adcock adds (with reference to the application of the retained Section 295A in India today) , violence has become " part of a legal strategy. Instead of simply responding to hurt feelings, the law has given strategic value to invoking and mobilizing wounded religious feelings ."[25]

This point is manifest in a more aggravated form in Pakistan, whereby the state cannot be seen as neutral in any sense of the word, and does not feigns this attribute.

11.3.2. Post- Partition

Upon the formation of Pakistan in 1947, the country inherited these "Offences against Religion," now predominantly referred to as blasphemy laws. Despite a

2016), 294–295; Gauri Viswanathan, *Outside the Fold: Conversion, Modernity, and Belief* (Princeton, NJ: Princeton University Press, 1988), 250–251.

[22] Asad Ali Ahmed, "Specters of Macaulay: Blasphemy, the Indian Penal Code, and Pakistan's Postc olonial Predicament," in *Censorship in South Asia: Cultural Regulation from Sedition to Seduction*, ed. Raminder Kaur and William Mazzarella (Bloomington: Indiana University Press, 2009), 173.

[23] Sudipta Kaviraj, *Plurality and Pluralism: Democracy, Religious Difference, and Political Imagination*.

[24] Ahmed, "Specters of Macaulay ," 173.

[25] C. S. Adcock, "Violence, Passion and the Law: A Brief History of Section 295-A and Its Antecedents," *Journal of American Academy of Religion* 84, no. 2 (2016): 337–351 .

common colonial origin, politics in India and Pakistan took very different forms, which impacted the way these laws were both interpreted and implemented within the new political context.

After partition, while India transitioned into a self-proclaimed secular constitutional democracy in 1950 s, Pakistan struggled in the constitution- making process, conclusively until 1973, as well as with democracy until much later. Pakistan oscillated between direct dictatorial rule, indirect dictatorial rule through politicians created by dictatorial rule, and brief periods of political rule by civilian political parties disrupted by coups. Under a dictatorial regime, these blasphemy laws were redefined, "as nearly all movement toward imposition of Sharia occurred during martial rule,"[26] and that says little on whether the populace needed or wanted these laws at the time or had any choice in the matter.[27] Subsequent democratic rule, often in the form of weak coalition- based governments, failed to reverse these changes either because they lacked the political will and courage to face the consequences (political and personal), or these governments consisted of political parties otherwise aligned ideologically with groups resisting reform in law and practice. Those advocating for change were victimized, silenced, or replaced.

Moreover, given Pakistan's unique status as a s tate created on a religious basis, the issue of the exact relationship between religion and state remained unresolved amid political liberals at one end and mullahs or clerics on the other.[28] As David Forte notes, "Pakistan was created in 1947 as a state for Muslims, but not necessarily as an Islamic State," until Islam was declared the state religion in 1973.[29] Over the years, Pakistan solidified its identity as the Islamic Republic of Pakistan, established for Muslims, while grappling with the definition and conditions of being Muslim and simultaneously a citizen of Pakistan; it is pertinent to note that at the time of independence, Pakistan retained considerable diversity, both among the Muslim majority, in the form of religious sects, ethnicity,

---

[26] Ayesha Jalal, *Democracy and Authoritarianism in South Asia: A Comparative and Historical Perspective* (New York: Cambridge University Press, 2009), 35. See further Mohammad Waseem, *Politics and the State in Pakistan* (Islamabad: National Institute of Historical and Cultural Research, 1989), 390– 400 ; I. A. Rehman, "Route of the Mullahs," *Newsline*, October 1993, 44–45; Lawrence Ziring, "From Islamic Republic to Islamic State in Pakistan, *Asian Survey* 24 (1984): 943 .

[27] The populace is not defined as members of religious organizations demonstrating on the streets; both politically and numerically, this does not constitute a significant majority.

[28] This is not to suggest that the "political liberals" did not use religion strategically for political gains, but that the relationship of the state with religion has remained unresolved. For a brief background see I. A. Rehman, " 40 Years of Zia: How Zia Redefined Pakistan," *Dawn*, 2 July 2017, at https://www.dawn.com/news/1342697/40-years-of-zia-how-zia-redefined-pakistan.

[29] For more on the constitutional evolution of Pakistan and the role of Islam within it see David F. Forte, "Apostasy and Blasphemy in Pakistan," *Conn. J. Int'l L.* 10 (1994–95): 29–43 .

culture, and language, and also among the non-Muslim community, which included representatives of all religions.

It is further relevant to mention that religious parties in Pakistan have never
been able to gain more than a handful of seats in major elections,[30] and so do
not necessarily enjoy widespread support in the political arena directly. However,
their position was consistently consolidated during military rule[31] and subsequent administrations dependent on coalitions, which continued to use religion
as a rallying point for their politics.[32] This political context also led to the transformation of the role of religious parties. Irfan Ahmad argues, tracing differences between Jamaat-e-Islami (Hind) and Jamaat-e-Islami (Pakistan), that despite both
groups originating from Jamaat-e-Islami and being founded in colonial India by
Abdul al-Maudadi, secular democracy played a key role in the moderation of the
Jamaat in India.[33] The Jamaat in Pakistan, a religious state, evolved in the opposite
direction. However, not only did an Islamic state empower these groups, but also
the lack of democracy—which created additional opportunities through the existence of power vacuums.

Being the Islamic Republic of Pakistan, the foundation and the politics of
the country have come to be based on "Islamic values and beliefs," the interpretation of which was given and imposed by the religious Right and
the dictators, who have represented those voices for political and personal
interests.[34] A natural, however unfortunate, consequence was the dominance
of a singular interpretation of Islam over not just the religious minorities

[30] Unless these elections were sham ones to validate a dictatorial rule, such as elections under
Musharraf.

[31] "The Pakistani military state partnered with religious parties... for the street power of these
groups that could exploit Islam for political power. " See Shemeem Abbas Burney, *Pakistan's
Blasphemy Laws: From Islamic Empires to the Taliban* (Austin: University of Texas Press,
2014,), 5.

[32] A r ecent addition to the list of prominent actors is the Tehreek-e-Labbaik, which staged the
2017 Faizabad sit- in against the Pakistani Muslim League (Nawaz) (PML-N) government for
changes in the electoral forms, wherein candidates are required to reaffirm the finality of the P
rophet. Hundreds of men led by Khadim Hussain of Tehreek-e-Labbaik (and joined by other religious groups) staged a sit- in, which ended after the government's assurance that it would not
change any laws and the resignation of a federal minister responsible for the "clerical" mistake.
See "How the Islamabad Protests Happened," *Dawn*, 25 November 2017, at https://www.dawn.
com/news/1372800.

[33] Irfan Ahmed, *Islamism and Democracy in India: The Transformation of Jamaat-e-Islami*
(Princeton, NJ: Princeton University Press, 2009).

[34] In Pakistan, the narrative around Islam has been informed by Wahhabism, which rose to prominence in the 1980s, when Saudi Arabia began funding Wahhabi madrasas in Pakistan. Saudi Arabia
has consistently funded Pakistan's political and military leadership. For example, Zia ul- Haq, who
was president of Pakistan between 1977 and 1988, as well as current Prime Minister Nawaz Sharif,
have received significant financial backing from Saudi Arabia. The Saudis also financed the growth
of various groups, including Jamat ud Dawa, Sipe Sahaba, and the Pakistani Taliban —which also
received patronage from the Sharif and Zia ul- Haq families—that have grown increasingly hostile
toward religious minorities over the last few decades. Wahhabism has also affected the s tate crack
down on Sufis and Sufism.

within the country, but also over the dissenting members of the majority in the country.[35] What is Islamic became lawful interchangeably and vice versa.[36]

From partition till 1977, before the military d ictator General Zia ul- Haq came into power, blasphemy laws were applied sparingly and fairly equally, affording punishments for offenses committed not only against Muslims, but also against religious minorities. For example, in *Okil Ali v . Behari Lal Paul PLD 1962*, an accused was sentenced to three months' imprisonment for damaging a Hindu place of worship.[37] Moreover, it has further been noted that during this time, most of the complaints under these provisions were made by Muslims against other Muslims, none on accounts of blasphemy against the Prophet or defiling the Quran; and a majority of the cases were dismissed in light of procedural safeguards, as under Section 295A of the Pakistan Penal Code: a case required the prior authorization from the p rovincial or entral government .[38]

However, since the 1980s, there has been an increase in the number of registrations of blasphemy cases as well as mob killings.[39] To fully understand the current application of blasphemy laws in Pakistan, it is pertinent to mention some key political developments post-independence and prior to amendments by Zia, which set the broader stage and, in some ways, facilitated what was to come.

11.3.3. The Ahmadi Question

Shortly after Pakistan's independence, religious groups such as the Majlis-ul-Ahrar-e-Islami (Ahrar), and the Jamaat-e-Islami (JI) raised questions on the

[35] Burney has stated that blasphemy laws during General Zia ul-Haq's time were instituted also for geopolitical control of the region, which included Afghanistan, in order to bring down the Soviet Union. She argues that Saudi Arabia and Western actors facilitated, through blasphemy laws, the creation of "a State sponsored 'infidel' ideology that not only has had an impact on citizens and led to social injustice but now affects international and global security as militant groups like the Taliban justify violence based on treating as infidels all Muslims and non-Muslims who do not subscribe to their militant interpretation of Islam." See Burney, *Pakistan's Blasphemy Laws*, 3.

[36] For an interesting comparative perspective on navigating the complex space between secularism and Islam and post-secularism in Turkey, see Ates Altinordu, Chapter 7 in this volume . It is insightful particularly to note how the politics of religion and against religion solidifies certain conceptions for the communities involved.

[37] Center for Research and Security Studies , "Blasphemy Laws in Pakistan ," 20 .

[38] Center for Research and Security Studies , "Blasphemy Laws in Pakistan ," 21 . See further International Commission for Jurists , "On Trial: The Implementation of Pakistan's Blasphemy Laws," November 2015, p. 9.

[39] Various national organizations, such as the Human Rights Commission of Pakistan, and international organizations have documented this increase. See Human Rights Commission of Pakistan, "State of Human Rights " (2014), 46–51; and "What Are Pakistan's Blasphemy Laws?," BBC, 6 November 2014, available at http://www.bbc.com/news/world-south-asia-12621225. See also Jinnah Institute, "State of Religious Freedom in Pakistan" (2015), 2.

relationship between Islam and the state, and in particular the status of Ahmadis within the newly formed Islamic state.[40]

In 1952– 53, these religious groups orchestrated the first anti-Ahmadi riots in Punjab, which led to mass killings of members of the Ahmadi community, with estimates of the number of dead going up to 2,000.[41] It is instructive to view the role of these religious groups as inherently political;[42] from time to time religious organizations have aligned with political elements for mutually beneficial ends and vice versa. For example, it was believed that the circumstances leading to the 1952– 53 riots were facilitated by the then chief minister of the Punjab (Muslim League), Mian Mumtaz Daultana, who used both the JI and the Ahrar in a plot to overthrow the prime minister (from his own party), Khawaja Nazimuddin, and to cover up his provincial government's failure in Punjab. He aimed to divert the blame for the economic crises in the province to the Ahmadi community, and to this end provided strategic support, through acts but also omissions in the form of ignoring ongoing activities of JI and Ahrar in their campaigns against the Ahmadi community.[43]

It may also be instructive to mention that before partition the above-mentioned religious organizations had opposed the creation of Pakistan as a separate state, and hence had very little political capital at the outset to influence decision-making within the political sphere. Their only recourse to regain prominence in the new state was through street demonstrations, riots, and strategic alliances invoking religion in a state that was unsure of its exact relationship with Islam. In contrast, members of the Ahmadi community had attained prominent positions within the government, bureaucracy, and other fields post-partition, and this reality may have contributed to the animosity toward them by the religious organizations.

---

[40] It is pertinent to mention that apart from the Ahmadi question, Pakistan has since independence grappled with the broader question of the state's relationship with Islam and the extent to which Pakistan's ideological creation on religious grounds is to influence institutional and governance structures and impact the substantive relationship of the state with citizens.

[41] These riots led to a declaration of Pakistan's first martial law.

[42] Sadia Saeed, in Chapter 1 in this volume, situates the riots and social mobilization of religious groups on this issue as "underpinned by political and not religious reasons" arising out of the needs of a modern nation- state. Her insights on the political use of religion in building a constituency in Pakistan are particularly relevant.

[43] The Nazimuddin government with the aid of the military establishment crushed the movement, dismissed Mian Mumtaz Daultana, and arrested the main leaders on charges of instigating violence against the state. See https://www.dawn.com/news/1057427. The *Justice Munir Commission Report on the Anti- Ahmadi Riots of Punjab in 1953* (1954), 283, also mentions the allegations against Dultana of conspiring to over throw the government. See the report at https://archive.org/stream/The1954JusticeMunirCommissionReportOnTheAntiAhmadiRiotsOfPunjabIn1953/The-1954-Justice-Munir-Commission-Report-on-the-anti-Ahmadi-Riots-of-Punjab-in-1953_djvu.txt
See further Seyyed Vali Reza Nasr, *The Vanguard of the Islamic Revolution: The Jama'at-i-Islami of Pakistan* (Berkeley: University of California Press, 1994), 132–134.

Therefrom, the period between 1953 and 1973 is reported to have witnessed irregular persecution of the Ahmadi community, but, in 1974, a new wave of anti-Ahmadi disturbances spread across Pakistan.[44]

The election in 1970 election brought Zulfiqar Ali Bhutto (Bhutto) of the Pakistan People's Party (PPP) into power. PPP was associated with democratic, socialist, and secular credentials,[45] and the Ahmadi community predominantly voted for the party in Punjab. There had been no major clash involving Ahmadis since the earlier riots in 1950s until the events that led to the 1974 riots.

The 1974 riots resulted from a clash between members of the Islami Jamiat-i-Talaba (IJT) student wing of the JI with Ahmadi youths in Rabwa—a predominantly Ahmadi town. IJT students were en route to Peshwar and stopped in Rabwa. At the train stop, IJT students got off and chanted anti-Ahmadi slogans and insulted the Ahmadi spiritual leader, and thereafter continued with their journey. When the incident was reported to Ahmadi leaders, they instructed Ahmadi youth to await IJT students' return at the train station. As the train stopped, the awaiting Ahmadi youth charged at members of IJT and a fight ensued, leading to 30 IJT men being severely beaten for insulting the religious sentiments of the Ahmadis.

After the Rabwa incident, IJT demanded accountability for perpetrators, and despite the apprehension of 71 Ahmadis and the creation of a judicial commission under Justice Samdani, IJT announced street protests[46] and issued ultimatums demanding "removal of Ahmadis from bureaucracy and the government; [that] Ahmadi youth outfits be disarmed; and [that] Rabwa be declared an open city because it had become 'a State within a State.'" These protests soon translated into mob violence leading to the loss of lives and properties of members of the Ahmadi community.

Amid this violent unrest, Zulfiqar Ali Bhutto was faced with two options. He could either continue to battle pressures from the right-wing groups [47] and risk losing his political rule in the process, as was communicated in threats to him and his party.[48] Or he could surrender to the circumstances and attempt to quell the unrest by creating national unity using religion (unanimity within the

---

[44] Human Rights Watch, "Pakistan: Massacre of Minority Ahmadis," 1 June 2010, https://www.hrw.org/news/2010/06/01/pakistan-massacre-minority-ahmadis.

[45] Nadeem F. Paracha, " The 1974 Ouster of the 'Heretics': What Really Happened?," *Dawn*, 21 November 2013, https://www.dawn.com/news/1057427.

[46] Other opposition parties, including the Muslim League and Majlis-i-Ahrar Tehrik-i-Istiqlal, headed by Asghar Khan, joined IJT. It i s instinctual to continue to see these alliances with a political lens.

[47] Prime Minister Bhutto resisted such an amendment. On 4 June , while speaking on the floor of the National Assembly, Bhutto refused to allow opposition members to speak on the Ahmadiyya issue. He accused the opposition of being "hell-bent on destroying the country." However, as the riots escalated, it became harder for him to oppose the amendment.

[48] Jamaat-i-Islami's Mian Tufail warned Bhutto that "his double-talk on the Ahmadiyya issue would trigger his downfall." See Paracha, " 1974 Ouster."

Muslims on the Ahmadi question) to counteract threats to his political rule by an impending military coup.[49]

The Bhutto government adopted a policy of appeasement in response to violence, to the detriment of the future peace.[50] In 1974, the Second Constitutional Amendment declared Ahmadis to be non-Muslims.[51] The parliament took this step, as opposed to the courts or any religious institution, albeit under duress and political expediency. The fact that this decision was taken by the parliament, as opposed to a dictator, provided a degree of legitimacy to it. Moreover, the fact that a liberal party such as the PPP did this greatly affected the scope for advocacy around the issue later for the same party.

A reported account of a non-Ahmadi man who witnessed the turmoil at the Rabwa station in 1974 best exemplifies the intricacies of the politics of the time, which are complex and outside the current scope of inquiry: " 'Someone wanted this to happen,' he said, without saying who that someone was."[52]

11.3.4. Blasphemy Laws Modified: The Zia Era

Even after the Second Constitutional Amendment in 1974, some protections for Ahmadis remained intact and were upheld by the courts. In *A.R. Mubashir v. A.A. Shah,* the Lahore High Court held that although constitutional recognition of the Ahmadi as Muslims had been barred, their fundamental right to peaceful religious practice was still intact. More specifically, the court held that the religious practices of the Ahmadi (including references to their places of worship as mosques) were neither a provocation amounting to public nuisance

---

[49] I. A. Rehman argues that Bhutto's tenure helped religious parties (even if he himself was not necessarily ideologically aligned) because he too invoked the religious identity of Pakistan. For example, in addition to declaring Islam the state religion, in "February 1974, Bhutto joined King Faisal's efforts to counter the forces of Arab nationalism with Islamic nationalism and organised the Islamic Summit." See Rehman, " 40 Years of Zia ."

[50] The same parties, who were appeased in 1974, took to the streets again in 1977 against Zulfiqar Ali Bhutto. This at the least is suggestive of politics being a key driving force, and religion a tool. In Pakistan, both the military regime and political parties have interchangeably used religion to consolidate their rule—religious groups have used religion as their bargaining chip. In any case, it has been manifest that the use of religion in politics does not provide opportunities for backtracking.

[51] In 1974, the Ahmadi community were declared to be non-Muslims, and hence a religious minority, by an a mendment to the Constitution of Pakistan (Section 260 (3)), based on their belief in Mirza Ghulam Ahmed. S ince then they have become one of the primary victims of blasphemy laws and of persecution as a religious minority . Section 260 (3) of the Constitution of Pakistan defines a Muslim as " a person who believes in the unity and oneness of Allah, in the absolute and unqualified finality of the Prophet-hood of Muhammad (PBUH), the last of prophets, and does not believe in, or recognize as a prophet or religious reformer, any person who claimed or claims to be a prophet, in any sense of the word or of any description whatsoever, after Muhammad (PBUH)"; and defines non-Muslims as including "persons belong to the Christian, Hindu, Sikh, Buddhist or Parsi community, a person of the Quadiani Group or the Lahori Group who call themselves Ahmadis . "

[52] Paracha, " 1974 Ouster."

nor a material threat to any special "property" held by Muslims. The promulgation of a constitutional amendment defining the Ahmadis as non-Muslims did not remove their fundamental rights as citizens. [53]

However, these protections did not last long after Zia's assumption of power.[54] As Eugene V. Debs, stated, "In every age it has been the tyrant, the oppressor and the exploiter who has wrapped himself in the cloak of patriotism, or religion, or both to deceive and overawe the People."[55] During Zia's reign (1977 to 1988), a period notorious for "Islamization,"[56] a new set of provisions were inserted to Pakistan's existing blasphemy laws that sought to cater only to the religious feelings of Muslims, the overwhelming majority of the population. A range of offenses specifically targeting the Ahmadi community, and broad enough to cover "the freedom to practice their religion" as well as that of Pakistan's other religious minorities were instituted; blaspheming against the Holy Prophet Muhammad and defiling of the Quran[57] were inserted as separate offenses. Section 295C of the Pakistan Penal Code prescribes punishment (death penalty)[58] for "defiling the sacred name of the Holy Prophet," without defining the exact nature of the offense and without making it an intention- based offense.[59]

---

[53] See Nelson, Chapter 8 in this volume, for a detailed analysis of the constitutional history relevant to religious freedom and the Ahmadi question in Pakistan.

[54] For jurisprudence of the c ourts, see also Sadia Saeed, "The Nation and Its Heretics: Courts, State Authority, and Minority Rights in Pakistan" (2011), http://web.law.columbia.edu/sites/default/files/microsites/law-culture/files/2011-files/Nation%26Heretics_SAEED.pdf.

[55] Eugene V. Debs, Voices of a People's History of the United States, (Canton, OH, Anti-war Speech, 16 June 1918).

[56] Islamization is a political concept in Pakistan —the use of religion as a political tool, as opposed to derived from Islamic j urisprudence. Zia ul-Haq's Islamization refers to a series of steps taken by him to make religion and its use more visible. During Zia 's rule, the Federal Shariat Court was established in 1980 to "examine and decide the question whether or not any law or provision of law is repugnant to the injunctions of Islam"; see Article 203D(1) of the Constitution of Pakistan . That court in 1990 mandated the death penalty for Section 295 C. The court held "the penalty for the contempt of the Holy Prophet . . . is death and nothing else" and held life imprisonment for this offense to be "repugnant to the injunctions of Islam as laid down in the Holy Quran and Sunnah." See Federal Shariat Court, *Muhammad Ismail Qureshi v . Pakistan through Secretary, Law and Parliamentary*, Shariat Petition No.6/L of 1987 (1990), http://khatm-e-nubuwwat.org/lawyers/data/english/8/fed-shariat-court-1990.pdf. Several measures taken by Zia have not been undone and the longer they remain in force become harder to undo. For additional specific measures taken by Zia, see Rehman, " 40 Years of Zia."

[57] Section 295 B states that "whoever willfully defiles, damages, desecrates a copy of the Holy Quran or of an extract therefrom or uses it in any derogatory manner or for any unlawful purpose shall be punishable with imprisonment for life."

[58] See *Muhammed Ismail Qureshi v. Pakistan* (PLD 1991, FSC10). However, it is pertinent to mention that this uniformity is constructed, and is not and has never been backed by Islamic jurisprudence. The work of Arafat Mazhar and his organization is illuminating in this regard. See Arafat Mazhar, "The Untold Story of Pakistan's Blasphemy Laws," *Dawn*, 13 August 2017, at https://www.dawn.com/authors/3757/arafat-mazhar.

[59] Section 295 C states: "Whoever by words, either spoken or written, or by visible representation or by any imputation, innuendo, or insinuation, directly or indirectly, defiles the sacred name of the Holy Prophet Muhammad shall be punished with death, or imprisonment for life, and shall be also liable for a fine."

The colonial blasphemy law inherited by Pakistan was meant to protect minorities and their freedom of religion. However, the deliberate additions by Zia to blasphemy laws shifted the focus from protection of religious diversity to protection of the dominant religion and religious sentiments of the majority. Generally applicable blasphemy laws were transformed into a tool to oppress religious minorities and threaten religious pluralism within the state.

It is pertinent to reiterate that the victims of these blasphemy laws are not only minorities, in the narrow sense of the word, but Muslims too, who when accused of blasphemy are instantly transformed into a minority.[60] The Muslim identity worthy of protection is subsumed into the dominant conception of Islam accepted and promoted by the state: that conception is overwhelmingly conservative and Sunni and over the years, anti-Ahmadi as well. Other sects within Islam, for example, the Shia sect, despite being the second main Muslim sect within the country, has consistently been persecuted for being different, from targeted killings of individuals to attacks at places of worship to imposition of laws that enforce the Sunni conception on their way of life.[61]

These laws have in essence confined what it means to be within the majority religion. When the state has the power to define the boundaries and decide membership of both those within and outside the religion, and further uses or condones the use of violence against individuals and groups who do not conform, notions of majority and minority can be distorted at will for the political interests of the state. The Ahmadis, who previously identified as Muslims, were subsequently redefined as a minority by the state. Minority sects, such as the Shia community, have been a victim of state-sanctioned and state-supported violence for a long time. This power of the state to define the terms and parameters of "Muslim-hood" has at a micro level empowered and continues to empower individuals to arbitrarily decide what is "Islamic" and not, as well as who is a Muslim and not, and enforce that conception in a vigilante-like fashion.

11.3.5. A Threat to Religious Pluralism: Restricting Minorities

Subsequent additions by Zia in Pakistan's blasphemy laws clearly stood on discriminatory grounds. No specific punishment or provision was incorporated for blaspheming against any of the religious minorities present within Pakistan,

---

[60] The Center of Social Justice has also reported that between 1987 and 2017, a majority of persons implicated under the blasphemy laws have been Muslims. See Asad Ahmed, "A Brief History of the Anti-blasphemy Laws," *Herald*, 31 October 2018, https://herald.dawn.com/news/1154036.

[61] Nosheen Ali refers to this victimization of Muslim minorities as sectism and includes women as well as "the more inclusive Sunni and Sufi lifeworlds that have historically overlapped with Shia beliefs in the heterogeneous sacred landscape of South Asia." See *"Stranger, Enemy": Anti-Shia Hostility and Annihilatory Politics in Pakistan* in this volume.

and neither was any penalty imposed for desecrating other religious texts, such as those of Hindus or Christians.[62] The death penalty, available only in cases of defiling the name of the H oly Prophet, has become an increasingly relied- upon provision.[63] The purpose was clearly not to protect religious pluralism or religious minorities within Pakistan. Contrary to that, the Ahmadis (also referred to as the Quadiani group) were particularly targeted through these new laws, not just in their application, but also in the express content of the added blasphemy laws, seriously curtailing their freedom to practice their religion (Articles 298 B and 298 C).

Article 298 B[64] barred, with threat of imprisonment and a fine, Ahmadis from referring to anyone other than "certain holy personages and places" of Muslims with specific holy titles; from reciting the azan , or "call to prayer " ; and from calling their places of worships mosques. This meant that for Ahmadis, it is a criminal offense to refer to their holy individuals with titles similar to those used by Muslims, as well as to use the same call to prayer—which the Ahmadi community had been using as an integral religious practice prior to their constitutional declaration as non-Muslims. Similarly, 298 C punished any Ahmadi " who directly or indirectly, poses himself as a Muslim, or calls or refers to his faith as Islam, or preaches or propagates his faith, or invites others to accept his faith, by words either spoken or written, or by visible representations, or in any manner whatsoever outrages the religious feelings of Muslims . . . with imprisonment [up to three years] . . . and . . . fine."[65]

These laws not only allow the state to dictate how Ahmadis can practice their religion— if at all possible with these restrictions— but also in essence are an attempt to ensure that no such belief system as that of Ahmadis is allowed to exist or be nurtured within the state of Pakistan. The vague yet expansive wording of

[62] "An amendment on blasphemy laws proposed by a minority Member of Parliament to criminalise desecration of other religious communities as well was rejected." See Aftab Mughal, "Parliament Rejects Amendment in Blasphemy Law," Countercurrent.org, 5 June 2007, http://www.countercurrents.org/mughal050607.htm.

[63] See Osama Siddique and Zahra Hayat, "Unholy Speech and Holy Laws: Blasphemy Laws in Pakistan—Controversial Origins, Design Defects, and Free Speech Implications," Minn. J. Int'l L. 17 (2008): 303.

[64] Section 298 B: "1) Any person of the Quadiani group [i.e., Ahmadis] a) refers to or addresses, any person other than a Caliph or companion of the Holy Prophet Muhammad (PBUH), as 'Ameer-ul-Mumineen,' 'Khalifat-Mumineen,' 'Khalifa-tul-Muslimeen,' 'Sahaabi,' or 'Razi Allah Anho'; b) refers to, or addresses, any person, other than a wife of the Holy Prophet Muhammad (PBUH), as 'Ummul-Mumineen'; c) refers to, or addresses, any person other than a member of the family 'Ahl-e-bait' of the Holy Prophet Muhammad (PBUH), as 'Ahle-bait'; or d) refers to, or names, or calls, his place of worship a Masjid'; shall be punished with imprisonment . . . for a term which may extend to 3 years, and shall also be liable to fine. 2) Any person of the Qaudiana Group . . . who . . . refers to the mode or form of call to prayers followed by his faith as ' Azan, ' or recites Azan as used by the Muslims, shall be punished . "

[65] Section 298 C, "Person of Quadiani Group, etc. . . . calling himself a Muslim or preaching or propagating his faith," Pakistan Penal Code 1860.

the provisions does not guide Ahmadi s on what they can or cannot do but, in short, makes their religious feelings subservient to the religious sentiments of the Muslim majority (to be determined by the majority itself). This is self-evidently contrary to the constitutional right to freedom of religion guaranteed under the Constitution of Pakistan to all citizens, and contrary to the values of religious pluralism.

Pakistan's amendments to blasphemy laws during the Zia regime reformed neutrally applicable and sparingly used blasphemy laws into a tool of persecution and religious domination in the hands of the majority religion. These laws have been used to raise public hostiliy toward Pakistan's other religious communities, and have increasingly sensitized the Muslim populace to offenses against their religion. Furthermore, such laws in content and in application signal to the majority that Pakistan's religious minority communities are not afforded protection, making them especially vulnerable to false blasphemy accusations. According to several human rights organizations, an overwhelming majority of the cases registered under blasphemy laws are false, instituted in the spirit of personal vendettas and property disputes, or simply to displace religious minority communities by burning more than a 100 houses at a time.[66]

It has been reported that from 1986 to 2010, approximately 1,274 people have been charged with offenses under the blasphemy laws, and 60 per cent of those have been non-Muslims.[67] Moreover, as many as 53 have been killed on mere allegations of blasphemy since 1986,[68] not to mention threats and attacks on communities and their assets. Statistics provided by human rights organizations show that there has been an increasing reliance on blasphemy laws since Zia's amendments—that trend continues and limits the breathing space of Pakistan's religious minorities and any dissenting viewpoints, as the next section will show through some practical examples.

11.4. Realities on the Ground

In the absence of a lack of any systematic research, data collection or evaluation on the part of the state to assess the impact of blasphemy laws, documentation efforts of national and international human rights organizations provide a much-needed occasion for introspection through detailed accounts of the context,

[66] "125 Christian Houses Burnt over Blasphemy," Dawn, 9 March 2013, https://www.dawn.com/news/791491/125-christian-houses-burnt-over-blasphemy.
[67] "Top Islamic Body Proposes Changes in Blasphemy Law," Express Tribune, 19 December 2010, http://tribune.com.pk/story/91838/council-of-islamic-ideology-top-islamic-body-proposes-changes-in-blasphemy-law/.
[68] See Malik Muhammad Mumtaz Qadri v. the State, Supreme Court of Pakistan, Criminal Appeals No. 2010 and 2011 of 2015, p. 26.

complexities, and circumstances in which blasphemy laws operate.[69] Several independent reports state that Pakistan's blasphemy laws, as they are implemented, threaten fundamental human rights guaranteed under the Constitution of Pakistan, by international human rights treaties Pakistan is a party to, under the core values of pluralism, tolerance, and equality of justice necessary in any democratic society.[70]

For the purposes of this section , fundamental rights violations through these blasphemy laws will be divided into violations taking place "outside the legal sphere"—referring to instances of violence perpetrated on individuals and communities, usually by vigilantes and mobs, prior to commencement of formal legal action—and violations stemming from within the legal sphere—referring to problems in the wording of the laws and the absence of safeguards, as well as lack of access to fair trial rights. However, th is division is not to suggest that one does not influence the other violation; in fact, it does so heavily. Moreover, while it is responsibility of the state and the legal regime to prevent mob violence and vigilantism, deliberate s tate action and inaction directly contribute to such violence.

11.4.1. Outside the Legal Sphere

Following the Zia amendments, an increase in extra judicial blasphemy incidents has been seen, with a multitude of incidents being "resolved" through vigilantism outside the jurisdiction of any courts or law enforcement agencies. Given the sensitivity of religious issues, those accused of blasphemy are at a risk to their life from the very moment such an accusation is made against them.

In April 2017, Mashal Khan, a Muslim student at Abdul Wali Khan University, was lynched by a mob on the premises of a university for alleged blasphemy;[71] in November 2015, an Ahmadi factory in Jhelum was torched by a mob on allegations of blasphemy, followed the next day by an attack on an Ahmadi Mosque in the same area.[72] It was also not too long ago when, on the basis of an accusation against Sawan Masih of insulting the Holy Prophet Muhammad

---

[69] See Amnesty International r eport titled *"As Good as Dead": The Impact of the Blasphemy Laws in Pakistan*, 2016, at https://www.amnesty.nl/content/uploads/2017/01/blasphemy_report_-_final_version_201216.pdf?x23787 . See further International Commission for Jurists , "On Trial."

[70] See further International Commission for Jurists , "On Trial . "

[71] "Pakistan Student Accused of Blasphemy Beaten to Death on Campus," Reuters, 13 April 2017, at http://www.reuters.com/article/us-pakistan-blasphemy-idUSKBN17F1ZL.

[72] Amir Kayani, "Ahmadi Place of Worship Set Ablaze in Jhelum, Riots Erupt after Blasphemy Allegations" *Dawn,* 21 November 2015, http://www.dawn.com/news/1221273; Kashif Chaudhry, "We Will Beat Them, We Will Lynch Them, They Chanted, before Setting Fire to the Ahmadi Factory," *Express Tribune Blogs,* 23 November 2015, http://blogs.tribune.com.pk/story/30468/we-will-beat-them-we-will-lynch-them-they-chanted-before-setting-fire-to-the-ahmadi-factory/.

during a conversation with a friend, approx imately 3,000 Muslims swarmed through Joseph colony, torching 100 Christian homes along the way.[73] Similarly, a Hindu temple in a southern city of Larkana was set on fire in 2014, by a mob angered by the alleged desecration of the Quran.[74] Other examples include the murder of Shahid Bhatti, f ederal m inister of minorities affairs and a Christian by faith, for speaking about reform within the legal paradigm in which blasphemy laws operate.[75] The governor of Punjab, Salman Taseer, was murdered by his security guard for criticizing the blasphemy laws in 2011.[76] A young professor, Junaid Hafeez, was accused of blasphemy in 2013, and in 2014 his lawyer, Rashid Rehman, was shot dead for taking up the case. Both Salman Taseer and Mashal Khan were from the dominant faith, as is Junaid Hafeez, who, after spending years in solitary confinement due to threat of violence from other inmates, has now been sentenced to death by the trial court. The case of Salman Taseer also highlights that even a critique of blasphemy laws is considered tantamount to blasphemy for the mob, and for Junaid Hafeez's lawyer, the act of defending an alleged blasphemy merits the same punishment.

Often times, even when formerly accused blasphemers are acquitted of all charges, they remain victims of threats and attacks, with little or no protection provided by the government or by legal agents. For example, in the case of a Christian girl Rimsha Masih, accused of burning pages from the Holy Quran but later proven innocent, she and her family were forced to remain in hiding to ensure their safety, before fleeing to Canada.[77] Similarly, 52-year- old Abid Mehmood Alias was shot dead a few days after his release from prison, where he had been detained for claiming prophet-hood.[78] Most recently, after much public pressure, Asia Bibi, formerly accused of blasphemy, was acquitted and se-cretly relocated outside the country, but still continues to get threats.

The current structure and content of Pakistan's blasphemy laws has thus strengthened the extremist, intolerant forces within the nation, instilling an

[73] "Blasphemy: Christian Sentenced to Death in Joseph Colony Case," Dawn, 28 March 2014, http://www.dawn.com/news/1095974.
[74] "Larkana: Hindu Worship Place Set Ablaze over ' Burning of Holy Pages,'" Geo News, 16 March 2014, http://www.geo.tv/latest/70279-larkana-hindu-worship-place-set-ablaze-over-burning-of-holy-pages.
[75] Umer Nangiana and Zia Khan, "Blasphemy Law Victim: One More Silenced," Express Tribune, 3 March 2011, http://tribune.com.pk/story/126757/blasphemy-law-victim-one-more-silenced/.
[76] "Punjab Governor Salman Taseer Assassinated in Islamabad," BBC, 4 January 2011, http://www.bbc.com/news/world-south-asia-12111831. See additional cases at "Timeline: Accused under the Blasphemy Law," Dawn, 18 August 2013, https://www.dawn.com/news/750512.
[77] "Rimshah Masih, Pakistani Girl Accused of Blasphemy, Finds Refuge in Canada," The Guardian, 1 July 2013, http://www.theguardian.com/world/2013/jul/01/pakistan-girl-accused-blasphemy-canada.
[78] "Mentally Unstable Blasphemy Suspect Shot Dead by Unknown Men after Prison Release," Global News Centre, 10 January 2015, http://www.globalnewscentre.com/mentally-unstable-blasphemy-suspect-shot-dead-by-unknown-men-after-prison-release/#sthash.0vIbf6S1.dpuf.

acute sense of fear within all citizens, most specifically those of other faiths, undermining the essence of religious pluralism.

11.4.2. Within the Legal Sphere

Those who initially escaped the mobs, such as Asia Bibi, Rimshah Masih, and Junaid Hafeez, who were falsely implicated in blasphemy cases, have struggled to defend themselves in biased courts, eventually ending up in jail for years in violation of their fair -trial rights.[79] Several problems with the law as well as procedures to enforce them make them especially harmful to minorities, leading to the persistent and systematic failure of the legal system to filter out malicious and frivolous complaints made in the wake of personal vendettas (which amount to up to 80 percent of the cases, according to various estimates).

11.4.3. Vague and Expansive Phrasing of the Laws

Vague and expansive language in Section 295, coupled with the absence of a clear intention required on the part of the accused, have allowed a larger net to be thrown in blasphemy cases under this provision, encompassing children and the mentally ill. Individual judges decide, in the absence of any clear guidelines, whether a particular "act" (irrespective of the intention of the alleged blasphemer) amounts to "defiling the Holy Prophet." This has resulted in subjectively variable and often contradictory jurisprudence of the courts, providing no guidance on or limit to what behavior could or could not constitute defilement . The problem of vagueness is true for other blasphemy provisions as well. For instance, in the case of 298 C, what does it mean for an Ahmadi to profess him- or herself to be a Muslim, while living in a Muslim state?

There is no provision within the law that excludes liability for statements made bona fide, in contrast to, for instance, the Canadian Criminal Code, which states: "No person shall be convicted . . . for expressing in good faith and in decent language, or attempting to establish by arguments used in good faith and conveyed in decent language, an opinion on a religious subject."[80] (Again, a very important point for the development of a genuine public sphere of democratic discussion, but it is not central to the theme of this chapter.) Neither has there

[79] At the time of writing, Junaid Hafeez has been sentenced to death, after having spent seven years in prison, most of it in solitary confinement. "Pakistan: Outrage over Death Sentence for ' Blasphemous' Lecturer," *The Guardian*, 21 December 2019, https://www.theguardian.com/world/2019/dec/21/death-sentence-for-pakistani-lecturer-junaid-hafeez-in-blasphemy-case-prompts-outcry.
[80] Section 296 (3) of the Canadian Criminal Code.

272 VIOLENCE AND DOMINATION

been any attempt by the courts to narrow acts amounting to blasphemy until very recently, when Justice Khosa of the Supreme Court of Pakistan stated that criticism of blasphemy laws is not blasphemy itself.[81] However, in the comparable example of India, the Supreme Court of India in 1957 held in relation to 295 A of the penal code (the same as 295 A of the Pakistan Penal Code) that " insults to religion offered unwittingly and without deliberate or malicious intent, which outraged the religious feelings of a class of citizens, did not come within Section 295 A of the Penal Code."[82] The prosecution further must prove offense was intended by the accused toward "a class" as opposed to an individual, under Section 295 A, Penal Code of India.[83]

Moreover, Section 295 C of the Pakistan Penal Code provides for a mandatory death penalty and further imposes the requirement that the presiding judge of the trial be a Muslim.[84] The fact that a judge is required to be Muslim has led to obvious concerns of bias and an expansive interpretation of the provision to the detriment of the accused, leading to mass persecution and detention. Often testimony of the accused is disbelieved by judges. In one judgment, *The State v. Younis Masih*, the judge stated that if the accused in fact believed "in the honour of the Holy Prophet PBUH . . . why [had] he up till now [not] embraced Islam?" The accused was subsequently convicted and sentenced to death.[85]

Further given the uncertainty surrounding what in fact constitutes blasphemy, lawyers have been accused of blaspheming for simply repeating words their client was alleged to have said in court, words that led to a blasphemy accusation in the first place. Other judges have refused to mention the specific charge in judgments to prevent reproducing blasphemous content.

Many blasphemy accusations occur in the context of a politically charged environment. Media coverage, coupled with the involvement of religious organizations in individual matters,[86] creates a hostile situation not just for the accused, but also for judges and lawyers dealing with a particular blasphemy case, who frequently face threats to their life. Violent demonstrations often accompany these cases and have led to violence within courtrooms. Justice Arif Iqbal Bhatti

Irfan Haider, "Criticizing Blasphemy Law Does Not Amount to Blasphemy: Justice Khosa," *Dawn*, 5 October 2015, www.dawn.com/news/1211047.

[82] Chief Justice S. R. Das in 1957. See Fali Nariman, "Freedom of Speech and Blasphemy: The Laws in India and UK," *I.C.J. Rev* 42 (1989): 54.

[83] Ratanlal and Dhirajlal's *Law of Crimes: A Commentary on the India Pen al Code* (1860) New Delhi: Bharat Law House, 2011, 1172.

[84] Schedule II of Pakistan's Code of Criminal Procedure.

[85] *The State v . Younis Masih*, 2007, pp. 83–84.

[86] " A religious organization, 'Jammat Alh-e-Sunnat ' announced a prize for a million rupees for the killing of Salamat and Rehmat, while another, ' Muttahida Ulema Council' of Sargodha, offered 300,000 rupees for the same task." See Osama Siddique and Zahra Hayat, " Unholy Speech and Holy Laws: Blasphemy Laws in Pakistan—Controversial Origins, Design Defects, and Free Speech Implications," *Minnesota Journal of International Law* 17: 333–335.

of the Lahore High Court was murdered within his chambers for acquitting two individuals accused of blasphemy. Lawyers have been victimized and killed for defending an accused in blasphemy cases. A recent example is the murder of Rashid Rehman . He had received multiple warnings by religious organizations to drop the case, and was eventually shot in his office.[87]

There are lack of effective protection measures in place for judges and lawyers from harassment and threats of personal violence that compromise the right of the accused to effective counsel and an independent and fair trial. The murder of Rashid Rehman is only one example, and reports have suggested that after that murder no lawyer was willing to take up the case. The Human Rights Commission of Pakistan confirmed in a statement that " during the hearing the lawyers of the complainant told Rehman that he wouldn't be present at the next hearing as he would not be alive."[88]

Given that many members of the bar hold strong anti-blasphemy opinions , the pool of lawyers available to an accused person is limited . For example, one of the lawyers, a former justice , representing Mumtaz Qadri, the guard who shot Salman Taseer, said,

"When it comes to the sanctity of the Prophet, the implementation of all man-made laws become different. . . . Those who insult Him have no rights, including no right to live. There is no need for trial or hearings . "[89]

No disciplinary action has been taken by bar councils against such statements by members of the legal and judicial community.

11.4.4. Inadequate Punishment for False Accusations

Under the blasphemy laws in Pakistan, there is little to deter false accusations, as no specific penalty is provided for falsely implicating someone in a blasphemy case. General safeguards, such as those provided under C hapter 11 of the Pakistan Penal Code dealing with punishment in cases of false evidence, are never utilized. However, the main problem remains effective engagement with these safeguards and their implementation, which is practically evident in the fact that no one, thus far, has been punished under these provisions in blasphemy cases. Judges, despite knowing false accusations and evidence exist in a case,

---

[87] "Rights Advocate Rashid Rehman Khan Gunned Down in Multan," *Dawn*, 8 May 2014, www.dawn.com/news/1104788.

[88] Naeem Sahoutara, "Lawyers Strike to Mourn Blasphemy Defense Lawyer," *Express Tribune*, 8 May 2014, http://tribune.com.pk/story/705770/lawyers-strike-to-mourn-blasphemy-defence-lawyer/.

[89] "Islamic Clerics Back Blasphemy Laws: Those Who Insult Mohammad Have No Right to Live," *Asia News*, 16 June 2015, http://www.asianews.it/news-en/Islamic-clerics-back-blasphemy-laws:-those-who-insult-Mohammed-have-no-right-tolive-34522.html.

have refrained from ordering action against the accuser and instead relied upon prayers of wisdom for the accuser to refrain from such acts in the future.[90]

In April 2017, the National Assembly unanimously passed a resolution[91] calling for the law to be reformed, for stronger safeguards, and for punishment of the perpetrators of false accusations . This is a step further than previous calls for amendments to the blasphemy laws,[92] including harsher penalties against false accusations.[93]

The imposition of no severe legal penalties on those responsible for false accusations of blasphemy, coupled with the failure of the state to investigate allegations of professional misconduct in blasphemy proceedings, impedes the rights of the accused and fuels a culture of impunity and selective lawlessness.

11.4.5. Blasphemy a Cognizable and Non- Bailable Offen se

In blasphemy cases under 295 , the lack of legal protection and the inability of those accused to defend him- or herself is visible from the outset, given that the police are allowed to arrest, and begin an investigation of, an accused person without a warrant from the court. The offense under section 295 C is a "cognizable ," meaning no prior judicial authorization is required for arrests and investigations. This shows the level of seriousness the law affords to this offense, as well as the absence of the requisite safeguards that ought to attach to serious criminal offenses.

Moreover, several blasphemy offenses are *non-bailable*, including Sections 295 A, 295 B, and 295 C of the Penal Code, meaning that bail is granted at the sole discretion of the courts, without regard to the rights of the accused. This has led individuals accused of blasphemy to undergo long periods of pre trial detention, as courts have been increasingly unwilling to grant bail to those accused specifically of blasphemy (compared to other capital offenses, such as m urder). Furthermore, within individual provisions, the courts have been much less

---

[90] PLD 2002 Lahore 587, p. 30 . The court concluded in the judgment with the prayer for those who falsely accused the acquitted victim of blasphemy: "God give them wisdom to understand and appreciate what is ordain(ed) and take care in the future before making such types of accusations and avoid the mischief in the future and Shaitaan (Satan) who is always ready to attac k."

[91] "NA Passes Resolution Condemning Mashal Khan's 'Barbaric, Cold Blooded' Murder," *Express Tribune*, 18 April 2017, https://tribune.com.pk/story/1386927/na-passes-resolution-condemning-mashal-khans-barbaric-cold-blooded-murder/.

[92] An earlier bill seeking amendments in Pakistan's blasphemy laws, tabled by Sherry Rehman in 2010, was withdrawn amid pressure. See Zia Khan, "Blasphemy Law Amendment: Sherry Rehman to Withdraw Bill, Says PM," *Express Tribune*, 3 February 2011, http://tribune.com.pk/story/113445/blasphemy-law-amendment-sherry-rehman-to-withdraw-bill-says-pm/.

[93] Azam Khan, "Penalties Proposed for False Accusers of Blasphemy," *Express Tribune*, May 27, 2015, http://tribune.com.pk/story/892895/blasphemy-law-penalties-proposed-for-false-accusers/.

likely to grant bail to an accused charged under 295 C (defiling the Holy Prophet) than other blasphemy provisions (295 A and 295 B).

11.4.6. Arbitrary Distinction between Offens es

There exist arbitrary distinctions within blasphemy offenses, with lesser safeguards in the face of harsher punishments for some, raising fair- trial concerns. For instance, only 295 C provides for a mandatory death penalty and imposes the requirement that the presiding judge of the trial be Muslim, yet it dispenses with the requirement of a prior approval from a f ederal or p rovincial government before a court can take cognizance of a blasphemy complaint. The requirement of prior approval is also absent under 295 B, and only reserved for 295 A.

Despite such dismal state of affairs with blatant fair- trial violations, an alarming trend has been noted by the International Commission of Jurists, whereby courts have upheld a greater number of blasphemy convictions after 2005, a total of five, while only one conviction was upheld during the period 1986–2005. Moreover, despite eventual acquittals in most cases, the innocent yet maliciously accused members of these religious minorities undergo long periods of prison time awaiting the outcome of their cases, in deplorable conditions and often in solitary confinement (to protect them from attacks from other inmates).

These incidents not only confirm the atrocities committed against the minorities of Pakistan under the blasphemy laws, but also project the aforementioned failure of the justice system in providing the accused with the means to defend him- or herself in the face of such accusations.

11.5. Conclusion

Given that the creation of Pakistan was premised itself on the ideal of a n ation providing for a fuller realization of minority rights (i.e., tThe Muslims then in united India), it is ironic to witness the appalling treatment religious minority groups within Pakistan receive at the hands of the state and its laws. The state has continued to assume the role of an oppressor through its use of blasphemy laws catering exclusively to a dominant religion, while depriving religious minorities of corresponding legal safeguards. The added failure of law enforcement and other institutions has enabled the creation of an atmosphere where mobs repeatedly and conveniently ravage and torch colonies, destroying property, businesses, and lives of those communities, who above all are citizens of Pakistan. Pakistan's blasphemy laws, far from upholding the principles of religious equality

276 VIOLENCE AND DOMINATION

and religious pluralism, have resulted instead in justifying religious intolerance and further propagating and inciting acts of violence against the minority religious groups .

Not only have members of religious minorities been implicated under these laws and prevented in all ways possible from freely practicing their faith, all voices of dissent have been hushed through their use. Intolerance has become entrenched within segments of Pakistani society and manifests itself in violence, such that others who do not conform have chosen to remain silent in the face of blatant persecution of fellow citizens, mostly members of Pakistan's religious minorities. This is often due to fear for their own lives, as those who have exercised their right to speak out in the past have experienced dire fates. However, it is important to remember, as Alan Moore reminds us, that " since mankind's dawn, a handful of oppressors have accepted the responsibility over our lives that we should have accepted for ourselves. By doing so, they took our power. By doing nothing, we gave it away. We've seen where their way leads, through camps and wars, towards the slaughterhouse."[94]

[94] Moore, Alan, David Lloyd, Steve Whitaker, and Siobhan Dodds. 2009. *The Absolute V for Vendetta*. New York: DC Comics.

12

Changing Modalities of Violence

Lessons from Hindu Nationalist India

Amrita Basu

Muslim men are murdered on suspicion that they are transporting cattle and consuming beef. Muslim women are raped to teach their community a lesson. Hindu women are abducted because they have married Muslim men. Christians are forced to convert to Hinduism and killed when they are suspected of prose-lytizing. Dalits are hounded and murdered for displaying pride in their identi-ties and demanding their rights. Journalists, scholars, and activists are harassed and imprisoned because their views are deemed seditious. As numerous as the targets are the forms of violence. They include murder, rape, abduction, coercion, and harassment, along with the destruction of homes, businesses, and places of worship. Such are the forms of Hindu nationalist violence in India today (Bal 2019; Griswold 2019; Jaffrelot 2019; United States Commission on International Freedom 2020).

Some observers are reassured that India has not experienced major "riots" since the Bharatiya Janata Party (BJP) first took office in 2014. However, such sanguine analyses fail to appreciate the extent and severity of violence since the BJP was elected in 2014 and re-elected in 2019. Relatedly, the issues that have provoked Hindutva (Hindu nationalist) violence have expanded. Along with long-standing concerns like prohibiting beef consumption, conversion out of Hinduism, and interfaith marriage, since seizing power, Hindu nationalists have repressed peaceful opposition to the government's hardline policy on Kashmir and its citizenship and farm laws, on the grounds that such dissent is anti-national. While in the past the BJP fostered Hindu-Muslim tensions prior to elections to influence their outcomes, it now does so more frequently and less predictably.

Drawing on recent developments in India, I argue in this chapter that we need to devise new ways of conceptualizing violence that recognize its significance, independent of the scale of any single incident; appreciate the links between discursive violence and physical assault; and identify the webs of complicity

Amrita Basu, *Changing Modalities of Violence* In: *Negotiating Democracy and Religious Pluralism*. Edited by: Karen Barkey, Sudipta Kaviraj, and Vatsal Naresh, Oxford University Press. © Oxford University Press 2021.
DOI: 10.1093/oso/9780197530016.003.0013

between the state, political parties, and civil society. This entails appreciating multiple forms of violence and systematic forms of humiliation and coercion by dominant groups that are designed to subjugate, denigrate, silence, and intimidate people on the basis of their identities and beliefs. I include in my account of violence hate speech that is violent in itself and is designed to provoke physical attacks.

I argue that the character and extent of violence result from the unprecedented success of Hindu nationalists in capturing state power and thereby being able to pursue their long-standing agenda of transforming India into a Hindu nation. Although Hindu nationalists are not the only group that engages in hate speech, they have been especially apt to do so in the current era, obviating the culpability of the violent words and actions of their leaders. Hindutva street violence reinforces discriminatory laws and policies that seek to alter the rules of citizenship and the relationship between state and society. Compared to the BJP-dominated National Democratic Alliance (NDA) government that occupied power in 1999–2004, the current BJP government is both stronger and more ideologically driven because it has tethered religious nationalism to right-wing populism.

There is an elective affinity between religious nationalism and right-wing populism. As Philip Gorski (2018) notes, religious nationalists often invoke notions of blood conquest and purity, portray the dominant majority as a persecuted religious minority, and claim there is a contest between good and evil. Similarly, right-wing populists tend to emphasize the moral purity of the common people, blame national decline on secular elites, and identify moral and/or religious others who can never become full members of the nation. Right-wing populism and religious nationalism are far more powerful when conjoined than either one is on its own.

The first section of this chapter critically evaluates contending analytic approaches to understanding violence and suggests that we turn our attention from riots to politically motivated hate crimes. The next section compares the changing modalities of Hindutva violence under the first and current BJP-led NDA governments (1999–2004 and 2014–). The section that follows documents the growth of politically motivated hate crimes and explores the role of the state, party, and civil society actors in executing them. I then analyze the effects of new modalities of violence on its victims and explore how the confluence of populism and religious nationalism normalize and encourage violence. I conclude by exploring the extent to which frequent, repetitive acts of violence have become the new norm, or an acceptable mode of political conduct. I assess Amartya Sen's claim that India is an argumentative democracy, and a resilient one, in which a large swath of society has met punctuated violence with largely nonviolent resistance (Sen 2005).

12.1. Scholarship on Violence

Political scientists who study ethnic conflict in India have focused on the role of the state, political parties, electoral systems, and civil society organizations in preventing or failing to prevent ethnic violence (Chhibber 1999; Kohli 1997; Varshney 2002; Wilkinson 2004). However, understanding Hindu nationalist violence entails shifting our focus from these actors' omission to commission. The BJP and affiliated civil society groups precipitate anti-minority violence. The role of the state is more complicated. The responsibility of both state and national governments for ethnic violence in India has historically been indirect; that is, they have failed to prevent the outbreak or escalation of violence rather than inciting it. However, this broad generalization must be qualified (Brass 2006). First, state governments have pursued policies that promote Hindu dominance and incite violence against minorities. Second, the national government has pursued violent and repressive policies in some states, especially in Kashmir and the northeast. Both of these tendencies have increased since 2014 and even more since 2019. Third, high-ranking government officials and party members have increasingly engaged in hate speech that provokes violence.

Furthermore, while most scholarship analyzes the role of the state *or* civil society *or* political parties, interlinkages among these institutions increase the likelihood of ethnic violence (Basu 2015). Such violence is generally sanctioned by high-ranking party and government leaders and orchestrated by civil society. In this respect, violence is both top down and bottom up—and the two are intertwined.

We must also rethink the modalities of Hindutva violence. Most existing scholarship on ethnic violence, my own included, has focused on politically motivated group violence, or what is commonly termed a "riot," which in the Indian context often refers to Hindu-Muslim conflict. The concept of "riot" implies a certain threshold of violence (without specifying that threshold) with respect to the number of people injured and killed, and the amount of property destroyed. However, the term "riot" has always been flawed because it ignores the pattern since the 1990s of well-planned Hindu nationalist attacks on Muslims. It is even less useful today because the modalities of Hindutva violence have changed. Although the targets of hate speech and state-condoned hate crimes are often individuals, this violence is designed to terrorize the groups to which these individuals belong in order to create docile subjects (Ray 2006).

Hindu nationalists instigate small-scale violence against a growing variety of targets. If in the past they engaged in extensive prior planning to engineer "riots" by spreading rumors and aggravating local tensions, they no longer need to do so. In the current political environment and amid the massive growth of social media, the mere suspicion that a Muslim or Christian is violating Hindu social codes is justification for violence. Thus, the individuals who attack minorities need not have formal affiliations with Hindutva organizations. Although the targets are generally religious minorities (Christians and especially Muslims), they include students, intellectuals, and human rights activists who challenge religious orthodoxy and government policy. They include Dalits who challenged upper-caste domination in Bhim Koregaon, Maharashtra, in January 2018, when they celebrated the defeat of an upper-caste Hindu ruler 200 years ago (Dutta 2018). They include women who sought to enter the Sabarimala temple in Kerala after the Supreme Court authorized them to do so in 2018 to affirm their equality in matters of faith (*India Today* 2019). They include students from Jamia Millia Islamia, Aligarh Muslim University, and Jawaharlal Nehru University (JNU).

Scholars have devoted little attention to hate crimes, perhaps because they appear to be apolitical, spontaneous responses to individual wrongdoing. However, the motivations for hate crimes are political and ideological. BJP electoral candidates often incite hatred and violence to polarize the electorate and win votes; they continue to do so after they are elected to promote their ideological commitments. Hate crimes seek to curb dissent, discriminate against citizens on the basis of their religious identities, undermine non-Hindus' abilities to practice their religious faiths, and strengthen the discretionary power of the police and bureaucrats. They have devastating political effects. Physical attacks against individuals who are accused of being terrorists, violating Hindu cultural norms, and breaching national security subject minorities to surveillance and repression.

12.2. Hindu Nationalist Violence: From Vajpayee to Modi

Hindu nationalist violence has a long ancestry. The Rashtriya Swayamsevak Sangh (RSS) and its affiliates have mounted violent campaigns around religious conversion and cow protection for decades. Their ability to organize and intensify these campaigns has been greatest when sympathetic regional and national governments are in office. However, there have been changes in the modalities of violence under the first (1999–2004) and second (2014–2019) and even between the second and third (2019–) NDA governments.

The most serious violence, under the first NDA government in Gujarat in 2002, claimed around 1,000 lives. The BJP's motivations were partly electoral: it had performed poorly in prior local elections in Gujarat and needed to broaden its caste base of support. The scale of the violence reflected the combined strength of Hindu nationalist forces, their success in defeating, repressing, and co-opting left, secular, and lower-class and lower-caste movements, and the soft Hindu nationalism of the opposition Congress party. The NDA government (1999–2004) failed to stop the escalation of violence by suspending the state government, and ruling by decree (as Article 356 of the Indian Constitution authorizes).

The recurrence of mass violence in Gujarat is unlikely. Although Narendra Modi—chief minister of Gujarat at the time of the violence—was not ultimately prosecuted, continued suspicions of his complicity will probably deter a recurrence of such violence in his home state. It is striking that "riots" in Gujarat declined dramatically a year after the Modi-led NDA government was formed. Of the 10 states in which violence was most extensive in 2015, Gujarat (with 55 incidents) ranked last (Engineer et al. 2017). By contrast, from 1980 to 2010, Gujarat experienced a larger number of Hindu-Muslim "riots" than any other state. This points to a larger pattern, discussed later, of a decline in "riots" and increase in politically motivated hate crimes.

The growth of politically motivated hate crimes results from deepening links between violent civil society organizations and the BJP government. This government has closer ties to the RSS and is less constrained by coalition parties than the previous NDA government (1999–2004). Furthermore, Prime Minister Modi is more of an ideologue than his BJP predecessor, Prime Minister Atal Behari Vajpayee. Although Vajpayee was a committed *pracharak* (RSS worker), his relations with the RSS affiliate, the Vishva Hindu Parishad (VHP), were sometimes strained. The VHP's support for the previous NDA government was conditioned on the government authorizing temple construction in Ayodhya. When the government refused to comply, the VHP openly opposed the government and organized mass campaigns around the temple from 2001 to 2003. Its senior leaders refused to campaign for the BJP in the 2004 national elections. The RSS shared the VHP's critique of the Vajpayee government. The RSS, which disseminates views that promote violence through official channels and affiliated civil society organizations, supported Modi throughout his career and was responsible for his ascendance both in Gujarat and nationally. RSS appointments to the cabinet and to major academic and cultural institutions have significantly increased under the current BJP government (Kanungo 2019). The RSS has grown in size and influence since 2010 and especially since 2014. By its own account, it currently runs 57,411 daily *shakhas* (training camps in militant Hindu nationalism); over 13,500 of these began after 2014 (Barik 2019). Shedding its old uniform of baggy khaki shorts and adopting more modern garb, the RSS has gained a following among tech-savvy elites by organizing 10,000 weekly Information Technology (IT) meetings exclusively for urban professionals (Bagchi 2019). The RSS has also grown in states like Kerala and West Bengal, where the Communist parties have declined, and in Uttar Pradesh (UP), where the BJP scored a major electoral victory in 2017 (*Indian Express* 2017a). The RSS's growing popularity signals the normalization of violence, while the BJP's prominent connections to the RSS demonstrate growing state support for this violent ideology.

In addition to espousing violence, RSS-affiliated organizations have increasingly engaged in it. The vigilante Bharatiya Gau Raksha Dal (Indian Cow Protection Group) has attacked Muslims and sometimes Dalits, whom it accuses of consuming beef and killing cows. The RSS-affiliated youth organization, the Akhil Bharatiya Vidyarthi Parishad (ABVP), has organized attacks on Indian students and faculty who criticize government policy. It claims that its membership doubled from 1.1 million in 2003 to 2.2 million a decade later and that it gained 900,000 new members in 2014 alone (Tiwary 2016). In February 2016, when students at JNU in New Delhi organized a public meeting to protest state repression in Kashmir, the ABVP alleged that the speeches were anti-national and encouraged the police to raid the university and arrest opposition student leaders, including student union president Kanhaiya Kumar. Ultimately, although the police admitted that they lacked evidence against Kumar and the court released him on bail, neither Modi nor other government officials condemned the police violence and the arrests. The ABVP continued to attack activists and charge them with sedition, including at an Amnesty International meeting in Karnataka in August 2016, and at Jai Narain Vyas University in Jodhpur and Ramjas College in Delhi University in February 2017. The police did nothing to stop the attacks and did not file charges against any of the assailants (Shafi 2017; *South Asia Citizens Web* 2017). The escalation of ABVP violence is just one example of how BJP leaders' silence and police complicity strengthens targeted Hindutva violence.

Hindutva activists have increasingly employed social media to propagate hatred and violence, contributing to the rapid and easy mobilization of aggressive perpetrators. Self-proclaimed "Ram *bhakts*" (devotees of the Hindu god Ram) post bigoted anti-minority views on social media, slandering Muslims and Pakistanis. They distort and invent news stories, attack opponents, and mobilize their followers to engage in violence, among other means through WhatsApp, a popular messaging application that over 230 million Indians use. Soma Basu's study (2019) of 140 pro-BJP WhatsApp groups found that a quarter of their messages contained anti-Muslim text, including claims that Muslims would carry out genocide against Hindus, all Muslims are terrorists and support Pakistan (#TerrorismHasReligion), and Muslim men would rape and kill Hindu women if Muslims become a majority in India. Several members of BJP

IT cells and BJP legislative assembly members are members of WhatsApp groups that incite anti-minority sentiment. The home minister, Amit Shah, has openly encouraged the public to demonstrate support for the BJP by making "real or fake . . . messages go viral" (Basu, Soma 2019).

The government has increasingly engaged in surveillance, censorship, incarceration, and physical assaults on those who criticize religious orthodoxy and government policy. It has curbed dissent in part by invoking laws that punish threats to national stability, such as Sections 124A (outlawing sedition) and 120B (outlawing criminal conspiracy) of the Indian Penal Code (IPC). Given its draconian provisions, the Supreme Court has limited its use to speeches that explicitly incite people to engage in violent action. Although convictions are unusual, the police frequently harass government critics by arresting them under the anti-sedition law. The Ministry of Home Affairs reported 179 sedition cases between 2014 and 2016 (Pattnaik 2019). According to the government's National Crime Records Bureau, 332 people were arrested on grounds of sedition from 2016 to 2018 (Yadav 2020). In October 2019, the state of Bihar charged 49 people with sedition for writing Prime Minister Modi an open letter expressing concern over the increase in anti-minority hate crimes and mob violence (Human Rights Watch 2020). The recent protests against the government's new citizenship laws have triggered more sedition charges, as the state brands protestors anti-national (*India Today* 2020a; *The Wire* 2020).

While strengthening Hindutva civil society groups, the government has undermined civil society organizations that defend marginalized communities and promote human rights. The Home Ministry has revoked the licenses of around 10,000 NGOs on grounds that they have violated the provisions of the Foreign Contributions Regulations Act. The government's suppression of dissent and of progressive civil society organizations, combined with its promotion of the RSS, normalizes hate speech and Hindu nationalist ideology. The government's failure to condemn repetitive and targeted acts of violence adds to the impunity with which Hindu nationalists are able to redefine citizenship and nationhood.

Although various laws proscribe hate speech on the basis of religion, ethnicity, and culture, and these forms of hate speech and related hate crimes are on the rise, they are rarely prosecuted.[1] It has become increasingly common for high-ranking government and party leaders to promote hatred and violence. Incendiary remarks by home minister and former BJP president Amit Shah, BJP member of parliament (MP) Sakshi Maharaj, former chief ministers (CMs)

---

[1] The Indian Penal Code under Sections 153A, 153B, 295A, 298, 505(1), and 505(2)25 declares that words, spoken or written, or employing signs or any kind of visual representation that "promotes disharmony, enmity, hatred or ill-will" or "offends" or "insults" on the basis of religion, ethnicity, culture, language, region, caste, community, race, etc., is a punishable offense.

Raman Singh in Chhattisgarh and Manohar Gopalkrishna Prabhu in Goa, and CMs Mohan Lal Khattar in Haryana, Yogi Adityanath in UP, and Manohar Gopalkrishna Prabhu in Goa, amount to calls for violence against Muslims and Christians.[2] Far from opposing the hate speech of its ministers and MPs, the national government has ignored or rewarded them.[3] This increases the likelihood of the recurrence of politically motivated hate crimes.

12.3. From "Riots" to Politically Motivated Hate Crimes

The most widely used data set (Varshney-Wilkinson 2006, updated by Basu 2015) shows a decline in "riots" from the early 1990s into the following decade. This pattern has continued; the number of riots declined from 38 in 2018 to 25 in 2019 according to the Centre for Study of Society and Secularism (CSSS), based on information it compiled from five leading newspapers. However, the CSSS emphasizes that while "riots" have declined, anti-minority violence has grown. For example, in 2018 there were 85 lynchings—over double the number of riots—stemming from claims that Muslims had abducted Hindu women and children and slaughtered cows (Engineer et al. 2020).

Gathering accurate data on hate crimes is exceedingly difficult. Newspapers and other journalistic outlets have ceased to track religiously motivated hate crimes. Although the Indian Home Affairs Ministry's National Crime Records Bureau has published reports on violent crimes since the 1950s, in 2017 it withheld information about violence against minorities and political dissidents (Schultz et al. 2019). Two years later, the citizens' religious hate crime watch website disappeared. However, Deepankar Basu (2021) provides reliable information on the growing incidence of what he terms religiously motivated hate crimes since the BJP was elected in 2014. Drawing on data from the Citizen's

[2] During the Bihar election in 2015, the BJP's president, Amit Shah, stated that if Nitish Kumar was elected and became CM, fireworks would go off in Pakistan—indeed, since he was so beloved in Pakistan, he should move there (*Indian Express* 2015; *India Today* 2015b). Sakshi Maharaj, who was elected BJP MP in 2014, called Nathuram Godse, Mohandas Gandhi's assassin, a "patriot and nationalist." He also defended the *ghar wapsi* (homecoming) campaign and advocated the death sentence for cow slaughter and religious conversion (Basu 2015).

[3] A government minister, Niranjan Jyoti, claimed that people faced a choice between a "government of followers of Ram and a government of bastards," rhyming the words *Ramzada* (Ram's children) and *haramzada* (illegitimate children / bastards) (*BBC News* 2014). Minister of Culture Mahesh Sharma described former Indian president A. P. J. Abdul Kalam as a nationalist and humanist "despite being a Muslim," supported a meat ban during the Hindu holiday Navaratra, and vowed to cleanse public discourse that he said had been westernized and "polluted" (Express News Service 2015; Venkataramakrishnan 2015). Both Niranjan Jyoti and Sharma retained their posts. In the 2014 national election campaign, Giriraj Singh exhorted those who did not vote for Modi to go to Pakistan (Ahmad 2014). He was subsequently elected to parliament and made a minister, where he continued to make hateful comments about Muslims and the skin color of Congress party leader Sonia Gandhi (*India Today* 2015a).

Religious Hate Crime Watch and the Election Commission of India's website, Basu shows that the BJP's electoral victory in 2014 was directly responsible for a rise in religiously motivated hate crimes, from 22 to 195, representing a 786 percent increase from 2009–2013 to June 2014–2018. During this time, hate crimes declined against Christians and Sikhs and increased against Muslims— from 36 percent to 83 percent of all hate crimes. Basu finds that hate crimes were greatest in the 10 states where the BJP won a high share of the popular vote.[4] He attributes weakened law enforcement by BJP state governments to the rise of hate crimes. The CSSS report similarly notes that state governments often extend patronage to those who engage in violence and fail to prosecute the culprits.

Hindu nationalists may achieve the same benefits from hate crimes as from riots, at less cost. Promoting hate crimes can serve to maintain or increase support for the BJP while minimizing the risk of alienating domestic and foreign groups who would oppose large-scale anti-minority violence. The state's willingness to permit Hindu nationalists to engage in violent discourses, while censoring critics of the regime, makes the state the arbiter of what constitutes secularism, freedom, and national well-being. It strengthens the repressive powers of the state in the name of protecting the very values that the state negates.

Modi risks domestic and international criticism if India experiences major "riots." The US government, whose support the Indian government has sought and achieved, has signaled its concern about religious freedoms. Although Modi remains extremely popular, his lowest approval ratings concern his handling of "communal" issues, in other words his treatment of minorities (Dutta 2017; Stokes 2016).

State governments are less culpable for frequent hate crimes than for "riots" that endanger stability. For example, UP has not experienced a single "riot" over the past few years that resulted in as many deaths and injuries as the one in Muzzafarnagar in August–September 2013 in which at least 62 people (42 Muslims and 20 Hindus) were killed and 93 people were injured.[5] However, according to both the CSSS and Deepankar Basu, UP has experienced more hate crimes (or what the CSSS calls "small-scale communal violence") than any state in the country. This violence contributed to the BJP's electoral success in the 2017 Legislative Assembly elections in UP, and its decision to appoint one of its most rabidly anti-minority legislators, Yogi Adityanath, as the state's CM (Puniyani 2017). Thus, as with the Muzzafarnagar "riot," the BJP uses small-scale violence to increase electoral success, but with fewer risks to its image.

[4] In descending order, they are Uttar Pradesh, Rajasthan, Karnataka, Haryana, Jharkhand, Gujarat, Maharashtra, Bihar, the national capital territory of Delhi, and Jammu and Kashmir.
[5] The "riot" in Muzzafarnagar resulted in the election of militant BJP leaders in UP. For example, Sanjeev Balyan, who had been imprisoned for 27 days for inciting violence, won a landslide victory and subsequently became a minister in the BJP government (Press Trust of India 2019).

The section that follows discusses the responsibility of national and state governments, local administrative officials, BJP leaders, and Hindutva civil society groups for violence against Christians, Muslims, and women. It discusses violence surrounding laws on religious conversion and beef consumption, and the love jihad campaign policing interreligious relationships. Hindutva-inspired civil society activists and pro-BJP local and state administrative officials are responsible for this violence. CM Adityanath actively encouraged it and Prime Minister Modi failed to condemn it. Modi's silences reveal his refusal to see hate crimes as politically motivated or as the government's responsibility.

12.4. State-Societal Linkages

Hindu nationalists have engaged in extensive violence against India's small Christian minority. Their rumors that Christians are forcibly converting Hindus has provided the pretext for vandalizing, burning, and destroying churches and assaulting, abducting, and murdering priests and nuns. According to one Christian human rights organization, there were 348 attacks on Christians in 2016 and 260 attacks from January to May 2017 (Thomas 2017). The targets are often people attending church services and celebrating Christmas. The perpetrators do not provide evidence that Christians are engaging in forcible conversions. The point of these attacks is to warn Christians that their religious identities make them suspect.

BJP state governments have fostered distrust of Christians by passing so-called Freedom of Religion legislation prohibiting conversion to Christianity. Five state governments have passed laws that require those who have converted out of Hinduism to inform the district magistrate and require community members to inform the police and administration if they suspect that pastors, nuns, and clergymen are proselytizing. Ironically, Freedom of Religion acts are only enforced when Hindus convert to another religion but not when religious minorities convert to Hinduism. Union Minister M. Venkaiah Naidu proposed that parliament extend anti-conversion laws from the state to the national level (Rao and Sinha 2014). Hindu nationalist organizations have gone one step further and organized *ghar wapsi* (homecoming, or return to the flock) campaigns to "reconvert" Christians and Muslims to Hinduism. What they term reconversion erroneously assumes that Muslims and Christians were forcibly converted out of Hinduism and must be converted back into it. Underlying this campaign is the assertion of Hindu domination and a refusal to recognize and affirm religious pluralism.

Currently, 24 of India's 29 states, most of which the BJP governs, prohibit either the slaughter or sale of cows. The BJP promised in its campaign for the 2017 Legislative Assembly elections in UP to close all illegal slaughterhouses and restrict mechanized ones. Upon being sworn in as CM of UP, Yogi Adityanath ordered the police and bureaucracy to shut down slaughterhouses (Barry and Raj 2017). Several NDA officials have supported a national beef ban.[6] In May 2017, the Ministry of Environment imposed a ban on the sale of cows and buffaloes for slaughter at animal markets across India. The following month the national government issued regulations requiring people selling livestock to produce a written guarantee that the animals would not be slaughtered. These regulations effectively ban the sale of buffaloes as well as cows for slaughter. Modi plans to assign unique 12-digit identification numbers to 88 million cattle in India to ensure that cows are properly cared for, a concern that the government fails to display for many of its citizens (Moon 2017).

The complicity between state and national governments becomes evident in several incidents of beef lynchings. For example, a mob brutally assaulted a 55-year-old dairy farmer, Pehlu Khan, and four others in Alwar, Rajasthan, in April 2017. Khan died two days later. The police filed charges against Khan's relatives although the family had documents certifying that they had purchased the cows for dairy production. The police did not arrest the men who attacked Khan (Angad 2017). BJP Union minister for parliamentary affairs (currently union minister for minority affairs) Mukhtar Abbas Naqvi initially denied that the attack occurred. Later, BJP Union home minister (current defense minister) Rajnath Singh defended the assailants. In another incident, BJP minister of state (currently MP) Jayant Sinha garlanded eight men convicted of murder in a cow vigilante lynching case (*India Today* 2018).

Narendra Modi has stoked passions around butchering cows and failed to condemn violence against people who are wrongly accused of engaging in it. During the 2014 national election campaign, he attacked the Congress party for introducing a "pink revolution" that resulted from increased cow slaughter. He delivered fiery speeches on the subject during the 2015 Bihar state election campaign. In September 2015, in what came to be known as the Dadri lynching, a group of men who heard a rumor that Mohammad Akhlaq had killed a cow and consumed beef, stormed his home near Delhi, murdered him, and wounded his son. Modi waited eight days before addressing the Dadri lynching and even then denied government responsibility for this and other such incidents. Neither that statement nor one he issued shortly thereafter stopped attacks on Muslims who were accused of consuming beef and killing cows.[7] Modi spoke up again after a

[6] Union Minister Mukhtar Abbas Naqvi remarked that "those who want to eat beef can go to Pakistan" ("Those who want to eat beef" 2015). Home Minister Rajnath Singh called for a nationwide ban on beef slaughter (Press Trust of India 2015).

[7] For example, on October 6, 2015, a group of men in Ahmednagar, Maharashtra, set a van on fire in response to a rumor that it contained 100 kilos of beef. On October 9, 2015, a group in Udhampur district of Jammu and Kashmir threw gasoline bombs at a truck because they wrongly suspected the driver of transporting beef. He died at a hospital 10 days later. On October 14, 2015, a group of

video went viral showing a group of Hindu men brutally beating several Dalit youth who were skinning a cow carcass in Una Gujarat in July 2016. He criticized the actions of cow vigilante groups but ignored their links to the police in BJP ruled states. Just days after his speech, the Haryana government created a police task force with 15 officers in each district to detect cow smugglers, and licensed cow protection groups to assist the police (Raj 2016).

A particularly insidious Hindutva campaign alleges that Muslim men are engaging in so-called love jihad, that is, coercing Hindu women into romantic relationships, converting them to Islam, and abusing them.[8] The campaign entails several levels of institutional complicity. Informants in the courts tell Hindutva activists when an interfaith couple is getting married so that activists can file contrived rape and kidnapping charges against Muslim men and fabricate documents stating that the women are minors. The police and local administration often support these groups, in part because of the presence of RSS members in the police force.[9] Major BJP and NDA government leaders have supported the love jihad campaign, particularly in advance of elections.

In UP, where the love jihad campaign has been especially active, the RSS English-language magazine *Organiser* and Hindi-language magazine *Panchjanya* featured love jihad on their front covers just a week before the 2014 UP elections. Adityanath alleged that Muslims were organizing an international conspiracy to seduce and corrupt Hindu girls prior to the 2014 and 2017 elections in UP. One of his videos instructed supporters to convert 100 Muslim women through marriage every time a Muslim man married a Hindu woman (Bidwai 2015). Senior BJP leaders, including Sanjay Balyan, endorsed his views and participated in the campaign, which included trying to prevent young women from using cell phones and the internet to avoid their falling into the love jihad trap.[10] UP has passed a law (the Prohibition of Unlawful Religious Conversion Ordinance) that is designed to criminalize interfaith marriage. It requires inter-faith couples to inform district magistrates of their plans to marry; these officials can sentence men who they believe are forcibly converting women for up to ten years.

Hindus at Sarahan village, near Simla, beat a man to death because they suspected he was smuggling cows. On March 18, 2016, a Muslim cattle trader and his 12-year-old son were found hanging from a tree in Jharkhand state, their hands tied behind their backs and their bodies bruised (*Indian Express* 2017b; *First Post* 2017). At least 44 people—36 of them Muslims—have been killed by cow vigilante groups between May 2015 and December 2018 (Human Rights Watch 2019).

[8] See, for example, Faleiro 2014; Sarkar 2014; and Raja 2014.

[9] A BJP member of the Legislative Council from Mangalore, Captain Ganesh Karnik, stated that the RSS had infiltrated the police force and claimed that 60 percent of the police are "our students" (Bhatnagar 2015).

[10] BJP MP Sakshi Maharaj; union minister and senior BJP leader Kalraj Mishra; former head of the National Commission on Women, Lalitha Kumaramangalam; and president of the BJP in UP, Laxmikant Bajpai, have all asserted, without substantiation, that Muslim men are engaging in love jihad and encouraged retribution for this practice (Hasan 2016).

Government officials are engaging in increased surveillance of the private sphere to regulate what people are eating and whom they are dating or marrying. It is difficult to determine whether the people who are skinning a carcass killed the cow and whether cooked meat is beef or buffalo. (The two taste similar but the former, unlike the latter, is banned in many places.) After Akhlaq was murdered, the police sent the meat he was consuming to a laboratory, which determined that it was goat, not beef. Some BJP state governments have taken absurd measures to decide whether beef is being consumed. In the predominantly Muslim district of Mewat, Haryana, just days before the Muslim Eid festival, the police sent samples of biryani (rice cooked with meat) they collected from street vendors to a laboratory to determine whether it was mutton, not beef (*BBC News* 2016). However ineffective these "scientific" tests may be, they, and other campaigns, send out important messages about what people should eat, what faith they should adopt, who they should love, and what they should believe.

12.5. The Impact of Hate Crimes

Coercive and violent Hindu nationalist campaigns claim, without substantiation, to be protecting religious sensibilities, national stability, and women's safety. They curtail the freedom of students to protest and scholars to dissent. They use the language of freedom to advance what they consider the interests of the majority community, thereby distorting what freedom entails, how the majority is constituted, and what its interests are. Freedom-of-religion bills for example, limit the freedom of Hindus to convert to other religions and limit the freedom of Christians to practice their faith.

Both the love jihad and *ghar wapsi* campaigns are coercive by definition. They do not ask people whether they want to convert or whom they want to marry. Those who engage in "reconversions" disregard the protestations of Christians (often from Dalit backgrounds) that they converted voluntarily. It does not matter if a young Hindu woman says that she freely decided to become involved with a Muslim man. She is presumed to be a victim and gullible; and Muslim men are presumed to be treacherous predators. The love jihad campaign seeks to regulate and control Hindu women's sexuality and reinforce gender hierarchies. Hindutva activists abduct (or in their language rescue) Hindu women who are dating or married to Muslim men, berate and threaten them and their partners, send them to "counseling centers," and pressure them to marry Hindu men.

All of these campaigns imply that those who are subject to violence are responsible for their own victimization. The notion that women should avoid the trap of "love jihad" conforms to the RSS view that women are responsible for sexual assault when they exercise freedom from familial constraints. RSS campaigns convey the message that women should not be out in public at night and should be modestly dressed, just as Muslims should stop having so many children, eating beef, and adhering to Muslim personal law.

Many of the people who are subject to Hindu nationalist violence are among the poorest and most vulnerable members of society. There are multiple accounts of poor Muslims and Christians being lured into conversion with material inducements.[11] Opposition to beef consumption denies the material reality of people's lives. Although the largest beef consumers are Muslims and Christians, the vast majority of the 12.5 million Hindus who eat beef (2 percent of the population) are Dalits and Adivasis (tribals, 70 percent), followed by so-called Other Backward Classes (21 percent). Poor rural cattle owners often sell their cows because they cannot afford the cost of feeding unproductive cattle. The threat of violence against anyone found in possession of a cow carcass denies people the income they have historically received from leather-related trades.

12.6. The Deepening of Populism and Religious Nationalism: 2014 to 2019

Populism promises a more perfect democracy, shorn of liberal constraints and devoid of self-seeking, corrupt leaders. It purports to empower ordinary citizens by encouraging them to circumvent institutional barriers and take power into their own hands. The commitment to expanding executive power, dismantling autonomous representative institutions, and strengthening civil society organizations that support the regime is a hallmark of populist regimes. So too is intolerance of criticism and dissent. Some scholars describe populists as anti-political because they promote moral absolutes and deny the legitimacy of dissent and conflict.

Modalities of Hindutva violence are significantly influenced by the populist and religious nationalist character of the current regime. The BJP's success rests on continual populist-style mobilization, accompanied by violence, to secure and expand its base. In this respect, the BJP government has a decisive advantage over many other populist regimes because it has strong and enduring ties to a network of RSS-affiliated civil society organizations. As the regime has become

---

[11] In Bastar, a district in the state of Chhattisgarh, BJP-dominated panchayats (village councils) prohibited Below the Poverty Line rations for Christian Adivasis unless they participated in a *ghar wapsi* in October 2014. In Agra, nearly 200 impoverished Muslim slum dwellers converted en masse to Hinduism in December 2014 because they were promised that they would thereby receive ration cards, school admission for their children, and basic amenities (Harris 2014). Hindu nationalists have branded these Bengali-speaking immigrants "Bangladeshi infiltrators" and Amit Shah has compared them to termites (Ghoshal 2019).

more populist, it has become increasingly intolerant. This reflects a common trend among populist regimes to shift from promises of a perfect democracy to the stifling of democratic deliberation and dissent.

Modi's leadership style is both populist and religious nationalist. Modi, who often claims that better days lie ahead, has lofty ambitions: to rid India of corruption, return power to the people, and improve India's global standing. Like other populists, Modi opposes political and cultural pluralism and draws a sharp distinction between "the people" and elites. In keeping with his religious nationalist commitments, he identifies the people as Hindus, and Muslims as anti-national outsiders. Modi's populist and religious nationalist commitments have deepened since he has been in office. In contrast to the 2014 election campaign, in which he emphasized economic issues, his 2019 election campaign was xenophobic and anti-minority. He repeatedly provoked fears about illegal migration and threats to national security by terrorist groups in Pakistan (Bal 2019). The government's decision to launch air strikes on Pakistan in response to a terrorist attack that killed Indian soldiers in Jammu and Kashmir in February 2019 played a major role in the BJP's election and Modi's increased popularity. In this and other instances, Modi has spoken not merely of a threat to Hindu identity but also of a threat to Indian identity, deeming opposition to government's actions anti-Indian and anti-Hindu.

The policies the government has pursued since its re-election in 2019 stem from its populist style centralization of power and its religious nationalist attempts to promote Hindu dominance. In August 2019, it revoked Article 370 of the Constitution, which for over 70 years allowed Jammu and Kashmir to form their own state legislature and create their own laws. In order to encourage non-Kashmiris, primarily Hindus, to purchase land and settle in the region, it also revoked Article 35A, which protected Kashmiris' rights to landownership and permanent residency. Following this sudden decision, the state deployed tens of thousands of Indian troops to the region, arrested opposition politicians and public figures, closed down the telephone and internet, and banned travel to and from Kashmir. This has curtailed opportunities for the peaceful expression of dissent and increased the likelihood of violent opposition to government policies.

In 2019 the government published an updated version of the National Register of Citizens (NRC) for Assam, which excluded the names of approximately two million people, many of them Muslims, who had lived in India for decades. Those who were unable to produce documentation of citizenship before foreigners tribunals (which is impossible for many displaced and impoverished people) will be separated from their families and sent to government detention centers, where conditions are deplorable (Hussain 2020). The BJP's 2019 national election manifesto promised to implement the NRC throughout India.

Within months of the BJP's re-election in 2019, the Indian parliament passed the Citizenship Amendment Act (CAA), which provides undocumented immigrants from Pakistan, Bangladesh, and Afghanistan an accelerated path to citizenship—unless they are Muslims. The act further reduces the period of time required for naturalization for non-Muslim immigrants who arrived in India before 2015, from Muslim majority neighboring countries. There is clearly a link between CAA and the government's actions in Assam. CAA enables tens' of thousands of Bengali Hindu migrants in Assam who were excluded from the NRC to become citizens. The cabinet also approved funding for a National Population Register that will include a question about parents' birthplaces; suggesting that people whose citizenship the government questions will have to establish their Indian lineage. As Mukul Kesavan (2020) points out, the real targets of this legislation are Muslim citizens. It empowers government functionaries to profile Muslims and requires that Muslims—and only Muslims—provide documentation of their citizenship.

The government's response to protests against the CAA has been repressive. The police arrested and injured thousands of students who protested the citizenship laws at two predominantly Muslim universities, Jamia Millia Islamia and Aligarh Muslim University in mid-December 2019. Less than three weeks later, the police, and allegedly the ABVP, assaulted student and faculty protesters at JNU. Adityanath incited violence against peaceful protestors at Shaheen Bagh in Delhi at a political rally in the capital, where he said that terrorists (i.e., the protestors) should be fed with "bullets not biryani" (Ellis-Peterson 2020).

In UP, several fact-finding reports provide extensive evidence of the police failing to protect innocent people, issuing arrests on false charges, and attacking protesters, especially Muslims, including Muslim children (Bhattacharya 2020).[12] An umbrella body of about 70 organizations issued a report that contended that there was "little doubt" that Chief Minister Adityanath was responsible for the violence:

> He publicly announced a doctrine of revenge against the protesters. In a shocking audio tape in wide circulation, a senior police official can be heard saying that he has the CM's instructions and full immunity to beat the violent protesters to pulp, so as to teach everyone a lesson. Sadly, none other than the Prime Minister has openly supported this wanton cruelty and breakdown of law and order. (Sabrangindia 2019)

---

[12] The police allegedly beat up a Muslim boy of age 9 or 10 emerging from a mosque; a 14-year-old boy was beaten in police custody, and a 16-year-old boy was shot in the thigh while riding a cycle (Bhattacharya, 2020). A 70-year-old Muslim man in Muzaffarnagar said nearly 20 policeman stormed and looted his house, beat him, and told him that there are two places for Muslims, "Pakistan or Kabristan (grave)" (Siddiqui 2019).

Rather than condemning police violence, Modi has blamed protestors for destroying property and supposedly attacking the police (*Hindustan Times* 2019a). In December 2019, he tweeted a video in which spiritual leader Jaggi Vasudev justified police violence against university students (*Hindustan Times* 2019b).

The BJP government's endorsement of targeted violence and discrimination against religious minorities, combined with its growing centralization of power and suppression of dissent, demonstrates the dangerous imbrication of right-wing populism and religious nationalism. Modi embodies and performs both traditional Hindu values, and the perspective of the "common man" against the elite. His leadership enables the BJP government to advance legislation like the abrogation of Article 370, the CAA, and the NRC, which redefine citizenship along populist and religious nationalist lines. Thus, when the BJP speaks of "the people," it refers to Hindus and excludes religious minorities and those whose views supposedly threaten the unity of the people. The normalization of hate speech deepens the linkages between populism and religious nationalism, as the BJP is able to increasingly claim that Hindu nationalism expresses the popular will.

12.7. Conclusion

My chapter illuminates the modalities and causes of Hindutva violence in contemporary India. Compared to preplanned "riots," organized from above, multiple, decentralized acts of violence appear to reflect a groundswell of Hindutva sentiment. Hate crimes unnerve and intimidate because their timing, location, and targets are unpredictable. They are not confined to "riot prone" regions and have multiple victims. While the major targets are Christian and Muslim minorities, they also include Dalits and women who allegedly violate upper-caste social codes. Much as the BJP seeks Dalit electoral support, Hindu nationalism is at its core an upper-caste project.

The result is the normalization of violence against minorities and political dissidents. A single murder, such as that of Mohammad Akhlaq, or single instance of police violence, such as against JNU student leader Aishe Ghosh, has demonstration effects. The individuals who are targeted serve as examples of what can happen to others who hold the same identities and views and sends shock waves throughout society. Hindutva violence signals that Muslims and political dissidents do not have equal citizenship rights, including security and equality before the law. The perpetrators of hate crimes are unlikely to be punished, and the victims are unlikely to be compensated. It refashions identities by prescribing what it means to be a Hindu, a Muslim, a moral woman, and a good citizen. The message it conveys to Muslims is that they cannot be safe in India unless they adhere to Hindu norms; to Hindu women, that their place is in the home, not in the university, streets, or even temple, and that they should marry only men of their faith; to Dalits, that their assertion of pride in challenging upper-caste dominance is an affront to Hindus. The list could be extended but the point is clear: politically motivated hate crimes have implications not only for those who are attacked verbally, physically, and legally, but for the entire society.

However, to recall Amartya Sen's argument about India's argumentative democracy, opposition to Hindu nationalist hate crimes is growing. Writers have returned their literary awards. Scientists have opposed government inaction in face of religious bigotry. Students and faculty have protested ABVP attacks on academic institutions. Dalits have protested atrocities against the community by demonstrating on the streets and running for political office. Thousands of people bearing placards proclaiming, "Not in My Name," have protested anti-Muslim violence in several Indian cities. High courts have struck down BJP state government policies to withdraw slaughterhouse licenses in UP and restrict the transportation of cattle in Maharashtra. The Supreme Court has challenged Modi's contention that security and anti-corruption concerns outweigh citizens' rights to privacy. Four senior Supreme Court justices took the audacious step of criticizing the biases of the government-appointed chief justice. Thousands of people across Indian cities opposed the CAA in months-long protests. Although Muslims, particularly Muslim women, were at the forefront of these protests, they were joined by people of all backgrounds who supported secular, inclusive citizenship.

Mounting civil society opposition to Hindu nationalism's violent and exclusionary agenda, suggest that the BJP's long-term prospects may be less secure than they once seemed. The BJP's decisive loss to the Aam Aadmi Party (AAP) in the Delhi 2020 elections signals a rejection of divisive politics, as the BJP campaign characterized protesters as rapists, and AAP members as terrorists and Pakistan supporters (Pal and Ghoshal 2020).

However, it is too early to determine the outcome of these protests. Thus far the government has refused to concede to protesters' demands and has empowered the police to violently punish them. Although his popularity rating dropped by 3 percent from August 2019 to January 2020 (*India Today* 2020b), Modi remains very popular. It's not clear how much the broad electorate will be influenced by the government's repressive actions.

One of the most important questions is whether and how effectively the opposition will challenge populists' discursive power. Rather than questioning deeply cherished democratic ideals, Modi has cleverly deployed them by ostensibly opposing established elites in the name of returning power to the people. The perversion of "people power" is most evident in the support—tacit or explicit—by BJP leaders for hate crimes. The BJP's penchant for providing easy answers to popular grievances reflects the long-term failure of Indian democracy to adequately address poverty, inequality, and minority well-being. Thus a viable alternative to the BJP must challenge the material and institutional structures that foster myriad forms of inequality and violence. It must re-interpret "power to the people" to entail secular, inclusive, peaceful, and genuinely democratic politics.

Acknowledgments

I am grateful for the valuable feedback I received from the volume editors, Karen Barkey, Sudipta Kaviraj, and Vatsal Naresh, and from Raka Ray, Uday Mehta, and other conference participants. Thanks also to Mark Kesselman, Amna Pathan, and Deepankar Basu for excellent comments, suggestions, and/or editorial advice.

References

"After BJP victory, RSS in Uttar Pradesh plans expansion." 2017a. *The Indian Express*. Updated March 26. http://indianexpress.com/article/india/after-bjp-victory-rss-in-uttar-pradesh-plans-expansion-4585863/.

"After 15-hour meditation at Kedarnath PM Modi urges nation to vote in final phase of Lok Sabha elections." 2019. *India Today*. Updated May 19. https://www.indiatoday.in/elections/lok-sabha-2019/story/after-15-hour-meditation-at-kedarnath-pm-modi-urges-nation-to-vote-in-final-phase-1528494-2019-05-19.

Ahmad, Faizan. 2014. "Those opposed to Narendra Modi should go to Pakistan, BJP leader Giriraj Singh says." *Times of India*. Updated April 20. https://timesofindia.indiatimes.com/news/Those-opposed-to-Narendra-Modi-should-go-to-Pakistan-BJP-leader-Giriraj-Singh-says/articleshow/33971544.cms.

Angad, Abhishek. 2017. "Alwar attack: Gau rakshasa killed a dairy farmer, not cattle smuggler." *Indian Express*. Updated April 7. http://indianexpress.com/article/india/alwar-gau-rakshaks-killed-a-dairy-farmer-not-cattle-smuggler-4601434.

Bagchi, Suvojit. 2019. "Number of shakhas has doubled in 10 years: RSS leader." *The Hindu*. Updated August 15. https://www.thehindu.com/news/national/number-of-shakhas-has-doubled-in-10-years-rss-leader/article29096977.ece.

Bal, Hartosh Singh. 2019. "Modi's Campaign of Fear and Prejudice." *New York Times*. April 17. https://www.nytimes.com/2019/04/17/opinion/modi-india-election.html.

Barik, Satyasundar. 2019. "51 percent rise in shakhas since 2010, says RSS." *The Hindu*. Updated October 16. https://www.thehindu.com/news/national/51-rise-in-shakhas-since-2010-says-rss/article29698348.ece.

Barry, Ellen and Suhasini Raj. 2017. "Buffalo Meat Industry Facing Government Shutdowns in India." *The New York Times*. March 24. https://www.nytimes.com/2017/03/24/world/asia/buffalo-meat-industry-india-shutdowns.html.

Basu, Amrita. 2015. *Violent Conjunctures in Democratic India*, New York: Cambridge University Press.

Basu, Deepankar. 2021. "Majoritarian politics and hate crimes against religious minorities: Evidence from India, 2009–2018." *World Development*, 146, p.105540.

Basu, Soma. 2019. "Manufacturing Islamophobia on WhatsApp in India." *The Dispatch*. May 10. https://thediplomat.com/2019/05/manufacturing-islamophobia-on-whatsapp-in-india/.

Bhatnagar, Gaurav Vivek. 2015. "BJP, RSS Leaders Caught Using 'Love Jihad' Bogey to Fuel Communal Polarisation." *The Wire*. October 5. https://thewire.in/12409/bjp-rss-leaders-caught-using-love-jihad-bogey-to-fuel-communal-polarisation.

Bhattacharya, Anirban. 2020. "A dangerous pattern of police violence in Uttar Pradesh has been masked by clever propaganda." *Scroll.in*. February 4. https://scroll.in/article/951187/a-dangerous-pattern-of-police-violence-in-uttar-pradesh-has-been-masked-by-clever-propaganda.

Bidwai, Praful. 2015. "Politics of 'love jihad': Spreading fear through stereotypes." *Daily Star*. Updated March 8. http://www.thedailystar.net/politics-of-love-jihad-40364.

"Biryani beef ban: Indian police check Mewat rice dishes." 2016. *BBC News*. September 7. https://www.bbc.com/news/world-asia-india-37295774.

Brass, Paul R. 2006. *Forms of Collective Violence: Riots Pogroms, and Genocide in Modern India*. New Delhi: Three Essays Collective.

Chhibber, Pradeep K. 1999. *Democracy without Associations: Transformation of the Party System and Social Cleavages in India*. Ann Arbor: University of Michigan Press.

Dutta, Prabhash K. 2017. "After nearly 3 years of Narendra Modi government, 61 percent people happy but dissatisfaction rises over last year." *India Today*. Updated May 16. http://indiatoday.intoday.in/story/3-years-of-narendra-modi-government-61-per-cent-people-happy/1/954809.html.

Dutta, Prabhash K. 2018. "What happened at Bhima Koregaon." *India Today*. Updated August 29. https://www.indiatoday.in/india/story/what-happened-at-bhima-koregaon-1326175-2018-08-29.

Ellis-Peterson, Hannah. 2020. "Feed them bullets not biryani: BJP uses Delhi elections to stoke religious hatred." *The Guardian*. February 6. https://www.theguardian.com/world/2020/feb/06/feed-them-bullets-not-biriyani-bjp-uses-delhi-elections-to-stoke-religious-hatred.

Engineer, Irfan, Neha Dabhade, and Suraj Nair. 2017. "Communal violence in 2016." *Matters India*. January 8. http://mattersindia.com/2017/01/communal-violence-in-2016/.

Engineer, Irfan, Neha Dabhade, and Suraj Nair. 2020. "Mob Lynching in 2019—Continuing Expression of Hegemony." *The Secular Perspective*, Center for the Study of Society and Secularism (CSSS). February 1–15. https://csss-isla.com/secular-perspective/mob-lynching-in-2019-continuing-expression-of-hegemony/.

Express News Service. 2015. "Culture Minister Mahesh Sharma speaks: Despite being a Muslim, APJ Abdul Kalam was a nationalist." *Indian Express*. Updated September 18. https://indianexpress.com/article/india/india-others/culture-minister-speaks-despite-being-a-muslim-kalam-was-a-nationalist/.

"Fact finding report reveals excesses by Meerut police against Muslims." 2019. Sabrangindia. December 28. https://www.sabrangindia.in/article/fact-finding-report-reveals-excesses-meerut-police-against-muslims.

Faleiro, Sonia. 2014. "An Attack on Love." *New York Times*. October 31. https://www.nytimes.com/2014/11/02/opinion/sunday/its-not-jihad-its-just-love.html.

"Five held after two Muslim cowherds hanged to death in India." 2016. *Reuters*. March 19. http://www.reuters.com/article/us-india-killings-idUSKCN0WL0FU.

Ghoshal, Devjyot. 2019. "Amit Shah vows to throw illegal immigrants into Bay of Bengal." *Reuters*. April 12. https://www.reuters.com/article/india-election-speech/amit-shah-vows-to-throw-illegal-immigrants-into-bay-of-bengal-idUSKCN1RO1YD.

Gorski, Philip. 2018. "Religious nationalism and right wing populism: Trumpism and beyond." *Contending Modernities*. August 6. https://contendingmodernities.nd.edu/theorizing-modernities/religious-nationalism-and-right-wing-populism-trumpism-and-beyond/.

Griswold, Eliza. 2019. "The violent toll of Hindu nationalism in India." *New Yorker* March 5, https://www.newyorker.com/news/on-religion/the-violent-toll-of-hindu-nationalism-in-india.

Harris, Gardiner. 2014. "'Reconversions' of religious minorities roils India's politics." *New York Times*. December 23. https://www.nytimes.com/2014/12/24/world/asia/india-narendra-modi-hindu-conversions-missionaries.html.

Hasan, Zoya. 2016. "Politics without the minorities." *The Hindu*. Updated May 23. https://www.thehindu.com/opinion/lead/politics-without-the-minorities/article6380445.ece.

"Heat on Sharjeel Iman: Sedition cases filed against anti-CAA activist in six states." 2020a. *India Today*. Updated January 28. https://www.indiatoday.in/india/story/heat-on-sharjeel-imam-sedition-cases-filed-against-anti-caa-activist-in-six-states-1640742-2020-01-27.

"'Hindu rashtra' to 'love jihad': A look at UP CM Yogi Adityanath's most controversial remarks." 2017. *First Post*. May 19. http://www.firstpost.com/politics/hindu-rashtra-to-love-jihad-a-look-at-up-cm-yogi-adityanaths-most-controversial-remarks-3341946.html.

Human Rights Watch. 2019. *Violent Cow Protection in India: Vigilante Groups Attack Minorities*. February 18. https://www.hrw.org/report/2019/02/18/violent-cow-protection-india/vigilante-groups-attack-minorities.

Human Rights Watch. 2020. "India: Events of 2019." In *World Report 2020*. https://www.hrw.org/world-report/2020/country-chapters/india.

Hussain, Tawqeer. 2020. "'How is it human?': India's largest detention centre almost ready." *Al-Jazeera*. January 2. https://www.aljazeera.com/news/2020/01/human-india-largest-detention-centre-ready-200102044649934.html.

"If BJP loses in Bihar, crackers will go off in Pakistan, says Amit Shah." 2015b. *India Today*. Updated November 3. http://indiatoday.intoday.in/story/if-bjp-loses-fireworks-will-go-off-in-pakistan-says-amit-shah-in-raxaul/1/510481.html.

"If BJP loses Bihar by mistake, crackers will be lit in Pakistan: Amit Shah." 2015. *Indian Express*. Updated December 25. http://indianexpress.com/article/india/politics/if-bjp-loses-crackers-will-go-off-in-pakistan-amit-shah/.

"India: Protect universities and academic freedom from threat of violence and intimidation—say human rights groups." 2017. *South Asia Citizens Web*. February 22. http://www.sacw.net/article13119.html.

"India 'hate speech' minister Niranjan Joshi keeps job." 2014. *BBC News*. December 4. http://www.bbc.com/news/world-asia-india-30326774.

Jaffrelot, Christophe. 2019. "A Defacto Ethnic Democracy? Obliterating and Targeting the Other, Hindu Vigilantes and the Ethno-State." In *Majoritarian State. How Hindu Nationalism is Changing India*, edited by Angana P. Chatterjee, Thomas Blom Hansen, and Christophe Jaffrelot, 41–67. London: Hurst.

"Kairana 'exodus,' love jihad key issues for BJP: Yogi Adityanath." 2017b. *Indian Express*. February 4. http://indianexpress.com/article/india/kairana-exodus-love-jihad-key-issues-for-bjp-yogi-adityanath/...

Kanungo, Pralay, 2019. "Sangh and Sarkar: The RSS power centre shifts from Nagpur to New Delhi." In *Majoritarian State: How Hindu Nationalism is Changing India*, edited by Angana P. Chatterjee, Thomas Blom Hansen and Christophe Jaffrelot, 133–149. London: Hurst.

Kesavan, Mukul. 2020. "The attacks on two Delhi universities reveal Modi's targets: Muslims and their allies." *The Guardian*. January 13. https://www.theguardian.com/commentisfree/2020/jan/13/attacks-delhi-universities-modi-muslims-allies.

Kohli, Atul, 1997. "Can democracies accommodate ethnic nationalism? Rise and decline of self-determination movements in India." *Journal of Asian Studies* 56, no. 2: 325–344.

Moon, Louise. 2017. "India plans to give 88 million cows 'identity cards' which can be tracked online." *The Telegraph*. January 4. https://www.telegraph.co.uk/news/2017/01/04/india-plans-give-88-million-cows-identity-cards-can-tracked/.

"On protests over Citizenship Act PM Modi tweets Sadhguru's video explainer." 2019b. *Hindustan Times*. Updated December 30. https://www.hindustantimes.com/india-news/pm-modi-launches-outreach-campaign-with-a-tweet-in-support-of-citizenship-act/story-7fXiDacIHlDbdtlfP2HkiL.html.

Pal, Alasdair and Devjyot Ghoshal. 2020. "India's divisive protests could help Modi's party in election test." *Reuters*. February 5. https://www.reuters.com/article/us-india-politics/indias-divisive-protests-could-help-modis-party-in-election-test-idUSKBN2000DO.

Pattnaik, Ayesha. 2019. "Long read: The art of dissolving dissent. India's sedition law as an instrument to regulate public opinion." South Asia @ LSE. October 4. https://blogs.lse.ac.uk/southasia/2019/10/04/long-read-the-art-of-dissolving-dissent-indias-sedition-law-as-an-instrument-to-regulate-public-opinion/.

"PM Modi remains popular despite mounting criticism since Lok Sabha win, shows MOTN poll." 2020b. *India Today*. Updated January 24. https://www.indiatoday.in/mood-of-the-nation/story/pm-modi-remains-popular-despite-mounting-criticism-since-lok-sabha-win-shows-motn-poll-1639581-2020-01-23.

Press Trust of India. 2015. "Will try to bring nationwide ban on cow slaughter: Rajnath Singh." *Economic Times*. Updated March 30. https://economictimes.indiatimes.com/news/politics-and-nation/will-try-to-bring-nationwide-ban-on-cow-slaughter-rajnath-singh/articleshow/46736863.cms?from=mdr.

Press Trust of India. 2019. "Sanjeev Balyan: Muzaffarnagar riots cast shadow over him." *Business Standard*. Updated May 30. https://www.business-standard.com/article/pti-stories/sanjeev-balyan-muzaffarnagar-riots-cast-shadow-over-him-119053001353_1.html.

Puniyani, Ram. 2017. "UP elections 2017: BJP's divisive agenda." *The Citizen*. February 7. https://www.thecitizen.in/index.php/en/NewsDetail/index/4/9879/UP-Elections-2017-BJPs-Divisive-Agenda.

Raj, Suhasini. 2016. "Indian state to license cow protection groups to aid police." *New York Times*. August 11. https://www.nytimes.com/2016/08/12/world/asia/indian-state-to-license-cow-protection-groups-to-aid-police.html.

Raja, Aditi. 2014. "VHP steps up campaign against 'love jihad.'" *Indian Express*. September 20. http://indianexpress.com/article/india/india-others/vhp-steps-up-campaign-against-love-jihad/.

Rao, Raghvendra and Rakesh Sinha. 2014. "Under opposition fire, centre counters: Bring anti-conversion law." *Indian Express.* Updated December 12. http://indianexpress.com/article/india/politics/cornered-govt-counters-bring-anti-conversion-law/.

Ray, Raka, 2006. "A Slap from the Hindu nation." In *Violence, Modernity and Democracy in India,* edited by Amrita Basu and Srirupa Roy, 83–100. Calcutta: Seagull India Press.

Sarkar, Tanika. 2014. "Love, control and punishment." *Indian Express.* Updated October 16. http://indianexpress.com/article/opinion/columns/love-control-and-punishment/.

Schultz, Kai, Suhasini Raj, Jeffrey Gettleman, and Hari Kumar. 2019. "In India, release of hate crime data depends on who the haters are." *New York Times.* October 24. https://www.nytimes.com/2019/10/24/world/asia/india-modi-hindu-violence.html.

Sen, Amartya. 2005. *The Argumentative Indian: Writings on Indian History, Culture and Identity.* Basingstoke: Macmillan.

Shafi, Showkat. 2017. "Nationalist group ABVP accused of Delhi campus violence." *Al Jazeera.* February 27. http://www.aljazeera.com/indepth/features/2017/02/nationalist-group-abvp-accused-delhi-campus-violence-170226050247696.html.

Siddiqui, Imran Ahmed. 2019. "'You've only two places, Pakistan or Kabristan.'" *The Telegraph.* Updated December 26. https://www.telegraphindia.com/india/youve-only-two-places-pakistan-or-kabristan/cid/1730395.

"Sonia Gandhi's skin colour made her Congress president: Giriraj Singh." 2015a. *India Today.* Updated April 1. https://www.indiatoday.in/india/north/story/giriraj-singh-sonia-gandhi-skin-colour-made-her-congress-president-246664-2015-04-01.

Stokes, Bruce. 2016. "India and Modi: The honeymoon continues: 2. How is Modi doing?" *Pew Research Center.* September 19. http://www.pewglobal.org/2016/09/19/2-how-is-modi-doing/.

"'They have died for you': PM Modi backs police amidst charges of brutality, firing." 2019a. *Hindustan Times.* Updated December 22. https://www.hindustantimes.com/india-news/they-have-died-for-you-pm-modi-backs-police-amid-charges-of-brutality-firing/story-B9BZRziGpmz0DzQkD1q1HI.html.

Thomas, Saji. 2017. "Anti-Christian violence on the rise in India." *UCA News.* May 18. https://www.ucanews.com/news/anti-christian-violence-on-the-rise-in-india/79257.

"Those who want to eat beef should go to Pak: Mukhtar Abbas Naqvi." 2015. *Hindustan Times.* Updated May 22. http://www.hindustantimes.com/india/those-who-want-to-eat-beef-should-go-to-pak-mukhtar-abbas-naqvi/story-kTyciMp58MrUhrWJfp5kFK.html.

Tiwary, Deeptiman. 2016. JNU row: Behind ABVP's confidence, govt and growth." *Indian Express.* Updated February 24. http://indianexpress.com/article/india/india-news-india/jnu-protests-jnusu-behind-abvp-confidence-govt-and-growth-rohith-vemula/.

"Union minister Jayant Sinha garlands 8 convicted for Ramgarh mob lynching." 2018. *India Today.* Updated July 6. https://www.indiatoday.in/india/story/union-minister-jayant-sinha-garlands-8-convicted-for-ramgarh-mob-lynching-1279601-2018-07-06.

US Commission on International Freedom, Annual Report, 2020. https://www.uscirf.gov/sites/default/files/USCIRF percent202020 percent20Annual percent20Report_Final_42920.pdf. (Accessed May 15, 2020)

Varshney, Ashutosh. 2002. *Ethnic Conflict and Civic Life: Hindus and Muslims in India.* New Haven: Yale University Press.

300 VIOLENCE AND DOMINATION

Varshney, Ashutosh and Steven Wilkinson. 2006. "Varshney-Wilkinson Dataset on Hindu-Muslim Violence in India, 1950–1995, Version 2." Ann Arbor: Inter-university Consortium for Political and Social Research. https://doi.org/10.3886/ICPSR04342.v1.

Venkataramakrishnan, Rohan. 2015. "Five quotes from India's culture minister who is on a quest to 'cleanse' public discourse." *Scroll.in*. September 15. https://scroll.in/article/755543/five-quotes-from-indias-culture-minister-who-is-on-a-quest-to-cleanse-public-discourse.

Wilkinson, Steven I. 2004. *Votes and Violence: Electoral Competition and Ethnic Riots in India*. New York: Cambridge University Press.

"Woman says 'Pakistan Zindabad . . . Hindustan Zindabad' at CAA protest, booked for sedition." 2020. *The Wire*. February 21. https://thewire.in/politics/amulya-leona-bengaluru-caa-protest-sedition-owaisi-waris-pathan.

Yadav, Anumeha. 2020. "How India uses colonial-era sedition law against CAA protesters." *Al-Jazeera*. January 21. https://www.aljazeera.com/news/2020/01/india-colonial-era-sedition-law-caa-protesters-200120100338578.html.

13

Legal Contention and Minorities in Turkey

The Case of the Kurds and Alevis

Senem Aslan

13.1. Introduction

When the Turkish Republic was established in 1923, the founders of the state sought to transform its society into an ethnically and culturally homogeneous whole, requiring ethnic and religious minorities to fit into a thick definition of Turkishness. Speaking the Turkish language and having a modern, western-ized lifestyle were pillars of the state's idealized image of Turkishness. Although the Republic defined itself as secular, the definition of Turkish national identity was intertwined with Sunni Muslim identity as the common denominator of the majority of the population (Lord 2018). The thick definition of Turkish national identity generated a coercive and exclusionary nation-building process. Religious and ethnic minorities were expected to assimilate, and expressions of difference were interpreted as disloyalty to the nation. It was in the 1990s that identity-based mobilizations increased, making minorities more expressive of their differences in the public sphere.

This chapter analyzes state-minority relations in Turkey over the last three decades. Since the late 1980s, Turkey has faced increasing pressure from the European Union (EU) and international human rights organizations to improve its treatment of minorities. Turkey applied for membership in the European Economic Community, the predecessor of the EU, in 1987. Two years later, Turkey approved the compulsory jurisdiction of the European Court of Human Rights (ECtHR), giving minority activists a major opportunity to challenge state policy in an international venue. In the 1990s, the issue of minority rights also became more important for the EU than before. Its accession criteria adopted in the 1993 Copenhagen summit explicitly emphasized respect for human rights and protection of minorities as preconditions for membership negotiations. In 1999, the EU declared Turkey's candidacy, giving the Turkish government the incentive to alleviate its minorities' grievances. EU pressure succeeded in pushing the Turkish government to undertake several legal reforms that addressed minority

Senem Aslan, *Legal Contention and Minorities in Turkey* In: *Negotiating Democracy and Religious Pluralism*. Edited by: Karen Barkey, Sudipta Kaviraj, and Vatsal Naresh, Oxford University Press. © Oxford University Press 2021.
DOI: 10.1093/oso/9780197530016.003.0014

demands. The EU process also encouraged minority activists' mobilization in the legal sphere, contesting the Turkish state's policies in courts.

In this chapter, I argue that progressive court decisions and legal reforms have not been adequate to reduce state discrimination against minorities. Rather than legislative reforms and court judgments, we need to shift our attention to enforcement on the ground to assess whether there is real change in minority policy. In contexts like Turkey, where the rule of law is weak, the implementation of legal reforms and court decisions that expand minority rights can be uneven, inconsistent, and incomplete. The concept of the rule of law is broad and contested and its measurements vary. However, an effective justice system with an independent and impartial judiciary that can enforce its decisions is a minimum criterion for any system with a strong rule of law.[1] Many scholars studying the Turkish judicial system call attention to the violations of the basic principles of the rule of law in the country. For example, Ceren Belge (2006) and Hootan Shambayati (2008) underline the partisan role the judiciary had played in Turkish politics, guarding the hegemonic status of the Kemalist ideology, and its unwillingness to expand political and civil liberties. Dilek Kurban and Haldun Gülalp (2013: 175) emphasize the statist mentality of the judges and prosecutors who prioritize the state's interests in their judgments. The executive and judicial branches of government can effectively sanction those who diverge from it. More recent works have focused on the Justice and Development Party (AKP) government's successful efforts in creating a dependent and compliant judiciary (Özbudun 2015). In this chapter I also call attention to the Turkish judiciary's weakness in enforcing its decisions vis-à-vis the executive and the bureaucracy.

In Turkey, legal mobilization and progressive court decisions could have pushed for political reform and, in certain cases, might have resulted in favorable legislative changes for minorities. However, these changes largely stayed on paper and did not get implemented. State officials could act with impunity, enjoying wide discretionary authority. Extralegal and informal forms of official discrimination were common, constituting an opaque context for minorities to substantiate and publicize legal violations. Examining the implementation of reforms and court decisions that related to the cultural demands of the two largest minorities in Turkey, the Kurds and the Alevis, this chapter underlines the

---

[1] For a literature review that discusses the concept of the rule of law, see Krygier (2012). The World Bank's Worldwide Governance Indicators takes into consideration a number of measures, such as degree of judicial independence vis-à-vis the state, timeliness of judicial decisions, degree of enforcement of court orders, private property protection, and confidence in the police force to assess the condition of the rule of law in a country. For more, see http://info.worldbank.org/governance/wgi/index.aspx#doc-over. World Justice Project's Rule of Law Index's assessment is based on 44 indicators organized around eight themes: constraints on government powers, absence of corruption, open government, fundamental rights, order and security, regulatory enforcement, civil justice, criminal justice, and informal justice. These criteria can be examined at https://worldjusticeproject.org/our-work/wjp-rule-law-index/wjp-rule-law-index-2016/factors-rule-law.

LEGAL CONTENTION AND MINORITIES IN TURKEY 303

importance of social and political mobilization for a real change in state policy. A strong movement creates broader opportunities for legal mobilization. But more importantly, it increases public awareness about a new court judgment or legislative change, organizes sustained collective action challenging the arbitrary exercise of state authority, and provides resources to individuals to put pressure on local authorities for the enforcement of court decisions and legal reforms. In other words, it helps people assert their newly gained rights on an everyday basis.

In the next brief section, I provide basic information on the Kurds and Alevis, their main issues of contention with the state, and their mobilizations. Second, I discuss the legal contentions involving Alevis conducted through the ECtHR and the domestic courts, exploring to what extent these lawsuits became successful in changing state policy on the ground. I examine the court decisions that related to three major Alevi demands: the exemption of Alevi children from mandatory religious education in Turkey's primary and secondary schools, legalization of and state support for the cem houses, and the removal of religious affiliation from national identity cards. These examples suggest that while the Alevis have achieved significant victories at courts due to their persistence at legal mobilization, these legal judgments have not had a significant impact on transforming actual state policy on the ground. Third, I examine the legal reforms and court cases that related to the Kurdish demands for the expansion of linguistic and cultural rights. Even though the implementation of favorable court decisions and legal reforms has not been immediate and has gone through a rugged process, Kurds' strong political and social mobilization has managed to challenge state agents who resisted reforms and pushed them to enforce some changes on the ground.

This chapter covers the period from the early 1990s to 2016, excluding the period after the State of Emergency declared on July 20, 2016, five days after the abortive coup attempt. It is important to note that the authoritarian shift of the AKP government that accelerated after the coup attempt restricted the ability of all political groups, let alone minorities, to express themselves freely and challenge state policy. The emergency rule allowed President Recep Tayyip Erdoğan to concentrate more power through the use of executive decrees without legislative and judicial oversight, imposing significant restrictions over individual liberties (Esen and Gümüşçü 2018). Even after the end of the emergency rule, the executive control over the judiciary increased, leading to a more repressive political environment. Minority mobilizations were hit hard as the space for political activism shrank. State repression over the Kurdish mobilization reversed many of the gains achieved in cultural and linguistic spheres in the 2000s.[2] The

---

[2] For more on state-Kurdish relations after the failed coup of 2016 see https://www.nytimes.com/2017/06/29/world/middleeast/amid-turkeys-purge-a-renewed-attack-on-kurdish-culture.html.

crackdown also affected the Alevi movement, and its demands for equal rights continued to be unmet. To make matters worse, the pro-government circles began to play on the Alevi-Sunni divide to unify the AKP constituents, alleging that the Alevis are potential fifth columns trying to destabilize the country. Such allegations increased communal tensions (Lord 2018: 157–159). At the time of writing, the situation of minorities under the AKP government looks grim.

13.2. Alevi and Kurdish Mobilizations

Kurds are the largest ethnic minority in Turkey, constituting between 15 and 20 percent of the population, according to estimates. Since the beginning of the Turkish Republic Kurdish speakers have been the main targets of coercive, and at times violent, Turkification policies (Aslan 2015; Üngör 2011; Watts 2010). For a long time, Kurdish cultural expressions, such as using the Kurdish language, were banned in Turkey. While succeeding in assimilating many Kurds into Turkishness, the predominantly coercive nature of state policies also sharpened a strong Kurdish national identity. In the 1980s, the Kurdish activists' cultural and linguistic demands gave way to demands for secession, led by an armed insurgency, the PKK (Kurdistan Workers' Party). State repression in the Kurdish provinces during the armed struggle was critical in raising the political consciousness of ordinary Kurds and contributed to the growth of support for the PKK within Kurdish society (Marcus 2007). While this chapter focuses on the legal contentions, the Kurdish struggle for rights goes beyond the legal sphere, playing out in the context of violent conflict between the state and Kurdish insurgents since the 1980s. Successive political parties and several nongovernmental organizations have represented the political wing of the movement (Watts 2010). The emergence of the armed conflict weakened the belief in the assimilatory potential of the Kurds into Turkishness, reinforcing the state and public hostility against the Kurds (Yeğen 2007).

Alevis represent the largest religious minority in Turkey and they are estimated to be between 15 and 25 percent of the population (Lord 2018: 128). Both in theology and religious practice Alevis set themselves apart from the Sunni majority. They do not attend mosques but perform their rituals in gathering places called cem houses. They do not consider pilgrimage to Mecca or praying five times daily as religious obligations. Unlike non-Muslim religious communities, such as Jews, Armenians, and Greek Orthodox Christians, the state does not recognize Alevis as a separate religious minority. The state considers Alevism to be an interpretation of Sunni Islam influenced by Sufism, not a branch of Islam. Many Alevis today complain that they cannot benefit from the services provided by the Directorate of Religious Affairs (hereafter Diyanet) in accordance with the Alevi faith. Diyanet is a state institution responsible for the provision of religious services, regulating religious affairs, and administering places of worship for Muslim citizens (Soner and Toktaş 2011: 420). Nor do the Alevis enjoy special rights that non-Muslim minorities have,[3] such as the rights to be exempt from compulsory religion courses in schools and to establish their own schools and places of worship.

Alevi mobilization is a more recent phenomenon than the Kurdish mobilization. The Kemalist regime sought to establish state control over religion through the Sunni-centered Diyanet and used Sunni identity as a symbolic resource to build national identity, without officially recognizing the Alevi faith (Lord 2018). Like Kurdish demands, Alevism was perceived as a threat to national homogeneity. Despite their exclusion, the Alevis have formed a conciliatory relationship with the state. They considered the Kemalist state a constraint on the Sunni majority and a bulwark against a possible Sunni-Alevi communal conflict. Many Alevis, however, hid their identity for fear of social discrimination and prejudice. In the polarized and violent political environment of the late 1970s, many Alevis were brutally targeted by right-wing groups (Lord 2018: 147). In the early 1980s, state-Alevi relations became more tense as the military junta relied more on Sunni Islam to counter the leftist and pro-Kurdish challenge. Together with the growing urbanization of Alevi communities and the rise of identity politics in the late 1980s, Alevis began to mobilize through various associations, cultural activities, cem houses, and publications (Soner and Toktaş 2011: 421–422). The rise of the Islamist parties that appeal to the conservative Sunni constituencies in the 1990s and the AKP government in the 2000s made state-Alevi relations more contentious.

Compared to the Kurdish case, Alevi mobilization has been weaker and more limited. The movement is fragmented and not supported by a pro-Alevi political party. Alevis' wide geographic spread also weakens their political weight in Turkey's elections. More importantly, unlike the Kurds, there is no organization like the PKK that has the ability to unite the movement and mobilize the Alevi masses, either by force or by using its influence (Massicard 2013). Challenging state policy at courts has become an important mode of action for the Alevi groups since the early 1990s. These lawsuits did not result from mass mobilization but rather were initiated by Alevi lawyers and leaders of Alevi organizations (Massicard 2013: 160). In the next section I discuss the legal contentions involving Alevis conducted through the ECtHR and the domestic courts,

[3] The Lausanne Treaty was a peace treaty that settled the conflict since the First World War between Turkey and the Allies in 1923. It recognized only non-Muslim religious communities, such as Jews, Armenians, and Greeks, as minorities with certain linguistic and religious rights.

exploring to what extent these lawsuits became successful in bringing legislative changes and/or transforming discriminatory practices on the ground.

13.3. Contention over Mandatory Religious Education

After the 1980 military coup, religious culture and ethics courses became mandatory in primary and secondary schools in Turkey. Arguing that the content of these courses is based predominantly on a Sunni interpretation of Islam, Alevi groups have complained that Alevi students are obliged to take religion classes that neglect their belief system. Many Alevis have considered these courses as an official tool to assimilate the Alevi minority into the Sunni culture. They asked the state to either change the content of the courses to incorporate the teaching of different interpretations of Islam and other religions or to turn them into elective courses.

A legal battle started in February 2001 when Hasan Zengin, an Alevi parent, submitted a request to the provincial education office in Istanbul, asking to have his daughter exempted from the religion course. He argued that he did not want his daughter to learn only the Sunni perspective and that compulsory religion courses were incompatible with secularism. His request was denied based on Article 24 of the Constitution stating that religious instruction should be conducted under state supervision and is compulsory in primary and secondary schools. Following the denial of his request, Zengin applied to the Istanbul Administrative Court for judicial review, but his application was dismissed. In 2003 Zengin took the case to the Supreme Administrative Court, which also dismissed the appeal, holding that the local court complied with the procedural rules and legislation. Subsequently, Zengin applied to the ECtHR. In its judgment in 2007, the court ruled that the religion courses were not conducted in an objective and pluralist manner and did not respect Zengin's religious and philosophical convictions, presenting a violation of Article 2 of the First Additional Protocol of the European Convention. The court underlined that an exemption procedure would not be an appropriate method, forcing parents to disclose their religious identity to authorities, which could lead to further stigmatization and discrimination. In order to comply with the Convention, Turkey had to either make the religion courses optional or change the courses' content to incorporate all religious cultures.[4]

The judgment of the ECtHR initially had an effect on altering the Turkish courts' stance on the religion courses. In two separate cases in 2007 and 2008,

---

[4] *Case of Hasan and Eylem Zengin v. Turkey*, Application Number 1448/04, October 9, 2007. Available at http://hudoc.echr.coe.int/eng?i=001-82580#{%22itemid%22:[%22001-82580%22]}.

Turkey's highest administrative court, the Council of State (Danıştay), ruled in favor of parents who demanded the exemption of their children from the compulsory religion courses. In line with the ECtHR judgment, the court ruled that the content of these courses failed to be inclusive of other religions and did not respect parents' freedom of religion and conscience. Nevertheless, these rulings did not have an effect in practice. School administrators, unaware of the higher court's decision, continued to force Alevi children to take religion courses (Kurban 2014: 108). Most Alevi parents refrained from petitioning the schools, fearing that their children would be stigmatized. Even those parents who challenged the Ministry of Education in lower courts did not always get rulings in line with the higher court's decision (Altıparmak 2013: 13).

The Ministry of Education revised the religious education textbooks to add a new section on Alevism, which the Alevi groups found inadequate and biased. They criticized the textbook's representation of Alevism as a "mystic interpretation of Sunnism" and argued that the revised textbooks still inculcated a Sunni interpretation of Islam (Shakman Hurd 2014: 429). Following the textbook revisions, the Council of State reversed its earlier decisions. Solely based on expert opinions stating that the revisions made these classes pluralistic and inclusive, the Council of State closed off the option of exemption from religion classes. The Alevi criticisms of the revised textbooks were confirmed by another ECtHR ruling in 2014. The court found that the Turkish education system was still inadequately equipped to ensure respect for parents' religious convictions.[5] Several reports evaluating religious freedom in Turkey underline that information on beliefs and religions other than Sunni Islam in textbooks is very brief and superficial. A 2015 report states that the government ignored the ECtHR's decisions even though they are binding on the Turkish government under Article 90 of the Constitution. Going against these judgments, the Ministry of Education instructed all schools in 2015 to exempt only Jewish and Christian children (Meral 2015: 8).[6] The government closed off the option of exemption for Alevi students.

The contention between the state and Alevis over compulsory religion classes shows the government's reluctance to address Alevi demands as well as the inadequacy and weakness of Turkey's judicial system in dealing with issues of discrimination. There is no consistency between the decisions of courts at different levels, and the higher courts do not necessarily have a binding effect on

[5] *Case of Mansur Yalçın and Others v. Turkey*, Application Number 21163/11, September 16, 2014. Available at http://hudoc.echr.coe.int/eng?i=001-146381#{%22itemid%22:[%22001-146381%22]}.

[6] Also see Türkiye'de İnanç Özgürlüğü Hakkını İzleme Raporu, Norwegian Helsinki Committee, Temmuz 2014-Haziran 2015, available at http://inancozgurlugugirisimi.org/wp-content/uploads/2015/10/T%C3%BCrkiyede-%C4%B0nan%C3%A7-%C3%96zg%C3%BCrl%C3%BC%C4%9F%C3%BC-Hakk%C4%B1n%C4%B1-%C4%B0zleme-Raporu-2015.pdf.

the lower courts. For example, in 2013 a local administrative court in Samsun decided to exempt an Alevi student from religion classes, citing the ECtHR's judgment, but contradicting the later decisions of the Council of State.[7] As a result, the legal system in Turkey creates uncertainty for Alevis. Even though the Turkish Constitution states that the international treaties that were duly ratified (i.e., European Convention of Human Rights) have the force of law, it is not uncommon for state officials, including the judicial establishment, to liberally violate the clauses of these international treaties and neglect the decisions of the ECtHR. The Alevi community has not yet shown a unified response backed by social mobilization to challenge state practice about compulsory religious education. Legal contention has been ineffective in changing state policy. Furthermore, the AKP government increased student exposure to religion classes by introducing a number of elective courses on Islam in secondary schools (Kurban 2014: 106). Even though they are presented as elective courses, many schools make them compulsory in practice by not providing other elective classes.[8]

13.4. Contention over the Recognition of Cem Houses

Another contention that has been very hard to resolve for the Alevis is the provision of legal status to cem houses as places of worship. Cem houses have been officially closed since the early days of the Republic. The 1925 Law on the Closure of Dervish Monasteries and Tombs (hereafter Law no. 677) closed down dervish lodges and prohibited the use of religious titles. The law closed down the cem houses because the state perceived them as a type of monastery (*tekke*). The use of religious titles related to Alevism, such as *dedelik* and *seyitlik*, was also banned. Only mosques and prayer rooms (*mescid*) remained operational. Their construction and administration as well as the employment of local imams went under the control of Diyanet. In Turkish legislation only mosques, churches, and synagogues are classified as places of worship. Such recognition comes with certain benefits from the state. For example, they are exempted from numerous taxes. Their electricity bills are paid out of the Diyanet's budget.[9] While numerous cem houses have been operating across Turkey, built and supported by local Alevi communities, the absence of official recognition means that they do not receive any benefits from the state, such as exemption to pay electricity bills

---

[7] See http://t24.com.tr/haber/alevi-aile-dava-acti-mahkeme-din-dersi-zorunlu-olamaz-dedi, 223866.

[8] http://t24.com.tr/yazarlar/yilmaz-murat-bilican/hukumetin-zorunlu-din-dersi-inadi,11310.

[9] *Case of İzzettin Doğan and Others v. Turkey*, Application Number 62649/10, April 26, 2016, 25. Available at http://hudoc.echr.coe.int/eng#{%22fulltext%22:[%22izzettin%20dogan%22],%22documentcollectionid2%22:[%22GRANDCHAMBER%22,%22CHAMBER%22],%22itemid%22:[%22001-162697%22]}.

and the employment of their religious leaders by the state.[10] Alevis' sense of discrimination with regards to cem houses became more acute after 1980. After the military coup, the junta promoted the idea of Turkish-Islamic synthesis to deal with the rise of leftism. The consequent increase in the construction of mosques, including in Alevi villages, as well as the official emphasis on Sunni Islam in schools, fueled Alevis' resentments (Çarkoğlu and Bilgili 2011: 354).

While some cem houses were allowed to operate, they continued to encounter several problems due to the absence of a clear legal framework that governed unrecognized religious minorities. Until 2003 there was a ban on associations founded on the basis of ethnic, religious, and sectarian differences. Cem houses could operate as part of an association, and yet these associations encountered obstacles when they sought official registration. As a result, many associations could not identify themselves explicitly as Alevi in their statues and hinted at their identity through symbolism (Massicard 2013: 156). According to Massicard, Alevis encountered "frequent but not systematic legal difficulties" for the registration of their organizations.

Alevi groups became more persistent in using the Turkish courts to address the problem of opening and operating cem houses in the 1990s. Usually decisions to deny registration to an Alevi organization were overturned on appeal. For example, a local court ordered the Cem House Culture, Arts, and Folklore Association of Emirdağ to dissolve in 1998 because it used the word "cem house" in its name. In 2000, the Court of Cassation overturned the decision, underlining that the Alevi reference in the association's name would not be adequate for its dissolution. Nevertheless, the decision by the highest court of appeal did not necessarily set a precedent for similar cases in the future. Although the ban on associations founded on the basis of racial, ethnic, religious, and regional differences was lifted in 2003, state officials continued to create problems for the construction of cem houses (Massicard 2013: 156). In brief, the attitude of different state institutions toward cem houses has not been consistent.

An important legal process with regards to cem houses started in 2010. Ankara's Chief Prosecutor's Office applied to a court to shut down the Çankaya Cemevi Construction Association, which aims to build cem houses. The Prosecutor's Office argued that Alevism was not a religion and cem houses were not places of worship. The local court ruled against the request of the prosecutor, stating that Alevis have been using cem houses to worship. The case went to the Court of Cassation, which overruled the lower court's decision, underlining that no place other than a mosque can be recognized as a place of worship according

---

[10] The Turkish government stated to the ECtHR that there were 1,151 *cemevis* across Turkey while the Alevi applicants claimed that there were 895 *cemevis* in the cities and about 3,000 *cemevis* in villages. *Case of İzzettin Doğan*, 19.

to the Law no. 677. It also stated that only Diyanet could establish mosques. In its decision the court went against both its earlier decision of 2000 and the ECtHR's rulings. The case was sent back to the local court, which insisted on its earlier decision in favor of the Cemevi Construction Association, underlining the principle of the freedom of religion in the European Convention of Human Rights and the principle of secularism in the Turkish Constitution (Kurban 2014: 22–23). In the final round of this legal battle the case was sent to the Legal Council of the Court of Cassation, which ruled that an association could be established with the goal of constructing cem houses. The Court of Cassation underlined that although operating cem houses was against Law no. 677, the European Convention of Human Rights has precedence over national laws.[11]

Although the Court of Cassation's latest decision was a major legal victory for the Alevis, constructing and operating cem houses still remain at the mercy of local authorities. The AKP government, with a strong bent of Sunni Islam, has not yet taken any initiative to legalize cem houses as places of worship. In 2015 the Court of Cassation issued another judgment saying that the cem houses were places of worship and Diyanet should pay their electricity bills.[12] The court based its decision on an earlier ECtHR ruling, stating that the state discriminated against Alevis by not granting cem houses exemption from payment of electricity bills.[13] Despite these legal rulings, the government continues to argue that the Alevi faith should be considered as a Sufi order, denying cem houses the same legal status enjoyed by mosques. In 2013 a case was filed at the ECtHR by İzzettin Doğan, chairman of the Cem Foundation, and 202 other citizens, accusing the Turkish state of violating its duty of neutrality toward religion. The Grand Chamber of the ECtHR issued its judgment in favor of the Alevi community leaders in 2016, stating that the failure of the Turkish authorities to recognize the cem houses as places of worship amounted to discrimination in violation of the Convention.[14] In its defense the government maintained that Alevi citizens were free to practice their religion in cem houses despite Law no. 677. While the government underlined that the law was not enforced anymore, allowing Alevis to practice their religion freely, it cited the same law as a justification not to recognize cem houses as places of worship, as such recognition would be contrary to the law.[15] This defense indicated the government's stance toward the law. The government perceives the law not as a constraint on its authority but as a flexible tool that can be used inconsistently to conform to its goals.

---

[11] http://www.milliyet.com.tr/yargitay-dan-tarihi-cemevi-karari-gundem-1979090/.
[12] http://www.hurriyet.com.tr/yargitaydan-cemevi-karari-29834823.
[13] *Case of Cumhuriyetçi Eğitim ve Kültür Merkezi Vakfı v. Turkey*, Application Number 32093/10, December 2, 2014. Available at http://demo.eurocases.eu/Doc/CourtAct/4574714.
[14] *Case of İzzettin Doğan*, 73–74.
[15] *Case of İzzettin Doğan*, 10 and 42.

Despite the recent rulings of the ECtHR and the Court of Cassation, Alevi communities still face significant problems on the ground with regards to their places of worship. For instance, in March 2016 an Alevi organization went to court in Çorum complaining that a tomb (*türbe*) that has been an important religious center for Alevis was converted into a prayer room (*mescid*) with a newly appointed imam.[16] Some municipalities that are run by the Republican People's Party (RPP) gave cem houses the status of religious sites, paying their water and electricity bills and making provision for the construction of cem houses in their urban development plans.[17] Nevertheless, such recognition is not uniform across all municipalities. Particularly in the case of granting a legal status to cem houses, lawsuits helped Alevis attract publicity to their demands but were inconsequential in affecting state policy.

13.5. The Controversy over Identity Cards

The government's unwillingness to address Alevis' sense of discrimination can also be seen in its stance toward the regulation of national identity cards. Until 2006 Turkish ID cards had a space for religious identity that was obligatory to fill. While many Alevis saw no problem to indicate their religion as Islam, others preferred to specify their religious identity as Alevi. When individuals applied to registration offices, state authorities rejected the demand to identify one's religion as Alevi on the ground that Alevism was part of Islam and not a separate religion of its own. In its opinion issued to a local court, Diyanet stated that designation of a subgroup within Islam was incompatible with national unity, republican principles, and the principle of secularism. The Court of Cassation upheld the judgment of the lower court.[18]

In 2006, as part of reforms to comply with EU membership criteria, the government lifted the obligation to fill the space for religion on ID cards, allowing individuals to leave the space empty by petitioning the Directorate of Population. This change, however, hardly satisfied the Alevis, along with other religious minorities and secularists. They argued that leaving the space blank could subject them to discriminatory treatment, as it would mean that the bearer of the card did not belong to Sunni Islam. In 2010, the ECtHR ruled that the new regulation requires individuals to disclose their religious identity, violating the freedom not

---

[16] http://direnisteyiz3.org/alevi-turbesini-mescit-yapip-imam-atadilar/.

[17] http://bianet.org/bianet/ifade-ozgurlugu/162094-agbaba-100-civari-belediye-cemevlerine-ibadethane-statusu-verdi.

[18] *Case of Sinan Işık v. Turkey*, Application Number 21924/05, February 2, 2010, 2–4. Available at http://hudoc.echr.coe.int/eng#{%22fulltext%22:[%22sinan%20isik%22],%22documentcollectionid2%22:[%22GRANDCHAMBER%22,%22CHAMBER%22],%22itemid%22:[%22001-97087%22]}.

to manifest one's religious convictions. The court recommended that removal of the religion box from identity cards would be the best option. No initiative was taken by the government to implement the ECtHR judgment until 2016, when the Turkish parliament passed a law regarding the new biometric identity cards. According to the law, the new cards do not contain a space displaying religious affiliation, but registration officers still ask for applicants' religious affiliation, keeping this information on the electronic chips embedded in cards.[19] The applicants are free not to identify with any religion. The new regulation fails to resolve the problem of religious discrimination because it still records religious information in the national register and forces individuals to disclose their religious identity to state authorities.

Adding to the controversy, a news report revealed in 2013 that the national registry records have contained confidential racial codes for different minorities, such as Greek Orthodox, Jewish, Syriacs, and Armenians, since the early days of the Republic. In response, the government stated that such coding was necessary to determine citizens' eligibility to enroll in minority schools, in accordance with the Treaty of Lausanne (Kurban 2014: 64–65). Sezgin Tanrıkulu, an RPP parliamentarian, submitted a written query to the then-prime minister, Recep Tayyip Erdoğan, asking whether Alevi identity was also separately coded. No response was given to the query.[20] The news about coding increased minority communities' worries about ethnic and racial profiling by the state.

The Alevis' experience indicates that legal mobilization and contention is inconsequential in transforming state policy in the absence of a strong social and political movement. As Massicard (2013: 160) underlines, legal action has not involved Alevi mass mobilization. The movement's elites, such as the leaders of Alevi associations and lawyers, initiate the lawsuits without the awareness and support of Alevis who are outside the organizational milieu. As will be discussed in the next section, unlike the Kurdish case, legal contention does not result in social mobilization among Alevis that would put further pressure on the government to make the necessary legal changes and force the bureaucracy to implement favorable court decisions. The relatively late politicization of Alevis, the movement's fragmentation, and the absence of a political leadership account for the movement's weakness compared to the Kurdish movement. Alevis gained increased publicity through legal contention but not much influence.

---

[19] http://armenianweekly.com/2016/02/18/turkey-id-cards/.
[20] http://www.egeninsesi.com/127024-alevilere_soy_kodlamasi_iddiasi.   Also   see the minister of interior's answers to Garo Paylan, an Armenian MP who belongs to the opposition party Halkların Demokratik Partisi (HDP) at http://t24.com.tr/haber/icisleri-bakani-efkan-ala-soy-kodunun-tum-vatandaslar-icin-uygulandigini-soyledi,328285.

Compared to the situation of the Alevis, there have been more official policy changes that addressed Kurdish grievances in the 2000s.[21] Kurdish mobilization helped bring modest changes in state policy, allowing some freedom to Kurdish linguistic and cultural expressions. These changes, nevertheless, did not result from a smooth and linear process of implementation. Court decisions and legal reforms that expanded Kurdish cultural rights took years to be put in practice, with many day-to-day confrontations between the state and the Kurds.[22]

13.6. Ban on the Kurdish Language

The Kurdish language ban was one of the most infamous violations of minority rights in Turkey. After the coup the military government issued a law (hereafter Law no. 2932) that banned the use of the Kurdish language in public and private. The law also prohibited the spread of any language, other than Turkish, as the mother tongue. Until its repeal in 1991, the law was used to justify several arrests of, interrogations of, and litigations against those who spoke, sang, or published in Kurdish. Additionally, in many cases the Turkish authorities considered the use of Kurdish to be a violation of the Turkish Penal Code's Article 142, which banned advocating separatism and propagating ideas that weaken national sentiments (Aslan 2015: 134).

Law no. 2932 was lifted in 1991, but restrictions on the use of Kurdish remained de facto in force. Two reasons account for this. First, the armed conflict between the PKK and the state security forces and the conditions of emergency rule in the Southeast increased the opportunities for state officials to act with impunity. Second, the broad and ambiguous provisions of laws allowed authorities to legally justify their interventions over the use of Kurdish. For example, the use of Kurdish language could be prosecuted under the Anti-Terror Law as constituting separatist propaganda or support for the PKK (Aslan 2015: 141).

The encounters of Kurdish publishers with state authorities exemplify how official restrictions over Kurdish remained in force. Many Kurdish publications could stay on the market without any official interruptions, while others were confiscated and banned by the local police. According to an editor of a Kurdish publishing company, the practice of the police toward Kurdish language publications was random and unpredictable. Neither the title nor the content of

---

[21] Given the length and violent nature of the Kurdish conflict, the Kurdish minority's demands have gone beyond the issue of ethno-cultural rights. These demands now involve regional administrative autonomy, general amnesty for PKK militants, including Abdullah Öcalan, the imprisoned leader of the PKK, and accountability for human rights violations by the state. These demands are more difficult to resolve and beyond the scope of this chapter.

[22] The discussion on the Kurds includes material from the author's previous work. For a detailed discussion, see Aslan (2015).

the publication determined the likelihood of confiscations. In general, the courts acquitted the publishers and the authors. Nevertheless, a court decision in favor of a publishing company did not deter the police from seizing publications. Some publishers printed the court decisions of acquittal at the end of the book to prove to the authorities that the book was legal, but it was not uncommon for local authorities to disregard these court decisions.[23] Despite state authorities' continuing restrictions over the use of Kurdish through legal and extralegal measures, the number of publications in Kurdish increased in the 1990s.

After the abolition of Law no. 2932, playing Kurdish music in public, on radio, and on TV also became legal. Popular singers from the Kurdish regions started to include Kurdish songs on their albums. A representative of a major music company complained that even after the Ministry of Culture authorized a music album, it could be banned in the entire Southeastern region with an order from a governor.[24] As in the case of Kurdish publications, local authorities frequently ignored the legal stipulations. For instance, a local radio station in Şanlıurfa, Radio Karacadağ, repeatedly faced criminal charges for broadcasting Kurdish songs, all of which had permission from the Ministry of the Interior. In the two-year period until 1998, around 20 legal investigations were opened against the radio station about these songs. Many times, the police renewed accusations about the same songs to the prosecutor, who consistently dropped the charges, being unable to find any grounds for litigation (Aslan 2015: 153–154). The police harassment eventually led to the closure of the radio station.

The prospect of becoming a full member of the EU in 1999 pushed the Turkish state to undertake a series of reforms that addressed some of the long-awaited Kurdish demands for linguistic rights. However, the implementation of these reforms on the ground has been contentious and often met with the resistance of the bureaucracy. Administrative regulations could limit rights that were accorded by the parliament. For example, the amendments to the broadcasting law in 2002 and 2003 allowed for Kurdish broadcasting in public and private radio and TV stations. Despite the change in the law, administrative requirements made Kurdish broadcasting difficult. Accordingly, programs in the Kurdish language had always to be accompanied by Turkish subtitles and could not exceed forty-five minutes a day or four hours a week. The content of the programs was strictly limited to news, culture, and music. Radio and TV stations also had to send Turkish translations of the Kurdish programs to the Supreme Board of Radio and Television in Ankara every week. These requirements presented additional costs for Kurdish media owners, discouraging them from broadcasting in Kurdish.

---

[23] Author's interview with a Kurdish editor, September 2006, Istanbul.
[24] "Kürtçe Sözlü Hafif Türk Müzigi," Nokta, May 1–7, 1994, 84–85.

Many complained that they encountered bureaucratic difficulties while trying to get permission to broadcast in Kurdish (Aslan 2015: 158).

Such measures by local authorities did not thwart the use of the Kurdish language. On the contrary, they politicized its use, giving more incentives to Kurdish activists to mobilize Kurds on the basis of language rights. The use of Kurdish became the most important marker for Kurdish intellectuals, politicians, and activists to assert the existence of Kurdish national identity. Starting in 1999, the pro-Kurdish party candidates increasingly won high numbers of mayoral offices and seats in provincial councils in the Kurdish Southeast in local elections (Watts 2010). These electoral victories provided an opportunity for Kurdish politicians to emphasize the use of the Kurdish language, increasing its visibility and gradually eroding the ability of the Turkish state to control the public space. Mayors used Kurdish in their rallies and encounters with the locals. Municipalities organized conferences where panelists presented in Kurdish, book fairs where Kurdish books were sold, and concerts where Kurdish music was played. Municipal posters and newsletters used both Kurdish and Turkish. Despite bureaucratic difficulties, many private Kurdish TV stations opened across the region. The increased use of Kurdish in the Southeast fueled more contention with state authorities. In 2007, the mayor of Diyarbakır's Sur municipality, Abdullah Demirbaş, was removed from office by an order of the Council of State (Danıştay) for providing municipal services in both Turkish and Kurdish (Watts 2010: 142–153). Demirbaş was reelected as the mayor of Sur in 2009 local elections. The mayor of Diyarbakır, Osman Baydemir, was taken to court many times on the charge that his use of Kurdish in public speeches violated the Law on Political Parties (Aslan 2015: 160). Nevertheless, as Nicole Watts (2010: 151) writes, Kurdish activists managed to routinize the use of the Kurdish language in public spaces, gradually eroding state power on the ground.

The EU accession process coupled with the pressures of persistent Kurdish mobilization eventually gave way to meaningful implementation of legal changes in linguistic rights. The administrative restrictions on Kurdish broadcasting were eventually abolished. In 2009, the state-owned Turkish Radio and Television established a new channel, TRT 6, to broadcast in Kurdish. In 2013, the Turkish parliament passed a law that allowed the use of Kurdish by defendants in courts.[25] The use of Kurdish in electoral campaigns was decriminalized. In 2014 local elections, not only the pro-Kurdish Peace and Democracy Party (BDP), but also the AKP, used Kurdish in its campaign.[26]

---

[25] http://www.ntv.com.tr/turkiye/ilk-kurtce-savunma-yapildi,_5hOKYPqkk2W5pGQZpeHeg.
[26] See http://www.aljazeera.com.tr/haber/kamuda-kurtceye-dolayli-serbestlik and https://t24.com.tr/haber/akpden-diyarbakirda-kurtce-secim-afisi,251823.

13.7. Contention over Kurdish Names

Another example of official discrimination against Kurds was the ban on Kurdish names.[27] The ban rested on a weak legal foundation. Article 16/4 of the 1972 Registration Law stated that names that do not conform to national culture, moral norms, customs, and traditions and which offend the public could not be given to children. Which names conformed to national culture was left to the discretion of registration officers. After the military coup of 1980, parents increasingly encountered problems giving Kurdish names to their children. As the war between the state and the Kurdish insurgency intensified, names increasingly became a tool for the symbolic construction of Kurdish national identity. As more parents insisted on giving Kurdish names to their children and more Kurds wanted to change their Turkish names to Kurdish, facing rejection by state officials, the issue turned into a legal contention in the late 1990s and early 2000s.

In general, the public registration offices and the local courts were not sympathetic to Kurdish naming. An analysis of the rulings of the Court of Cassation, however, shows that the highest court of appeal was consistently permissive of non-Turkish names. In 1990, it overruled a decision by a lower civil court that ruled that the parents should annul the Kurdish name, Berivan, that they had given their child. The Court of Cassation ruled that naming their child was a right of parents and no individual could be stripped of a name by a court decision according to basic human rights norms.[28] In 1993, it overturned a lower court's decision that refused a parent's demand to change his daughter's name from Berrin to a Kurdish name, Berfin. While the lower court refused this demand on the ground that Berfin was not Turkish, the Court of Cassation ruled that a name's foreign origin could not be a justification for the rejection of a name.[29] In all the other lawsuits that relate to naming, the highest court of appeal consistently ruled that individuals were free to take any name, unless the meaning of the name was insulting, humiliating, or profane.

State authorities frequently ignored these rulings of the highest court. Registrars continued to refuse to register Kurdish names, the gendarmerie searched for Kurdish names to inform legal authorities, and local public prosecutors occasionally indicted parents who gave Kurdish names to their children. Many local courts continued to interpret the Registration Law as a ban against Kurdish names. In 2002, a militarily weakened PKK declared that it promoted a political uprising as a solution to the Kurdish problem and began to emphasize human rights, democracy, and multiculturalism in its discourse to

---

[27] This section is drawn from the author's previous article on the issue. For more, see Aslan (2009).

[28] Yargıtay İlamı, T.C. Yargıtay 3. Hukuk Dairesi, Esas no: 8859, Karar no: 516.

[29] Yargıtay İlamı, T.C. Yargıtay 18. Hukuk Dairesi, Esas no: 9708, Karar no: 0832, October 13, 1993.

attract European and international support. The PKK's announcement mobilized Kurds over Kurdish naming as more people demanded to replace their names with Kurdish names or give their children Kurdish names, starting a wave of contention with the state. Officials interpreted demands for Kurdish names to be in line with the new civil disobedience strategy of the PKK and undertook legal action against them (Aslan 2009).

The controversy pushed the Turkish parliament in 2003 to clarify the Article 16 of the Registration Law. The amendment dropped the terms "national culture" and "Turkish customs and traditions," stating that only names that disregard moral norms or offend the public could not be given as first names. Kurdish mobilization did not end after the legal change. Activists encouraged people to give Kurdish names to their children. The Diyarbakır Municipality, run by the pro-Kurdish party, published a 105-page reference book that listed Kurdish names. Several websites were established advertising Kurdish names with their meanings. Soon after the amendment was passed, the pro-Kurdish Democratic People's Party (DEHAP) organized a campaign for the registration of Kurdish names that include the letters *q*, *x*, and *w*, which do not exist in Turkey's official alphabet. Kurdish activists applied to courts to change their names to explicit Kurdish names like Xemgin, Berxwedan, and Warjin. Turkish courts, including the Court of Cassation, did not allow the registration of such names, underlining that registration of names that were spelled with letters that did not exist in the Turkish alphabet could create administrative problems and confusion (Aslan 2009). The case went to the ECtHR, which ruled in favor of the Turkish state in 2010. The court argued that that states have the right to require their official language to be used in identity papers and that the transcription of Kurdish names into the Turkish alphabet did not cause the applicants a social inconvenience.[30]

The Kurdish activists' continued insistence on the legalization of the use of the letters *x*, *q*, and *w* managed to put pressure on the government. As Kurban (2014: 5) underlines, municipalities run by the pro-Kurdish party "have already created a de facto situation in the Kurdish region whereby the local authorities use these letters in official correspondence and documents, as well as in names of public spaces." The democratization package announced by Erdoğan in September 2013 included the legalization of the use of the letters *x*, *q*, and *w* in official documents.[31] Kurdish names began to be registered without any major problems, indicating a real change in state policy.

---

[30] *Affaire Kemal Taşkın et Autres c. Turquie*, Requêtes nos 30206/04, 37038/04, 43681/04, 45376/04, 12881/05, 28697/05, 32797/05 et 45609/05, February 2, 2010. Available at http://hudoc.echr.coe.int/eng#{%22languageisocode%22:[%22FRE%22],%22appno%22:[%2230206/04%22,%2237038/04%22,%2243681/04%22,%2245376/04%22,%2212881/05%22,%2228697/05%22,%2232797/05%22,%2245609/05%22],%22documentcollectionid2%22:[%22CHAMBER%22],%22itemid%22:[%22001-97088%22]}.

[31] http://www.radikal.com.tr/turkiye/q-w-xin-85-yillik-yasagi-bitiyor-1152737/.

13.8. The Issue of Kurdish Education

Education in the Kurdish language has been an important demand of the Kurdish movement since its early days. The prohibition on the teaching of the Kurdish language was binding for both public and private educational institutions. According to the Turkish Constitution, no language other than Turkish can be taught to citizens as a mother tongue in any educational institution (Kurban 2003: 179). Kurdish activists have demanded the teaching of the Kurdish language in public schools. They have argued that this education should be provided by the state because the majority of the Kurds could not afford private education given the poverty of the Kurdish regions.

As part of the EU reforms the parliament changed the Law on the Teaching of Foreign Languages in 2002. The amendment allowed for the establishment of private courses for teaching "different languages and dialects traditionally used by Turkish citizens in their daily lives." With this amendment, the ban on teaching Kurdish in private classes was abolished, but the law also included a provision that these classes could not violate the indivisible integrity of the state and the main principles of the Republic as written in the Constitution. The new law also stipulated that no language other than Turkish could be taught as a mother tongue in private and public educational institutions (Kurban 2003: 205).

Opening private courses to teach Kurdish encountered resistance from the state authorities. The administrators of the Kurdish private courses, who could get approval from the Ministry of Education after a long struggle that lasted for months, encountered several obstacles from the local bureaucracy. In Urfa, a school owner was asked to change the name of his school, Urfa Private Kurdish Language School, to Urfa Private Kurdish Dialects Language School on the grounds that Kurdish was not a language but was composed of two local dialects.[32] The opening of other schools was postponed because the buildings did not have a fire escape or the width of the interior doors did not conform to regulations. There was another problem. A regulation of the Ministry of Education that clarified rules for teaching foreign languages required teachers to have a bachelor's degree in education in the language they would teach. Because there were no university departments for the Kurdish language, there was practically no one who would be eligible to teach Kurdish in private classes. In the end, the ministry agreed to approve a number of Kurdish language schools to operate in the region and accepted some of the candidates that the private schools proposed as teachers (Aslan 2015: 158–159).

The opening of private schools did not stop demands for Kurdish education in state schools. Activists organized petition campaigns, demonstrations, and

[32] http://bianet.org/bianet/insan-haklari/30857-bakanlik-kurt-dili-denilmesine-karsi.

conferences, achieving extensive coverage by the media. They raised money from local businesses and parents to open schools to teach exclusively in Kurdish.[33] The pro-Kurdish party supported their efforts in the parliament.[34] They initially encountered repressive measures but gradually affected state policy. In September 2009, the Council of Higher Education (YÖK) permitted graduate study in Kurdish in the new Mardin Artuklu State University at the Institute for Living Languages. Since 2011, YÖK has allowed undergraduate study in Kurdish, and it has established Kurdish language and literature departments in five universities, signaling that it recognizes the shortage of Kurdish language teachers. The Ministry of Education included elective Kurdish language classes in the curriculum of secondary education starting with 2012–2013 academic year (Kurban 2014: 162–163). While these changes did not satisfy the Kurdish movement's demand for instruction in Kurdish language in state schools, they indicated substantial improvement in language rights compared to the past.

13.9. Conclusion

This chapter has examined how the state addressed the demands of the two largest minorities in Turkey, the Kurds and the Alevis, as it sought closer relations with the European Union in the last three decades. Examining the implementation of decisions by the European Court of Human Rights and the domestic courts as well as of legal reforms passed by the Turkish parliament, I have argued that international incentives and pressure are important for the initiation of legal reforms that improve minority rights, but they are not sufficient. This is because in the absence of a strong political will and domestic public support in favor of minority rights as well as an impartial and independent judiciary, legislative reforms and progressive court judgments do not have much effect on state policy on the ground. The Kurdish and Alevi examples have shown that levels of official discrimination can be best examined by focusing on administrative implementation rather than legal texts.

This study has also shown that the implementation of minority rights reforms is a contentious process that largely depends on bottom-up pressures through persistent social and political mobilization. Despite judgments of the ECtHR and some domestic courts in favor of their demands, none of the Alevi grievances have yet been addressed in Turkey. With regards to Kurds, however, there has been some change in state policy toward official recognition of linguistic and

[33] http://www.al-monitor.com/pulse/originals/2014/09/turkey-kurds-education-in-mother-tongue-schools.html.
[34] For example, see Kadri Yıldırım's query to the minister of education in January 2016, http://www2.tbmm.gov.tr/d26/7/7-1468s.pdf.

cultural rights in the 2000s. I have argued that this difference can be explained through different levels of strength of Kurdish and Alevi mobilizations. State policy on the ground is less likely to change through international pressure and legal contention if the minority in question has not yet formed a strong movement that has the ability for mass mobilization, as in the case of Alevis. As McCann underlines,

> Legal mobilization does not inherently disempower or empower citizens. How law matters depends on the complex, often changing dynamics of the context in which struggles occur. Legal relations, institutions, and norms tend to be double-edged, at once upholding the larger infrastructure of the status quo while providing limited opportunities for episodic challenges and transformations in that ruling order. (2006: 19)

As the recent political developments in Turkey indicate, whether or not legal reforms are consequential for minority rights is still contingent on the broader political context. The failure of the peace process, the resumption of violence between the state and Kurdish militants in 2015, and the increasing shift to authoritarianism by the AKP government led to a renewed crackdown on Kurdish activism as well as on cultural rights. Several Kurdish associations, media outlets, and language schools were shut down, and some of the language restrictions have made a comeback.[35] As of 2019, the ability of Kurdish activists to challenge the renewed state repression of Kurdish cultural rights is extremely limited.

Bibliography

Altıparmak, Kerem. 2013. *Hasan ve Eylem Zengin/Türkiye Kararının Uygulanması İzleme Raporu.* Ankara: Kapasite Geliştirme Derneği. Available at http://aihmiz.org.tr/files/01_Hasan_ve_Eylem_Zengin_Rapor_TR.pdf.

Aslan, Senem. 2009. "Incoherent State: The Controversy over Kurdish Naming in Turkey." *European Journal of Turkish Studies* 10. Available at http://ejts.revues.org/4142.

Aslan, Senem. 2015. *Nation-Building in Turkey and Morocco: Governing Kurdish and Berber Dissent.* New York: Cambridge University Press.

Belge, Ceren. 2006. "Friends of the Court: The Republican Alliance and Selective Activism of the Constitutional Court of Turkey." *Law and Society Review* 40 (3): 653–692.

Çarkoğlu, Ali and Nazlı Çağın Bilgili. 2011. "A Precarious Relationship: The Alevi Minority, the Turkish State, and the EU." *South European Society and Politics* 16 (2): 351–364.

---

[35] See https://www.thenation.com/article/in-turkey-repression-of-the-kurdish-language-is-back-with-no-end-in-sight/ and https://www.al-monitor.com/pulse/originals/2018/11/turkeys-kurds-in-new-effort-against-linguistic-assimilation.html#ixzz64vRqKzdu.

Esen, Berk and Şebnem Gümüşçü. 2018. "The Perils of Turkish Presidentialism." *Review of Middle East Studies* 52 (1): 43–53.

Krygier, Martin. 2016. "The Rule of Law: Pasts, Presents, and Two Possible Futures." *Annual Review of Law and Social Science* 12: 199–229.

Kurban, Dilek. 2003. "Confronting Equality: The Need for Constitutional Protection of Minorities on Turkey's Path to the European Union." *Columbia Human Rights Law Review* 151 (35): 151–214.

Kurban, Dilek. 2014. *Report on Measures to Combat Discrimination Country Report-Turkey, 2013*. Migration Policy Group. Available at http://www.refworld.org/docid/541acf1e4.html.

Kurban, Dilek and Haldun Gülalp. 2013. "A Complicated Affair: Turkey's Kurds and the European Court of Human Rights." In *The European Court of Human Rights: Implementing Strasbourg's Judgments on Domestic Policy*, edited by Dia Anagnostou, 166–187. Edinburgh: Edinburgh University Press.

Lord, Ceren. 2018. *Religious Politics in Turkey: From the Birth of the Republic to the AKP*. Cambridge: Cambridge University Press.

Marcus, Aliza. 2007. *Blood and Belief: The PKK and the Kurdish Fight for Independence*. New York: New York University Press.

Massicard, Elise. 2013. *The Alevis in Turkey and Europe: Identity and Managing Territorial Diversity*. New York: Routledge.

McCann, Michael. 2006. "Law and Social Movements: Contemporary Perspectives." *Annual Review of Law and Social Science* 2: 17–38.

Meral, Ziya. 2015. *Compulsory Religious Education in Turkey: A Survey and Assessment of Textbooks*. US Commission on International Religious Freedom. Available at http://www.uscirf.gov/sites/default/files/TurkeyTextbookReport.pdf.

Özbudun, Ergun. 2015. "Turkey's Judiciary and the Drift toward Competitive Authoritarianism." *International Spectator* 50 (2): 42–55.

Shakman Hurd, Elizabeth. 2014. "Alevis under Law: The Politics of Religious Freedom in Turkey." *Journal of Law and Religion* 29 (3): 416–435.

Shambayati, Hootan. 2008. "Courts in Semi-Democratic/Authoritarian Regimes: The Judicialization of Turkish (and Iranian) Politics." In *Rule by Law: The Politics of Courts in Authoritarian Regimes*, edited by Tom Ginsburg and Tamir Moustafa, 283–303. New York: Cambridge University Press.

Soner, Bayram Ali and Şule Toktaş. 2011. "Alevis and Alevism in the Changing Context of Turkish Politics: The Justice and Development Party's Alevi Opening." *Turkish Studies* 12 (3): 419–434.

Üngör, Uğur Ümit. 2011. *The Making of Modern Turkey: Nation and State in Eastern Anatolia, 1913–1950*. Oxford: Oxford University Press.

Watts, Nicole F. 2010. *Activists in Office: Kurdish Politics and Protest in Turkey*. Seattle: University of Washington Press.

Yeğen, Mesut. 2007. "Turkish Nationalism and the Kurdish Question." *Ethnic and Racial Studies* 30 (1): 119–151.

14

"Stranger, Enemy"

Anti-Shia Hostility and Annihilatory Politics in Pakistan

Nosheen Ali

This chapter examines the question of religious pluralism in Pakistan by examining its exact opposite: the attitudes and practices that perpetuate humiliation and hostility toward religious others, thus hampering the creation of an inclusive social being. My focus is on the ways in which the biggest Muslim minority group in the country—the Shia—are minoritized in everyday life, and how this violence is connected to the politics of Muslim religious majoritarianism in Pakistan. Informed by feminist thought, the chapter seeks to make three distinct contributions. First, it proposes that in order to make sense of the violence against the Shia in contemporary Pakistan, we need to go beyond the typical analysis couched in the framework of Islam, religion, theological difference, and sectarianism. Instead, I argue that the social dimension of Shia minoritization in Pakistan is better understood through the concept of "sectism," which theoretically draws upon the ways in which racism, casteism, and sexism have been understood as projects of majoritarian privilege and domination. Second, the chapter investigates new forms and prescriptions of Sunni religiosity that are radically redefining Islam and the meaning of being Muslim in Pakistan today, in ways that promote a de-pluralization of Muslim sociality instead of the ethic of religious pluralism. Finally, I argue that questions of sect and gender have become intrinsically linked in contemporary Muslim contexts, and hence must be understood relationally in order to examine the religio-political, hegemonic formations of military-militant Islam in Pakistan. At the end, I offer broader reflections on the question of Islam, feminism, and democracy in Pakistan.

Pakistan today is witnessing a resurgence of violence against Shia Muslims, with more than twenty-five attacks on *imambargahs* between 2012 and 2017, and at least two thousand Shias killed in individual and group attacks.[1] This involves

---

[1] *Imambargahs* are the congregation and community spaces of Shia Muslims. Reliable and complete statistics on anti-Shia violence are hard to find, as the documentation of such atrocities is itself a political act and structurally de-prioritized within state and media discourses. As one useful source, see http://jinnah-institute.org/violence-against-the-shia-community-in-pakistan-2012-2015/.

Nosheen Ali, *"Stranger, Enemy"* In: *Negotiating Democracy and Religious Pluralism.* Edited by: Karen Barkey, Sudipta Kaviraj, and Vatsal Naresh, Oxford University Press. © Oxford University Press 2021. DOI: 10.1093/oso/9780197530016.003.0015

systematic murder campaigns against "high-profile" Shia professionals such as doctors—more than 150 Shia doctors have been killed simply for being Shia—and of particular Shia communities such as the Hazaras in Balochistan.[2] While there are attacks on Ahmadis, Christians, and Hindus in Pakistan and often silence in the face of these attacks, the focus of this chapter is on the specific predicament faced by Twelver Shia Muslims in the country. I argue that when it comes to intra-Islam killings of Pakistan's biggest Muslim minority group, the public, intellectual, and activist silence is of a particular order. This is because the state in Pakistan has increasingly promoted an aggressive form of Sunni Islam, under which the Shia have come to be seen as internal others, deviant and disposable.

Sunni Islam is a complex and heterogenous social formation. As Tareen (2019) has insightfully pointed out, research on political Islam often implies that Deobandi-Sunni Islam defines militancy and extremism in Pakistan, while Barelvi-Sunni Islamic interpretations alongside Sufi and Shia ones offer a more peaceful and tolerant Islam.[3] As he goes on to demonstrate, Islamic discursive formations do not lend themselves so neatly to such binaries, nor to imperial frameworks of bad Muslims versus good Muslims. Beyond theological formations and histories of Sunni Islam, my concern in this chapter is with the affective practices associated with Muslim majoritarianism in Pakistan, which embody and perpetuate the hegemonic violence of Sunni privilege in Pakistan, heightening anti-Shia hostility and what we might call a *logic of annihilation* in everyday practice.

The everyday, of course, is structured by hegemonic constellations of power. The military establishment that rules Pakistan has historically used and abused Sunni Islam for its own political imperatives, in the process authorizing a warped and violent form of Sunnism for the nation. This militant and militarized Sunnism has multiple historical antecedents, and is connected to the jihad in Afghanistan as part of the Cold War, the Iranian Revolution in 1979, as well as to General Zia's legal regime of Sunnification in the 1980s, which sought to impose a narrow, puritanical, and deeply misogynist version of Islam as state and societal practice in Pakistan.[4] This period coincides with the first, prominent genocide against Shia Muslims in Pakistan, in the contested border territory of the Northern Areas—now Gilgit-Baltistan—in 1988, when around eight hundred Shia were massacred with conscious government support (Ali 2019).

[2] According to a New York–based activist group, 1,454 members of the Hazara community have been murdered between 1999 and 2016. See also https://www.dawn.com/in-depth/i-am-hazara/.

[3] Deobandis and Barelvis are two of the most prominent subsects within the practice of Sunni Islam in Pakistan.

[4] For relevant studies of General Zia's "Islamization" project, the rise of sectarian violence in Pakistan, and the multiple pasts and presents of the Shia in South Asia, see Zaman (1998), Nasr (2002), Jones and Qasmi (2015), Rieck (2016), and Ali (2019).

The fact that the Sunni-privileging project of General Zia continues to be called "Islamization" in Pakistan is revelatory—both of the hegemonic universality associated with Sunni Islam as the only/real/true definition of Islam, as well as the invisibilization of this hegemonic order. In such an order, the Shia are constructed as particular, different, and threatening—indeed, the opposite of true Islam—and thus need to be disciplined, minimally tolerated, or reformed and annihilated altogether. My purpose in this chapter is to explore the sociocultural dimensions of this minoritization and violence from a feminist perspective, while also offering broader insights on the question of religious diversity and citizenship in Pakistan.

14.1. Sunni Privilege, Sectism, and an Anti-Sectist Feminist Politics

In 1994, an Islamic studies teacher at a school in Lahore tells her ninth-grade students, "Shias have strange beliefs, thank God that there are no Shias in this classroom." In 2019, a female Quran teacher in Karachi requests a Shia mother to not mention to neighbors that the Shia mother's children are taught by the Quran teacher, because the teacher would lose the Sunni clients living in the same apartment building. Sunni privilege, hence, is not just part of the legal and "moral regulation" by the state (Corrigan and Sayer 1985). It also embodies prejudice suffused in everyday social imaginaries and emotions, reflecting a collective distancing of the national self from Shia others.

This hegemonic violence of Sunni privilege in Pakistan is often eclipsed in discourses centered on "Shia-Sunni conflict," "sectarianism," "religious violence," and "theological differences." Discourses on "sectarianism" often assume a false equivalence between the Sunni and Shia in Pakistan. While members of both sects grow up prejudiced toward the other and of course hold their own perspective as true and the other as incorrect, it is crucial to note that Sunni theology can pass as universal Islam, Sunni-fundamentalist groups in Pakistan have extensive state support and protection, and Sunni worship places and residential colonies are not being blown up by Shia Muslims. In the first three months of 2013, for example, bombs in Quetta took the lives of 200 members of the Shia community, while another bomb in Karachi killed 48, injuring a further 150 in a targeted attack on a Shia neighborhood.[5] The discourse of sectarianism is sometimes used to silence this reality of anti-Shia violence in Pakistan, by claiming that "all Pakistanis are dying under terrorism." This is a form of denialism, and not unlike the "All Lives Matter" response to "Black Lives Matter"—a response

---

[5] See https://www.bbc.com/news/world-asia-21651956.

ridden with denial of structural modes of oppression, as well as majoritarian entitlement, erasure, and escape. This denialism embodies a sectarian silence that
characterizes even feminist activism in Pakistan. The eminent Pakistani poet
Fahmida Riaz related to me in 2016 that when she was speaking to some of her
feminist activist-friends about condemning the brutal campaign of violence
against the Shia in Pakistan, she was told, "Let's not talk about Shia rights. Let's
talk about human rights."

I suggest that we need new vocabularies to understand the multiple discourses
and practices of Islam in Pakistan today, as scholars, as feminists, and as citizens. To analyze sect-based, structural-everyday violence, I propose the term
"sectism" as one aspect of Muslim sociality that has remained undertheorized.
Through the category of sectism, what I am arguing for is an analytic and political attention to the normalization of violent minoritization, hate, and murder
of the Shia in contemporary Pakistan, under the hegemonic conditions of Sunni
privilege. As will become evident later, I also include anti-shrine and anti-Sufi
violence as part of sectism in Pakistan.

The concepts of racism, sexism, and casteism offer important referents and
connected processes that help us understand the working of sectism in Pakistan.
Put simply, racism is "the belief in the inherent superiority of one race over all
others and thereby the right to dominance," while sexism is "the belief in the
inherent superiority of one sex over the other and thereby the right to dominance" (Lorde 2007: 115). Sectism, likewise, is the belief in the inherent superiority of one sect over all others and thereby the right to dominance. While I am
not suggesting that sectism is the same as racism, it is important to recognize that
there are "broad similarities in the ways in which discrimination and otherness
characterize racism and sectarianism as lived experience" and that "the experience and threat of racist and sectarian harassment and intimidation is what
defines racism and sectarianism" (McVeigh 1998: 17). If Shias are being discriminated against and disadvantaged in the classroom, in the workplace, and even in
the civil service exam, then the meaning of sectism is in effect anti-Shia racism.[6]

The second critical point that I wish to make here is that the sect and gender
questions have become inextricably linked in contemporary Pakistan and must
be understood relationally. Violent sectism and violent sexism have gone hand
in hand. The same militia who are attacking Shia places of worship are also
blowing up girls' schools in the country.[7] These same agents are even killing

---

[6] For a detailed analysis of Sunni dominance and Shia exclusion in school curricula in Pakistan,
see Ali (2019).

[7] More than one hundred schools for girls have been blown up in the Khyber-Pakhtunkhwa and
FATA regions of Pakistan, and especially in the Swat Valley. See http://nation.com.pk/politics/24-
Jan-2009/170-schools-bombed-torched-UN and http://www.violenceisnotourculture.org/content/
pakistan-taliban-bans-school-girls.

Deobandi Sunni clerics who oppose the Taliban or Lashkar-e-Jhangvi version of Sunni, political Islam. The militant-Sunni ideologies that have been promoted in Pakistan since the 1970s have simultaneously been anti-Shia, anti-minority, anti-pluralism, and anti-women. Yet, because of the exigencies of struggle, different social groups organized along the lines that concerned them the most. In Pakistan, the project of marking, managing, and silencing women continues in ways similar to how religious minorities are marked. Most significantly, shrines have historically been spaces of women's devotion and rituals. In Pakistan's history, Sufi shrines have never been bombed the way they have been over the last decade in Pakistan with more than eighteen shrines attacked since 2009. These attacks have been accompanied by a significant containment and curtailment of women's activities in the space of the shrines.

Sectism thus describes a violent de-pluralization of Islam that simultaneously victimizes women and the Shia, alongside devastating the dominant Sunni and Sufi lifeworlds that have historically blended with Shia beliefs in the heterogeneous sacred landscape of South Asia. It is important to note that this de-pluralization is often most intensely targeted on impoverished and already vulnerable communities. Yet, because of the narrow conceptual apparatus of resistance politics, our analysis often ignores that the attacks on Sufi shrines or on girls' schools should also be theorized as class issues. In adopting an anti-sectist feminist politics, thus, I wish to argue for an intersectional critique of power and draw attention to how sectist violence has impacted both women and the rural poor alongside the Shia in Pakistan.

Moreover, feminist theorists working on Pakistan such as Shahnaz Rouse have earlier interrogated the connections between militarism, masculinities, and fundamentalism (Rouse 1998). I am proposing that we go further by unpacking the category of fundamentalism, and name, interrogate, and challenge institutionalized, everyday, and felt modes of sectism. We need to call out sectism by investigating how state-sponsored fundamentalism has promoted a hegemonic militarized Sunnism and what this has meant for the lives of women, the impoverished, and Muslim minorities in Pakistan.

To understand sectism and articulate an anti-sectist feminist politics, it is also imperative, first, that we understand and problematize the majority-minority discourse that dominates discussions of Islam, democracy, nationalism, and sectarianism in Pakistan today. When minority rights were being talked about in earlier periods in Pakistan, the reference was essentially to non-Muslims and specifically to Hindus and Christians. It is a telling comment on the contemporary state of affairs in Pakistan that reports on minorities today focus on the violence against the Shia.[8] The term "minority" has thus been a shifting and expanding category in the political discourse and reality of Pakistan. What, then, about

---

[8] See, for example, http://minorityrights.org/2014/06/12/shia-muslims-in-pakistan-face-unprecedented-violence-new-report/.

the category of the "majority"? How do we understand the cultural majority in Pakistan, and what do readily used statements such as "75 percent of Pakistan is Sunni" reveal and erase? Such generalizations are problematic because they make assumptions about the heteroreligious, social milieu of the country and actively reduce it to a majoritarian category, in the name of which certain practices can be prescribed as legitimate and hegemonic.

The problem thus begins precisely with the taken-for-granted, colonially inherited logics of enumerative classification. First, the majority-minority discourse assumes that homogeneous cultural groups exist that can be neatly parceled into "majority" and "minority." However, cultural identities—whether minority or majority—cannot be construed as pure, unified, and fixed. At this moment of renewed, communitarian ossification, it is important to remember again that the socio-religious domain in South Asia was never neatly classifiable into "Hinduism," "Islam," and "Sikhism," let alone into "Sunni" and "Shia." Sindh and Gilgit-Baltistan in particular—two regions where I have conducted field research—have a long history of pluralist religious identities, with heteroreligiosity and shared, devotional piety being the norm instead of the exception.

Second, constructions of majority and minority privilege one particular form of identity in defining and numerically dividing a population, as if the reality of people's multiple social positions and complex subjectivities—stemming from the interacting identities of class, gender, ethnicity, religion, and language, among others—can be simplistically reduced to a single, determining essence. The majority/minority distinction then comes to constitute a critical discourse through which the hegemonies of particular collectivities are sustained, and their access to the apparatus of the state naturalized. Hegemonic power asserts itself as the legitimate authority by appealing to the logic of "majority rule"—defined in terms of religious, ethnic, class, and other identities. Simultaneously, by constructing various others as "minority," it renders them somehow less legitimate, as assumed deviants because they are not "normal," and hence, justifiably deprived from a recognition of identity and participation in structures of authority (Anthias and Yuval-Davis 1992). This utility of the majority-minority distinction in maintaining hegemonic power makes it effective for the accomplishment of state-making. Not surprisingly, then, the minority/majority distinction has been deeply embedded in legitimizing discourses of nationalism. In nationalist projects across the world, the "imagined community" (Anderson 1991) of the nation was frequently constructed as one in which an imagined majority personified the nation, and a "minority tolerated only insofar as it proved able to accommodate the demands of the fictitious majority represented by the state" (Benbassa and Rodrigue 2000: 105). The distinctiveness of the minority was "to receive expression only in private, and destined eventually to disappear within the majority" (Benbassa and Rodrigue 2000: 105).

For these reasons, I argue that we need to abandon the very language of "majority" and "minority" when it comes to an understanding of Islam and of polity in South Asia. In the language of secular as well as religious nationalism, minorities are always-already reduced to being less than equal—at best beneficiaries under a "politics of protection and patronage" (Fazl 2014: 31). But an anti-sectist politics needs to emphasize the history of blended religiosities, as well as an ethic of pluralism that promotes equality and an equal respect for diversity—the very opposite of hegemonic nationalism.[9] Can Pakistanis, as citizens, acknowledge that diversity is intrinsic to Islam and has always been present in the historical, sociocultural, and religious milieus of Muslims? Can they embrace this diversity as beautiful, good, and legitimate? Can they say that multiple ways of Islam are beautiful, good, and legitimate?[10] These questions may seem like philosophical queries for those benefiting from Sunni privilege in Pakistan, but for their others, it is a matter of life and death.

To promote an inclusive approach toward religious coexistence in Pakistan through an anti-sectist, feminist consciousness, it is important to explore in more detail the structural and everyday meaning of the majority-minority discourse as it operates in the case of the Shia in Pakistan, as well as the multiple ways in which the attitude toward intra-Muslim religious diversity has changed in Pakistan in recent years. These are the concerns that I examine in the following sections.

14.2. Faith Interrogations: The Burden of Majoritarian Questioning

In state practice as well as in social life in Pakistan today, the Shia perspective on Islam is routinely presumed as particular and different, while the Sunni one is assumed to be universal and normal. When one narrow interpretation of Sunni Islam comes to stand for "Islam," this in itself produces domination as it becomes the only acceptable script against which all others must be evaluated. In practice, this means that followers of one sect see and feel themselves to be both normal and neutral, and their perspective as the correct, true, and objective one. A minority perspective is thus always marked, against a hegemonic one that operates as the normative, unmarked ideal. The presumption of neutrality also means

---

[9] On plurality and pluralism, see Sudipta Kaviraj, Chapter 10 in this volume.
[10] I am inspired here by Aime Cesaire's "Qu'il est beau et bon et légitime d'être nègre": "It is beautiful and good and legitimate to be black" (Scharfman 2010: 110).

that not just the difference of belief but even the discourse and analytic insight of those seen as "minority" will always be perceived as such: as a particular perspective and hence a *partial* one. Hegemonic power otherizes difference and silences its own critique precisely by assuming this control over reality and the right to its objective interpretation. A minoritized person's knowledge and analysis are thus reduced to partial experiences that can only ever be personal, particular, or limited, instead of being seen as real and objective, and reflecting an equal capacity for grounded observation and theory. This is a simultaneous denial of equality, authority, legitimacy, and epistemic voice, and lies at the heart of minoritized subjection.

What accompanies this hegemonic assumption of considering one's own Sunni Muslim lifeworld as universal, normal, and neutral in Pakistan is then a presumed right to question those who are perceived to be *different*. Indeed, the very fact of difference has increasingly come to be seen as deviance instead of diversity. For Shias in everyday life in majoritarian settings in Pakistan, then, the most basic form of sectism and minoritization that they have to encounter is a culture of judgmental questioning and suspicion that stems from being seen as different and deviant.

Majoritarian interrogation can come up anytime when one's Shia-ness is revealed or suspected: Why is your prayer different? Do you think Ali is more important than Muhammad? Why do you visit shrines in Iraq and Iran? The tone of these questions is that of the normalized toward the not-normal. This means that the tone is often one of assumed righteousness instead of genuine curiosity, and may readily degenerate into suggestions, declarations, and accusations that Shia beliefs are not properly Muslim. It is a tone of power and privilege, reflecting the naturalized right to question the beliefs and practices of others but never having to face questioning oneself. In its primal manifestation, power is revealed precisely in this observation: who has the right to question whose beliefs and behavior. This is a hegemonic right and embodies a form of both *structural* and *everyday* violence against Muslim minorities in Pakistan. This right is structurally assumed and assured due to occupying a position of majoritarian power; it is felt as an everyday form of injury and humiliation by those on the receiving end. To be put on the defense merely for having one's own interpretation of Islam, to have to answer for and justify one's history, belief, and ways of being, to constantly have to prove one's Muslim credentials—is a burden of routinized inquisitions that children from minority households learn to carry all too early, even when they attend the most liberal-secular, privileged schools. They also learn that the risk of discovery might mean more widespread discrimination than just individual questioning. Hence, many learn themselves—or are specifically taught by their parents—to self-silence, and avoid answering even when provoked. To escape public interrogation and humiliation, Shia and other

Muslim minorities regularly learn that the best means of survival is to pretend to belong to the Sunni sect.

In 2014, Hyder Ali, a Lahori banker from the Shia sect received aggressive and repeated questioning from a senior colleague when he was observed to be praying differently in the workplace. It became a heated matter, involving different levels of the management. Whereas in this particular case the situation was resolved in his favor, he realized in relation to his future career that such encounters are best avoided in the workplace by pretending to be Sunni and praying the Sunni way—which is what he does in his current job. There is always implicit lack of acceptance and fear of open hostility lurking in any given situation. A potential confrontation when exposed is also draining, demeaning, and economically threatening. Hence, one learns that in order to belong, one must not be oneself, and instead pass off as the hegemonic Sunni "normal" assumed to be the national self of Pakistan.

Maham Rizvi, a ten-year-old student at a progressive school in Islamabad, was called to the Islamic Studies teacher's desk in front of all the students along with another Shia student. Both were subjected to a series of questions by the teacher:

> You are Shias, do you believe Hazrat Ali is a caliph? Do you believe in the other three caliphs? Why don't you pray the Sunni way? What is the "Shia" *kalma* and why is it different? Who are the twelve imams and why do you believe in them? Do you believe Bibi Fatima is the best of all the Prophet's children?

This public interrogation reflects an intimidatory use of a teacher's authority to otherize and humiliate, and left the children in a totally disturbed state. Maham's mother reported it to the principal, and refused to have her daughter sit in the Islamic Studies class again. In the classroom and the playground, Maham had already learned to silence her identity, even when provoked and harassed by her classmates in everyday interaction. In response to the persistent format of questioning, "Are you Shia? Why do Shias . . . ?" she had learned to say: "I'm just Muslim." We must witness the nature of the assertion and appeal here: I'm just as Muslim as you are. Do not target me, just regard me as an equal. However, this desire for respect comes at the cost of repressing one's Shia identity. Moreover, the desire not to be singled out, and to be treated like a regular Muslim and classmate, is not always possible with Shia-normative last names like "Rizvi" that reveal potential Shia-ness either way and render a child vulnerable to shaming and hostility.

In cases such as the ones just discussed, it is not uncommon that once Shia colleagues or classmates or even neighbors have been identified as visible others, they are now seen as outcasts to be distanced and actively disassociated from because of being perceived as improper and impure. My choice of the word "impure" here is conscious, because in analyses of Muslim social life the language of impurity is often not used. It is assumed that the construction of pure and impure is a central feature of a Brahminical social order, and solely of casteist practice in India. The message of Islam, one is told from childhood, promotes equality and the *huqooq*, or rights, of human beings. We are told that Islam embodies a rejection of caste and difference, and is inclusive of diversity even within. My use of the word "impure' is also, in fact, true and actively used for the Shia; Shia as well as Sufi beliefs are routinely vilified as heterodox, tainted by Hindu rituals, insufficiently authentic, and thus illegitimate. The exclusionary logics of majoritarian Islam and nationalism thus coalesce on the bodies of those constructed as minority Shia.

For many Sunni Muslims in Pakistan, hence, Shia Muslims have been turned into objects of aversion and contempt, and seen as social pariahs. My use of the word "pariah" here is also intentional. It originates from Tamil, referring to a member of a low caste in south India. It also intriguingly resonates with the Urdu-Hindi word *paraia*—which literally means "other" and "not one's own." The reduction of the Shia to being pariah—other, and not one of us—has come to operate in ways that denies the Shia equal belonging both within Islam and within the Pakistani nation. The feeling of un-belonging is especially acute among elderly Shia who migrated to Pakistan at the time of partition. Fearing exclusion in Hindu-majoritarian India, they never suspected that what awaited them was exclusion and violence in Sunni-majoritarian Pakistan. Hence, "a minority community's political dilemma" (Bose and Jalal 1997: 174) that Muslims faced in British India ironically continues for Shias in Sunni-dominated Pakistan.

14.3. Humiliation, Hostility, and Annihilation: The Killable Shia

The recent intervention of Dalit studies has productively framed the question of humiliation and dignity as the central dynamic of history and historiography in India, in place of the dominant framework of colonialism and nationalism (Rawat and Satyanarayana 2016). Continuing my earlier work on affective politics, sectarian imaginaries, and citizenship in Gilgit-Baltistan, I find this attention to the question of dignity and everyday affective experience as a particularly useful way for understanding social relations more broadly in contemporary Pakistan. I would argue that alongside humiliation, it is *hostility* that increasingly defines the experience of being a Muslim minority in Pakistan today. The word "hostility" originates from the Latin words *hostis*, which means "stranger, enemy" (Stevenson and Waites 2011: 689). While all religious groups may regard themselves as true and others as incorrect, the ability to declare infidel or unbeliever within Islam is a privilege of the dominant sect, a tool for it, and a source of oppression. It cultivates active and dormant hostility, a hostility that brings fear, intimidation, and silencing into the lives of the minoritized.

In everyday situations of interrogation and hostility toward Shia Muslims, the questions that Shias in Pakistan routinely faced till recently tended to focus on their different style of prayer, the significance of mourning and wearing black in the month of Muharram, and the place of the imams in Shia belief. In the last five years in Pakistan, a new kind of anti-Shia questioning has emerged that is astounding "beyond belief": the denigration of Shia Islam is now being realized through a hostility toward the Prophet's own family. Devotion and love for the *ahl-e-bait* or the members of the Prophet's family—the Prophet himself, his daughter Fatima, his son-in-law Ali, their children Hassan and Hussain, and including their descendants as well—is a core aspect of Shia belief, and widely adhered to by Muslims in general. Today, the veneration of Ali, Fatima, Hassan, and Hussain is being bizarrely constructed as evidence of the lack of respect and love for the Prophet by the Shia, and hence as proof of potential blasphemy. That the Shia are unbelievers and should be thrown out of the fold of Islam is an old demand of many Sunni groups in Pakistan. However, a renewed everyday suspicion that Shia are blasphemous comes in an atmosphere where blasphemy charges have been used with a ferocious vengeance to demonize everyone from Ahmadis and Christians to progressive politicians, women activists, literature professors, and qawwali singers in Pakistan.

To understand this atmosphere, recall the Islamic Studies teacher's question posed earlier to the ten-year-old Maham about whether Fatima is considered the "best of all of Prophet's children." There is a comparative and competitive spirit here, and one gets the impression that the Prophet's family itself is being constructed as Shia. Moreover, it was never as common as it is now to ask a Shia, "Do you think of Ali as the Prophet?" The insinuation here is that Shias are challenging the finality of the Prophet—the same whip that has been used to dehumanize and punish Ahmadis in Pakistan under charges of blasphemy.

Further examples abound. The first of Muharram—signifying the beginning of Muslim and especially Shia mourning for the murder of Hussain, the Prophet's grandson—has now been turned into a "Happy New Year" among some segments of Sunnis in Pakistan. Qawwals report that in Sunni households as well as in the public at large, they now recite a *naat* for the Prophet before the *qaul* for Ali—going against what has been normative in the qawwali tradition that they were trained in. Hence, in multiple registers, we are now being tuned to divide up the Prophet's family, pitting the Prophet against his own son-in-law, cousin, and closest follower-companion, Ali, and his grandson Hussain. This is an entirely new construction of Sunni Muslimness in Pakistan, under the influence of imperial as well as nationally sponsored, vehemently anti-Shia Islam.[11]

In this new construction, the devotional spirit of Islam that dominates Pakistan as embodied particularly through shrines, spirituality, and women's rituals is demonized and threatened alongside the promotion of anti-Shia vitriol. This is not a coincidence. Sufism and Shiism blend fluidly in many ways, most evidently because Ali—the Prophet's son-in-law and cousin who is revered as the first imam for Shia Muslims—is also the spiritual head of almost all well-known Sufi orders in Islam. The veneration toward Ali is central to Islam and Muslim thought, and historically, shrines of the Alids reflected an "architecture of co-existence" and shared piety (Mulder 2014). Today, in Pakistan, such widely followed religious practices as saint veneration are being delegitimized as contrary to Islam, and the veneration of Ali is being produced as solely a "Shia" belief.

This narrow interpretation of Islam is striving to replace the vast, overlapping, and connected ground across Shia and Sunni Islam—an ethos that is mainstream in Pakistani and South Asian Islam and because of which easy categorizations and objectification of Pakistan as a "Sunni majority" country are misleading. To highlight the shared Muslim sensibility across Shias and Sunnis in Pakistan, it is worth quoting Arif Rafiq (2014: 13) at length here:

> Sectarian identities were often ambiguous in South Asia. In contrast to Gulf Arab states, Sunni Islamic culture in South Asia is, like that of the Shi'a, infused with reverence for Ali and the Ahl al-Bayt. For example, today, the Pakistan Army's highest award, the Nishan-e-Haider, is named after Ali. In Pakistan and elsewhere in the subcontinent, Sunni Barelvis and Shi'a both attend many of the same shrines and often pay tribute to the same saints. Even Hindus in India have taken part in Muharram processions, with some becoming devotees of Hussain. And Islamic devotional Qawwali music—popular with Sunnis, Shi'a, and even non-Muslims in the region—is replete with lyrics and themes praising Ali and the Ahl al-Bayt. A verse in "Man Kunto Mawla"—which relates the aforementioned tradition of the Prophet Muhammad: "For whom I am their master / Ali is their master"—was penned by the thirteenth-century Sufi poet, Amir Khusro, a Sunni, and sung in the late twentieth century by the popular Qawwali singer Nusrat Fateh Ali Khan, also a Sunni.

Given this shared ethos, it is problematic to minoritize the veneration of Ali and construct a majoritarian Islam that purges the valorization of Ali, of other members of the Prophet's family, and of Muslim saints from the definition of

---

[11] For histories of imperial as well as state constructions of violent Islamist politics, see Mamdani (2004) and Abbas (2005).

real Islam. Because of this violent construction of a majoritarian Sunni Islam, attacking Shia thought and attacking Sufi traditions have gone hand in hand in present-day Pakistan as well as in India. A *sajjada nashin*, or spiritual heir of Khwaja Moinuddin Chishti's shrine in Ajmer, related to me that when he went to Mashad in Iran during Muharram in 2014, he was asked for the first time in his city about why he was going since he was a Sunni. He was flabbergasted that mourning the Prophet's grandson Hussain was now been deemed a negative act and a Shia practice. Hence, there is an attempt to purify and purge Islam, Sunnism as well as Sufism, in the process dividing Sufis too along sectarian lines. Very soon, we might hear of good Sunni Sufis and bad Shia Sufis.

The purging that I am highlighting here is not just of tradition and socio-religious practice, but also one of history. Ustad Inayat Khan, a sitar player from Pakistan reported to me a conversation he once had with a fellow musician. The ustad said to his colleague: "Just hearing the name of Ali makes my blood alive in the veins. And why not? Who else is born in Khana-e-Kaaba and dies in a mosque?" To this, the other musician responded: "Hmm. How do you know Ali was born in the Khana-e-Kaaba?" Ustad Inayat related this incident to me in a state of disbelief, because of the renewed disdain it embodied for the Prophet's cousin Ali, who is central to Sufi, poetic and musical traditions within Islam. As the Ustad said, even basic, long-taken-for-granted, shared understandings of Islamic history in Pakistan are now being rejected and reformulated. Indeed, there is an attempt to breed hostility toward this *shared history* itself and replace it with a new history altogether.

Such theological, historical, and social modes of otherizing and pernicious prejudice mean that the dominant mode of feeling toward Shias in Pakistan is increasingly one of antipathy instead of empathy. This explains the deep-seated indifference and callousness that one witnesses in Pakistan when a Shia *imambargah* or procession is attacked. Indeed, such violent attacks have come to be casualized, expected, ignored. A Sunni female journalist who was condemning the violence against the Shia on Twitter was puzzled when male journalists started asking her: why are *you* so concerned about Shias dying? Hence, Sunnis raising their voice for Shias may also be considered out of place, and be disciplined.

Today in Pakistan, the Shia perspective is not just considered *other* but also wrong and illegitimate. Declaring the Shia or another Muslim as *kafir*—un-Islamic, heretic, and infidel—embodies a specific mode of hostility and otherizing, related to but distinct from declaring a group "unclean" and "inferior." Not just in theory but in political theology itself, we might speak of the "killable bodies" of the Shia in Pakistan.[12]

---

[12] I am borrowing from Agamben (1998) here, and the powerful framing of the "killable Kashmiri body" by Ather Zia (2019).

The killable body is "one that can be killed without remorse or accountability" (Zia 2019: 50). Beyond hostility and denigration, thus, what the infidelization of the Shia other makes possible is the unleashing of a particular kind of annihilatory violence that condemns a group based on a difference of belief and theologically declares them *wajib-ul-qatl*, or "deserving of murder." Sunni militancy against the Shia in Pakistan stems from this authorizing practice of *takfir*, which is the act of rendering fellow Muslims as *kafir*, or unbelievers. As Ahmed (2007: xvii) has argued, the "patterns of state-backed and vigilante persecution after *takfir* follows the patterns of genocide noticed in the tribal warfare in Africa." In a situation of targeted, organized violence against the Shia and continued state support for Sunni fundamentalist organizations that openly promise and promote such annihilation, it is not surprising that Shias fear for their lives when they go to their prayer areas and workplaces. They are aware that the right to abuse—which is a key element of patriarchal, casteist, and racist regimes—can translate into the denial of the very right to life at any moment.

Analyses of such annihilatory violence in Pakistan often focus on how Saudi Arabia and Iran have waged proxy sectarian warfare in Pakistan since the 1970s.[13] It is important to point out that the "What about Iran?" argument is often used to evade critiques of the rise of a Sunni-fundamentalist Pakistani state, silence the reality of Sunni privilege and the targeting of Shias in genocidal massacres, and erase the asymmetry of violence that structures Sunni-Shia conditions in Pakistan today. In a perverse way, it also obliquely serves as a rationale for anti-Shia violence in Pakistan, suggesting to Shias that they themselves are to blame for the violence being committed against them. Recognizing Iran's role is critical and correct, alongside the existence of Shia militancy. But it need not be used as a means to deflect, and deny the hegemonic and horrific scale of Sunni-majoritarian violence against the Shia in Pakistan.

Tracing sectarian hostility to "Saudi Arabia" and "Iran" also serves to perpetuate the myth of a pure and innocent Pakistani nation-state, derailed by conniving external forces—a discourse that protects the internal self and state from culpability, renders invisible the defining role of the Pakistani military-intelligence establishment, and shields how Sunni privilege has been intrinsic to Pakistani nationalism since the establishment of the state in 1947. While the current situation of nurtured sectarianization and sectist violence began in the 1970s due to conscious government policy as well as external forces, the very fact that as early as 1948 the "founder," Muhammad Ali Jinnah, had to have two burials—first the family, Shia one and then a public, Sunni one—demonstrates

---

[13] See Hashemi and Postel (2017) for a recent analysis of regional sectarianization.

how the discomfort and antipathy toward the Shia has been part of state-making since the inception of Pakistan.[14]

This is deeply ironic given that Shias formed a significant part of the Muslim political elite and of the Pakistan movement itself. The Shia and other Muslim sects did not see themselves as a "minority," as the struggle was perceived to be a "Muslim" one against a Hindu-majority India. Arab nationalism, on the other hand, has predominantly been Sunni in nature, and this has to do with the markedly different nature of how Islam developed in South Asia versus elsewhere. Middle-class Pakistani Sunnis, for example, are often struck when they visit a place in the Gulf or even countries like Indonesia and Malaysia and realize that Muharram is not revered there as a significant Islamic event the way it is in Pakistan.[15] That the lived experience of Islam and its history is so different as one goes from South Asia to elsewhere is simply not recognized enough in blanket discourses on "Islam versus the West" or the "Sunni versus the Shia axis."

This lived Islam has been brutally damaged by the military and political elite in Pakistan, who have used "Islam" to justify an anti-India posture as well as to bolster their own rule. In the process, they have created a new puritanical and sectist version of Sunni Islam as well as of Pakistani nationalism—one that purges diversity and fosters antipathy toward minority Muslims, non-Muslims, and women. Even worse, Sunni militant groups such as the SSP (Sipah-e-Sahaba Pakistan) and ASWJ (Ahle Sunnat Wal Jamat) have come to have a "privileged status" in Pakistan, and operate with "relative impunity" (Rafiq 2014: 4). These banned outfits, which "want the state to excommunicate the Shia and relegate them to second-class status," are "mainstreamed" in Pakistan's dominant province of Punjab (Rafiq 2014: 43). While Shia militancy exists, it is "essentially retaliatory" and does not match the scale, infrastructure, everyday power and structural support of Sunni Deobandi militancy in Pakistan (Rafiq 2014: 4).

As indicated earlier, the state-sponsored mobilization of a Deobandi identity to foster Sunni militancy has been a result of the Pakistani military establishment's use of jihad as a tool of foreign policy and "strategic depth" in Afghanistan and Kashmir since the 1980s. The arming of numerous Sunni militias has not only activated violence toward the Shia but also had the effect of radicalizing Sunni Barelvis. Followers of Deobandi Islam are generally regarded to be a minority in Pakistan; however, today there are "approximately 9,500 Deobandi madrasas registered across Pakistan, compared to 6,500 associated with other Muslim sects" (Rafiq 2014: 21). As Rafiq explains:

---

[14] For details about the deaths of Jinnah and his sister Fatima Jinnah and how the questions of gender, sect, and property have intersected following their deaths, see Ahmed (2007).

[15] See http://brownpundits.blogspot.com/2015/01/shia-killing-in-pakistan-background-and.html.

During the past two decades, the Pakistani state effectively looked away as Sunni Deobandis took over Sunni Barelvi mosques, forcing the latter group to form the Sunni Tehreek, which violently reclaimed some of its mosques. When the Pakistani state turns a blind eye to Sunni Deobandi mosque grabbing, it sends the message that Pakistan is a Sunni Deobandi state and it contributes to the militarization of Pakistani society as other sects, such as the Sunni Barelvis, resort to violence to defend their houses of worship. (2014: 108)

This militarization of society driven by new constructions of Sunni Muslimness and competing, militant Sunni factions has led to a vicious, downward spiral of violence in Pakistan—a dynamic that has set in motion a hollowed-out, misogynist, and anti-minority Islam that cannot be easily undone through pluralistic military postures such as the Kartarpur corridor.

14.4. Islam, Feminism, and the Secular

In this final section, I wish to take up the larger academic discourse on Islam, feminism, and the secular to find analytical and political pathways forward. In such a search, it is important to consider not just Muslim-majority countries but also the shared South Asian historical context within which Pakistan is located. Feminist scholars in India, for example, have powerfully illuminated the question of Hindutva fundamentalism and secularism in India in ways that are pertinent to the situation in Pakistan. Sujata Patel (2007) historicizes the emergence of majority-minority discourse as a binary of colonial modernity in the subcontinent, and examines how it served as a "language of domination and power" (p 1090). She goes on to explain how this language is uncritically adopted in sociological analyses in contemporary India in ways that shields *savarna*, upper-caste majoritarianism, under the guise of objective analysis of religion. Patel (2007) argues that Hindu majoritarianism in India has become "not only a movement that fuels an aggressive integration of Hindu identity but also legitimises everyday caste and gender violence" (p 1090). Such histories of the "master narrative of majority and minority" (2007: 1089) are inherited by, and applicable to, Pakistan as well, and yet similar analysis of the connections between Muslim majoritarianism, sectist discrimination, and gendered violence is missing from studies in Pakistan. I have sought to advance such an anti-sectist, feminist analysis in this chapter, but we must also probe more deeply as to why such an analysis has been lacking in studies of Pakistan. One reason, I suggest, is the limiting, analytical framework for discussing Islam, secularism, and feminism within which academic discourses are taking place today.

Recent scholarship on Muslim histories and politics has offered important challenges to the dominant discourse on "radical Islam" by exposing the violent, causative histories of Western modernity, and articulating a powerful critique of the secular. Beginning most notably with Talal Asad (2003), we have learned to unpack the secular-religious binary itself as a technique of power and mode of regulation, one that selectively defines the domain of the religious and authorizes particular imaginaries of the secular as universal. Moreover, as Saba Mahmood (2009) has detailed, the desire for a "liberal" and "moderate" Islam has been tied in the West to political imperatives of empire—imperatives that have been both erased and justified through comfortable collusions with Euro-American feminism and spurious claims of bringing "democracy." And as Devji and Mohaghegh (2014: 4) have argued, the "naming as well as the reality of 'extremism' or 'militancy' tells us as much about the violence of modern politics as it does about that of 'radical Islam.'"

Yet these interventions do not address or help us grasp the political terrain in places like Pakistan, where—as a result of colonialism, imperialism, and militarized Sunnism—particular imaginaries of Islam have come to be defined as right while others have been delegitimized and systematically attacked. Talking back to empire is critical, but so is talking back to hegemonic formations within Islam that have perpetuated violence against minorities and women. Unfortunately, among scholars writing on Pakistan today, the secular and feminist question has reached a divisive impasse. On the one hand are academics who expose the pernicious histories of secular modernity, and emphasize the agency and lived meanings of Muslims otherized as "pious" or "radical." On the other hand, there are feminist scholars and activists within Pakistan who face and witness violence in the name of Islam everyday—from the blowing up of girls' schools to attacks on Christian churches to the forced conversions of Hindu women. Critiquing this violence of the "Islamic" is deemed necessary for them, and holding on to an understanding of the "secular"—however flawed and historically complicated— is felt as an urgent political need in order to fight for a democratic society.

In this political and historical conjuncture, I contend that it is essential to first recognize this divide, and see it as an unhelpful impasse to be caught in, as academics, feminists, activists, and also as Muslims—a category through which the beings and bodies of one billion people are perceived, irrespective of their own relationship with it. Second, I contend that academic inquiries on Islam and feminist scholarship are being shaped by the political, geographical, and intellectual locations one is inhabiting and seeking to intervene in. My third observation is that we must see the question of liberal-secular empire and the question of political Islam as relational instead of oppositional, and do the simultaneous work of external and internal critique. We need to ask: why is anti-Shia violence not seen or described as anti-Muslim hate and Islamophobia? Muslims are certainly facing unflinching xenophobic racism in the West, but in Muslim-dominated states like Pakistan, they are also held hostage by the proclaimers of faith within Islam who are simultaneously victimizing Muslim and non-Muslim citizens. As journalist discourse in Pakistan routinely asserts, Islam, in fact, has been "hijacked." We do not even have words to describe this violence of the internal self with the clarity that terms like "Hindutva" and "Zionist" suggest in other contexts—this, in itself, is partly a reflection of Sunni privilege and sectist prejudice.

A cohesive term is additionally difficult in the Muslim context for a number of other reasons: because Islam reflected an aspirational idiom of anti-colonial nationalism; because of the continuing use of Islam as a framework of resistance against imperial politics and against "democratic violence" in contexts such as Indian-controlled Kashmir; because terms like "Islamofascism" have been used by neocons across Europe and the United States to systematically perpetuate empire and Islamophobia; and because violent, fundamentalist, and suprema-cist visions of Islamist politics have had diverse roots in colonial, imperial, and nationalist imperatives. This analytical lacuna has translated into a failure of scholarship to attend to hegemonic constellations of annihilatory politics and Islam within Pakistan in discussions of contemporary Muslim societies. For this reason, I have proposed sectism as one specific analytic to recognize the reality of Sunni privilege and interrogate the religio-political, masculinist project of majoritarian violence in the specific context of Pakistan.

In terms of alternate vocabularies and conceptualizations, I find Hasso's discussion of feminist politics and pro-democracy movements in Egypt as deeply instructive as well. Hasso critiques Saba Mahmood's work for overestimating "the impact of external forces on 'local' forms of sectarianism in Egypt and elsewhere in the region" (2015: 613). Acknowledging Mahmood's "valid critique of Western geopolitical machinations," Hasso simultaneously emphasizes how religions like Judaism, Islam, and Christianity promoted problematic discourses of gender and minority violence before the era of secularism, modern nation-alism, and Western colonialism. She goes on to argue that the term *madani*, or "civil," in Egypt—despite being used in multiple ways for "competing arrangements of power"—has nevertheless come to advance a "radically plural and emancipatory politics," and has served as "a solution to the exclusions of mil-itarism, Islamism, and sectarianism, as well as the authoritarian baggage of post-colonial 'secularism' in the region" (Hasso 2015: 606).

Majoritarian practices of humiliation, hostility, and anti-Shia violence in Pakistan today cannot be wished away, and we must enlarge the scope of our analytical gaze, accept discomfort, and recognize processes of othering, discrimination, and violent annihilation within the Sunni-dominant Muslim state of Pakistan. The everyday creates the conditions of possibility for large-scale violence, and hence it is as necessary to challenge the supposedly harmless, casual sectism of daily life as it is to organize against incremental genocides. Alongside, I also find it critical to attend to the intertwined histories of Muslim piety, Islamic philosophy, and poetic thought that have long imagined faith as formative of justice and resistance (Ali 2016). Complicating our imagining of South Asian and Muslim history along with the language of democratic, human, and civil rights is indispensable toward creating an inclusive polity, particularly in the context of patriarchal, militarized sectism that Pakistan is witnessing today. In such a context, a robust feminist praxis demands not just a concern for the condition of women but also a rigorous analysis and resistance toward larger sectist state projects that are deepening religious oppression and annihilation.

Bibliography

Abbas, Hassan. 2005. *Pakistan's Drift Into Extremism: Allah, the Army, and America's War on Terror.* London: M.E. Sharpe.

Agamben, Giorgio. 1998. *Homo Sacer: Sovereign Power and Bare Life.* Palo Alto, CA: Stanford University Press.

Ahmed, Khalid. 2007. *Sectarian War: Pakistan's Sunni-Shia Violence and Its Link to the Middle East.* Karachi: Oxford University Press.

Ali, Nosheen. 2016. "From Hallaj to Heer: Poetic Knowledge and the Muslim Tradition." *Journal of Narrative Politics* 3(1): 2–26.

Ali, Nosheen. 2019. *Delusional States: Feeling Rule and Development in Pakistan's Northern Frontier.* Delhi: Cambridge University Press.

Anderson, Benedict. 1991. *Imagined Communities: Reflections on the Origin and Spread of Nationalism.* London: Verso.

Anthias, Floya and Nira Yuval-Davis. 1993. *Racialized Boundaries: Race, Nation, Gender, Colour and Class and Anti-racist Struggle.* London: Routledge.

Asad, Talal. 2003. *Formations of the Secular: Christianity, Islam, Modernity.* Stanford, CA: Stanford University Press.

Benbassa, Esther and Aron Rodrigue. 2000. *Sephardi Jewry: A History of the Judeo-Spanish Community, 14th to 20th Centuries.* Berkeley: University of California Press.

Bose, Sugata and Ayesha Jalal. 1997. *Modern South Asia: History, Culture, Political Economy.* Delhi: Oxford University Press.

Corrigan, Philip and Derek Sayer. 1985. *The Great Arch: English State Formation as Cultural Revolution.* Oxford: Basil Blackwell.

Devji, Faisal and Jason Bahbak Mohaghegh. 2014. "Point of No Return: Extremism, Sectarian Violence, and the Militant Subject," SCTIW Interlocutors Series, *SCTIW Review*, September 3, http://sctiw.org/sctiwreviewarchives/archives/232.

Fazl, Tanweer. 2014. *Nation-State and Minority Rights in India: Comparative Perspectives on Muslim and Sikh Identities.* New York: Routledge.

Hashemi, Nader and Danny Postel, eds. 2017. *Sectarianization: Mapping the New Politics of the Middle East.* Oxford: Oxford University Press.

Hasso, Frances S. 2015. "Civil and the Limits of Politics in Revolutionary Egypt." *Comparative Studies of South Asia, Africa and the Middle East* 35(3): 605–621.

Jones, Justin and Ali Usman Qasmi, eds. 2015. *The Shi'a in Modern South Asia: Religion, History and Politics*. Cambridge: Cambridge University Press.

Lorde, Audrey. 2007. *Sister/Outsider: Essays and Speeches*. Reprint ed. Berkeley, CA: Crossing Press.

Mahmood, Saba. 2009. "Feminism, Democracy, and Empire: Islam and the War on Terror." In *Gendering Religion and Politics: Untangling Modernities*, edited by Hanna Herzog and Anne Braude, 193–215. New York: Palgrave Macmillan.

Mamdani, Mahmood. 2004. *Good Muslim, Bad Muslim: America, the Cold War, and the Roots of Terror*. New York: Pantheon Books.

McVeigh, Robbie. 1998. "Is Sectarianism Racism? The Implications of Sectarian Division for Multiethnicity in Ireland." In *The Expanding Nation: Towards a Multi-ethnic Ireland*, edited by Ronit Lentin, 16–20. Dublin: Department of Sociology, Trinity College Dublin.

Mulder, Stephennie. 2014. *The Shrines of the 'Alids in Medieval Syria: Sunnis, Shi'is and the Architecture of Coexistence*. Edinburgh: Edinburgh University Press.

Nasr, Seyyed V. R. 2002. "Islam, the State and the Rise of Sectarian Militancy in Pakistan." In *Pakistan: Nationalism without a Nation?*, edited by Christophe Jaffrelot, 85–114. Delhi: Manohar.

Patel, Sujata. 2007. "Sociological Study of Religion: Colonial Modernity and 19th Century Majoritarianism." *Economic and Political Weekly*. March 31.

Rafiq, Arif. 2014. Sunni Deobandi-Shi'i Sectarian Violence in Pakistan: Explaining the Resurgence since 2007. *MEI Report*. Middle East Institute.

Rawat, Ramnarayan S. and K. Satyanarayana. 2016. *Dalit Studies*. Durham, NC: Duke University Press.

Rieck, Andreas T. 2016. *The Shias of Pakistan: An Assertive and Beleaguered Minority*. Oxford: Oxford University Press.

Rouse, Shahnaz. 1998. "The Outsider (s) Within: Sovereignty and Citizenship in Pakistan." In *Appropriating Gender: Women's Activism and Politicized Religion in South Asia*, edited by Patricia Jeffery and Amrita Basu, 53–70. New York: Routledge.

Scharfman, Ronnie. 2010. "Aimé Césaire: Poetry Is/and Knowledge." *Research in African Literatures* 41(1): 109–120.

Stevenson, Angus and Maurice Waite, eds. 2011. *Concise Oxford English Dictionary*. 12th ed. Oxford: Oxford University Press.

Tareen, SherAli. 2019. *Defending Muhammad in Modernity*. Notre Dame, IN: University of Notre Dame.

Zaman, Muhammad. 1998. "Sectarianism in Pakistan: The Radicalization of Shia and Sunni Identities." *Modern Asian Studies* 32(3): 687–716.

Zia, Ather. 2019. *Resisting Disappearance: Military Occupation and Women's Activism in Kashmir*. Seattle: University of Washington Press.

15

Thinking through Majoritarian Domination in Turkey and India

Karen Barkey and Vatsal Naresh

15.1. Introduction

In this chapter, we argue that recent developments in India and Turkey constitute a vital reorganization of political belonging that moves into a phase of majoritarian domination, which we define as the majority's avoidable and illegitimate exercise of governmental power that compromises minorities' basic interests. Although both Turkey and India, as modern states in the twentieth century, emerged in the context of widespread violence and imperial dissolution, their founding elites adopted substantially different positions toward the challenge of extant religious difference. Differing notions of modernity, history, nationalism, and diversity motivated distinctive state-society compacts and arrangements for diversity. Turkish leaders believed they could forge a unified and unitary nation built on a Turkish Sunni identity. More than two decades later, Indian elites adopted a more intricate view of diversity that accommodated, constrained, and constitutionalized difference. However, by the time of this writing, both Turkey and India have developed into regimes that uphold majoritarian domination.[1] In this chapter, we modify the theoretical intuitions underlying "majoritarianism," a concept that has often described regimes where identitarian rather than decisional political majorities prevail. We then describe how India and Turkey became states of majoritarian domination through a comparative history of three mechanisms. Before setting out our argument, we briefly revisit the basis for comparing India and Turkey.

The Armenian Genocide and forced exchanges, and the Partition of India and Pakistan, unfolded while political elites sought to establish new states. In India, the Congress elite acknowledged the violence and struggled to find imperfect compromises to uphold peace and adherence to what would come to be called

---

[1] This chapter was revised in early 2020 as Covid-19 spread in India and Turkey, and we offer here a theoretical statement, that we hope, through extension or refutation, will further efforts to understand the historical sociology of political regimes.

Karen Barkey and Vatsal Naresh, *Thinking through Majoritarian Domination in Turkey and India* In: *Negotiating Democracy and Religious Pluralism*. Edited by: Karen Barkey, Sudipta Kaviraj, and Vatsal Naresh, Oxford University Press. © Oxford University Press 2021. DOI: 10.1093/oso/9780197530016.003.0016

Indian secularism (Bajpai 2011; Mehta 2016; Prakash 2018). Turkish elites, situated in the former imperial metropole, had lost an empire and many territories and refused to acknowledge the violence around them, and their legatees deny it to this day. As a result, violence did not act as a prospective restraint upon elites in Turkey. While India's constitutional settlement was a meaningful restriction on minority discrimination, in Turkey, elites ruled out accommodation toward any group, creating a burden for minorities to prove their loyalty to the state (Rodrigue 2014; Tambar 2016).

Both countries' leadership saw secularism as indispensable for national unity, justice, and development. However, they interpreted the role of religion and diversity in different ways (Madra 2015). India established a "state-nation" while Turkey established a nation-state (Stepan, Yadav, and Linz 2011; Kaviraj 2020). The Turkification project completed the transformation from empire to a linguistically and religiously homogeneous republic. The Indian republic regulated and constrained religious pluralism, and shortly thereafter institutionalized linguistic diversity.

Indian secularism, more an interpreted ethic than articulated state policy, emphasized negotiation, while Turkish secularism forbade public religiosity even as it privileged one ethnoreligious community. Kemalist laicism's original and continuing refusal to take diversity as a premise to guide the building of institutions regulating the relation between state and religion differed from that of another unitary state, France (Akan 2017a, 2017b). Thereafter, however, long-standing opposition to secularism and the globalization of economic and ideological worldviews have produced striking similarities. Turkey's and India's respective journeys into majoritarian domination are indicative of a convergence on understandings of pluralism.

The AKP (Adalet ve Kalkinma Partisi), which has ruled Turkey since 2002, emerged amid an economic crisis set within the context of decades of corrupt and caustic multiparty alliance politics. The AKP has, over time, eroded an already weak apparatus of the rule of law and decisively shaped an electorate identified by conservative, religious, Sunni, and ethnic Turkish markers. In India, political competition through the 1960s consisted of contests between ideological and ethnic parties in opposition, and the Congress, the default party of power. Then, as the Congress atrophied nationally in the 1970s and 1980s, Hindu nationalist and oppressed-caste movements altered the terms of political contest. The political parties that grew from these movements staked their claim to power, in coalition nationally, and in many states. The Bharatiya Janata Party (BJP), the latest iteration of Hindu nationalism in party politics, first formed the government in 1996. This chapter discusses the second national BJP regime, which began in 2014, and has since sought to remake Indian politics and society in its image of a "Hindu Rashtra"—or Hindu nation.

The AKP and BJP found electoral success through a combination of long-running identity scripts championed by affiliated social organizations and more temporally proximate economic promises. These identity scripts disavow the founding secular compact and deny the plurality of religious and ethnic life, converting the logic of democratic majorities from uncertain, changing coalitions to permanent, ethnoreligious categories and reinscribing difference as disloyalty. Once in power, these parties undermined state institutions and constrained civil society organizations to reflect the majoritarian narrative, thereby eroding pluralism in another realm of social and political life (Kaviraj 2010). Diversity and pluralism—of religious belief and political disposition—are anathema to these regimes. They frame such diversity and the criticism that stems from it as disloyalty, punishable with violence. Therefore, despite differences in the respective histories of democracy and the management of pluralism since their modern founding, we suggest these regimes have arrived at a similar equilibrium: majoritarian domination.

15.2. Majoritarian Domination

We define majoritarian domination as the majority's avoidable and illegitimate exercise of governmental power that compromises minorities' basic interests. Majoritarianism refers to the belief that the governing majority must act in the interests of the enumerated majority—as might be produced by a census—in society.[2] Put another way, it refers to the privileges a member of the enumerated majority must enjoy over government *because* of her membership in that community.[3] Domination, following Ian Shapiro (2015: 5), connotes "the avoidable and illegitimate exercise of power that compromises people's basic interests." We offer this definition to specify rather than repudiate existing usages of "majoritarianism."[4]

We explain the development of majoritarian domination through three different features: discursive, epistemic, and institutional. First, majoritarian domination arises from the conflation of decisional majorities with social groups

---

[2] The enumeration of the majority is a contested process: groups dispute how they and others are classified and enumerated by the state.

[3] Akin to what Avigail Eisenberg (2020) labels the "entitled majority."

[4] The prospect of an oppressive majority has long captivated political theorists. Alexis de Tocqueville's discussion of "the moral empire of the majority" contains a potent critique of the tendencies toward pluralistic ignorance and conformism in majority rule (Elster 2014). Oliver Wendell Holmes and James Fitzjames Stephens also worry about the possibility of "national majorities" (Vermeule 2014). More recently, in the context of debates about multiculturalism, scholars have examined the appropriateness of "majority rights" and the limits that should be placed upon them (Eisenberg 2020; Patten 2020).

bound by ascriptive identities, such as religion.[5] When the majority is identified with a specific community, rather than an episodic coalition of individuals, the majority attains the capacity to interfere, illegitimately, in the basic interests and activities of minorities. Elections and social movement organizing, as we will elaborate, provide the discursive context in which majorities acquire this *permanence*. A permanent majority undermines a central tenet of modern democracy: that anyone might hope to be in the majority and have their political will enacted by a government of their choosing. It attacks, in this sense, democratic pluralism.[6]

Second, majoritarian domination relies on the suspension of criticality to secure claims of the majority's support. Uncertainty about other individuals' beliefs is a ubiquitous fact of social life. The right to free expression, a staple of democratic regimes, notionally removes all formal constraints upon expression. Indeed, democratic societies do have greater diversity in expressed opinion and include protections for this diversity, most influentially in the form of the news media. The publication of different opinions reveals the existence of diversity. The agents of majoritarian domination seek to undermine this diversity by stifling free expression in the news media. In this sense, they attack *epistemic* pluralism.

Third, majoritarian domination entails that those in power insist that the majority's will prevail in all political matters and that all state institutions must reflect the will of the permanent majority. Majoritarian domination undermines pluralism by weakening institutions designed to temper majoritarian impulses and by attacking mechanisms for accountability that supplement democratic elections. These institutions include constitutional organs of the state, such as the judiciary; statutory institutions, such as election bodies; as well as nongovernmental organizations, such as human rights watchdogs. This feature of majoritarianism is similar to authoritarianism, except that majoritarian domination uses its electoral victory as a justification for striking against other democratic institutions.[7] We rely heavily upon excellent scholarship on institutional domination in Turkey and India. In the following sections, we examine each of the three facets—discursive, epistemic, and institutional.

[5] See Urbinati's (2017) discussion of the threat populism poses to the principle of majority rule when it claims to consist of a more "dense majority."

[6] An ethnic majority's exercise of political power is not inherently unjust. For instance, in post-apartheid South Africa, the Black majority had a strong, justified case to bring redress to historical domination under apartheid (Patten 2020). Chaturvedi (2019) illuminates the distinction between political and numerical minority status in her study of democratic violence in post-apartheid South Africa.

[7] See Scheppele's (2018) account of autocratic legalism, which establishes how elected leaders undertake change to the content and structure of law to favor supporters and entrench their rule.

15.3. Majoritarianism and Discursive Pluralism

The first feature of majoritarian domination is the transformation of majority from an uncertain and episodic enumeration to a permanent declaration of popular will. Permanence undermines democratic pluralism discursively. India, Pakistan, and Turkey all negotiated the imperatives of founding modern states with fluctuating, yet still legible, communities.[8] Elites, especially in India and Turkey, somewhat disingenuously presumed abstract decisional majorities would replace the logics of communal mobilization in competitive democracies. Majoritarian domination occurs when an abstract majority is made salient as a permanent political majority. In other words, the majoritarian identity needs to be activated for majoritarian domination to occur. This process of activation unfolds in three phases. First, social movements and political parties undertake the discursive labor of producing an identity script that describes the boundaries of belonging and invents the majority's victimhood. Second, political parties secure electoral power through strategic alliances as well as neoliberal styles and strategies (Grewal and Purdy 2014). Third, the majoritarian party and accompanying movements frame challenges to the identity script as disloyalty and punish minorities with violence. In what follows we will describe the activation of majoritarianism and its attack on discursive pluralism, through an account political Islam in Turkey, led by the Milli Görüs, the Fethullah Gülen movement, and the AKP; and Hindu nationalism in India, led by the Rashtriya Swayamsevak Sangh, the Bharatiya Janata Party, and their affiliates.

15.3.1. Turkey

The history of majoritarian discourse in Turkey has three crucial components. First, Turkish nationalism produced an identity script that connected Sunni Islam and Turkishness during the transition from empire to nation-state. This

---

[8] Ottoman and British systems of difference negotiation entrenched political contestation along communal lines and institutionalized a state that saw this as a problem for it to "manage," albeit in different sequences. James Scott (1998) and many postcolonial scholars demonstrate states' efforts to create legibility through categorical distinctions to exercise coercive rule more effectively. The census is one such tool. In recording the various social identities of individuals under a handful of categories like "Hindu," "Muslim," "Jew," "Orthodox Christian," and so on, the state produced enumerated communities. The imperial state also created incentives for the mobilization of these communities in the selection of their representatives and in the competition for state resources. In the Ottoman Empire, the state's management of diversity preceded the modern census; in British India, the census became a tool in the management of religious diversity as the colonial state positioned itself as a neutral arbiter. See Lieberman and Singh (2017) for a global study of the exacerbating effect censuses have had on ethnic conflict between groups.

identity script was embellished through the twentieth century. Then, in the early twenty-first century, the AKP transformed this latent identity script and activated it through the discursive labor of electioneering. It produced a political Islam that exploited a long-standing secular-religious divide through a moral language of imagined victimhood, resulting in continuous electoral success with "unprecedentedly comfortable majorities" (Yabanci 2016; see also Cinar 2015).

Finally, challenges to this identity script—which already existed uneasily during the republican period—were framed as disloyalty and compounded with threats of violence against political dissidents and religious and ethnic minorities. The Ottoman Empire had a Sunni majority, in that most of its subjects were Sunni. After the genocide of Armenians (1914–23) and the population transfers with Balkan countries in 1923, this majority was more pronounced in Turkey. In the early years of the republican period, the state conducted multiple "nationalization" campaigns, legislated enforcement of the Turkish language, and sanctioned discriminatory treatment of minorities. Together, these initiatives activated a boundary between the Sunni majority and Turkish minorities. Nevertheless, the state's favor for Sunnis was not explicitly stated—it was embedded in the ostensibly secular label of "Turkishness." Christian and Jewish minorities were the visible "other," and, over time, Alevi and Kurdish minorities found their belonging circumscribed and loyalty questioned. For instance, the imposition of a "pure" Turkish language was supplemented by public admonitions directed at minorities ("Citizens speak Turkish"), and speaking Greek, Armenian, or Judeo-Spanish was punished by humiliation. The Turkish nation-state broke decisively with the Ottoman Empire, discarding the inclusive disposition to diversity and the traditional millet system (Barkey 2008). Ironically, state-sponsored laicity, which relegated religion to the private sphere, contained within it the enabling discourses of the Sunni majoritarian identity script. The modern Turkish state's Directorate of Religious Affairs, responsible for managing religious affairs, sacral and financial, reflected a more complicated legacy than the ideal-typical laicity (Adar 2013).

During the 1960s, opposition to the terms of this national identity project emerged in the form of political Islam. Emboldened by the rise of pan-Arab Islamism, Necmettin Erbakan, who would go on to found many Islamist parties, organized a coalition of Islamist groups under the platform of "Milli Görüs," which consistently argued for a geopolitical and cultural turn toward the world of Islam (White 2014b). The electorally dominant political party through the 1950s and 1960s, the Democrat Party, and its successor, Adalet (Justice) Party, were less sanguine about Turkish laicity. Jenny White (2014a) describes this combination of an Islamic response to laicity with electoral politics as "vernacular politics," encapsulating its connectivity with preexisting non-elite discourses.

Support for this agenda—intellectual and financial—also came from abroad. White (2014b) recounts the influence of Islamist writers like Abul A'la Maududi and Hassan al-Banna. Behlül Özkan (2017) argues that during the 1960s and later, Saudi influence among Islamists increased, only to multiply through the influx of Saudi capital in 1983 after the election of Prime Minister Turgut Özal. The military's relaxation of its hostility to religion began during this period. Cold War politics, and a fear of the Left in Turkey, motivated the military to restructure control over public religiosity after its coup in 1980, initiating the production of a new Turkish-Islamic synthesis (Kaplan 2002; Magnarella 1993). In order to promote a counterweight to Kurdish and leftist politics, the military allowed Quranic schools and expanded religious programs, paving the way for a state-sponsored political Islam (Hemmati 2013). Islamist political parties and the Turkish-Islamic synthesis together transformed the unstated exclusions of "Turkishness" into a majoritarian identity script that excluded and vilified, above all, Kurdish and Alevi minorities. The Sivas Massacre of 37 Alevi intellectuals in 1993 was a critical expression of how the majority would punish minority disloyalty. The Turkish state subjected Kurdish minorities to more intense, systematic, violent suppression after 1980. These campaigns, did not, however, have uniform effects: many Alevis continued to support republican Cumhuriyet Halk Partis politics, and many Kurds who had moved or forcibly relocated to the west escaped violent domination.

In the new century, the AKP emerged as a new political party and associated itself with an already flourishing social movement led by Fethullah Gülen, which had built a robust network among Sunni Muslims. The AKP was able to bridge decades of Islamist discourse, bringing conflicting parties and organizations together. It provided them with a language to claim political power through electoral politics, the second feature of permanence.

The Gülen movement flourished after the 1980 coup. Fethullah Gülen carved a global, partly progressive, partly illiberal social movement with a focus on uniformity and an Islamic concept of service, *hizmet* (Turam 2007). Marshaling education and counseling in schools and dormitories through a networked and loyal set of business organizations, and media outlets that disseminated their message, the Gülen movement developed a "communitarian synthesis of faith and nationalism, of social conservatism and economic power" (Hendrick 2011: 40). The AKP, which emerged in 2001, constructed the local political apparatus that reached out to previous Islamic party and social movement networks, framing its development and anti-corruption message as a new politics of mass empowerment (Karaveli 2016; White 2014a; Sayari 2011).

This campaign resonated with voters, especially in the Anatolian heartland, tired of the endemic corruption of secular elites. Simultaneously, the AKP courted liberal elite opinion by heralding an encouraging outlook on EU accession and the military's devolution. September 11, 2001, and the events in its wake produced an eagerness for "good," "moderate" Islamic politics in liberal circles. The AKP was able to build upon its initial success in subsequent elections, moving from 34 percent of the vote in 2001 to surpassing 50 percent of the votes in its third election in 2011.

Once in power, the AKP acted on its promised neoliberal reforms and fiscal conservatism. The economy recovered from the crisis of 2001 through "politically supported capital accumulation" (Bugra and Savaðskan 2014:20). This process empowered new actors separate from the privileged elite, which was also the secular elite, producing business associations that supported scripts of political Islam. As electoral successes multiplied, the AKP's discursive emphasis on its majoritarian script increased. They forwarded a new conception of the Turkish identity, inspired by a rehabilitation of the Ottoman past: glorification of the conquest of Istanbul and symbolic re-enactment of Ottoman splendor. Performing this imaginary reinscribed a vision of the nation at odds with its modern founding, and signaled the intensification of the domination of minorities.

Non-Muslim minorities—Christians and Jews—had been targets of majoritarian domination from the beginning of the republican regime, and their demographic insignificance has sustained persistent discrimination. After the Gezi Park protests in 2013 and the attempted coup in 2016, government discourse, in speeches, proclamations, and legal proceedings against all political opponents, framed dissidence in a vocabulary of treason and disloyalty. Post-coup rallies attacked non-Muslims by labeling imagined coup-plotters "crusaders" and a "flock of infidels," and state-sanctioned incitement by the media encouraged attacks against sacred sites, community organizations, and buildings (Erdemir 2019).

The domination of Alevis and Kurds intensified, with the latter subjected to a prolonged civil war. The state-led construction of the Taksim Mosque, a controversial project in Istanbul, encapsulates the regime's preoccupation with rewriting the founding scripts of the secular Turkish Republic and Ottoman toleration. By activating a latent privilege for Sunni, deploying scripts that privilege majority belonging in elections, and subjecting minorities to violent domination, the AKP has made the Sunni majority permanent and social, rather than fluctuating and uncertain.

15.3.2. India

The history of Hindu nationalism precedes the rise of the BJP, and the numerical majority of Hindus, as a proportion of India's population, has been a fact since the colonial census began in the nineteenth century. The founding script of

350 VIOLENCE AND DOMINATION

Hindu nationalism, drawn from V. D. Savarkar's writings, prescribes hierarchical belonging for India's many religious groups. Those whose ancestral *and* holy land lay in the subcontinent could claim the first right, while those whose holy land lay abroad could only pledge partial loyalty to India.[9] This script formalized local antagonisms that had emerged in British India by the 1920s, around contests over physical space, such as temples and mosques, as well as religious conversion and cow slaughter.

The Congress party led India's movement for independence. It was consistently criticized by the Muslim League and Dalit groups, led by B. R. Ambedkar, as the party of caste Hindu interests.[10] By 1947, the Congress elite asserted its support for secularism, even as the party disagreed internally about the concept's meaning and the extent of its application. Gandhi's assassination in 1948 by a self-professed Hindu nationalist led to a yearlong ban on the Rashtriya Swayamsevak Sangh (RSS). After the ban was lifted, the RSS resumed and intensified widespread social mobilization along "cultural issues." While many members of the Congress held and retained their links with the RSS, the Bharatiya Jana Sangh emerged as the political party championing Hindu nationalism in many parts of North India. The BJS enjoyed limited electoral successes nationally, consistently falling short of securing a majority throughout its existence. However, it did succeed in forming state governments with other non-Congress parties after 1967. After Indira Gandhi revoked the Emergency in 1977, the Jana Sangh joined an array of other parties and formed the first non-Congress national coalition government that fell apart twice in three years, leading to Indira Gandhi's return in 1980.

The BJP emerged from the BJS, which unraveled that same year. Since then, the BJP has been the torchbearer of Hindutva in the party-political arena. As one of the RSS's satellite organizations, the party has maintained personnel and ideology-level relationships with the larger Sangh Parivar (the "family" of RSS affiliates). The party's national electoral fortunes reversed in the late 1980s, when Hindu nationalist mobilization upended the discursive vocabulary that dominated Indian democracy. The Shah Bano case, the Mandal Commission's report and implementation, and the Babri Masjid mobilization are well-documented episodes that accelerated and intensified the Hindu nationalist polarization program (Bajpai 2011; Blom Hansen 1996).

[9] See Iqtidar, Chapter 5 in this volume, for a comparison of Savarkar's and Maududi's theories of democracy.

[10] Gandhi's fast unto death in 1932—perhaps his most coercive—to protest the classification of depressed classes as a separate electorate that would choose its representatives to colonial legislatures was motivated by a desire to prevent a fracturing of the Hindu community. Demographic anxiety was not limited to Hindu nationalists.

Then-prime minister Rajiv Gandhi's decisions to support Muslim orthodoxy in the Shah Bano case in 1985 and leave unchallenged the opening of the Babri Masjid to Hindu devotees in 1986 catalyzed the emergence of Hindutva as the defining cultural fault-line in Indian politics. The destruction of the Babri Masjid in 1992 and the riots that followed instantiated the potential of majoritarian domination under Hindutva. Mythic revivalism was an essential component of the RSS's project—an appeal for Brahmanical primacy and caste order projected backward to antiquity and forward into an epoch of the assertive Hindu nation. Through mass mobilizations in the 1980s the BJP and the RSS developed the capacity to contest a hitherto dominant ideological narrative of the Indian state—that of flawed but significant secularism.

The BJP's acquisition of political power at the national level in 1998 facilitated a further discursive transformation—through state policy rather than in confrontation against it. The first BJP government altered education policy through curricula and made scientific appointments to promote an alternative historical and scientific ethos that celebrated a mythic Hindu past and caricatured Muslims and Christians as foreign invaders and proselytizers respectively. The government altered the basis of citizenship to center a *jus sanguinis* conception over the *jus soli* basis that preceded it (Jayal 2013; Roy 2019). In doing so, it created the framework to enact the script Savarkar authored. Only those whose ancestral lineage and religious homeland lay within India were Indians, with the result that Christians and Muslims had split loyalties and therefore could never fully belong.

The RSS has numerous affiliated organizations that provide a variety of services—education, martial training, health services, and militant activism in the service of Hindutva. Some—like Seva Bharati and the Vanvas Kalyan Ashram—pursue political ends by discreetly encouraging support for the BJP in elections (Thachil 2014). In contrast, others provide ideological manpower and overt assistance in mobilization efforts (Valiani 2011). The RSS's ideological labor produced a majoritarian identity script through decades of mobilization, resulting in the "thinning" of the ethical and practical core of religion into a majoritarian political identity.[11] Religion in politics provides an alphabet, which could be used in many different choreographies. It can be deployed to create animosity, but it has also been used to promote harmony and solidarity.[12]

[11] Sudipta Kaviraj (2010) convincingly argues that secularization can occur even as religion ostensibly remains the locus of contestation in politics when the ethical and practical core of religion is stripped away but its importance to identity is retained. In this context, Hindu nationalists' preoccupation with othering Muslims and Christians translates into political proposals that are mistaken as the only possible expression of Hinduism in politics.
[12] A growing literature examines the practices, networks, and ideologies of religious sharing. For instance, Anna Bigelow (2010) describes the practice of religious sharing in Malerkotla in Northern India. Also see Barkan and Barkey (2014).

Different religious traditions also offer discourses of ethical goods, such as justice and compassion. The effort to instead prioritize political proposals that dominate minorities is a political choice, not the inevitable consequence of religion in politics.

Although the BJP government under Vajpayee through 1998–2004 furthered many majoritarian projects, it did not succeed in retaining power. Vajpayee called early elections in 2004 and led the BJP's National Democratic Alliance coalition as it lost power to the Congress-led United Progressive Alliance coalition.[13] The BJP had ruled in a coalition with parties that included lower-caste parties, Dravidian parties, and other regional parties that ostensibly rejected many of their majoritarian positions. The party itself changed its position on economic policy in the aftermath of India's "liberalization," initiated in 1991 following a foreign reserve crisis. In the 2014 general elections, the BJP's campaign deployed selective messaging about "development" and Hindutva to different audiences. Campaign speeches were replete with sharp criticisms of corruption and dynastic malaise in the Congress government. Simultaneously, through its affiliates and election candidates, the BJP orchestrated violence between Hindus and Muslims in the state of Uttar Pradesh, where it then won an astounding number of seats.

The BJP also turned a corner on the challenge initiated by the Mandal Commission's report recommending the expansion of caste-based reservations to other backward classes (OBCs) above existing reservations for scheduled castes and scheduled tribes, as had been constitutionally agreed in 1949. In 1990, and thereafter, the BJP opposed the expansion of reservations on a caste basis because the deepening of caste categories underscored divisions within Hindu society, instead backing reservations along economic deprivation, which would include poor upper castes. Through the 1990s, regional parties with support among Dalit and OBC castes won state-level elections and were important coalition partners in short-lived national governments in 1996 and 1997 (Yadav 1996). The rise of the BJP in 2014 and 2019 demonstrated its success in defeating not only the Congress, which had failed to find support in these communities, but also the regional parties that represented assortments of "backward castes."[14] The BJP actively courted these caste groups in its mid-level leadership, and the prime minister himself campaigned on his OBC identity (Bhan 2014). In the 2019 elections, the BJP nationalized what had hitherto been a state-level strategy by instituting reservations for the economically deprived, which was widely recognized as a quota for upper castes (Deshpande 2019).

[13] It is sometimes argued that the BJP's role in the 2001 Gujarat riots impacted their electoral prospects in 2004 (see Dhattiwala 2019).
[14] See Ahuja's (2019) account of the conditions that explain the success of caste-based party organization in different Indian states.

The BJP has consistently framed disagreement as disloyalty. The identity script imperils minorities in quotidian ways as well as through monumental legislative change. Through its first term from 2014–2019, targeted atrocities, such as lynchings, against Muslims, Adivasis, Christians, and Dalits, rose manifold. Then, early in the BJP's second term, in 2019, the Citizenship Amendment Act initiated, rather than settled, contestation around the basis for Indian citizenship. The act allows persons of all South Asian religious communities in Pakistan, Bangladesh, and Afghanistan except Muslims to seek asylum from persecution in India. It waives a five-year waiting period for seeking citizenship. When combined with other proposals for population control and citizenship restriction, such as the National Register of Citizens, it signals the possibility of the incarceration and expulsion for hundreds of millions of Indian Muslims. Majoritarian domination seeks to find "permanent solutions" for minorities and to ensure the majority's permanence is undisturbed.

15.4. Epistemic Pluralism

The second feature of majoritarian domination is its attack on epistemic pluralism through the production of pluralistic ignorance. Elections aggregate and enumerate support for candidates and parties. The news media represent the diversity of political opinions, albeit without enumerating and aggregating support for those opinions. However, unlike elections, which occur on a specific date, the news media represent opinion daily. They become a source of diversity that, if opposed to the majoritarian agenda, can challenge the basis of the majority's permanence and universalism. In other words, they can suggest to their audience that those among the majority may have reason to disagree with the majoritarian agenda and that political positions on a wide range of issue domains may vary even if the agents involved have a single shared identity marker. We demonstrate in what follows how AKP and BJP governments have attacked the media to stifle diversity of opinion by attacking perceived opponents, and by encouraging the amplification of long-standing scripts drawn from their repertoires by compliant media houses.

15.4.1. Turkey

As of this writing, there are no independent media left in Turkey, which now has more journalists in jail than any other country. In 2018 alone, the government imprisoned 159 journalists and has pressured more than 190 press institutions into closure since the 2016 coup (Tangen 2019). This intimidation is lawful: the

AKP government has made liberal use of the Anti-Terror Law and the Turkish Penal Code to charge journalists. According to a report on media freedom in Turkey, the most used charges are those of "leading . . . or being a member of or aiding a terrorist organization," or "denigrating state institutions or religious values" ("Media Freedom in Turkey" 2019). The few independent journalists still active are often intimidated, and some experience violent assaults by AKP supporters, self-appointed purveyors of the majoritarian script (Wyatt 2019). Whether their behavior is induced or voluntary, the print and television media are complicit in manipulating and manufacturing news sources and information, ardently labeling opposition as disloyalty.

While the AKP regime entrenched its hold on a growing and supportive conservative Muslim population, groups that opposed the AKP became more vocal in their disapproval. The Gezi Park protests, which started over environmental concerns, lasted from May to August 2013 and involved more than 5,000 demonstrations across cities. Police violence wounded about 8,000 people and killed 22. Gezi Park was the first large-scale protest against AKP and Erdoğan. It crystallized conflict between a coalition of social forces and a neoliberal regime remaking Istanbul into a playground and shopping center for a rising, wealthy, conservative religious elite. Gezi Park unleashed police brutality, ordered and supported by the AKP regime. The media's absence from the scene decimated its credibility, and only the media houses allied to the regime have survived the onslaught of acquisition and reformulation that followed (Orucoglu 2015). When the Gezi Park protests began, many television channels opted to air nature programming instead.[15]

Gezi Park became the moment of a new confrontation between two worldviews; an opposition view with little airtime and a strong social media presence, and a pro-regime public with an AKP-controlled media amplified the majoritarian identity script. State media portrayed pro-government groups as "the authentic representations of the nation." The AKP organized a mass counterdemonstration labeled "A Meeting That Respects the National Will." Erdoğan declared, "If they bring 20.000 people to Taksim, I can bring 500.000 people to Kazlıdere. We have that power, and we have that opportunity" (*Hürriyet Daily News* 2013). He evoked past republican state violence toward the followers of the AKP, and through its repetition on state media channels, he mobilized the countermovement (Aytaç and Öniş 2014; Tambar 2016).

At the same time, state media, and allied private media houses insulted minority religious traditions and goaded members of these communities to prove their loyalty. In Aykan Erdemir's (2019) summary, the "scapegoating of, and

---

[15] "Rosa Engels" (2019) discusses the preponderance of penguin programming in TV broadcasts at the time.

incitement against, minorities to mobilize the electorate, solidify the ranks of loyalists, and strengthen majoritarian hegemony at home" and "propagating conspiracy theories about minorities to divert the Turkish public's attention from the government's policy failures" occur together. The state-controlled and allied media have been zealously loyal, producing misinformation and propaganda and spreading falsehoods that have undermined opposition. The result of persecuting critics and bolstering support in the sphere of news media has been an amplification of the majoritarian will and the decimation of epistemic pluralism in Turkey.

15.4.2. India

The destruction of epistemic pluralism relies upon control over the news media and state institutions that perform essential informational and transparency functions. In India, the Congress-initiated Central Information Commission responded to "Right to Information" requests that assisted activists in exposing the government's corruption. Many other institutions perform the task of providing public information—such as the comptroller and auditor general, and the National Statistics Office. These institutions exist to provide information to citizens as a check on the government of the day. By contrast, the news media show both a diversity of opinion and a political identity that is not totalizing—they vary across issue positions. Information-providing state institutions have been *disabled* through a lack of appointments as well as a withholding of statistics by executive decision; and the state's restrictions on information, demands of fealty, and vicious punishment of dissent have reshaped the news media.

In 2005, after decades of ardent activism, the Congress-led government legislated a right to information and created a Central Information Commission to oversee the government's disclosure of information to citizens that sought it. Through this very mechanism, nongovernmental organizations and lawyers were able to expose corruption in the bureaucracy's lower and higher levels. Along with the comptroller and auditor general's report in 2011, the government itself revealed the scandals that precipitated the Congress's defeat in 2014. Since 2014, the executive has understaffed the Central Information Commission, denied requests that it would earlier comply with, and captured the comptroller and auditor general's office by appointing loyalists. In 2018, a news magazine exposed the suppression of a statistical report that placed unemployment an unprecedented level, based on an unpublished National Sample Survey Organization report (Jha 2019). The experts who had authored the report resigned in protest against its suppression, and the government actively sought to discredit a report its appointees had authored (Seth et al. 2019).

The news media's diversity has also shrunk. Non-state television channels proliferated upon deregulation in 2001 (KPMG India 2017). Neoliberal reforms reoriented the communication industry's institutional apparatus from its use in the service of state-led development and poverty alleviation to commercial profit and advertising.[16] The 2011–12 India Against Corruption protests, partly in response to Right to Information and comptroller and auditor general disclosures, mark a pivotal moment in the media's transformation. The protests, aimed against the Congress party's ostensibly persistent corruption scandals, received unprecedented media coverage, and mainstream English and Hindi media were instrumental in shaping support for the protests. Congress corruption and nepotism, and a choreographed confrontational newsroom, have since become the hallmarks of successful television journalism. The BJP has promoted, through various measures, a group of channels that unapologetically demanded military aggression against Pakistan, repression in Kashmir, and the suppression of student protesters. This television discourse frequently condemns dissenters, students, minorities, activists, and the political opposition as "anti-nationals," "urban naxals," and "sickulars," furthering the Hindutva agenda. It is not that the BJP exercises direct and complete control. On occasion, the media exceeds its brief: TV channels arguably escalated the government's response to terrorist attacks in 2016 and again in 2019 (Shukla 2016).

The media's role in destroying epistemic pluralism is undeniably sinister. With government support, the Indian media, especially television media, have conflated opposition with disloyalty and sought to eradicate the space for diverse opinions. Two mechanisms, not unique to India, have been at work. First, news channels have echoed government directives and cited each other to justify their position. Second, news channels have resorted to brazenly selective coverage, both in the time they give to different political views, and in the normative values they attach to issue positions. The consequence is that the institution most capable of reproducing diversity has become complicit in destroying it. The news media's promotion of the majoritarian narrative, often more ardently than the government itself pushes, leads viewers to believe it is a more widely shared view than it is and discredits critics by making them feel isolated. As Alexis de Tocqueville wrote of the tyranny of the majority, it operates as a "moral empire," producing conformism where criticality once existed. Timur Kuran's (1997) scholarship on the collapse of the Soviet Union suggests that pluralistic ignorance is less likely in democracies because freedoms of expression are protected. In this instance, however, the presumption of democratic legitimacy for the

---

[16] In Rajagopal's (2016) words: "Publicly traded business conglomerates own the leading television channels that broadcast nationwide[;] state-level political parties and companies with family ties to these parties control regional television channels."

majoritarian position is what makes the multiplicity of news sources more pernicious.

15.5. Institutional Pluralism

The third feature of majoritarian domination is its institutional holism. Majoritarian domination takes a form similar to what some scholars have termed electoral authoritarianism. Democratic institutions in modern states are tasked with executing the will of the people, and with ensuring that the exercise of state power is accountable and just. At an abstract level, they consist of organs such as the executive, legislature, judiciary, military, police, and the bureaucracy. Electoral victory empowers the executive and legislature and affords the power to act through the bureaucracy and military. Judicial power, and especially judicial review, maintains a check on the power of any majority to legislate and execute untrammeled power. Some power-limiting institutions are formally empowered, as in the judiciary, whereby their authority and legitimacy are independent of the elected majority. Other institutions, such as the bureaucracy and military, are empowered (and required) to execute the majority's will. However, these institutions might also challenge the exercise of majoritarian will if it inheres against the higher authority of the constitution. Majoritarian domination attacks the legitimacy of all these challenges. It insists that electoral power is absolute, delegitimizes opposition from non-elected institutions, and seeks to replicate the expression of majority will in these institutions. In what follows, we selectively redescribe research on Turkish and Indian democratic institutions and their corrosion under majoritarian domination in this section.

15.5.1. Turkey

The AKP in Turkey first undermined the military, and then reshaped the judiciary, the Diyanet and civil society organizations into institutions of majoritarian control that act in concert with its elected regime. Its crowning achievement came in the form of Turkey's transition to a presidential system (Öniş 2015). After winning the 2002 election, the AKP upended settled civil-military relations in three phases. First, it enacted legislative reforms that circumscribed the military's policymaking power and discretionary influence. Second, through two important and scandalous judicial trials (Ergenekon and Balyoz), it discredited the earlier leadership. Between 2002 and 2013, the military was weakened and subdued, ending military tutelage with all its supporting institutions (Bardakçi 2013). Third, through purges after the unsuccessful coup of July 15, 2016, the AKP remade the personnel to its liking. As Lars Haugom (2019: 7) argues, "Turkey's new strong presidential system will increase civilian *political* control and oversight with the armed forces, but not civilian *democratic* control, as we usually understand this concept." The military had always led the conflict against the Kurdish opposition. However, the recent intensification of violence against Kurds within Turkey and in Syria connotes the amalgam of the Sunni identity script and the institutional subjugation of the military.

The aftermath of the failed coup also reveals the transformation of the Turkish judiciary. More than 4,000 judges were purged from their positions and replaced by young, ideologically pliable aspirants (PPJ 2018; Gall 2019; Felter and Didem Aydin 2018). The lack of judicial independence has had varied effects, especially in the manipulation of legislation to further state patronage for loyal interests (Bugra and Savaðskan 2014: 79). It helped AKP consolidate a class of loyal businessmen, as it worked through a weak judiciary to provide allies with significant public resources, in return for contributions and donations of various kinds (Esen and Gumuscu 2018). More worryingly, the state's post-coup repression has included the severe curtailment of the civil rights of many academics, journalists, civil society leaders, and opposition politicians.

The Diyanet, the primary religious administrative institution, is not formally equal to the executive, like the military or the judiciary. Under this regime, it has flourished into an essential instrument of the state ideology, growing in size and heft (Gözaydın 2013). Ahmet Erdi Öztürk's study of Erdoğan's speeches and the sermons to the Diyanet between 2002 and 2016 shows the conformity of this state institution with the party, and further, the degree to which "the *Diyanet* was used to suppress dissent against the AKP and Erdoğan" (2016: 629). Crucially, as Murat Akan argues, the strategic motivation underlying the Diyanet in the AKP period is strangely similar to the Kemalist period. Both sets of elites were interested in building a homogenous society. The difference is that the AKP's identity script is less abstract and more interested in what Akan (2017b: 275) calls "state-religion religionism."

Finally, the AKP sought to build a deep network of intermediary organizations. Following the 2013 Gezi protests, and especially in the post-July 2016 coup period, there was "increasingly selective [repression] targeting Civil Society Organizations perceived as 'politically motivated,' such as those working on human rights monitoring and minority rights" (Yabanci 2017). Simultaneously, the AKP fostered the emergence of docile civil society organizations that promoted the majoritarian identity script. In the case of unions, a decline of traditional unions gave way to confederations closely associated with the AKP.[17]

[17] Two such unions, Hak-Is and Memur-Sen, use the party's discourse and imply a distinction between themselves and the older pre-AKP unions (Duran and Yildirim 2005).

In the case of women's associations, Yabanci shows the displacement of feminist organizations by regime-supported, patriarchal counterparts.[18] These organizations mobilize against "elitist feminism," emphasizing traditional gender roles. These new organizations subvert the task of civil society. Rather than increasing diversity and furthering citizens' efforts at securing redress for economic, ethnic, religious, sexual, or linguistic disadvantage, they further the identity scripts of the government, prolonging and deepening the suffering of minorities (Yabanci 2016, 2017).

15.5.2. India

The Hindu nationalist project in India has attempted to remake, replace, or remove institutions such that they collectively, and seamlessly, espouse the majoritarian will. The BJP government has also undermined India's federal structure by striking at the autonomy of state governments. The Indian judiciary, through appointment and scandal, is less able, and possibly less willing, to exercise its powers of review over the executive and legislation than it has been since the Emergency of 1975–77. The BJP has also altered the capacity and standing of a series of "fourth branch" institutions, and punished civil society activists and dissenters with prolonged incarceration.[19]

In August 2019, the BJP achieved what no national government had succeeded in since 1956: stripping a state of statehood. By bifurcating Jammu and Kashmir, revoking the constitutional article that granted it special status, and dissolving its legislature, the BJP altered the terms of Indian federalism and effectively signaled that self-rule in any Indian state is subject to the whim of the national government. Horizontally, as Khaitan (2020) puts it, the executive has tried to "disable" or "capture" other institutions. It has stifled legislative opposition, as though to suggest that the electoral majority renders debate nugatory. The executive also struck judicial independence through appointments to higher courts; first, it legislated a change to its appointment rules. Then, it rejected the courts' chosen nominees and left high courts widely understaffed in an already overburdened judicial system (Khaitan 2020). The courts' jurisprudence seems to track a similar trajectory of increasing "bonhomie" with the executive, with a predilection to defer to the executive in matters ranging from writ petitions for detained

[18] Organizations such as KADEM (Women and Democracy Organization), AK-DER (Women's Rights Organization against Discrimination), and KASAD-D (Women's Health and Education Organization) are products of this initiative.

[19] Tarunabh Khaitan's (2020) essay provides an extensive and illuminating examination of institutional attacks against three forms of democratic accountability: "vertical," "horizontal," and "diagonal."

persons to constitutional challenges to government legislation (Chelameswar 2018; Bhatia 2019).

"Fourth-branch institutions" such as the Reserve Bank of India, Central Bureau of Investigation, and the national ombudsman, Lokpal, have also been undermined to seek the replication of majoritarian will across institutions.[20] In downstream institutions such as the bureaucracy, the government has used its power over appointments to subvert their ostensible neutrality. Its efforts in this domain have somewhat resembled preceding regimes. On the other hand, the army has been actively co-opted by the executive to further long-standing majoritarian scripts. The executive has pushed the army to engage Pakistan along the Line of Control aggressively and to commit human rights abuses in Kashmir (ANI 2017). Discursively, the BJP has framed the army as an institution that is not accountable for its actions, and thereby, in everyday nationalist imaginations, superior to other state institutions.

The BJP also initiated an unprecedented attack on civil society organizations and activists, targeting a range of groups that defended environmental protection and human rights, in addition to students and activists, with fiscal intimidation, sedition laws, and modified antiterrorism legislation. These myriad institutional attacks may be common to many regressions from democracy. However, the motivation and justification for the attack on institutional pluralism rest on the primacy of the majoritarian identity script.

15.6. Conclusion

India and Turkey do not have a monopoly on majoritarian domination. Scholarly and journalistic work has lamented the demise of pluralism in societies around the world over the past decade. Some scholars have also long believed that democracy cannot survive in diverse societies, and especially not outside the West. We have argued here that majoritarian domination has replaced imperial pluralism, albeit following a dramatically different interlude. However, we do not romanticize the imperial past, nor do we believe majoritarian domination is the inevitable fate of democracy in societies with long-standing religious diversity.

The danger of majoritarian domination lies both in what it destroys and in what it constructs. It destroys democracy with its own instruments by constructing a majority emboldened to believe it is there for good. It ejects coexistence, tolerance, and pluralism from political discourse, and produces a vengeful, violent public. Majoritarian domination also deepens the oppression

---

[20] We would add the comptroller and auditor general and the now defunct Planning Commission to Khaitan's (2020) extensive list of fourth-branch institutions.

of minorities whose experience of democracy and religious pluralism has always been checkered. For Kashmiris and Kurds, for instance, majoritarian domination has escalated long-standing oppression by intensifying violence and sanctifying repression by legalizing it. As of this writing, the future of democracy and religious pluralism in these societies is bleak. However, movements for democracy, and for religious pluralism, have succeeded in more adverse conditions.

Acknowledgments

We thank Murat Akan, Henri Barkey, Udit Bhatia, Sumedha Chakravarthy, Bhoomika Joshi, Sudipta Kaviraj, Melis Gulboy Laebens, and Karuna Mantena for their comments on various drafts.

Works Cited

Adar, Sinem. 2013. "Longing for the Past, "Waiting for the Future: Ambiguities of Belonging in Turkey and Egypt." PhD dissertation, Brown University.

Ahuja, Amit. 2019. *Mobilizing the Marginalized: Ethnic Parties without Ethnic Movements.* New York: Oxford University Press.

Akan, Murat. 2017a. "Diversité: Challenging or Constituting Laïcité?" *French Cultural Studies* 28 (1): 123–137.

Akan, Murat. 2017b. *The Politics of Secularism: Religion, Diversity, and Institutional Change in France and Turkey.* New York: Columbia University Press.

ANI. 2017. "Human Shield Row: Army Chief Bipin Rawat Praises Major Gogoi." *Business Standard India*, May 29. https://www.business-standard.com/article/current-affairs/human-shield-row-army-chief-bipin-rawat-praises-major-gogoi-117052900052_1.html.

Aytaç, S. Erdem, and Ziya Öniş. 2014. "Varieties of Populism in a Changing Global Context: The Divergent Paths of Erdoğan and Kirchnerismo." *Comparative Politics* 47 (1): 41–59.

Bajpai, Rochana. 2011. *Debating Difference: Group Rights and Liberal Democracy in India.* New York: Oxford University Press.

Bardakçi, Mehmet. 2013. "Coup Plots and the Transformation of Civil-Military Relations in Turkey under AKP Rule." *Turkish Studies* 14 (3): 411–428.

Barkan, Elazar, and Karen Barkey, eds. 2014. *Choreographies of Shared Sacred Sites: Religion, Politics, and Conflict Resolution.* New York: Columbia University Press.

Barkey, Karen. 2008. *Empire of Difference: The Ottomans in Comparative Perspective.* New York: Cambridge University Press.

Bhan, Rohit. 2014. "Congress Calls Modi a 'Fake OBC,' His Office Hits Back." *NDTV. Com* (blog). Accessed May 18, 2020. https://www.ndtv.com/elections-news/congress-calls-modi-a-fake-obc-his-office-hits-back-560872.

Bhatia, Gautam. 2019. "The Absentee Constitutional Court." *The Hindu*, September 12, sec. Lead. https://www.thehindu.com/opinion/lead/the-absentee-constitutional-court/article29394699.ece.

Bigelow, Anna. 2010. *Sharing the Sacred: Practicing Pluralism in Muslim North India*. New York: Oxford University Press.

Bugra, Ayðse, and Osman Savaðskan. 2014. *New Capitalism in Turkey: The Relationship between Politics, Religion and Business*. Cheltenham: Edward Elgar.

Chaturvedi, Ruchi. 2019. "Violence, Democracy, and the Major-Minor Question." *Comparative Studies of South Asia, Africa and the Middle East* 39 (1): 49–62. https://doi.org/10.1215/1089201X-7493766.

Chelameswar, J. 2018. "Chelameswar Letter Text: 'Bonhomie between Judiciary, Government Sounds Death Knell to Democracy.'" Scroll.In. March 29. https://scroll.in/article/873787/full-text-bonhomie-between-judiciary-and-government-sounds-the-death-knell-to-democracy.

Cinar, Kursat. 2015. "Local Determinants of an Emerging Electoral Hegemony: The Case of Justice and Development Party (AKP) in Turkey." *Democratization* 23 (7): 1216–1235.

Deshpande, Satish. 2019. "Quotas, Theirs and Ours." *The Indian Express* (blog). January 11. https://indianexpress.com/article/opinion/columns/reservation-general-category-bill-parliament-modi-quotas-theirs-and-ours-5532691/.

Dhattiwala, Raheel. 2019. *Keeping the Peace: Spatial Differences in Hindu-Muslim Violence in Gujarat in 2002*. Delhi: Cambridge University Press.

Duran, Burhanettin, and Engin Yildirim. 2005. "Islamism, Trade Unionism and Civil Society: The Case of Hak-İş Labour Confederation in Turkey." *Middle Eastern Studies* 41 (2): 227–247.

Eisenberg, Avigail. 2020. "The Rights of National Majorities: Toxic Discourse or Democratic Catharsis?" *Ethnicities* 20 (2): 312–330.

Elster, Jon. 2014. "Tyranny and Brutality of the Majority." In *Majority Decisions: Principles and Practices*, edited by Stéphanie Novak and Jon Elster, 159–176. New York: Cambridge University Press.

Engels, Rosa. 2019. "Trees vs Tyranny: Erdogan and the Gezi Park Protests." *Diggit Magazine*, June 26. https://www.diggitmagazine.com/articles/trees-vs-tyranny-erdogan-and-gezi-park-protests.

Erdemir, Aykan. 2019. "Scapegoats of Wrath, Subjects of Benevolence: Turkey's Minorities under Erdoğan." April 19. http://www.hudson.org/research/14970-scapegoats-of-wrath-subjects-of-benevolence-turkey-s-minorities-under-erdo-an.

Esen, Berk, and Sebnem Gumuscu. 2018. "Building a Competitive Authoritarian Regime: State-Business Relations in the AKP's Turkey." *Journal of Balkan and Near Eastern Studies* 20 (4): 349–372.

Felter, Edwin L., Jr., and Oyku Didem Aydin. 2018. "The Death of Judicial Independence in Turkey: A Lesson for Others." *Journal of the National Association of Administrative Law Judiciary* 38: 34–44.

Gall, Carlotta. 2019. "Erdogan's Purges Leave Turkey's Justice System Reeling." *New York Times*, June 21, sec. World. https://www.nytimes.com/2019/06/21/world/asia/erdogan-turkey-courts-judiciary-justice.html.

Gözaydın, İştar. 2013. *Religion, Politics and the Politics of Religion in Turkey*. Berlin: Liberales Institute.

Grewal, David Singh, and Jedediah Purdy. 2014. "Introduction: Law and Neoliberalism." *Law & Contemporary Problems* 77: 1–23.

Hansen, Thomas Blom. 1999. *The Saffron Wave*. Princeton, NJ: Princeton University Press.

Haugom, Lars. 2019. "The Turkish Armed Forces and Civil-Military Relations in Turkey after the 15 July 2016 Coup Attempt." *Scandinavian Journal of Military Studies* 2 (1): 1–8.

Hemmati, Khash. 2013. "Turkey Post 1980 Coup d'État: The Rise, the Fall, and the Emergence of Political Islam." *Illumine* 12 (1): 58–73.

Hendrick, Joshua D. 2011. "Media Wars and the Gülen Factor in the New Turkey." *Middle East Report*, no. 260: 40–46.

Hürriyet Daily News. 2013. "'Patience Has Its Limits,' Turkish PM Erdoğan Tells Taksim Gezi Park Demonstrators." June 9. http://www.hurriyetdailynews.com/patience-has-its-limits-turkish-pm-erdogan-tells-taksim-gezi-park-demonstrators-48516.

Jayal, Niraja Gopal. 2013. *Citizenship and Its Discontents: An Indian History*. Cambridge, MA: Harvard University Press.

Jha, Somesh. 2019. "Unemployment Rate at Four-Decade High of 6.1% in 2017–18: NSSO Survey." *Business Standard India*, January 31. https://www.business-standard.com/article/economy-policy/unemployment-rate-at-five-decade-high-of-6-1-in-2017-18-nsso-survey-119013100053_1.html.

Kaplan, Sam. 2002. "Din-u Devlet All over Again? The Politics of Military Secularism and Religious Militarism in Turkey Following the 1980 Coup." *International Journal of Middle East Studies* 34 (1): 113–127.

Karaveli, Halil. 2016. "Erdogan's Journey: Conservatism and Authoritarianism in Turkey." *Foreign Affairs* 95 (6): 121–130.

Kaviraj, Sudipta. 2010. "On Thick and Thin Religion: Some Critical Reflections on Secularization Theory." In *Religion and the Political Imagination*, edited by Ira Katznelson and Gareth Stedman-Jones, 336–355. Cambridge: Cambridge University Press.

Khaitan, Tarunabh. 2020. "Killing a Constitution with a Thousand Cuts: Executive Aggrandizement and Party-State Fusion in India." *Law & Ethics of Human Rights* 14 (1): 49–95.

KPMG India. 2017. "Indian Media and Entertainment Industry Report 2017." FICCI. https://home.kpmg.com/in/en/home/events/2017/03/kpmg-india-ficci-media-entertainment-report-2017.html.

Kuran, Timur. 1997. *Private Truths, Public Lies: The Social Consequences of Preference Falsification*. Cambridge, MA: Harvard University Press.

Lieberman, Evan S., and Prerna Singh. 2017. "Census Enumeration and Group Conflict: A Global Analysis of the Consequences of Counting." *World Politics* 69 (1): 1–53.

Madra, Aysel. 2015. "Interventionist Secularism: A Comparative Analysis of the Turkish Grand National Assembly (1923–1928) and the Indian Constituent Assembly (1946–1949) Debates." *Journal for the Scientific Study of Religion* 54 (2): 222–241.

Magnarella, Paul J. 1993. *Human Materialism: A Model of Sociocultural Systems and a Strategy for Analysis*. Gainesville: University Press of Florida.

"Media Freedom in Turkey." 2019. European Centre for Press and Media Freedom. January 31. https://www.rcmediafreedom.eu/Dossiers/Media-Freedom-in-Turkey.

Mehta, Uday S. 2016. "Indian Constitutionalism: Crisis, Unity, and History." In *The Oxford Handbook of the Indian Constitution*, edited by Sujit Choudhry, Madhav Khosla, and Pratap Bhanu Mehta, 38–54. Oxford: Oxford University Press.

Öniş, Ziya. 2015. "Monopolising the Centre: The AKP and the Uncertain Path of Turkish Democracy." *International Spectator* 50 (2): 22–41.

Orucoglu, Berivan. 2015. "How President Erdogan Mastered the Media." *Foreign Policy* (blog). August 12. https://foreignpolicy.com/2015/08/12/how-president-erdogan-mastered-the-media/.

Ozkan, Behlul. 2017. "The Cold War–Era Origins of Islamism in Turkey and Its Rise to Power." *Current Trends in Islamist Ideology* 22: 41–58.

Öztürk, Ahmet Erdi. 2016. "Turkey's Diyanet under AKP Rule: From Protector to Imposer of State Ideology?" *Southeast European and Black Sea Studies* 16 (4): 619–635.

Patten, Alan. 2020. "Populist Multiculturalism: Are There Majority Cultural Rights?" *Philosophy & Social Criticism* 46 (5): 539–552. https://doi.org/10.1177/0191453720903486.

PPJ. 2018. "The Most Comprehensive Report on the Turkish Judiciary Is Updated." *Platform for Peace and Justice* (blog). March 1. http://www.platformpj.org/2917-2/.

Prakash, Gyan. 2018. "Anxious Constitution-Making." In *The Postcolonial Moment in South and Southeast Asia*, edited by Gyan Prakash, Nikhil Menon, and Michael Laffan, 141–162. Bloomsbury.

Rajagopal, Arvind. 2016. "Indian Media in Global Context." *History Compass* 14 (4): 140–151. https://doi.org/10.1111/hic3.12308.

Rodrigue, Aron. 2014. "Reflections on Millets and Minorities: Ottoman Legacies." In *Turkey between Nationalism and Globalization*, edited by Riva Kastoryano. New York: Routledge.

Roy, Anupama. 2019. "The Citizenship (Amendment) Bill, 2016 and the Aporia of Citizenship." *Economic & Political Weekly* 54 (49): 28–34.

Sayari, Sabri. 2011. "Clientelism and Patronage in Turkish Politics and Society." In *The Post-modern Abyss and the New Politics of Islam: Assabiyah Revisited. Essays in Honour of Serif Mardin*, edited by Faruk Birtek and Binnaz Toprak. Istanbul: Istanbul Bilgi University.

Scheppele, Kim Lane. 2018. "Autocratic Legalism." *University of Chicago Law Review* 85 (2): 545–584.

Scott, James C. 1998. *Seeing Like a State: How Certain Schemes to Improve the Human Condition Have Failed.* New Haven: Yale University Press.

Seth, Dilasha, Abhishek Waghmare, Somesh Jha, and Ishan Bakshi. 2019. "NSC Members Feel 'Sidelined by Govt,' Resign on Row over Jobs, GDP Data." *Business Standard India*, January 29. https://www.business-standard.com/article/economy-policy/nsc-members-feel-sidelined-by-govt-resign-on-row-over-jobs-gdp-data-119012901079_1.html.

Shapiro, Ian. 2015. *Politics against Domination.* Cambridge, MA: Belknap Press.

Shukla, Sonia Trikha. 2016. "Is the Indian Media Forcing the Government into a War with Pakistan?" *The Caravan*, September 25. https://caravanmagazine.in/vantage/indian-media-forcing-government-war-pakistan.

Stepan, Alfred C., Yogendra Yadav, and Juan J. Linz. 2011. *Crafting State-Nations: India and Other Multinational Democracies.* Baltimore: Johns Hopkins University Press.

Tambar, Kabir. 2016. "Brotherhood in Dispossession: State Violence and the Ethics of Expectation in Turkey." *Cultural Anthropology* 31 (1): 30–55.

Tangen, Ole, Jr. 2019. "An Ongoing Crisis: Freedom of Speech in Turkey." DW.com. February 26. https://www.dw.com/en/an-ongoing-crisis-freedom-of-speech-in-turkey/a-47405671.

Thachil, Tariq. 2014. *Elite Parties, Poor Voters.* New York: Cambridge University Press.

Turam, Berna. 2007. *Between Islam and the State: The Politics of Engagement.* Stanford, CA: Stanford University Press.

Urbinati, Nadia. 2017. "Populism and the Principle of the Majority." In *The Oxford Handbook of Populism*, edited by Cristóbal Rovira Kaltwasser, Paul Taggart, Paulina Ochoa Espejo, and Pierre Ostiguy. New York: Oxford University Press. https://doi.org/10.1093/oxfordhb/9780198803560.001.0001.

Valiani, Arafaat A. 2011. *Militant Publics in India: Physical Culture and Violence in the Making of a Modern Polity*. New York: Palgrave Macmillan.

Vermeule, Adrian. 2014. "The Force of Majority Rule." In *Majority Decisions: Principles and Practices*, edited by Stéphanie Novak and Jon Elster, 132–158. New York: Cambridge University Press.

White, Jenny. 2014a. *Islamist Mobilization in Turkey: A Study in Vernacular Politics*. Seattle: University of Washington Press.

White, Jenny. 2014b. "Milli Görüs." In *Islamic Movements of Europe: Public Religion and Islamophobia in the Modern World.*, edited by Frank Peter and Rafael Ortega. London: I.B. Tauris. http://qut.eblib.com.au/patron/FullRecord.aspx?p=1834039.

Wyatt, Tim. 2019. "Turkish Journalist from Opposition Newspaper Beaten with Baseball Bats outside Home." *The Independent*, May 11, sec. Europe. https://www.independent.co.uk/news/world/europe/turkey-journalist-baseball-bats-yavuz-selim-demirag-yenicag-erdogan-istanbul-a8909586.html.

Yabanci, Bilge. 2016. "Populism as the Problem Child of Democracy: The AKP's Enduring Appeal and the Use of Meso-Level Actors." *Southeast European and Black Sea Studies* 16 (4): 591–617.

Yabanci, Bilge. 2017. "Turkey Is Getting More Authoritarian. Here's Why Funding Nongovernmental Organizations Won't Help Democracy." *Washington Post*, December 21. https://www.washingtonpost.com/news/monkey-cage/wp/2017/12/21/turkey-is-getting-more-authoritarian-heres-why-funding-nongovernmental-organizations-wont-help-democracy/.

Yadav, Yogendra. 1996. "Reconfiguration in Indian Politics: State Assembly Elections, 1993–95." *Economic and Political Weekly* 31 (2/3): 95–104.

Index

For the benefit of digital users, indexed terms that span two pages (e.g., 52–53) may, on occasion, appear on only one of those pages.

Shia, hostility to and annihilatory practices against
blasphemy charges, 332
difference, right of the majority to
question, 328–31
faith interrogations, 328–31
feminist politics, anti-sectist, 324–28
hegemonic constellations of power, 323–24
indifference to, 334–35
introduction, 322–24
Islam, feminism, and the secular, academic
discourse on, 337–40
the killable Shia, 331–37
logic of, 323
majoritarian questioning, 332
murder statistics, 323n.2
pathways forward, 337–40
religious practices, delegitimizing, 332–34
sectism, 324–28
Sunni privilege, hegemonic violence of,
323, 324–28
Shia, othering, 301–2
Shia Islam, historically, 11
Shia Muslims
persecution of, 266
status, 26
violence against, 322–23
Shirazi, Sayyid ʿAli Muhammad, 52
Shirur Mutt, 209
Shirur Mutt case, 206–9, 210–11
Shourie, Arun, 244–47
Sikhism, 151–52, 221–22
Sikhs, 19, 118, 244, 284–85
Singh, Charan, 232–33, 236–38
Singh, Manmohan, 146
Singh, Raman, 283–84
Sivas Massacre, 168–69
social media, violence and, 280, 282–83
social science, stages of development, 3
society, Gandhi's views on, 107–9
South Asian Muslims, 13–14, 18–19
sovereign / sovereignty, 5–6, 126–27
Spencer, Herbert, 119–20
state
ownership of the, 5–6
secular power of the, 96–98
Stepan, Al, 148–49
Stoeckl, K., 158
Subrahmanyam, Sanjay, 38–39, 42
Sufism, 44, 333–34
Sunni-Alevi conflict, 305, 306–8
Sunni Barelvi, 337
Sunni Islam. See also Alevi
defining, 304–5
hegemony of, 165
historically, 11
prioritization in religion courses, 165–68,
307, 308–9

public religiosity, 18
sectist version of, 336
social formation, 323
state-controlled, 10, 16, 165
Sunni Muslim identity, 26
Sunni Muslimness, 332–33, 337
Sunni Muslims
lived experience of, 336
militant and militarized, 323
persecution of, 10, 44
public religiosity, 18
religious primacy, Turkey, 6–7, 16
state support and protection, 324–25
survival in passing as, 329–30
Sunni nationalism, 10
Sunni privilege, 13–14, 323, 324–28, 339
Sunni Tehreek, 337
Swaminarayan, 211–12

Tahmasp, Shah, 42–43, 44
Tamir, Yael, 127–28
Tanrıkulu, Sezgin, 312
Tanzimat reforms, 16, 60–61
Tareen, S. A., 323
Tarkishduz, Ustad Yusuf, 41–42
Taseer, Salman, 269–70, 273
Tejani, S., 131–32
temple entry legislation, 211–15
Tevfik, Riza, 73
Tocqueville, Alexis de, 356–57
toleration
Gandhi's view on, 101–3
Gandhi's views on, 109–13
meaning of, 224
Mughal Empire, 33–34, 42–45
Ottoman Empire, 14–15
toleration and secularism
conflict, a response to, 95, 102
constitutional requirement, India, 97–98, 103
linked idea of, 101–3
treason, liberalism and
Ottoman Empire (1908-1913), 62–63,
70, 73–74
Treaty of Lausanne, 9, 62–63
Treaty of Sèvres, 9, 62–63, 73
Turkey
anti-minority violence, 25–26
Anti-Terror Law, 313, 353–54
democracy, internal heterogeneity, 4
democracy, transformation to, 18–21
empire to nation-state transition, 7–10
EU preconditions for membership, 301–2,
311–12, 314–15
identity script and nationalism in, 346–47,
358
judicial independence, end of, 358
liberal reformist, persecution of, 16